THE CONFEDERATE AND
NEO-CONFEDERATE READER

THE CONFEDERATE AND NEO-CONFEDERATE READER

The "Great Truth" about the "Lost Cause"

Edited by James W. Loewen
and Edward H. Sebesta

UNIVERSITY PRESS OF MISSISSIPPI / JACKSON

www.upress.state.ms.us

Designed by Peter D. Halverson

The University Press of Mississippi is a member of the Association of
American University Presses.

First printing 2010

∞

Library of Congress Cataloging-in-Publication Data

The Confederate and neo-Confederate reader : the great truth about the
lost cause / edited by James W. Loewen and Edward H. Sebesta.
p. cm.
Includes bibliographical references and index.
ISBN 978-1-60473-218-4 (cloth : alk. paper) — ISBN 978-1-60473-219-1
(pbk. : alk. paper) — ISBN 978-1-60473-788-2 (ebook) 1. Confederate
States of America—Sources. 2. Southern States—History—19th
century—Sources. 3. Southern States—History—20th century—Sources.
4. United States—History—Civil War, 1861–1865—Causes—Sources. 5.
United States—History—Civil War, 1861–1865—Influence—Sources. I.
Loewen, James W. II. Sebesta, Edward H.
F215.C75 2010
973.7'13—dc22   2010008340

British Library Cataloging-in-Publication Data available

THE CONFEDERATE AND NEO-CONFEDERATE READER

The "Great Truth" about the "Lost Cause"

Edited by James W. Loewen
and Edward H. Sebesta

UNIVERSITY PRESS OF MISSISSIPPI / JACKSON

www.upress.state.ms.us

Designed by Peter D. Halverson

The University Press of Mississippi is a member of the Association of
American University Presses.

First printing 2010

∞

Library of Congress Cataloging-in-Publication Data

The Confederate and neo-Confederate reader : the great truth about the
lost cause / edited by James W. Loewen and Edward H. Sebesta.
p. cm.
Includes bibliographical references and index.
ISBN 978-1-60473-218-4 (cloth : alk. paper) — ISBN 978-1-60473-219-1
(pbk. : alk. paper) — ISBN 978-1-60473-788-2 (ebook) 1. Confederate
States of America—Sources. 2. Southern States—History—19th
century—Sources. 3. Southern States—History—20th century—Sources.
4. United States—History—Civil War, 1861–1865—Causes—Sources. 5.
United States—History—Civil War, 1861–1865—Influence—Sources. I.
Loewen, James W. II. Sebesta, Edward H.
F215.C75 2010
973.7'13—dc22   2010008340

British Library Cataloging-in-Publication Data available

CONTENTS

ACKNOWLEDGMENTS AND PHOTO CREDITS   XIII

INTRODUCTION: UNKNOWN WELL-KNOWN DOCUMENTS   3

CHAPTER 1: THE GATHERING STORM (1787–1860)   22

Debate over Slavery at the Constitutional Convention, August 21–22, 1787   25

John C. Calhoun (1782–1850), "On Abolition Petitions," U.S. Senate,
February 6, 1837   30

Alabama Platform, February 14–15, 1848   36

John C. Calhoun (1782–1850), "Address to the Southern People," U.S. Senate,
January 22, 1849   40

James H. Thornwell (1812–62), *The Rights and the Duties of the Masters*,
May 26, 1850   50

Resolves of the Southern Convention at Nashville, June 10–11, 1850   55

Journal, Resolution, and Ordinance, State Convention of South Carolina,
April 26–30, 1852   60

Two Images of Slavery: Confederate $100 Bill (1862) and Obelisk, Fort Mill,
South Carolina (1895)   62

Samuel A. Cartwright (1793–1863), "Diseases and Peculiarities of the
Negro Race," 1851   64

Slave Jail, Alexandria, c. 1859   71

Jefferson Davis (1808–89), "Endorsement"; T. L. Clingman (1812–97),
"Endorsement"; and J. H. Van Evrie (1814–96), "Negroes and Negro 'Slavery',
The First an Inferior Race—The Latter, Its Normal Condition," 1853   73

George Fitzhugh (1806–81), *Cannibals All! Or Slaves Without Masters*, 1857   80

Alexander H. Stephens (1812–83), "Speech on the Bill to Admit Kansas as a State
under the Topeka Constitution," House of Representatives, June 28, 1856   82

Jefferson Davis (1808–89), Speech at State Fair, Augusta, Maine,
September 29, 1858   87

John B. Gordon (1832–1904), "An Address Delivered Before the Thalian &
Phi Delta Societies of Oglethorpe University," June 18, 1860   89

CHAPTER 2: SECESSION (1859–1861)   92

South Carolina General Assembly, "Resolutions for a Southern Convention,"
December 22, 1859   94

Jefferson Davis, Congressional Resolutions on "Relations of States,"
U.S. Senate, March 1, 1860   96

Official Proceedings of the Democratic Convention, April 28–May 1, 1860   98

Benjamin Palmer (1818–1902), "Thanksgiving Sermon," November 29, 1860   104

Christiana Banner, 1994 (1911, 1851)   109

South Carolina Secession Convention, "Declaration of the Immediate Causes
Which Induce and Justify the Secession of South Carolina from the Federal
Union," December 24, 1860   111

South Carolina Secession Convention, "The Address of the People of South
Carolina, Assembled in Convention, To the People of the Slaveholding States
of the United States 1861," December 24, 1860   118

Mississippi Secession Convention, "A Declaration of the Immediate Causes
Which Induce and Justify the Secession of the State of Mississippi from the
Federal Union," January 26, 1861   127

Florida Secession Convention, "Cause for Secession," January 7, 1861   130

Alabama Secession Convention, "Resolution of Resistance," January 7, 1861,
and "Ordinance of Secession," January 11, 1861   131

Georgia Committee of Seventeen, "Report on Causes for Secession,"
January 29, 1861   133

Texas Secession Convention, "A Declaration of the Causes Which Impel the
State of Texas to Secede from the Federal Union," February 2, 1861   140

George Williamson (1829–82), Louisiana Secession Commissioner, "Letter
to President and Gentlemen of the Convention of the People of Texas,"
February 11, 1861   145

Henry L. Benning (1814–75), "Address Delivered Before the Virginia State
Convention," February 18, 1861   149

Virginia Secession Convention, "Resolutions," March 28–April 5, 1861   153

Arkansas Secession Convention, "Resolutions," March 11, 1861   156

Isham Harris (1818–97), Governor of Tennessee, "Message to the Legislature,"
January 7, 1861   160

John W. Ellis (1820–61), Governor of North Carolina, "Proclamation,"
April 17, 1861   166

CHAPTER 3: CIVIL WAR (1861–1865)   167

Jefferson Davis (1808–89), "Farewell to the U.S. Senate," January 21, 1861   170

Jefferson Davis (1808–89), "Message to the Confederate Congress about
Ratification of the Constitution," April 29, 1861   175

The Constitution of the Confederate States of America, March 11, 1861   182

Alexander H. Stephens (1812–83), "African Slavery: The Corner-Stone of the
Southern Confederacy," March 22, 1861   187

Governor H. M. Rector (1816–99), Letter to Colonel Sam Leslie,
November 28, 1861   191

Three National Flags of the Confederacy, 1861, 1863, 1865   193

William T. Thompson (1812–82), "Proposed Designs for the 2nd National
Confederate Flag," April–May 1863   194

Jefferson Davis (1808–89), "Message to the Confederate Congress,"
January 12, 1863   198

Confederate Congress, "Response of the Confederate Congress to Message
from Jefferson Davis on the Emancipation Proclamation," May 1, 1863   201

Richard Taylor (1826–79), Edmund Kirby Smith (1824–93), "Treatment of
African American Prisoners of War," June 8, 13, 16, 1863   203

Fort Pillow Massacre, April 12, 1864   206

John R. Eakin (1822–55), "The Slave Soldiers," June 8, 1864   209

Henry Hotze (1833–87), "The Negro's Place in Nature," December 10, 1863   213

Robert E. Lee (1807–70), Letter to Hon. Andrew Hunter, January 11, 1865   216

Macon Telegraph, Editorial Opposing Enlistment of African Americans,
January 6, 1865   219

Howell Cobb (1815–68), Letter to James A. Seddon, Secretary of War,
January 8, 1865   221

J. H. Stringfellow (1819–1905), Letter to President Jefferson Davis, February 8, 1865   223

General Orders, No. 14, An Act to Increase the Military Force of the Confederate
States, approved March 13, 1865   228

CHAPTER 4: RECONSTRUCTION AND FUSION (1866–1890)   230

Edmund Rhett Jr., "Letter to Armistead Burt," October 14, 1865   234

Mississippi's Black Code, November 24–29, 1865   237

Robert E. Lee (1807–70), Testimony before the Congressional Joint Committee
on Reconstruction, February 17, 1866   240

Rushmore G. Horton (1826–68), "A Youth's History of the Great Civil War in the
United States from 1861 to 1865," 1867   242

Jack Kershaw (1913–), Statue of Nathan Bedford Forrest, 1998   247

Edward A. Pollard (1831–72), "The Lost Cause Regained," 1868   249

Alexander H. Stephens (1812–83), "Conclusion," *A Constitutional View of the
Late War Between the States*, 1868   251

Robert E. Lee (1807–70), "The White Sulphur Manifesto," August 26, 1868   254

John B. Gordon (1832–1904), "To the Colored People," address in Charleston, South Carolina, September 11, 1868   257

Ku Klux Klan Postcard, c. 1937   259

R. L. Dabney (1820–98), "Women's Rights Women," 1871   260

Jubal A. Early (1816–94), "Speech to the Southern Historical Society," August 14, 1873   267

Jefferson Davis (1808–89), "Slavery Not the Cause, but an Incident," 1881   271

CHAPTER 5: THE NADIR OF RACE RELATIONS, 1890–1940   277

J. L. M. Curry (1825–1903), *The Southern States of the American Union*, 1895   283

Stephen D. Lee (1833–1908), "The Negro Problem," 1899   286

White Mob Burns Black Businesses in Wilmington, North Carolina, November 10, 1898   294

S. A. Cunningham (1843–1913), "M'Kinley, Roosevelt, and the Negro," January 1903   296

S. A. Cunningham, "Problem of the Negroes," January 1907   299

John Sharp Williams (1854–1932), "Issues of the War Discussed," November 1904   301

John Singleton Mosby (1833–1916), Letter to Sam Chapman, July 4, 1907   304

E. H. Hinton (1852–1916), "The Negro and the South: Review of Race Relationships and Conditions," August 1907   306

South Carolina Confederate Women's Monument, 1912   312

C. E. Workman, "Reconstruction Days in South Carolina," July 1921   314

Mildred Rutherford (1852–1928), "The War Was Not a Civil War," January 1923   320

Susan Lawrence Davis (1862–1939), "The First Convention," 1924   322

John E. Rankin (1882–1960), "Forrest at Brice's Cross Roads," August 1925   324

CHAPTER 6: THE CIVIL RIGHTS ERA, 1940–   330

Richard Weaver (1910–63), Selections from *The Southern Tradition at Bay*, 1943   334

M. Clifford Harrison (1893–1967), "The Southern Confederacy—Dead or Alive?"
December 1947   336

Dixiecrat Convention, Birmingham, Alabama, July 1848   338

Birmingham Post Staff Writers, Untitled Sidebars about the Dixiecrat Convention,
July 17, 1948   339

Strom Thurmond (1902–2003), "Address to the State Convention of the United
Daughters of the Confederacy at Winthrop College, South Carolina,"
October 17, 1957   341

Sumter L. Lowry (1893–1985), "The Federal Government and Our Constitutional
Rights," Address to the United Daughters of the Confederacy, October 15, 1958   348

The Citizens' Council Logo, March 1957   354

"His Example Inspires Our Efforts of Today," *The Citizens' Council*, June 1956   355

W. E. Rose, "The Warning of Robert E. Lee," *The Citizens' Council*, February 1957   357

The Citizens' Councils, "Old Censored Joe," November 1957   359

The Citizens' Councils, "Mau Mau Party," December 1958   360

The Citizens' Council, "Conditions in U.S. Today Offer Alarming Parallel to First
Reconstruction Era of a Century Ago," August 1960   361

Richard Quinn (c. 1945–), "Martin Luther King Day," Fall 1983   366

James Ronald Kennedy (1947–) and Walter Donald Kennedy (1947–),
"Equality of Opportunity," 1994   368

"Sic Semper Tyrannis" T-shirt, 1999   370

Alister C. Anderson (c. 1924–), "Address at Arlington National Cemetery,"
June 6, 1999   371

Sons of Confederate Veterans, "Postcard Objecting to Mention of Slavery at
Civil War Sites," 2000   375

John J. Dwyer (1956–), "Introduction" to *The War Between the States:*

America's Uncivil War, 2005   376

"Lincoln's Worst Nightmare," 1996–99   379

States Voting for Lincoln (Republican, 1860) and Kerry (Democrat, 2004)   380

Sonny Perdue (1946–), "Confederate History Month Proclamation," March 5, 2008   382

Frank Conner, "Where We Stand Now: And How We Got Here," September 2003   384

CONCLUDING WORDS   392

NOTES   394

INDEX   417

ACKNOWLEDGMENTS

The editors would like to thank the following readers for comments and suggestions that were of extraordinary value: John Coski, John Dittmer, James O. Horton, Dwight Pitcaithley, Gregory Urwin, David Williams, and an anonymous reviewer.

PHOTO CREDITS

Figures 2, 12, and 18, courtesy of James W. Loewen
Figure 9, courtesy of James B. Jones Jr.
Figure 11, courtesy of North Carolina Department of Cultural Resources, Iconographic Collection # N.66.7.120.
Figures 17 and 19, courtesy of Edward H. Sebesta

THE CONFEDERATE AND
NEO-CONFEDERATE READER

THE CONFEDERATE AND
NEO-CONFEDERATE READER

UNKNOWN WELL-KNOWN DOCUMENTS

James W. Loewen

Anyone who knows the history of the Civil War and its aftermath and who talks with members of the public quickly grows frustrated. Most recent high school graduates, many history and social studies teachers, and even some professional historians whose training is in other areas hold basic misconceptions about the era. Questions about why the South seceded, what the Confederacy was about, and the nature and later use of its symbols and ideology often give rise to flatly untrue "answers." In turn, these errors persist because most Americans do not know and have never read key documents in American history about the Confederacy.

The documents included here also make a case for teaching every American the word and the concept "historiography." Most concisely, historiography means "the study of history," but not just "studying history." Historiography asks us to scrutinize how a given piece of history came to be written. Who wrote it? When? With whom were they in debate? What were they trying to prove? Who *didn't* write it? What points of view were omitted? Especially on the subjects of slavery, secession, and race—the core of this volume—Confederate and neo-Confederate statements change depending upon where people wrote or spoke, and when and why. Why did Confederates say they seceded for slavery in 1861 but not in 1891? Why did neo-Confederates claim in 1999, but not in 1869, that thousands of African Americans served in the Confederate armed forces? Teachers can use questions like these to get students to understand and do historiography on the documents in this collection.

By no means is this the only selection of Confederate and neo-Confederate writings and speeches that could be made. Jefferson Davis's *Rise and Fall of the Confederate Government* runs two volumes and more than 1,500 pages by itself. The Confederate and neo-Confederate literature is vast. Any book-length selection is bound to be arbitrary, at least to some degree. But not all writing by Confederate or neo-Confederate leaders is part of that literature. Before Virginia seceded, for example, Robert E. Lee wrote eloquently against such a move. We do not include his piece, because his was not a Confederate position. During Reconstruction, his corps commander, James Longstreet, became a Republican and favored equal rights for all; we do not include excerpts from his autobiography, because his was not a neo-Confederate position. Of course, not all Confederates or neo-Confederates held identical points of view, and our selections show considerable diversity. Nevertheless, a core of Confederate and neo-Confederate thought evolved over time that we have tried to present here.

WHY DID THE SOUTH SECEDE?

In 1998, I was honored to give the fourteenth Dortch Lecture at the Greensboro Historical Museum in North Carolina. The auditorium was full and overflowed to another room with closed-circuit TV. This was an audience of people deeply interested in history, including many members of the museum. During my talk, I asked the crowd, "Why did we have a Civil War?" All knew that the Civil War resulted from the secession of South Carolina, followed by ten other states, so the question became, "Why did South Carolina, followed by ten other Southern states, secede?" The group generated four answers: slavery, states' rights, tariffs and taxes, and the election of Lincoln.

They agreed that those answers exhausted the likely alternatives. I then asked them to vote. "This is not Chicago," I said. "You may only vote once."

States' rights drew half the votes. Slavery received a fourth. Tariffs and taxes and the election of Lincoln split the remaining 25%, about evenly.

Then I asked, "What would be the best evidence to resolve the matter?" Individuals volunteered "diaries from the time" and "newspaper articles"; not bad answers but hardly the best. Then one man asked, "Wasn't there some sort of convention? Didn't it *say* why South Carolina was leaving the Union?"

Such a convention did meet, of course, in Charleston; in December 1860 it voted to take South Carolina out of the United States. As it did so, it indeed explained why, in a document titled "Declaration of the Immediate Causes Which Induce and Justify the Secession of South Carolina from the Federal Union." The Declaration begins with a biased and incomplete history of the formation of the United States. Then it lists South Carolina's grievances against the North: "We assert that fourteen of the States have deliberately refused, for years past, to fulfill their constitutional obligations, and we refer to their own statutes for the proof." The only constitutional obligation that concerned South Carolina in 1860 was the fugitive slave clause, which the Declaration proceeds to quote. Delegates then note "an increasing hostility on the part of the non-slaveholding states to the institution of slavery." The document immediately lists those states and the rights they tried to exercise to avoid being complicit with slavery: "The States of Maine, New Hampshire, Vermont, Massachusetts, Connecticut, Rhode Island, New York, Pennsylvania, Illinois, Indiana, Michigan, Wisconsin and Iowa, have enacted laws which either nullify the acts of Congress, or render useless any attempt to execute them. In many of these States the fugitive is discharged from service of labor claimed, and in none of them has the State Government complied with the stipulation made in the Constitution." A few Northern states further infuriated South Carolina by letting African Americans vote, even though who could vote was a state matter until the Fourteenth and Fifteenth amendments to the U.S. Constitution, adopted after the Civil War. South Carolina was also upset that Northern states "have permitted the open establishment among them of [abolitionist] societies." To South Carolina "fire eaters," Northern states did not have the right to let their citizens assemble and speak freely—not if what they say might threaten slavery.

In short, South Carolina was not *for* states' rights, but *against* them. This was only to be expected, of course, because Southern planters had been in power during the Buchanan administration, indeed, throughout most of our history. In an oft-quoted phrase, James Henry Hammond, senator from South Carolina, noted in 1858 that Southerners had ruled the nation "for sixty out of seventy years of her existence."[1] The party in power *always* opposes states' rights. It's in their interest to do so.

Instead, as these excerpts show, the document is suffused with concern about slavery. None of the 50% of my audience who had voted for states' rights meant that South Carolina seceded because it was *against* states' rights, that it was *outraged* at states' rights. Yet that would be more accurate. Many audience members actually sat with their mouths open as I read from the South Carolina document, taking in this information, brand new to them.

Lincoln's election triggered secession, of course, and South Carolina says so, but it acted as a trigger precisely owing to his opposition to slavery. Debating Stephen A. Douglas in 1858, for example, even in southern Illinois, Lincoln had referred to the crisis over slavery in these words:

> It is the eternal struggle between two principles—right and wrong— throughout the world. . . . It is the same spirit that says "You toil and work and earn bread—and I'll eat it." No matter what in shape it comes, whether from the mouth of a king who seeks to bestride the people of his own nation and live by the fruit of their labor, or from one race of men as an apology for enslaving another race, it is the same tyrannical principle.[2]

When South Carolina's declaration denounced "the election of a man to the high office of President of the United States whose opinions and purposes are hostile to Slavery," it described Lincoln accurately. Indeed, Lincoln's words were anathema to slaveowners, who increasingly defined slavery as right. Hence, the eighth of my audience that had chosen that answer were not wrong, although "the election of Lincoln" amounts to another way of saying the South seceded for slavery. Unfortunately, only a relative handful in my audience had chosen that alternative.

That was North Carolina, I thought to myself afterward. The audience was overwhelmingly white. Most were over 50 years old. Many had taken U.S. history before or during the civil rights movement, when public education in the South was deliberately used as a tool of white supremacy.

By chance my next speaking engagement was at St. Cloud State University, northwest of Minneapolis. On a whim, I asked students the same question I had posed in Greensboro. To my surprise, I got the same responses in almost the same proportions. Miseducation about why we had a civil war was hardly limited to Dixie or to those educated long ago.

Lest readers imagine that we are making too much of a single source, we hasten to point out that at least four other states, when seceding from the Union, incorporated passages and ideas from South Carolina's document in their statements telling why. These statements are included in this collection. The secession convention in Texas, for example, proclaims: "The States of Maine, Vermont, New Hampshire, Connecticut, Rhode Island, Massachusetts, New York, Pennsylvania, Ohio, Wisconsin, Michigan, and Iowa, by solemn legislative enactments, have deliberately, directly or indirectly violated the 3rd clause of the 2nd section of the 4th article of the federal constitution, and laws passed in pursuance thereof."

Texas lists about the same states, in about the same order, and the constitutional clause they are charged with violating is of course the same fugitive slave clause about which South Carolina complains. Mississippi even copies South Carolina's title in its "Address Setting Forth the Declaration of the Immediate Causes Which Induce and Justify the Secession of Mississippi," and again, concern over slavery permeates the document: "Our position is thoroughly identified with the institution of slavery. . . . [A] blow at slavery is a blow at commerce and civilization. That blow has been long aimed at the institution, and was at the point of reaching its consummation. There was no choice left us but submission to the mandates of abolition, or a dissolution of the Union."

As well, South Carolina and other Deep South states sent ambassadors to other states that allowed slavery, to persuade them to secede. These envoys use similar language, stressing slavery first, last, and foremost. Georgia's Henry Benning, for instance, speaking to Virginia's secession convention, begins by asking: "What was the reason that induced Georgia to take the step of secession?" He then continues, "That reason may be summed up in one single proposition. It was a conviction; a deep conviction on the part of Georgia, that a separation from the North was the only thing that could prevent the abolition of her slavery."

No one doubted in the 1860s that secession was for slavery. When Abraham Lincoln said in his "Second Inaugural," "All knew that this interest [slavery] was somehow the cause of the war," he was not trying to convince his audience. He was merely stating the obvious, en route to some searing statements about slavery, God, and justice. The documents prove it—including Lincoln's "Second Inaugural," for that matter—if only we would read and teach them.[3]

TEACHERS ESPECIALLY NEED THESE DOCUMENTS

That verb "teach" holds a special relevance. In 2008–9, teachers underscored to me the need for this book. I led workshops for teachers of U.S. history and social studies in school systems across the United States (California, Florida, Illinois, Iowa, Louisiana, Maryland, Michigan, Minnesota, North Dakota, Ohio, Oregon, and Tennessee). During the workshops, I asked the teachers the same question I had posed in Greensboro a decade earlier, "Why did we have a Civil War?" Again, all the teachers understood that the Civil War resulted from the secession of South Carolina et al., so again the question became, "Why did South Carolina, followed by ten other Southern states, secede?" Quickly the teachers supplied the same four answers that had come from my Greensboro and St. Cloud audiences. Again, I asked them to vote, but with one twist: "You *have* to vote once. No abstentions. OK?" They agreed.

When the polls closed, teachers had done even worse than college students in Minnesota or history enthusiasts in North Carolina. About 15% had voted for slavery, 2% to 5% for the election of Lincoln, 60% to 75% for states' rights, and 2% to 20% for tariffs and taxes. In short, just 17% to 20% got it right.[4] Professional historians find it "incredible" that "some sort of abstract commitment to states' rights" is still widely believed to have motivated secession, rather than "preserving slavery and racial subordination," in the words of historian Christopher Olsen, and they are right: evidence to the contrary has always been available, in plain view.[5] Yet most teachers continue to present and misrepresent this issue to the next generation of Americans. Let me hasten to point out that none of these school systems was an educational backwater. Many of these teachers participated in special seminars under the national Teaching American History program. Nevertheless, most of them had been presenting an untrue version of why the South seceded—*because they didn't know the key documents.*

The declarations supplied by the eleven Confederate states as they left the Union are among the more important documents in the history of our nation. South Carolina's is particularly central. They are all on the web and are hardly obscure. Yet they remain little known. In *The Confederate Reader: How the South Saw the War*—which came out in 1957, has been repackaged by two other publishers since then, and remains in print today—Richard Harwell included only the formal one-paragraph "Ordinance to Dissolve the Union" that the South Carolina convention passed to notify the nation "that the union now subsisting between South Carolina and the other States . . . is hereby dissolved." Harwell thus dodged entirely the crucial question of why. So did Rod Gragg, editor of *Illustrated Confederate Reader*, in 1991.[6] Recently the National Archives put "100 Milestone Documents" on its website for Americans to ponder but included nothing about secession.[7] No high school history textbook quotes any statement about why the South seceded.[8] *Holt American Nation*, for example, says, "Within days of the election, the South Carolina legislature called a convention and unanimously voted to leave the Union. Alabama, Florida, Georgia, Louisiana, Mississippi, and Texas soon passed similar acts of secession." Similar to what? *Holt* does not quote a single word from any of these documents.

Not only do our textbooks avoid the documents, the accounts they do provide contradict the historical record. *Holt*, for example, writes, "The southern secessionists justified their position with the doctrine of states' rights. They asserted that since individual states had come together to form the Union, a state had the right to withdraw from the Union." If read literally, in a certain minimalist sense *Holt* is right: secessionists seceded while asserting their right to secede.[9] But this is hardly what people meant then by "states' rights"; nor is it how most people would read the passage today. Proponents of states' rights defend the power of individual states to make public policy vis-à-vis the power of the central government. The secession documents show that Southern states were outraged by the rather feeble attempts by Northern states *to* exercise states' rights, not by their own inability to do so.[10]

Other textbooks throw tariffs into the mix. *The American Pageant*, for instance, admits, "The low Tariff of 1857, passed largely by southern votes, was not in itself menacing." Nevertheless, it goes on to hypothesize, "But who could tell when the 'greedy' Republicans would win control of Congress and drive through their own oppressive protective tariff?" This seems plausible, because after senators from the Deep South left the U.S. Senate early in 1861, that body, now dominated by Republicans, passed a higher tariff in March. But it had bipartisan support: President Buchanan, of the proslavery wing of the Democratic Party, signed it into law. Moreover, as the timing implies, opposition to this tariff hardly explains why seven states seceded before it passed, and war broke out before it took effect. Not one state said anything substantive about tariffs when seceding in 1860–61.[11]

Older textbooks were even less clear. *Triumph of the American Nation* was the best-selling textbook in the 1970s and 1980s, when most of today's teachers went to high school. Its 1990 edition offers only obfuscation:

> Why did the North and South go to war in 1861? What was the immediate cause of the tragic conflict? There is no easy way to answer these two questions. Historians have studied the issues for years and still reach different conclusions.
>
> Some historians have stressed the basic economic and social differences of the North and the South. Other historians have pointed to disagreements over tariffs, internal improvements at public expense, money and banking, the disposal of public lands, and slavery. Still other historians have emphasized the issue of states' rights.[12]

Thus today's teachers are not exactly uneducated. Their problem is, they have read their textbooks but not the documents.

Why do textbooks get secession wrong? Why would their authors not quote the critical documents, easily available to them?

Four basic reasons explain this failure. First, textbook authors have gotten into the habit of not quoting anything. One textbook even gives students two paragraphs *about* William Jennings Bryan's famous "Cross of Gold" speech while not quoting a single word of it, other than its title. Authors drone on in an omniscient monotone, rather than letting the voices of the past speak.

Second, publishers don't want to offend. Flatly saying that slavery was why Southern states seceded might cause state textbook adoption boards across the South to reject a textbook. Or at least so worry publishers' marketing departments. As historian William C. Davis put it in 1996, "All peoples part with their myths reluctantly, and historians are at some risk when they try to dismantle those of the Confederacy."[13] At its best, history embodies the triumph of evidence over ideology. Textbooks do not embody history at its best.

Third, authors are too busy to write "their" textbooks. Most K–12 textbooks—especially as they age—aren't really by the scholars whose names grace their covers. *The American Journey*, for example, lists James McPherson as one of its authors. McPherson wrote *Battle Cry of Freedom*, perhaps our best one-volume history of the Civil War. Two passages in *Journey* "explain" why the South seceded. According to the first:

> Lincoln and the Republicans had promised not to disturb slavery where it already existed. Nevertheless, many people in the South mistrusted

the party, fearing that the Republican government would not protect Southern rights and liberties. On December 20, 1860, the South's long-standing threat to leave the Union became a reality when South Carolina held a special convention and voted to secede.

"Would not protect Southern rights and liberties"—what might this mean? It is vague to the point of mystification. In *Battle Cry of Freedom*, McPherson asks precisely this question: "What were these rights and liberties for which Confederates contended?" And he answers immediately: "The right to own slaves; the liberty to take this property into the territories. . . ."[14] Readers of *The American Journey* get no such help.

Journey then claims:

> Southerners justified secession with the theory of *states' rights*. The states, they argued, had voluntarily chosen to enter the Union. They defined the Constitution as a contract among the independent states. Now because the national government had violated that contract—by refusing to enforce the Fugitive Slave Act and by denying the Southern states equal rights in the territories—the states were justified in leaving the Union.

Again, in a literal and minimalist sense, the first half of that passage is right: South Carolina's declaration does point out that the original thirteen states had voluntarily chosen to enter the Union, and South Carolina did claim secession as a state's right. Otherwise, however, South Carolina made no states' rights claim of any kind in 1860. Indeed, South Carolina voiced no complaint with any policy of the federal government. Why would it? Lincoln had not even taken office, and Southern slaveowners dominated the Buchanan administration. The South also enjoyed a majority on the Supreme Court. As McPherson himself writes in an article published the same year as his textbook, "Of all these interpretations, the state's-rights [*sic*] argument is perhaps the weakest."[15]

The two reasons for secession that the last sentence of the textbook passage concocts—"refusing to enforce the Fugitive Slave Act" and "denying the Southern states equal rights in the territories"—are flatly wrong. South Carolina specifically noted that the national government had *not* refused to enforce the Fugitive Slave Act. Nor had it denied to Southern states equal rights in the territories. Quite the opposite: the 1857 *Dred Scott* decision, supported by Buchanan, denied *free* states equal rights in the territories. It declared that territories *had* to be open to slavery, regardless of their residents' desires.[16] This paragraph in *Journey* is not what we would expect from America's premiere Civil War historian. It is hard to believe that McPherson even read it and impossible to believe that he wrote it.

Fourth, downplaying slavery as the chief reason for secession got established in our culture as well as our textbooks during the Nadir of race relations. We shall discuss that terrible period—from 1890 to 1940, when race relations deteriorated—a few pages later. Here let us simply note, since the "states' rights" alternative became dominant around 1900, by now it has become a textbook tradition. It's hard for publishers to buck tradition, especially since the people who actually write their textbooks are often temporary workers who lack the independence and sometimes the credentials and knowledge to start a new custom. Indeed, given the remarkable inertia built into the textbook industry, just getting slavery back in as a secondary cause in recent books probably could not have happened without the civil rights movement.

WHAT WAS THE CONFEDERACY ABOUT?

The documents collected here make various other eye-opening points. If the South seceded for slavery, obviously the Confederacy was about the perpetuation of that institution. Intertwined with slavery, however, and underlying the fervor with which white Southerners had defended slavery before the war and seceded for slavery in 1860–61, was the idea of white supremacy.[17] This idea won considerable sympathy from white Northerners, especially Democrats, who called their party "the white man's party," tarred Republicans as "black Republicans," and raised the specter of massive black immigration northward, were slavery to end.

Slavery had not always been caught up with race. Europeans had enslaved each other for centuries; the word itself derives from "Slav," the group most often enslaved by other Europeans before 1400. Native Americans and Africans likewise enslaved their neighbors long before Europeans arrived. Indeed, Europeans did not think of themselves as a group before the slow increase of racially based slavery, beginning around 1400. As Europeans sailed down the west coast of Africa, they traded with coastal tribes for captives from the interior. Slaves came to be more and more identified as dark-skinned Africans, and vice-versa. Increasingly whites viewed enslavement of whites as illegitimate, while enslavement of Africans was acceptable, maybe even good for them. Unlike in earlier slaveries, children of African American slaves would be slaves forever. They could never achieve upward mobility through intermarriage with the owning class.

The rationale for this differential treatment was racism. As Montesquieu ironically observed in 1748: "It is impossible for us to suppose these creatures to be men, because, allowing them to be men, a suspicion would follow that we ourselves are not Christian."[18] Therefore racism gradually increased in Western culture. At first, Europeans considered Africans exotic but not necessarily inferior. Shakespeare's 1604 depiction of Othello, derived from a story written in 1565 by Giovanni Battista Giraldi, fits this description.[19] As more and more European nations joined the slave trade, followed by the United States, whites increasingly characterized Africans as stupid, backward, and uncivilized. Concurrently, they came to see themselves as "white." By the 1850s, many white Americans, including some Northerners, claimed black people were so hopelessly inferior that slavery was a proper form of education for them. After all, it removed them physically from the alleged barbarism of the "dark continent."

Racism was not just an expedient adopted to rationalize the otherwise indefensible unfairness of slavery. Slavery had given rise to white supremacy as an ideology—a way of making sense of the social world. Now white supremacy prompted a fierce defense of slavery. Consequently, to a considerable degree, the Confederacy was about white supremacy. The "Cornerstone Speech" by the vice president of the Confederacy, Alexander Stephens, delivered to a huge audience in Savannah, Georgia, as the Confederacy was forming, speaks to this issue. After telling several ways that he deems the new constitution for the Confederate States of America superior to the U.S. Constitution, Stephens reaches the central point of his speech. He notes that Jefferson and other founders believed that all men were created equal, "that the enslavement of the African was . . . wrong in *principle*, socially, morally and politically." He continues: "Our new Government is founded upon exactly the opposite idea. Its foundations are laid, its cornerstone rests, upon the great truth that the negro is not equal to the white man; that slavery—subordination to the superior race—is his natural and moral condition." Again, no textbook quotes Stephens. None quotes Jefferson Davis or Robert E. Lee or any other Confederate leader on the idea of race.

Under great pressure, Confederate leaders rapidly formed a government, mobilized a people, and recruited an army. Their constitution incorporated much of the U.S. Constitution, but with certain changes and interesting additional features. As the war progressed, Confederate leaders put Stephens's "great truth" into practice. In May 1861, they had to decide what to do with 800 light-skinned African Americans (in today's terms) who wanted to enlist in the Confederate army. These were members of the "Native Guards," a New Orleans paramilitary group. James Hollandsworth calls them "representatives of a free black community in New Orleans that was both prosperous and well-educated." Some owned slaves. Confederates let them form as a militia but "never intended to use black troops for any mission of real importance," notes Hollandsworth.[20] Soon the Native Guards' enthusiasm for the Confederate cause waned. On February 15, 1862, the Louisiana legislature disbanded them.

A month later the governor reinstated them, desperate to hold New Orleans, but they never saw combat. After the United States took New Orleans in April, many Native Guardsmen eventually enlisted in the U.S. Army.[21]

Confederate leaders did recruit Native Americans. But they could not bring themselves to recruit African American troops until March 1865, just three weeks before Appomattox. Confederate ideology blocked acceptance of such troops. As a letter we include by Howell Cobb, provisional president of the Confederacy before Jefferson Davis took office, puts it, "You cannot make soldiers of slaves, nor slaves of soldiers. . . . The day you make soldiers of them is the beginning of the end of the revolution. If slaves will make good soldiers our whole theory of slavery is wrong." Stephens had encapsulated that theory in his "great truth that the negro is not equal to the white man." From time to time a Confederate officer or civilian leader, notably General Patrick Cleburne, advocated enlisting African Americans, but the central government always said no. Near the end, with Richmond almost surrounded, Jefferson Davis finally changed his mind, but no time remained to put the new policy into effect.[22] Nevertheless, in the late twentieth century, neo-Confederate accounts of the Civil War came to include dozens, even thousands, of black soldiers in gray.

Just as race precluded Confederates from using African Americans as soldiers, so race kept them from treating captured black soldiers as prisoners of war. Documents in this reader show that the repeated Confederate massacres of black POWs and their white officers—after Fort Pillow, Honey Springs, Saltville, Plymouth, the Crater, etc.—were not chance mishaps in the heat of battle. Rather, they reflected Confederate policy from the top down.

Confederates even showed their preoccupation with race in their flag. Civil War buffs know that "the Confederate flag" waved today was never the official flag of the Confederate States of America. Rather, it was the battle flag of the Army of Northern Virginia. During the war, the Confederacy adopted three official flags. The first, sometimes called "the Stars and Bars," drew many objections "on account of its resemblance to that of the abolition despotism against which we are fighting," in the words of the editor of the *Savannah Morning News*, quoted herein. The second, often called "the Stainless Banner," included the battle flag in its upper corner but was otherwise pure white. The Georgia editor shows this to be no accident: "As a people, we are fighting to maintain the Heaven-ordained supremacy of the white man over the inferior or colored race; a white flag would thus be emblematical of our cause." The third flag, adopted near the end of the war, retained the white field but added a red strip at the end because the second flag too often was mistaken for a flag of surrender.

HOW DID CONFEDERATE IDEOLOGY CHANGE AFTER THE WAR?

After the Civil War, the United States passed new laws, including the Fourteenth and Fifteenth amendments, making African Americans full citizens with equal rights. Considerable numbers of former Confederates, including such leaders as General James Longstreet, Lee's second in command at Gettysburg, and General William Mahone, came to agree with these measures. To these men, the performance of black troops in the last two years of the war helped put to rest Stephens's "great truth."

Most Confederates, having seceded and fought for slavery, found it hard to admit they had been wrong about African Americans. Some did admit that slavery was wrong; almost no ex-Confederate claimed it was still viable. Many white Southerners now emphasized that they had fought to defend their homes and states against Northern invasion, a point made in postwar documents in this collection.

With slavery ended, some former Confederates had no use for African Americans at all. In 1866, in testimony before a congressional committee included in this collection, Robert E. Lee suggests, "I think it would be better for Virginia if she could get rid of them." But Lee's was a minority position, and he never took steps to implement it.

Stephens's "Cornerstone Speech" had stated that the Confederacy's "cornerstone rests, upon the great truth that the negro is not equal to the white man; that slavery—subordination to the superior race—is his natural and moral condition." The war had settled the matter of slavery. Simply dropping that word from Stephens's sentence leaves the crux of his position intact, however. Indeed, in an 1868 document in this volume, Stephens writes, "What was called Slavery amongst us, was but a legal subordination of the African to Caucasian race."

In 1868, Edward A. Pollard made clear the continuity between the Confederate cause and what Southern Democrats worked for during Reconstruction. Pollard was a secessionist who in 1866 famously renamed the Confederacy "the Lost Cause" in a pro-Southern book of that title. In the "Introduction" to his next book, *The Lost Cause Regained*, included in this volume, Pollard argues that slavery's "greatest value" was as "a barrier against a contention and War of races." If white supremacy could be reestablished, Pollard writes, then the South "really triumphs in the true cause of the war, with respect to all its fundamental and vital issues."

At about the same time, Rushmore G. Horton, probably a co-conspirator in a Confederate plot to burn Manhattan in 1864, published *A Youth's History of the Great Civil War*, written expressly from a Southern viewpoint and reprinted by neo-Confederates in 1925 and again in the 1990s.[23] Horton focuses on alleged black inferiority to explain the necessity of white supremacy and the reason for secession: "[White Southerners] knew from their practical knowledge of the negro that he belonged to a distinct species of man; that his brain, his bones, his shape, his nerves, in fact that every part of his body was different from the white man's. They knew that he was liable to different diseases from the white man; that he required the care and protection of the superior race. They knew that to equalize the races was simply to follow the fate of Mexico and Central America." After extended analysis blaming everything bad in Mexico and Central America on the evil of "amalgamation with the black race," Horton concludes that interracial children "are *hybrids* or *mongrels*, and are always a weak, degraded, and wretched class of beings—as inferior to the white race as the mule is to the horse."[24] Avoiding such a result was among "the *policy* and *objects* of secession."

Horton's ideological purpose is to provide ex-Confederates with beliefs to justify the campaign of terror they were waging against black schools and black voters. As well, he supplies talking points to persuade outsiders to leave them alone while they reestablished white supremacy. Other documents and speeches by former Confederate leaders during and immediately after Reconstruction, included in this reader, show this same continuity of purpose with the Confederate era. They succeeded: ex-Confederates became the core— and the corps—of various paramilitary organizations calling themselves the Red Shirts, Knights of the White Camellia, and, most often, the Ku Klux Klan. Gradually, state by state, white supremacists overthrew by force and fraud the interracial Republican administrations.

As the 1870s passed, some ex-Confederates—whom we now must start calling "neo-Confederates"[25]—found themselves less able to admit they had been wrong about African Americans, since they were now dominating them politically. They also found it harder to admit they had seceded and fought a war on behalf of slavery. As a result, as documents in this collection show, the reasons for secession began to blur. Outrage that Northern states were not honoring the fugitive slave clause of the U.S. Constitution became "failure to adhere to Constitutional principles." Thus we see that *when* we write about secession influences *what* we write about secession.

NEO-CONFEDERATE IDEOLOGY DURING THE NADIR

In 1890, the Nadir of race relations began to set in. Mississippi passed a new state constitution making it impossible for most black Mississippians to vote or hold public office. The United States did nothing. Therefore all other Southern states followed suit. In 1894, Democrats in Congress repealed the remaining federal election statutes. Now the Fifteenth Amendment was lifeless, for it had no extant laws to enforce it. Neo-Confederates were delighted: at that point, Alexander Stephens's "great truth" again became national policy, as it had been in 1857. States as far north as North Dakota passed new laws outlawing interracial marriage. Lynchings rose to their all-time peak, and not just in the South. After 1890, again not just in the South, segregation swept through public accommodations. Describing the day-to-day interactions of whites and blacks in the Midwest, historian Frank Quillen observed in 1913 that race prejudice "is increasing steadily, especially during the last twenty years." In short, during the Nadir, white Americans—North and South—joined hands to restrict African Americans' civil and economic rights.[26]

How were white Americans—Northerners as well as Southerners—to understand these actions? How could whites harmonize them with our nation's stated belief "that all men are created equal"? Only by agreeing with Stephens that African Americans were subhuman. So it happened that racism as an ideology reached its highest point in American history in the Nadir, higher even than during slavery.[27]

With their triumph, neo-Confederates were able to rewrite the history of the Civil War. Again, *when* people wrote about the war influenced *what* they wrote. Selections from *Confederate Veteran*, the magazine of the Sons of Confederate Veterans; Mildred Rutherford's *Scrap Books*; and other sources after 1890 in this collection show history turned on its head. Now neo-Confederates claimed that secession had been misunderstood all along: South Carolina and the other Southern states had seceded *for* states' rights. They even renamed the war, at least in Dixie; for fifty years it became "the War Between the States."[28] States' rights also played an important contemporary function: since white Southerners no longer commanded the federal government during the Nadir, as they had during slavery, they stressed the need for each state to handle race relations as it saw fit.

During the Nadir, the role African Americans played in the Union army and navy lay forgotten. It did not fit with the racism of the era. Instead, from Virginia to Louisiana, Neo-Confederates erected a handful of monuments honoring African Americans who sided with the Confederacy. At the same time, paradoxically, neo-Confederates did recall that African Americans had enlisted in the U.S. armed forces and considered that fact a blot on Union honor.[29]

Neo-Confederates portrayed Reconstruction as a time of terror, imposed by the North on behalf of deluded and inferior African Americans who could not possibly benefit from the rights bestowed upon them. John W. Daniel, longtime senator from Virginia, speaking to the Reunion of the United Confederate Veterans held at New Orleans in 1892, termed Reconstruction "a seething caldron of ruin and corruption." Even though the historical record does not support such "analysis," Northerners did not really contest this revisionism. To do so was not in their ideological interest, since they had acquiesced in the reimposition of white supremacy. Fueled by such rhetoric, neo-Confederate documents mingle the terrorist organizations that ended Reconstruction—the Ku Klux Klan, Red Shirts, etc.—with the Confederate cause, as part of Confederate glory.

During the Nadir, neo-Confederates also came out against other aspects of liberal democracy that seemed to have little connection to the Civil War. For example, documents included in this collection show that they opposed women's suffrage. They influenced their legislatures; even after Congress passed the Nineteenth Amendment, Southern states refused to ratify it. This opposition lingered at least into the 1970s, when only Texas, among all former Confederate states, ratified the Equal Rights Amendment.[30] Neo-Confederates also opposed labor unions. Under the heading "What Has the Negro Meant to the South?" Mildred Rutherford, historian general of the United Daughters of the Confederacy, listed as a benefit, "The Negro has protected us from strikes in the South."[31] She was right; the labor movement has always been weak in the South.[32]

Today, no textbook tells how Confederate ideas triumphed during the Nadir. Doing so would not fit with their underlying storyline of uninterrupted progress. For that matter, that notion of progress has kept textbook authors from seeing that sometimes things grew worse, so most textbooks do not treat the Nadir of race relations at all. As a result, most Americans have no idea that in the 1890s and the first third of the twentieth century, race relations worsened all across America.

NEO-CONFEDERATE IDEOLOGY AFTER THE NADIR

After 1940, race relations slowly began to improve. During World War II, Nazi Germany was so outrageously hateful toward Jewish and Rom people that racism began to get a bad name. At war's end, the United States housed the United Nations. Our national interests were jeopardized when segregation embarrassed leaders from new nations in Asia and Africa as they traveled beyond New York City or Washington, D.C. In 1947, Jackie Robinson and the Brooklyn Dodgers desegregated Major League Baseball. The next summer, President Truman ordered the armed forces desegregated.

Neo-Confederates dusted off Confederate ideas and symbols to resist these changes. In 1948, Southern white supremacists formed the Dixiecrat Party. At their convention, students and delegates waved battle flags of the Confederacy in support of Strom Thurmond of South Carolina for president and Fielding Wright of Mississippi for vice president. After *Brown v. Board of Education* triggered the struggle for civil rights in 1954, white Mississippians founded Citizens' Councils to oppose the civil rights movement. Rapidly the Councils spread across the South. Again, the Confederate flag, now crossed with Old Glory, was their symbol.[33] In their speeches and articles opposing civil rights, neo-Confederate organizations and leaders made very clear the white supremacist meaning of their Confederate heritage.

Neo-Confederates correctly saw the struggle against the modern civil rights movement as a repeat of the postwar struggle of ex-Confederates against racial equality. To try to keep African Americans from becoming full citizens, the Citizens' Councils exhumed the horrific portrait of Reconstruction developed by neo-Confederates. In an editorial in this volume, *The Citizens' Council* makes the parallel between the two eras explicit. It quotes Margaret Mitchell's racist and inaccurate account of Reconstruction in *Gone With the Wind*, including her allegation of interracial sexual outrages, to inveigh against letting African Americans have the rights of citizenship (guaranteed them by the Fourteenth and Fifteenth amendments) a century later.

As in the Nadir, neo-Confederates controlled Southern state governments, but not the federal government. Therefore they continued to write bad history not only about Reconstruction but also about secession. They identified the 1960s struggle against federal civil rights laws—which was indeed a states' rights conflict—as a battle for the principles of the Confederacy—which had little to do with states' rights.

When he signed the 1964 Civil Rights Act, Lyndon Johnson is said to have remarked, "We have lost the South for a generation." Indeed, we shall see that the Republican Party became dominant in Dixie; conversely, Southerners came to have immense influence in the party. From 1960 through 2004, only two candidates for president from outside Dixie were successful. One of those, Richard Nixon, won partly owing to his "Southern strategy," appealing to white voters by using coded language that implied he would go slow on civil rights. The other, Ronald Reagan, kicked off his 1980 general election campaign at that most Southern of all locations, the Neshoba County Fair. This is a traditionally white venue in the Mississippi county whose law enforcement officers had notoriously helped to kill three civil rights workers in 1964. Reagan never mentioned that tragic event, although some of the perpetrators and their relatives and friends were in his audience. Instead, he focused his remarks on the need for "states' rights," a code phrase for getting the federal government to leave race relations alone. More recent Republican leaders, like former attorney general John Ashcroft, former Mississippi senator Trent Lott, and Richard Quinn, former spokesperson and campaign organizer for John McCain, have ties to some of the most extreme neo-Confederate organizations and publications.[34]

Confederate symbolism and ideology inevitably come with white supremacy baggage—a darker side to the neo-Confederate revival. In 1995, I chatted with a flag vendor at a flea market near Brattleboro, Vermont. He displayed more Confederate flags than any other single item, but not the usual battle flag of the Army of Northern Virginia. Embroidered across each were the words, "If the South had won, we'd have no trouble now." Consider that phrase for a moment. Who is "we?" Exactly what "trouble" would we not have? The implications are chilling. "What does this mean?" I asked him. "If the South had won, we'd have no trouble now," he answered. "I can read it," I replied, "but what does it *mean?*" "I don't know," he parried. "It's my best seller." Such symbols are quick to appear amid moments of racial tension. In 1999, at North High School in Appleton, Wisconsin, for instance, conflicts between Mexican Americans and whites were a frequent occurrence. On the day after whites had defaced a Mexican flag at North, white students came to school wearing Confederate battle flag symbols. For decades Appleton had been a sundown town, requiring African Americans to be outside its city limits after dark. Residents of such towns frequently own and display Confederate flags. Although Appleton allowed black residents in 1999, the fact that students already owned these symbols and saw this conflict as their chance to use them probably derived from Appleton's sundown past.[35]

Despite their new political connections and the general "Southernization of America," to use John Egerton's memorable phrase, the success of the civil rights movement disheartened many neo-Confederates. Now that the Voting Rights Act of 1965 has again enfranchised African Americans across the South, white Southern politicians are no longer so eager to fly the Confederate battle flag on state capitols and celebrate Jefferson Davis's birthday with effusive speeches. Organizations like Sons of Confederate Veterans and United Daughters of the Confederacy now fight rear-guard delaying actions, trying to preserve the monuments, celebrations, and holidays that they have long enjoyed. In the process, some neo-Confederates now emphasize that they stand for "heritage, not hate," a slogan popularized by Charles Lunsford, head of the Heritage Preservation Association. This represents an explicit abandonment of white supremacy as a Confederate cause.[36]

In a further twist of the black soldier issue, late in the twentieth century some neo-Confederates claimed that thousands of African Americans had served in the Confederate army. In 1992, Lunsford wrote in *Confederate Veteran*, "The truth is that the overwhelming majority of blacks during the War Between the States supported and defended, with armed resistance, the Cause of Southern Independence," and went on to claim, "more than 300,000 blacks, both free and slave, supported the Confederacy—far more than supported the Union."[37] Such service supposedly showed that the Confederacy was about neither race nor slavery.[38] Examined thoughtfully, these claims founder. Documents in this reader show black Confederates to be an imaginative late-twentieth-century creation rather than a reality in the 1860s. The contention does show a further attempt to distance the Confederate cause from slavery or race. It may get further use during the presidency of Barack Obama.

Some of today's neo-Confederates take heart from the rise of separatist movements around the globe, in such places as Scotland, Belgium, Quebec, even Russia. In the United States, however, anyone advocating secession looks like a fringe element. Although neo-Confederates point to success stories like the Baltic nations and Slovakia, it is hard to take them seriously. Nevertheless, their connections to major leaders of the Republican Party do mean that we must take their influence seriously, if not their secession proposals. Within that party, a substantial proportion of members favor such neo-Confederate principles as states' rights and white supremacy.[39] In 2008, the Republican candidate for vice president had ties to a fringe party advocating secession for Alaska. In 2009, the Republican governor of Texas and the leading Republican candidates for governor of Georgia refused to back away from secession and states' rights when discussing tax protests and potential congressional actions they disapproved.

THESE DOCUMENTS ARE IMPORTANT

Perhaps the most pervasive theme in U.S. history is the domination of black America by white America. Certainly race is the sharpest and deepest division in American life. Of all problems facing our nation, race relations is also the most historically embedded. Indeed, even the definitions of "race" and the various races we recognize today result from history. Yet most Americans cannot apply history usefully to today's race relations issues—partly because they do not know these documents.

Teaching that the Confederate states seceded for states' rights is not accurate history. It might be termed "white history." It bends—even breaks—the facts of what happened, seeking an explanation that will not upset neo-Confederate white students (or parents or potential book adopters). Taught that way, history especially alienates people of color. As a result, African American, Native American, and Latino students view U.S. history with a special dislike. They also learn it especially poorly; the racial achievement gap is larger in history/ social studies than in any other high school subject. Young African Americans may not realize why they are alienated or even *that* they are alienated, only that "I don't *like* social studies" or "I'm not good at history."[40]

Even scarier than historically ignorant and alienated minority children is the prospect of white children who "know" things that never happened. Across the country, teachers who have never read these documents are presenting se-cession, the Confederacy, and the aftermath of the Civil War to the next genera-tion of Americans. Even if we could fix this problem tomorrow morning, most of the people leading our government and other institutions in the year 2050 will have been miseducated on these points. But we have not fixed the problem. The fact that most teachers still misteach secession shows the extraordinary in-fluence of neo-Confederate ideas even today. So does the fact that most teach-ers—and most Americans—have never heard of the Nadir of race relations.

A stanza of the civil rights anthem "We Shall Overcome" repeats: "The truth will make us free." We believe that. We believe that if white Southerners knew what Confederate leaders like Jefferson Davis and Alexander Stephens and neo-Confederates like Mildred Rutherford and Strom Thurmond actually said and did, they would give up these men and women as role models. A realm of idealistic white leaders in the past—from James Longstreet to Robert Zellner—awaits discovery and recovery by young Southerners of all races.[41]

White history may be appropriate for a white nation. It is inappropriate for a great nation. The United States is not a white nation. It has never been a white nation. It is time for us to give up our white history in favor of more accurate history, based more closely on the historical record, such as these documents. Surely a great nation can afford to do that.

CHAPTER 1

THE GATHERING STORM (1787–1860)

Before 1776, every American colony allowed slavery. In 1720, 1,600 of New York City's population of 7,000 were African Americans, mostly enslaved; several hundred Native Americans were also in chains. In 1755, more than 10% of Rhode Island's people were in bondage. The utopian justification for the American Revolution, emphasizing the "rights of man," coexisted uneasily with the institution of slavery. So did the rhetorical tactics the colonists employed: Americans were fighting a war seeking "freedom" from "British tyranny," yet were keeping others in a bondage far more oppressive than any Britain had imposed.

As a result, a movement favoring emancipation coursed through the Northern states, formerly colonies, even making considerable headway in Virginia and North Carolina. One after another, beginning in New England and ending with New Jersey, the Northern states began to abolish slavery. By the Constitutional Convention in 1787, slavery had become a point of contention between North and South. Although the "s-word" appears nowhere in the document, Paul Finkelman points out that five passages in the Constitution directly treat slavery. All five guarantee it. To get those guarantees, Southern representatives threatened not to sign the evolving Constitution, hence to withdraw from the United States. In the summary of the discussion about the international slave trade included here, John Rutledge of South Carolina voices such a warning: "The true question at present is, whether the Southern States shall or shall not be parties to the Union." Thus he foreshadows the rhetoric to which his state would resort in the 1850s.[1]

By 1830, only vestiges of slavery remained in the North. Meanwhile Southern slavery flourished even as it tightened, making manumission harder and the lives of free blacks more restricted. In Maryland, Virginia, and Kentucky, owners were finding that their largest profits came from selling excess children and young adults to slave markets in Mobile, Natchez, and New Orleans. In the

Deep South, cotton was becoming so profitable that Natchez claimed more millionaires per capita in 1860 than anywhere else in America. Even Egypt and India could not compete with American cotton—planted, cultivated, and picked by unpaid labor. Unlike some Founding Fathers, politicians after 1830 could not realistically believe that slavery would somehow die out on its own. Conflict loomed.

By this time South Carolina senator John C. Calhoun had become slavery's most important spokesperson. In his 1837 speech "On Abolition Petitions," included here, Calhoun predicts secession if citizens in the North are left free to develop antislavery thought and flood Congress with petitions against slavery. In the "Address to the Southern People" in this collection, Calhoun lists key passages in the Constitution that protected slavery. He is incensed that Northern states let private citizens advocate abolition and circulate "incendiary publications in the South." His words here are a harbinger of Confederate efforts during the Civil War and neo-Confederate efforts during the civil rights movement to stifle dissent in the South.

In 1848, the Alabama Democratic Party adopted a platform with national implications. This platform instructs Alabama's delegates to the Democratic National Convention to require in the national party platform that all territory recently gotten from Mexico—as well as whatever other territories the United States might acquire anywhere—be open to slavery. Not only did Alabama pass this platform, the legislatures or Democratic conventions of several other Southern states also endorsed it. Alabama Democrats readopted this plank in 1860, and so did the majority report of the platform committee of the 1860 Democratic National Convention.[2]

Meanwhile, Protestant denominations began to separate regionally. Of course, the split was not mainly geographic. Rather, like the deepening political division, it had to do with slavery, overlaid by religious leaders with theological embellishment. Rev. James H. Thornwell was a prominent Southern Presbyterian. Neo-Confederates regard him highly today. They use the sermon we include to support their claim that the Civil War was a conflict between a heretical North and a more orthodox Christian South.

Some clergymen, even some Southern Presbyterians, disagreed with the extreme proslavery views of clerics like Thornwell. Southern politicians were similarly divided in 1850. They held a convention in Nashville that passed various resolutions, included here, that conflict with each other to a degree. Not satisfied with these resolutions, South Carolina, always taking the most extreme proslavery position, passed a law late that year providing for a state convention to consider secession. Eventually that convention passed a resolution, which we include, declaring that South Carolina had grounds to secede but would not do so at present.

Like ministers, secular ideologues increasingly provided rationales for enslaving African Americans. In 1851, Samuel A. Cartwright, a New Orleans doctor, wrote "Diseases and Peculiarities of the Negro Race." His purpose was partly to guide practitioners of medicine with enslaved African clienteles, partly to justify slavery as appropriate for African peoples for medical and religious reasons. J. H. Van Evrie was a medical doctor in New York City with strong pro-Confederate sentiments. He wrote a pamphlet, "Negroes and Negro 'Slavery'; The First an Inferior Race—The Latter, Its Normal Condition," which came out in 1853. Its purpose was to show "scientifically" that "the negro" is a "DIFFERENT AND INFERIOR SPECIES OF MAN"—capitalized in the original—for whom slavery is appropriate.[3] Important Confederates-to-be wrote blurbs for its inside cover, also included here. George Fitzhugh's sociological works agreed that African Americans were inferior, but in the passage we include, he claims that Southern racial slavery was kinder and gentler than Northern wage slavery.

As the 1850s wore on, Kansas became a flash point of conflict between pro- and antislavery forces. In 1856, Alexander Stephens, then congressman from Georgia, argued against accepting Kansas as a free state. Much of his speech, which we include, is a defense of slavery based on "Christian philanthropy" and the "laws of nature." Two years later, speaking in Maine in 1858, Jefferson Davis looks forward to U.S. expansion southward, but he cautions Americans against "the mingling of races" with Latinos. In July 1860, shortly before Lincoln's victory would trigger Southern secession, John B. Gordon gave a speech in Georgia that sums up budding Confederate precepts. Like Calhoun, he sees slavery to be a positive good. Like Davis, he foresees taking land to the south. Like Stephens, he holds that the federal government must protect the rights of slaveowners to enter any territory with their slaves. Ominously, Gordon also argues for "dismemberment of this Union" if the Republicans win in November.

* * *

DEBATE OVER SLAVERY AT THE CONSTITUTIONAL
CONVENTION, AUGUST 21–22, 1787.[4]

By the 1830s, slaveowners told opponents of slavery that the Constitution protected slavery, that representatives from the slave states would never have signed it otherwise, and that everyone at the Constitutional Convention knew it. This summary of the discussion of the international slave trade at that convention shows that they have a point. Some historians maintain that Southerners at the convention never really contemplated a separate nation. Indeed, the three South Carolina delegates who voice such threats in this extract supported a strong national government. Nevertheless, the belief that their threats were serious had become dogma by the 1850s. Thus this debate begins a pattern of threats by slaveowners that eventually resulted in secession.[5]

Mr. Luther Martin [MD] proposed to vary article 7, sect. 4, so as to allow a prohibition or tax on the importation of slaves. In the first place, as five slaves are to be counted as three freemen, in the appointment of representatives, such a clause would leave an encouragement to this traffic. In the second place, slaves weakened one part of the Union, which the other parts were bound to protect; the privilege of importing them was therefore unreasonable. And, in the third place, it was inconsistent with the principles of the revolution, and dishonorable to the American character, to have such a feature in the Constitution.

Mr. John Rutledge [SC] did not see how the importation of slaves could be encouraged by this section. He was not apprehensive of insurrections, and would readily exempt the other states from the obligation to protect the Southern against them. Religion and humanity had nothing to do with this question. Interest alone is the governing principle with nations. The true question at present is, whether the Southern States shall or shall not be parties to the Union. If the Northern States consult their interest, they will not oppose the increase of slaves, which will increase the commodities of which they become the carriers.

Mr. Oliver Ellsworth [CT] was for leaving the clause as it stands. Let every state import what it pleases. The morality or wisdom of slavery are considerations belonging to the states themselves. What enriches a part enriches the whole, and the states are the best judges of their particular interest. The old Confederation had not meddled with this point; and he did not see any greater necessity for bringing it within the policy of the new one.

Mr. Charles Pinckney [SC]. South Carolina can never receive the plan if it prohibits the slave trade. In every proposed extension of the powers of Congress, that state has expressly and watchfully excepted that of meddling with the importation of negroes. If the states be all left at liberty on this subject, South Carolina may perhaps, by degrees, do of herself what is wished, as Virginia and Maryland already have done.

Mr. Roger Sherman [CT] was for leaving the clause as it stands. He disapproved of the slave trade; yet, as the states were now possessed of the right to import slaves, as the public good did not require it to be taken from them, and as it was expedient to have as few objections as possible to the proposed scheme of government, he thought it best to leave the matter as we find it. He observed, that the abolition of slavery seemed to be going on in the United States, and that the good sense of the several states would probably by degrees complete it. He urged on the Convention the necessity of despatching its business.

Col. George Mason [VA]. This infernal traffic originated in the avarice of British merchants. The British government constantly checked the attempts of Virginia to put a stop to it. The present question concerns not the importing states alone, but the whole Union. The evil of having slaves was experienced during the late war. Had slaves been treated as they might have been by the enemy, they would have proved dangerous instruments in their hands. . . . Maryland and Virginia, he said, had already prohibited the importation of slaves expressly. North Carolina had done the same in substance. All this would be in vain, if South Carolina and Georgia be at liberty to import. The western people are already calling out for slaves for their new lands, and will fill that country with slaves, if they can be got through South Carolina and Georgia. Slavery discourages arts and manufactures. The poor despise labor when performed by slaves. They prevent the emigration of whites, who really enrich and strengthen a country. They produce the most pernicious effect on manners. Every master of slaves is born a petty tyrant. They bring the judgment of Heaven on a country. As nations cannot be rewarded or punished in the next world, they must be in this. By an inevitable chain of causes and effects, Providence punishes national sins by national calamities. He lamented that some of our eastern brethren had, from a lust of gain, embarked in this nefarious traffic. As to the state being in possession of the right to import, this was the case with many other rights, now to be properly given up. He held it essential, in every point of view, that the general government should have power to prevent the increase of slavery.

Mr. Oliver Ellsworth [CT], as he had never owned a slave, could not judge the effects of slavery on character. He said, however, that if it was to be considered in a moral light, we ought to go further, and free those already in the country. As slaves also multiply so fast in Virginia and Maryland, that it is cheaper to raise them than import them, whilst in the sickly rice swamps foreign supplies are necessary, if we go no further than is urged, we shall be unjust towards South Carolina and Georgia. Let us not intermeddle. As population increases, poor laborers will be so plenty as to render slaves useless. Slavery, in time, will not be a speck in our country. Provision is already made in Connecticut for abolishing it. And the abolition has already taken place in Massachusetts. As to the danger of insurrections from foreign influence, that will become a motive to kind treatment of the slaves.

Mr. Charles Pinckney [SC]: If slavery be wrong, it is justified by the example of all the world. He cited the case of Greece, Rome and other ancient states; the sanction given by France, England, Holland, and other modern states. In all ages, one half of mankind have been slaves. If the Southern States were let alone, they will probably of themselves stop importations. He would himself, as a citizen of South Carolina, vote for it. An attempt to take away the right, as proposed, will produce serious objections to the Constitution, which he wished to see adopted.

Gen. Charles C. Pinckney [SC] declared it to be his firm opinion that if himself and all his colleagues were to sign the Constitution, and use their personal influence, it would be of no avail towards obtaining the assent of their constituents. South Carolina and Georgia cannot do without slaves. As to Virginia, she will gain by stopping the importations. Her slaves will rise in value, and she has more than she wants. It would be unequal to require South Carolina and Georgia to confederate on such unequal terms. He said, the royal assent, before the revolution, had never been refused to South Carolina, as to Virginia. He contended, that the importation of slaves would be for the interest of the whole Union. The more slaves, the more produce to employ the carrying trade; the more consumption also; and the more of this, the more revenue for the common treasury. He admitted it to be reasonable that slaves should be dutied like other imports; but should consider a rejection of the clause as an exclusion of South Carolina from the Union.

Mr. Abraham Baldwin [GA] had conceived national objects alone to be before the Convention; not such as, like the present, were of a local nature. Georgia was decided on this point. That state has always hitherto supposed a general government to be the pursuit of the central states, who wished to have vortex for everything; that her distance would preclude her from equal advantage; and that she could not prudently purchase it by yielding national powers. From this it might be understood in what light she would view an attempt to abridge one of her favorite prerogatives. If left to herself, she may probably put a stop to the evil. As one ground for this conjecture, he took notice of the sect of ____, which, he said, was a respectable class of people, who carried their ethics beyond the mere *equality of men*, extending their humanity to the claims of the whole animal creation.

Mr. James Wilson [PA] observed that, if South Carolina and Georgia were themselves disposed to get rid of the importation of slaves in a short time, as had been suggested, they would never refuse to unite because the importation might be prohibited. As the section now stands, all articles imported are to be taxed. Slaves alone are exempt. This is, in fact, a bounty on that article.

Mr. Elbridge Gerry [MA] thought we had nothing to do with the conduct of the states as to slaves, but ought to be careful not to give any sanction to it.

Mr. John Dickinson [DE] considered it as inadmissible, on every principle of honor and safety, that the importation of slaves should be authorized to the states by the Constitution. The true question was, whether the national happiness would be promoted or impeded by the importation; and this question ought to be left to the national government, not to the states particularly interested. If England and France permit slavery, slaves are, at the same time, excluded from both those kingdoms. Greece and Rome were made unhappy by their slaves. He could not believe that the Southern States would refuse to confederate on the account apprehended; especially as the power was not likely to be immediately exercised by the general government.

Mr. H. Williamson [NC] stated the law of North Carolina on the subject, to wit, that it did not directly prohibit the importation of slaves. It imposed a duty of £5 on each slave imported from Africa; £10 on each from elsewhere; and £50 on each from a state licensing manumission. He thought the Southern States could not be members of the Union, if the clause be rejected; and that was wrong to force anything down not absolutely necessary and which any state must disagree to.

Mr. Rufus King [MA] thought the subject should be considered in a political light only. If two states will not agree to the Constitution, as stated on one side, he could affirm with equal belief, on the other, that great and equal opposition would be experienced from the other states. He remarked on the exemption of slaves from duty, whilst every other import was subjected to it, as an inequality that could not fail to strike the commercial sagacity of the Northern and Middle States.

Mr. John Langon [NH] was strenuous for giving the power to the general government. He could not, with a good conscience, leave it with the states, who could then go on with the traffic, without being restrained by the opinions here given, that they will themselves cease to import slaves.

Gen. Charles C. Pinckney [SC] thought himself bound to declare candidly, that he did not think South Carolina would stop her importations of slaves in any short time; but only stop them occasionally, as she now does. He moved to commit the clause, that slaves might be made liable to an equal tax with other imports; which he thought right, and which would remove one difficulty that had been stated.

Mr. John Rutledge [SC]. If the Convention thinks that North Carolina, South Carolina, and Georgia, will ever agree to the plan, unless their right to import slaves be untouched, the expectation is vain. The people of those states will never be such fools as to give up so important an interest. He was strenuous against striking out the section, and seconded the motion of Gen. Pinckney for a commitment.

Mr. Gouverneur Morris [PA] wished the whole subject to be committed, including the clauses relating to taxes on exports and a navigation act. These things may form a bargain among the Northern and Southern States.

Mr. Pierce Butler [SC] declared, that he never would agree to the power of taxing exports.

Mr. Roger Sherman [CT] said it was better to let the Southern States import slaves than to part with them, if they made that a *sine qua non*. He was opposed to a tax on slaves imported, as making the matter worse, because it implied they were *property*. He acknowledged that, if the power of prohibiting the importation should be given to the general government, it would be exercised. He thought it would be its duty to exercise the power.

Mr. George Read [DE] was for the commitment, provided the clause concerning taxes on exports should also be committed.

Mr. Roger Sherman [CT] observed, that the clause had been agreed to, and therefore could not be committed.

Mr. Edmund Randolph [VA] was for committing, in order that some middle ground might, if possible, be found. He could never agree to the clause as it stands. He would sooner risk the Constitution. He dwelt on the dilemma to which the Convention was exposed. By agreeing to the clause, it would revolt the Quakers, the Methodists, and many others in the states having no slaves. On the other hand, two states might be lost to the Union. Let us then, he said, try the chance of a commitment.

On the question for committing the remaining part of sections 4 and 5 of article 7, Connecticut, New Jersey, Maryland, Virginia, North Carolina, South Carolina, Georgia, ay, 7; New Hampshire, Pennsylvania, Delaware, no, 3; Massachusetts, absent.

* * *

John C. Calhoun (1782–1850), "On Abolition Petitions," U.S. Senate, February 6, 1837.[6]

Calhoun was elected vice president twice, with John Quincy Adams and Andrew Jackson. He also won election to the House of Representatives and as U.S. senator from South Carolina and served as secretary of war and secretary of state. Increasingly, as time passed, he placed the interests of his region as he perceived them ahead of the national interest, becoming a champion of slavery and secession. Here he claims that antislavery agitation poses a threat to the preservation of white supremacy. In its avowal of black inferiority, its consequent defense of slavery as a positive good for such an inferior people, and its warning that without slavery, racial conflict would drench the South in blood, his address foreshadows later Confederate and neo-Confederate thought. Contradictions lurk within it, however. If African Americans are inherently inferior, why is it important to keep them ignorant to keep them down? As well, if slavery is inherently good, why is it important to keep whites ignorant of the arguments against it? Finally, Calhoun notes that "a large portion of the Northern States believed slavery to be a sin" and would want to abolish it "if they should feel themselves in any degree responsible for its continuance." Subsequently, he pushed for a draconian federal fugitive slave act that he knew would indeed implicate Northerners in slavery's continuance. Never quite addressing those incongruities, Calhoun predicts that continued abolitionist activity would lead to disunion. In this he proved correct, in that it led to the election of Lincoln, which in turn prompted eleven slave states to secede.

The subject of the reception of abolition petitions being under consideration, Mr. Calhoun rose and said:

If the time of the Senate permitted, I would feel it to be my duty to call for the reading of the mass of petitions on the table, in order that we might know what language they hold towards the slaveholding States and their institutions; but as it will not, I have selected, indiscriminately from the pile, two: one from those in manuscript, and the other from the printed; and, without knowing their contents, will call for the reading of them, so that we may judge by them the character of the whole.

[Here the Secretary, on the call of Mr. CALHOUN, read the two petitions.]

Such, resumed Mr. C, is the language held towards us and ours; the peculiar institutions of the South, that on the maintenance of which the very existence of the slaveholding States depends, is pronounced to be sinful and odious in the sight of God and man; and this with a systematic design of rendering us hateful in the eyes of the world, with a view to a general crusade against us and our institutions. This, too, in the legislative halls of the Union, created by these confederated States for the better protection of their peace, their safety, and their respective institutions; and yet we, the representatives of twelve of these sovereign States, against whom this deadly war is waged, are expected to sit here in silence, hearing ourselves and constituents, day after day, denounced, without uttering a word; if we but open our lips, the charge of agitation is re-sounded on all sides, and we are held up as seeking to aggravate the evils we resist. Every reflecting mind must see in this a state of things deeply and dangerously diseased.

I do not belong, said Mr. C., to the school which holds that aggression is to be met by concession. Mine is the opposite creed, which teaches that encroachments must be met at the beginning, and that those who act on the opposite principle are prepared to become slaves. In this case in particular I hold concession or compromise to be fatal. If we concede an inch, concession would follow concession, compromise would follow compromise, until our ranks would be so broken that effectual resistance would be impossible. We must meet the enemy on the frontier, with a fixed determination of maintaining our position at every hazard. Consent to receive these insulting petitions, and the next demand will be that they be referred to a committee, in order that they may be deliberated and acted upon. At the last session we were modestly asked to receive them simply to lay them on the table, without any view of ulterior action. I then told the Senator from Pennsylvania, [Mr. BUCHANAN,] who strongly urged that course in the Senate, that it was a position that could not be maintained, as the argument in favor of acting on the petitions, if we were bound to receive, could not be resisted. I then said that the next step would be to refer the petitions to a committee; and I already see indications that such is now the intention. If we yield, that will be followed by another; and we would thus proceed, step by step, to the final consummation of the object of these petitions. We are now told that the most effectual mode of arresting the progress of abolition is to reason it down; and with this view it is urged that the petitions ought to be referred to a committee. That is the very ground which was taken at the last session in the other House; but, instead of arresting its progress, it has since advanced more rapidly than ever. The most unquestionable right may be rendered doubtful if once admitted to be a subject of controversy; and that would be the case in the present instance. The subject is beyond the jurisdiction of Congress; they have no right to touch it in any shape or form, or to make it the subject of deliberation or discussion.

. . . As widely as this incendiary spirit has spread, it has not yet infected this day, or the great mass of the intelligent and business portion of the North; but unless it be speedily stopped, it will spread and work upwards till it brings the two great sections of the Union into deadly conflict. This is not a new impression with me. Several years since, in a discussion with one of the Senators from Massachusetts, [Mr. WEBSTER,] before this fell spirit had showed itself, I then predicted that the doctrine of the proclamation and the force bill—that this Government had a right in the last resort to determine the extent of its own powers, and enforce it at the point of a bayonet, which was so warmly maintained by the Senator, would at no distant day arouse the dormant spirit of abolitionism; I told him that the doctrine was tantamount to the assumption of unlimited power on the part of the Government, and that such would be the impression on the public mind in a large portion of the Union. The consequence would be inevitable—a large portion of the Northern States believed slavery to be a sin, and would believe it to be an obligation of conscience to abolish it, if they should feel themselves in any degree responsible for its continuance, and that his doctrine would necessarily lead to the belief of such responsibility. I then predicted that it would commence, as it has, with this fanatical portion of society, and that they would begin their operation on the ignorant, the weak, the young, and the thoughtless, and would gradually extend upwards till they would become strong enough to obtain political control, when he, and others holding the highest stations in society, would, however reluctant, be compelled to yield to their doctrine, or be driven into obscurity. But four years have since elapsed, and all this is already in a course of regular fulfillment.

Standing at the point of time at which we have now arrived, it will not be more difficult to trace the course of future events now than it was then. Those who imagine that the spirit now abroad in the North will die away of itself, without a shout or convulsion, have formed a very inadequate conception of its real character; it will continue to rise and spread, unless prompt and efficient measures to stay its progress be adopted. Already it has possession of the pulpit, of the schools, and to a considerable extent of the press—those great instruments by which the mind of the rising generation will be formed.

However sound the great body of the non-slaveholding States are at present, in the course of a few years they will be succeeded by those who will have been taught to hate the people and institutions of nearly one half of this Union with a hatred more deadly than one hostile nation ever entertained toward another. It is easy to see the end. By the necessary course of events, if left to themselves, we must become, finally two people. It is impossible, under the deadly hatred which must spring up between the two great sections, if the present causes are permitted to operate unchecked, that we would continue under the same political system. The conflicting elements would burst the Union asunder, as powerful as the links are which hold it together. Abolition and the Union can not coexist. As the friend of the Union I openly proclaim it, and the sooner it is known the better. The former may now be controlled, but in a short time it will be beyond the power of man to arrest the course of events. We of the South will not, cannot, surrender our institutions. To maintain the existing relations between the two races inhabiting that section of the Union, it is indispensable to the peace and happiness of both. It cannot be subverted without drenching the country in blood, and extirpating one or the other of the races. Be it good or bad, it has grown up with our society and institutions, and is so interwoven with them that to destroy it would be to destroy us as a people. But let me not be understood as admitting, even by implication, that the existing relations between the two races in the slaveholding states is an evil—far otherwise. I hold it to be a good, as it has thus far proved itself to be, to both, and will continue to prove so if not disturbed by the fell spirit of abolition. I appeal to facts. Never before has the black race of Central Africa, from the dawn of history to the present day, attained a condition so civilized, and so improved, not only physically, but morally and intellectually. It came among us in a low, degraded, and savage condition, and in the course of a few generations it has grown up under the fostering care of our institutions, as reviled as they have been, to its present comparative civilized condition. This with the rapid increase of numbers, is conclusive proof of the general happiness of the race, in spite of all the exaggerated tales to the contrary.

In the mean time, the white or European race has not degenerated. It has kept pace with its brethren in other sections of the Union where slavery does not exist. It is odious to make the comparisons; but I appeal to all sides whether the South is not equal in virtue, intelligence, patriotism, courage, disinterestedness, and all the high qualities which adorn our nature. I ask whether we have not contributed our full share of talents and political wisdom in forming and sustaining this political fabric; and whether we have not constantly inclined most strongly to the side of liberty, and been the first to see first to resist the encroachments of power. In one thing only we are inferior—the arts of gain. We acknowledge that we are less wealthy than the Northern section of this Union; but I trace this mainly to the fiscal action of this Government, which has extracted much from and spent little among us. Had it been the reverse?—if the exaction had been made from the other section and the expenditure with us, this point of superiority would not be against us now, as it was not at the formation of this Government.

But I take higher ground. I hold that in the present state of civilization, where two races of different origin, and distinguished by color, and other physical differences, as well as intellectual, are brought together, the relation now existing in the slaveholding States between the two, is, instead of an evil, a good—a positive good. I feel myself called upon to speak freely upon the subject, where the honor and interests of those I represent are involved. I hold, then, that there never has yet existed a wealthy and civilized society in which one portion of the community did not, in point of fact, live on the labor of the other. Broad and general as is this assertion, it is fully borne out by history. This is not the proper occasion, but if it were, it would not be difficult to trace the various devices by which the wealth of all civilized societies has been so unequally divided, and to show by what means so small a share has been allotted to those by whose labor it was produced, and so large a share given to the non-producing class. The devices are almost innumerable, from the brute force and gross superstitions of ancient times, to the subtle and artful fiscal contrivances of modern. I might well challenge a comparison between them and the more direct, simple, and patriarchal mode by which the labor of the African race is among us commanded by the European. I may say with truth, that in few countries so much is left to the share of the laborer, and so little exacted from him, or where there is more kind attention to him in sickness or infirmities of age. Compare his condition with the tenants of the poor-houses in the most civilized portions of Europe—look at the sick and the old and infirm slave, on one hand, in the midst of his family and friends, under the kind superintending care of his master and mistress, and compare it with the forlorn and wretched condition of the pauper in the poor-house.

But I will not dwell on this aspect of the question; I turn to the political; and here I fearlessly assert that the existing relations between the two races in the South, against which these blind fanatics are waging war, forms the most solid and durable foundation on which to rear free and stable political institutions. It is useless to disguise the fact. There is and always has been, in an advanced state of wealth and civilization, a conflict between labor and capital. The conditions of society in the South exempts us from the disorders and dangers resulting from this conflict; and which explains why it is that the political conditions of the slaveholding States has been so much more stable and quiet than those of the North. The advantages of the former in this respect will become more and more manifest if left undisturbed by interference from without, as the country advances in wealth and numbers. We have in fact but just entered that condition of society where the strength and durability of our political institutions are to be tested; and I venture nothing in predicting that the experience of the next generation will fully test how vastly more favorable our condition of society is than that of other sections, for our free and stable institutions, provided we are not disturbed by the interference of others, or shall have sufficient intelligence and spirit to resist promptly and successfully such interference. It rests with ourselves to meet and repel them. I look not for aid to this Government, or to the other States; not but there are kind feelings towards us on the part of the great body of the non-slaveholding States; but, as kind as their feelings may be, we may rest assured that no political party in those States will risk their ascendancy for our safety. If we do not defend ourselves, none will defend us; if we yield, we will be more and more pressed as we recede; and if we submit, we will be trampled under foot. Be assured that emancipation itself would not satisfy these fanatics—that gained, the next step would be to raise the negroes to a social and political equality with the whites; and that being effected, we would soon find the present condition of the two races reversed. They and their Northern allies would be the masters, and we the slaves; the condition of the white race in British West India islands, as bad as it is, would be happiness to ours—there the mother country is interested in sustaining the supremacy of the European race. It is true that the authority of the former master is destroyed, but the African will there still be a slave, not to individuals, but to the community—forced to labor, not by the authority of the overseer, but by the bayonet of the soldiery and the rod of the civil magistrate.

Surrounded as the slaveholding States are with such imminent perils, I rejoice to think that our means of defence are ample, if we shall prove to have the intelligence and spirit to see and apply them before it is too late. All we want is concert, to lay aside all party differences, and unite with zeal and energy in repelling approaching dangers. Let there be concert of action, and we shall find ample means of security, without resorting to secession or disunion. . . .

* * *

Alabama Platform, February 14–15, 1848.[7]

When the Alabama Democratic Party convention met in 1848, its "Committee Appointed to Prepare Resolutions" proposed various resolutions about the new land taken from Mexico. The first six resolutions adopted by the convention, omitted here, mostly tell why Democrats should not ally with Whigs or support General Zachary Taylor for president. Resolution 7, which we include, pledges support for the presidential ticket nominated by the next Democratic National Convention, *if* they renounce "all claims to Federal interference with slavery in the territories." Then, after nine omitted resolutions defending the recently concluded Mexican War, the committee had proposed two final resolutions treating slavery in the territories. We include them, bracketed as in the original. They lie in some tension with each other. The first proclaims that slaveowners have the right to bring their slaves into *any* territory that has been or may be acquired by the United States. The second states that any territory ceded by Mexico must provide for slavery south of 36° 30' latitude, the Missouri Compromise line. Doing so would open what is now New Mexico, Arizona, and southern California to slavery, but not northern California, Nevada, and Utah.

The convention did not approve either resolution and also removed the last part of Resolution 7 (bracketed in the original). Instead, William Yancey, a proslavery extremist, persuaded the delegates to substitute seven other resolutions that he wrote. In the final document below, these are 9 through 15 and are prefaced by an important "Whereas." Curiously, there is no Resolution 8. Yancey rejects the Missouri Compromise line, insisting instead that *all* territory got from Mexico—and all other territories as well—be open to slavery. In 1848, this was a radical proslavery position, even in Alabama. No Southerner really imagined slavery taking hold in such places as present-day Montana, the Dakotas, or Nevada. But a relentless political dynamic was at work in the South: As soon as a significant political leader took a more extreme position favoring slavery, more moderate politicians felt pressure to identify with it, lest they be labeled "unsound on slavery."

7 h. *Resolved*, Accordingly, that we will support for the Presidency and Vice Presidency, the candidates nominated by a democratic National Convention, to be held in Baltimore on the fourth Monday in May next, as recommended by the democratic members of Congress and that we do appoint delegates thereto, to represent the democracy of this State. [Subject however to one special instruction not as necessary for them, but as a notice in all frankness to our brethren elsewhere, that they do not concur in, nor pledge our support to the nomination of any candidate who shall not be explicit in the renunciation of all claims to Federal interference with slavery in the territories.]

[Mr. Yancey Moved to amend the 7th resolution by striking out all after the words, "to represent the Democracy of the State," and insert the following resolutions, to be numbered 9, 10, 11, 12, 13 and 14 to which there was no objection made.]

Whereas, opinions have been expressed by eminent members of the Democratic party, and by a Convention of the party in New York assembled, for the purpose of selecting delegates to the Baltimore Convention, that the municipal laws of the Mexican territories, would not be changed in the ceded territory, by the cession to the United States, and that slavery could not to [*sic*] be *re-established* except by the authority of the U.S. or of the legislature of the territorial government—that no doubts should be allowed to exist upon a subject so important and at the same time so excited. Be it further

9 *Resolved*, That the treaty of cession should contain a clause securing an entry into those territories to all the citizens of the United States, together with their property of every description, and that the same should remain protected by the U.S. while the territories are under its authority.

10 *Resolved*, That if it should be found inconvenient to insert such a clause into the treaty of cession, that our Senators and Representatives in Congress should be vigilant to obtain before the ratification of such a treaty, ample securities that the rights of the southern people should not be endangered during the period the territories shall remain under the control of the U.S. either from the continuance of the municipal laws of Mexico, or from the legislation of the U.S.

11 *Resolved*, That the opinion advanced and maintained by some, that the people of a territory, acquired by the common toil, suffering, blood and treasure of the people of all the States, can, in other events than in the forming [of] a Constitution preparatory to admittance as a State into the Union, lawfully or constitutionally prevent any citizen of any such states from removing to, or settling in such territory with his property, be it slave property or otherwise, is a restriction as indefensible in principle and as dangerous in practice, as if such restriction were imposed by act of Congress.

12 *Resolved*, That the Democratic party is and should be co-extensive with the Union: and that while we disclaim all intention to interfere in the local division

and controversies in any of our sister States, we deem it a solemn duty, which we owe to the constitution, to ourselves, and to that party, to declare our unalterable determination neither to recognize as Democrats or to hold fellowship or communion with those who attempt to denationalize the South and its institutions, by restrictions upon its citizens and those institutions, calculated to array one section, in feeling and sentiment, against the other, and that we hold the same to be alike treason to party faith, and to the perpetuity of the Union of these states.

13 *Resolved*, That this Convention pledges itself to the country, and its members pledge themselves to each other, *under no political necessity whatever*, to support for the offices of President and Vice President of the United States, any persons who shall not openly and avowedly be opposed to either of the forms of excluding slavery from the territories of the U.S. mentioned in the resolutions, as being alike in violation of the constitution, and of the just and equal rights of the citizens of the slaveholding States.

14 *Resolved*, That these resolutions be considered as instructions to our delegates to the Baltimore Convention, to guide them in their votes in that body; and that they vote for no men for President or Vice President, who will not unequivocally avow themselves to be opposed to either of the forms of restricting slavery, which are described in these resolutions.

15 *Resolved*, That as democrats we are proud to find, that every statesman in the non slave holding States who has declared opinions favorable to the constitutional equality of southern Citizens in acquired territory, is of our own political brotherhood, and that every public meeting or other body political or legislative, which has taken sides for us, is, without exception, also democratic—and we commend this fact to the whigs of the South as an important element to be considered by them, when they are choosing friends, allies, or candidates "without distinction of party."

Then followed nine resolutions defending the Mexican War and blaming Mexican aggression for starting it.

[The following resolutions, reported by the committee, and numbered 17 and 18, were stricken out, inasmuch in the resolutions submitted by Mr. Yancy.

Resolved, That any territory which has been or may be acquired by the U. States, either by purchase or conquest, of right belongs to the people of all the States, and that they have the constitutional right to migrate to any such territories with their property of every description, and to be protected therein, and no power exists in Congress, *or elsewhere*, to deny to any of the people of any of the States the right to remove into and occupy with their property of whatever description any portion of such territory.

Resolved, That no cession of territory to the United States by the authorities of Mexico, will be acceptable to the people of this State unless, for the territory ceded south of 36° 30' it is distinctly provided in the treaty of cession that such territory shall be, and shall remain, so long as it remains a territory of the U. States, free and open to all the people of the U. States together with their property of every description.]

* * *

John C. Calhoun (1782–1850), "Address to the Southern People," U.S. Senate, January 22, 1849.[8]

Calhoun's 1837 speech "On Abolition Petitions" contains an interesting admission: "[A] large portion of the Northern States believed slavery to be a sin, and would believe it to be an obligation of conscience to abolish it, if they should feel themselves in any degree responsible for its continuance." Despite this reason to favor states' rights, twelve years later in his "Southern Address" Calhoun takes offense because Northern states have not done much to return fugitive slaves or shut down the Underground Rail Road. He wrote the "Address to the Southern People" on behalf of a Southern congressional bloc during the crisis that led to the Compromise of 1850. Forty-eight members of Congress from slave states signed it, including future Confederate president Jefferson Davis; William Rufus King of Alabama, shortly to become vice president under Franklin W. Pierce; David Atchison of Missouri, who suggested the Kansas-Nebraska Act and led "Border Ruffians" into Kansas to try to make it a slave state; Robert Barnwell Rhett, fire eater from South Carolina; and James M. Mason of Virginia, who would soon draft the Fugitive Slave Act. However, twice as many members of Congress from slave states did not sign. Only one Whig signed.

Interestingly, the address claims that the South does not ask that the federal government extend slavery into the territories, but only that it be neutral, while allowing slaveowners to bring their property, including slaves. That is hardly neutral, especially when considering the fugitive slave clause of the Constitution, which requires the government to act on behalf of slavery. As he did in 1837, Calhoun prophesies that if the North succeeds in ending slavery in the South, "wretchedness, and misery, and desolation would overspread the whole South." The address even foresees an era of black supremacy in the South, absent slavery.

We, whose names are hereunto annexed, address you in discharge of what we believe to be a solemn duty, on the most important subject ever presented for your consideration. We allude to the conflict between the two great sections of the Union, growing out of a difference of feeling and opinion in reference to the relation existing between the two races, the European and the African, which inhabit the southern section, and the acts of aggression and encroachment to which it has led.

The conflict commenced not long after the acknowledgment of our independence, and has gradually increased until it has arrayed the great body of the North against the South on this most vital subject. In the progress of this conflict, aggression has followed aggression, and encroachment encroachment, until they have reached a point when a regard for your peace and safety will not permit us to remain longer silent. The object of this address is to give you a clear, correct, but brief account of the whole series of aggression and encroachments on your rights, with a statement of the dangers to which they expose you. Our object in making it is not to cause excitement, but to put you in full possession of all the facts and circumstances necessary to a full and just conception of a deep-seated disease, which threatens great danger to you and the whole body politic. We act on the impression, that in a popular government like ours, a true conception of the actual character and state of a disease is indispensable to effecting a cure.

We have made it a joint address, because we believe that the magnitude of the subject required that it should assume the most impressive and solemn form.

Not to go further back, the difference of opinion and feeling in reference to the relation between the two races, disclosed itself in the Convention that framed the Constitution, and constituted one of the greatest difficulties in forming it. After many efforts, it was overcome by a compromise, which provided in the first place, that representative and direct taxes shall be apportioned among the States according to their respective numbers; and that, in ascertaining the number of each, five slaves shall be estimated as three. In the next, that slaves escaping into States where slavery does not exist, shall not be discharged from servitude, but shall be delivered up on claim of the party to whom their labor or service is due. In the third place, that Congress shall not prohibit the importation of slaves before the year 1808; but a tax not exceeding ten dollars may be imposed on each imported. And finally, that no capitation or direct tax shall be laid, but in proportion to federal numbers; and that no amendment of the Constitution, prior to 1808, shall affect this provision, nor that relating to the importation of slaves.

So satisfactory were these provisions, that the second, relating to the delivering up of fugitive slaves, was adopted unanimously, and all the rest, except the third, relative to the importation of slaves until 1808, with almost equal unanimity. They recognize the existence of slavery, and make a specific provision for its protection where it was supposed to be the most exposed. They go further, and incorporate it, as an important element, in determining the relative weight of the several States in the Government of the Union, and the respective burden they should bear in laying capitation and direct taxes. It was well understood at the time, that without them the Constitution would not have been adopted by the Southern States, and of course that they constituted elements so essential to the system that it never would have existed without them. The Northern States, knowing all this, ratified the Constitution, thereby pledging their faith, in the most solemn manner, sacredly to observe them. How that faith has been kept and that pledge redeemed we shall next proceed to show.

With few exceptions of no great importance, the South had no cause to complain prior to the year 1819—a year, it is to be feared, destined to mark a train of events, bringing with them many, and great, and fatal disasters, on the country and its institutions. With it commenced the agitating debate on the question of the admission of Missouri into the Union. We shall pass by for the present this question, and others of the same kind, directly growing out of it, and shall proceed to consider the effects of that spirit of discord, which it roused up between the two sections. It first disclosed itself in the North, by hostility to that portion of the Constitution which provides for the delivering up of fugitive slaves. In its progress it led to the adoption of hostile acts, intended to render it of non-effect, and with so much success that it may be regarded now as practically expunged from the Constitution. How this has been effected will be next explained.

After a careful examination, truth constrains us to say, that it has been by a clear and palpable evasion of the Constitution. It is impossible for any provision to be more free from ambiguity or doubt. It is in the following words: "No person held to service, or labor, in one State, under the laws thereof, escaping into another State, shall, in consequence of any law or regulation therein, be discharged from such service or labor, but shall be delivered up on claim of the party to whom such service or labor may be due." All is clear. There is not an uncertain or equivocal word to be found in the whole provision. What shall not be done, and what shall be done, are fully and explicitly set forth. The former provides that the fugitive slave shall not be discharged from his servitude by any law or regulation of the State wherein he is found; and the latter, that he shall be delivered up on claim of his owner.

. . . When we take into consideration the importance and clearness of this provision, the evasion by which it has been set aside may fairly be regarded as one of the most fatal blows ever received by the South and the Union.

Calhoun then quotes from Supreme Court Justices Story and Baldwin on the importance of the fugitive slave clause, concluding with these words by Baldwin: "Thus you see, that the foundations of the Government are laid, and rest on the right of property in slaves. The whole structure must fall by disturbing the corner-stone."

These are grave and solemn and admonitory words, from a high source. They confirm all for which the South has ever contended, as to the clearness, importance, and fundamental character of this provision, and the disastrous consequences which would inevitably follow from its violation. But in spite of these solemn warnings, the violation, then commenced, and which they were intended to rebuke, has been full and perfectly consummated. The citizens of the South, in their attempt to recover their slaves, now meet, instead of aid and co-operation, resistance in every form; resistance from hostile acts of legislation, intended to baffle and defeat their claims by all sorts of devices, and by interposing every description of impediment—resistance from judges and magistrates—and finally, when all these fail, from mobs, composed of whites and blacks, which, by threats or force, rescue the fugitive slave from the possession of his rightful owner. The attempt to recover a slave, in most of the Northern States, cannot now be made without the hazard of insult, heavy pecuniary loss, imprisonment, and even of life itself. Already has a worthy citizen of Maryland lost his life* [*Mr. Kennedy, of Hagerstown, Maryland.] in making an attempt to enforce his claim to a fugitive slave under this provision.

But a provision of the Constitution may be violated indirectly as well as directly; by doing an act in its nature inconsistent with that which is enjoined to be done. Of the form of violation, there is a striking instance connected with the provision under consideration. We allude to secret combinations which are believed to exist in many of the Northern States, whose object is to entice, decoy, entrap, inveigle, and seduce slaves to escape from their owners, and to pass them secretly and rapidly, by means organized for the purpose, into Canada, where they will be beyond the reach of the provision. That to entice a slave, by whatever artifice, to abscond from his owner, into a non-slaveholding State, with the intention to place him beyond the reach of the provision, or prevent his recovery, by concealment or otherwise, is as completely repugnant to it, as its open violation would be, is too clear to admit of doubt or to require illustration. And yet, as repugnant as these combinations are to the true intent of the provision, it is believed, that, with the above exception, not one of the States, within whose limits they exist, has adopted any measure to suppress them, or to punish those by whose agency the object for which they were formed is carried into execution. On the contrary, they have looked on, and witnessed with indifference, if not with secret approbation, a great number of slaves enticed from their owners, and placed beyond the possibility of recovery, to the great annoyance and heavy pecuniary loss of the bordering Southern States.

When we take into consideration the great importance of this provision, the absence of all uncertainty as to its true meaning and intent, the many guards by which it is surrounded to protect and enforce it, and then reflect how completely the object for which it was inserted in the Constitution is defeated by these two-fold infractions, we doubt, taking all together, whether a more flagrant breach of faith is to be found on record. We know the language we have used is strong, but it is not less true than strong.

There remains to be noticed another class of aggressive acts of a kindred character, but which instead of striking at an express and specific provision of the Constitution, aims directly at destroying the relation between the two races at the South, by means subversive in their tendency of one of the ends for which the Constitution was established. We refer to the systematic agitation of the question by the Abolitionists, which, commencing about 1835, is still continued in all possible forms. Their avowed intention is to bring about a state of things that will force emancipation on the South. To unite the North in fixed hostility to slavery in the South, and to excite discontent among the slaves with their condition, are among the means employed to effect it. With a view to bring about the former, every means are resorted to in order to render the South, and the relation between the two races there, odious and hateful to the North.

Calhoun then writes a long paragraph denouncing abolitionists; we omit three paragraphs on the Missouri Compromise of 1820. He continues:

For many years the subject of slavery in reference to the territories ceased to agitate the country. Indications, however, connected with question of annexing Texas, showed clearly that it was ready to break out again, with redoubled violence, on some future occasion. The difference in the case of Texas was adjusted by extending the Missouri compromise line of 36° 30', from its terminus, on the western boundary of the Louisiana purchase, to the western boundary of Texas. The agitation again ceased for a short period.

The war with Mexico soon followed, and that terminated in the acquisition of New Mexico and Upper California, embracing an area equal to about one half of the entire valley of the Mississippi. If to this we add the portion of Oregon acknowledged to be ours by the recent treaty with England, our whole territory on the Pacific and west of the Rocky Mountains will be found to be in extent but little less than that vast valley. The near prospect of so great an addition rekindled the excitement between the North and South in reference to slavery in its connection with the territories, which has become, since those on the Pacific were acquired, more universal and intense than ever. . . .

. . . [W]e hold that the Federal Government has no right to extend or restrict slavery, no more than to establish or abolish it; nor has it any right whatever to distinguish between the domestic institutions of one State, or section, and another, in order to favor one and discourage the other. As the federal representative of each and all the States, it is bound to deal out, within the sphere of its powers, equal and exact justice and favor to all. To act otherwise, to undertake to discriminate between the domestic institutions of one and another, would be to act in total subversion of the end for which it was established—to be the common protection and guardian of all. Entertaining these opinions, we ask not, as the North alleges we do, for the extension of slavery. That would make a discrimination in our favor, as unjust and unconstitutional as the discrimination they ask against us in their favor. It is not for them, nor for the Federal Government to determine, whether our domestic institution is good or bad; or whether it should be repressed or preserved. It belongs to us, and us only, to decide such questions. What then we do insist on, is, not to extend slavery, but that we shall not be prohibited from immigrating with our property, into the Territories of the United States, because we are slaveholders; or, in other words, that we shall not on that account be disfranchised of a privilege possessed by all others, citizens and foreigners, without discrimination as to character, profession, or color. All, whether savage, barbarian, or civilized, may freely enter and remain, we only being excluded.

We rest our claim, not only on the high grounds above stated, but also on the solid foundation of right, justice, and equality. The territories immediately in controversy—New Mexico and California—were acquired by the common sacrifice and efforts of all the States, towards which the South contributed far more than her full share of men, to say nothing of money, and is, of course, on every principle of right, justice, fairness and equality, entitled to participate fully in the benefits to be derived from their acquisition. But as impregnable as is this ground, there is another not less so. Ours is a Federal Government—a Government in which not individuals, but States as distinct sovereign communities, are the constituents. To them, as members of the Federal Union, the territories belong; and they are hence declared to be territories belonging to the United States. The States, then, are the joint owners. Now it is conceded by all writers on the subject, that in all such Governments their members are all equal—equal in rights and equal in dignity. They also concede that this equality constitutes the basis of such Government, and that it cannot be destroyed without changing their nature and character. To deprive, then, the Southern States and their citizens of their full share in territories declared to belong to them, in common with the other States, would be in derogation of the equality belonging to them as members of a Federal Union, and sink them, from being equals, into a subordinate and dependent condition. Such are the solid and impregnable grounds on which we rest our demand to an equal participation in the territories. . . .

Calhoun then provides evidence that we omit of the large number of Southern soldiers who fought in Mexico.

At the last session of Congress, a bill was passed, establishing a territorial government for Oregon, excluding slavery therefrom. The President gave his sanction to the bill, and sent a special message to Congress assigning his reasons for doing so. These reasons presupposed that the Missouri compromise was to be, and would be, extended west of the Rocky Mountains, to the Pacific Ocean. And the President intimated his intention in his message to veto any future bill that should restrict slavery south of the line of that compromise. Assuming it to have been the purpose and intention of the North to extend the Missouri compromise line as above indicated, the passage of the Oregon bill could only be regarded as evincing the acquiescence of the South in that line. But the developments of the present session of Congress have made it manifest to all, that no such purpose or intention now exists with the North to any considerable extent.

Calhoun then presents six paragraphs complaining of recent congressional efforts to end the slave trade in the District of Columbia, exclude slavery from California and New Mexico, and abolish it in forts and dockyards governed by Congress.

We have now brought to close a narrative of the series of acts of aggression and encroachment, connected with the subject of this address, including those that are consummated and those still in progress. They are numerous, great, and dangerous, and threaten with destruction the greatest and most vital of all the interests and institutions of the South. Indeed, it may be doubted whether there is a single provision, stipulation, or guaranty of the Constitution, intended for the security of the South, that has not been rendered almost perfectly nugatory. It may even be made a serious question, whether the encroachments already made, without the aid of any other, would not, if permitted to operate unchecked, end in emancipation, and that at no distant day. But be that as it may, it hardly admits of a doubt that, if the aggressions already commenced in the House, and now in progress, should be consummated, such in the end would certainly be the consequence.

Little, in truth, would be left to be done after we have been excluded from all the territories, including those to be hereafter acquired; after slavery is abolished in this District and in the numerous places dispersed all over the South, where Congress has the exclusive right of legislation, and after the other measures proposed are consummated. Every outpost and barrier would be carried, and nothing would be left but to finish the work of abolition at pleasure in the States themselves. This District, and all places over which Congress has exclusive power of legislation, would be asylums for fugitive slaves, where, as soon as they placed their feet, they would become, according to the doctrines of our Northern assailants, free, unless there should be some positive enactments to prevent it.

Under such a state of things the probability is, that emancipation would soon follow, without any final act to abolish slavery. The depressing effects of such measures on the white race at the South, and the hope they would create in the black of a speedy emancipation, would produce a state of feeling inconsistent with the much longer continuance of the existing relations between the two. But be that as it may, it is certain, if emancipation did not follow, as a matter of course, the final act in the States would not be long delayed. The want of constitutional power would oppose a feeble resistance. The great body of the North is united against our peculiar institution. Many believe it to be sinful, and the residue, with inconsiderable exceptions, believe it to be wrong. Such being the case, it would indicate a very superficial knowledge of human nature, to think that, after aiming at abolition, systematically, for so many years, and pursuing it with such unscrupulous disregard of law and Constitution, that the fanatics who have led the way and forced the great body of the North to follow them, would, when the finishing stroke only remained to be given, voluntarily suspend it, or permit any constitutional scruples or considerations of justice to arrest it. To these may be added an aggression, though not yet commenced, long meditated and threatened: to prohibit what the abolitionists call the internal slave trade, meaning thereby the transfer of slaves from one State to another, from whatever motive done, or however effected. Their object would seem to be to render them worthless by crowding them together where they are, and thus hasten the work of emancipation. There is reason for believing that it will soon follow those now in progress, unless, indeed, some decisive step should be taken in the mean time to arrest the whole.

The question then is, Will the measures of aggression proposed in the House be adopted?

They may not, and probably will not be this session. But when we take into consideration, that there is a majority now in favor of one of them, and a strong minority in favor of the other, so far as the sense of the House has been taken; that there will be in all probability a considerable increase in the next Congress of the vote in favor of them, and that it will be largely increased in the next succeeding Congress under the census to be taken next year, it amounts almost to a certainty that they will be adopted, unless some decisive measure is taken in advance to prevent it.

But, even if these conclusions should prove erroneous—if fanaticism and the love of power should, contrary to their nature, for once respect constitutional barriers, or if the calculations of policy should retard the adoption of these measures, or even defeat them altogether, there would still be left one certain way to accomplish their object, if the determination avowed by the North to monopolize all the territories, to the exclusion of the South, should be carried into effect. That of itself would, at no distant day, add to the North a sufficient number of States to give her three fourths of the whole; when, under the color of an amendment to the Constitution, she would emancipate our slaves, however opposed it might be to its true intent.

Thus, under every aspect, the result is certain, if aggression be not promptly and decidedly met. How is it to be met, is for you to decide.

Such then being the case, it would be to insult you to suppose you could hesitate. To destroy the existing relation between the free and servile races at the South would lead to consequences unparalleled in history. They cannot be separated, and cannot live together in peace, or harmony, or to their mutual advantage, except in their present relation. Under any other, wretchedness, and misery, and desolation would overspread the whole South. The example of the British West Indies, as blighting as emancipation has proved to them, furnishes a very faint picture of the calamities it would bring on the South. . . . [T]he British West India possessions are ruined, impoverished, miserable, wretched, and destined probably to be abandoned to the black race.

Very different would be the circumstances under which emancipation would take place with us. If it ever should be effected, it will be through the agency of the Federal Government, controlled by the dominant power of the Northern States of the Confederacy, against the resistance and struggle of the Southern. It can then only be effected by the prostration of the white race; and that would necessarily engender the bitterest feelings of hostility between them and the North. But the reverse would be the case between the blacks of the South and the people of the North. Owing their emancipation to them, they would regard them as friends, guardians, and patrons, and centre, accordingly, all their sympathy in them. The people of the North would not fail to reciprocate and to favor them, instead of the whites. Under the influence of such feelings, and impelled by fanaticism and love of power, they would not stop at emancipation. Another step would be taken—to raise them to a political and social equality with their former owners, by giving them the right of voting and holding public offices under the Federal Government. We see the first step toward it in the bill already alluded to—to vest the free blacks and slaves with the right to vote on the question of emancipation in this District. But when once raised to an equality, they would become the fast political associates of the North, act-ing and voting with them on all questions, and by this political union between them, holding the white race at the South in complete subjection. The blacks, and the profligate whites that might unite with them, would become the prin-cipal recipients of federal offices and patronage, and would, in consequence, be raised above the whites of the South in the political and social scale. We would, in a word, change conditions with them—a degradation greater than has ever yet fallen to the lot of a free and enlightened people, and one from which we could not escape, should emancipation take place (which it certainly will if not prevented), but by fleeing the homes of ourselves and ancestors, and by aban-doning our country to our former slaves, to become the permanent abode of disorder, anarchy, poverty, misery, and wretchedness.

With such a prospect before us, the gravest and most solemn question that ever claimed the attention of a people is presented for your consideration: What is to be done to prevent it? It is a question belonging to you to decide. All we propose is, to give you our opinion.

He concludes by calling for white Southern unity.

* * *

JAMES H. THORNWELL (1812–62),
THE RIGHTS AND THE DUTIES OF THE MASTERS,
MAY 26, 1850.[9]

Thornwell was born on a plantation in South Carolina, graduated from South Carolina College, and went on to Harvard. Eventually he became pastor of the First Presbyterian Church of Columbia, South Carolina. In 1850, soon to become president of what is now the University of South Carolina, he spoke at the dedication of a church in Charleston paid for by whites but intended for slaves. His address reflects paternalism—that slaveowners cared about their slaves as a parent might care for children, and in this case cared for their religious development. It also reveals owners' belief that Christianity would prod slaves toward docile behavior and away from revolt. The sermon is very long, forcing us to make several cuts.[10]

Thornwell describes "the disparity in resources of the parties in the war," by which he means the struggle with abolitionism in 1850, not an actual war. He aligns abolitionism with "atheists, socialists, communists," and contrasts "the friends of order and regulated freedom," such as slaveowners and Southern Christianity. Euan Hague and Edward Sebesta note that this view was "once a marginal revisionist reading of the Civil War," but in recent years neo-Confederates like the Sons of Confederate Veterans and the League of the South have used it to bolster their thesis that the war was not primarily about slavery. Founders of the Presbyterian Church of America—which split from the Southern Presbyterian Church in the 1970s as the latter grew more liberal and reunited with the Northern church—also cite Thornwell as a progenitor. The "Christian benevolence" to which he refers is, of course, the church for African Americans he is dedicating.[11]

... This triumph of Christian benevolence is the more illustrious, as having taken place in a community which has been warned by experience to watch with jealous care, all combinations of the blacks....

Time will show that they have acted wisely, and that this Church will prove a stronger fortress against insubordination and rebellion than weapons of brass or iron.

The juncture at which you have been led to begin and carry out this undertaking—it is but just to say—affords a proof of your homage to religion, and a vindication of your characters, as beautiful as they are conspicuous. The slave-holding States of this confederacy have been placed under the ban of the publick opinion of the civilized world. The philanthropy of Christendom seems to have concentrated its sympathies upon us. We have been denounced, with every epithet of vituperation and abuse, as conspirators against the dignity of man—traitors to our race, and rebels against God. Overlooking, with a rare expansion of benevolence, the evils which press around their own doors, the vices and crimes and sufferings of their own neighbours and countrymen, the philanthropists of Europe and this country can find nothing worth weeping for but the sufferings and degradation of the Southern slave, and nothing worth reviling but the avarice, inhumanity and cruelty of the Southern master, and nothing worth laboring to extirpate but the system which embodies these outrages and wrongs....

This insane fury of philanthropy has not been content with speculating upon our degradation and wretchedness at a distance. It has aimed at stirring up insurrection in our midst. In the sacred names of religion and liberty, private efforts have been made to turn the hearts of servants against their masters; and publick institutions, which the implied faith of the country should render only vehicles of convenience, have been treacherously converted into engines of sedition and organs of tumult....

That we should be passive spectators of these scenes of madness and confusion—that we should be indifferent to the condemnation of the civilized world, and especially to efforts to put in jeopardy our lives, as well as our property, is not to be expected.... The agitations which are convulsing the kingdoms of Europe—the mad speculations of philosophers—the excesses of unchecked democracy, are working out some of the most difficult problems of political and social science; and when the tumult shall have subsided and reason resumed her ascendancy, it will be found that the very principles upon which we have been accustomed to justify Southern slavery, are the principles of regulated liberty—that in defending this institution we have really been upholding the civil interests of mankind—resisting alike the social anarchy of communism and the political anarchy of licentiousness—that we have been supporting representative, republican government against the despotism of masses on one hand, and the supremacy of a single will on the other.

God has not permitted such a remarkable phenomenon as the unanimity of the civilized world, in its execration of slavery, to take place without design.

This great battle with the Abolitionists, has not been fought in vain. The muster of such immense forces—the fury and bitterness of the conflict—the disparity in resources of the parties in the war—the conspicuousness—the unexampled conspicuousness of the event, have all been ordered for wise and beneficent results; and when the smoke shall have rolled away, it will be seen that a real progress has been made in the practical solution of the problems which produced the collision.

What disasters it will be necessary to pass through before the nations can be taught the lessons of Providence—what lights shall be extinguished, and what horrors experienced, no human sagacity can foresee. But that the world is now the theatre of an extraordinary conflict of great principles—that the foundations of society are about to be explored to their depths—and the sources of social and political prosperity laid bare; that the questions in dispute involve all that is dear and precious to man on earth—the most superficial observer cannot fail to perceive. Experiment after experiment may be made—disaster succeed disaster, in carrying out the principles of an atheistic philosophy—until the nations, wearied and heart-sickened with changes without improvement, shall open their eyes to the real causes of their calamities, and learn the lessons which wisdom shall evolve from the events that have passed. Truth must triumph. God will vindicate the appointments of His Providence—and if our institutions are indeed consistent with righteousness and truth, we can calmly afford to bide our time—we can watch the storm which is beating furiously against us, without terror or dismay—we can receive the assault of the civilized world—trusting in Him who has all the elements at His command, and can save us as easily by one as a thousand. If our principles are true, the world must come to them; and we can quietly appeal from the verdict of existing generations, to the more impartial verdict of the men who shall have seen the issue of the struggle in which we are now involved. It is not the narrow question of abolitionism or of slavery—not simply whether we shall emancipate our negroes or not; the real question is the relations of man to society—of States to the individual, and the individual to the States; a question as broad as the interests of the human race.

These are the mighty questions which are shaking thrones to their centres—upheaving the masses like an earthquake, and rocking the solid pillars of this Union. The parties in this conflict are not merely abolitionists and slaveholders—they are atheists, socialists, communists, red republicans, Jacobins, on the one side, and the friends of order and regulated freedom on the other. In one word, the world is the battle ground—Christianity and Atheism the combatants; and the progress of humanity the stake. One party seems to regard Society, with all its complicated interests, its divisions and sub-divisions, as the machinery of man—which, as it has been invented and arranged by his ingenuity and skills, may be taken to pieces, re-constructed, altered or repaired, as experience shall indicate defects or confusion in the original plan. The other party beholds in it the ordinance of God. . . .

The Apostle briefly sums up all that is incumbent, at the present crisis, upon the slaveholders of the South, in the words of the text—Masters, give unto your servants that which is just and equal, knowing that ye also have a Master in Heaven. It would be a useless waste of time to spend many words in proving, that the servants contemplated by the Apostles were slaves. Finding it impossible to deny that slavery, as an existing element of society, is actually sanctioned by Christ and His Apostles, those who would preserve some show of consistency in their veneration of the Scriptures, and their condemnation of us, resolve the conduct of the founders of Christianity into motives of prudence and considerations of policy. While they admit that the letter of the Scriptures is distinctly and unambiguously in our favour, they maintain that their spirit is against us, and that our savior was content to leave the destruction of whatsoever was morally wrong in the social fabric, to the slow progress of changes in individual opinions, wrought by the silent influence of religion, rather than endanger the stability of governments by sudden and disastrous revolutions. . . .

Thornwell then provides a lengthy theological justification for slavery. He does admit:

That the design of Christianity is to secure the perfection of the race, is obvious from all its arrangements; and that when this end shall have been consummated, slavery must cease to exist, is equally clear. . . .

Slavery is a part of the curse which sin has introduced into the world, and stands in the same general relation to Christianity as poverty, sickness, disease or death. In other words, it is a relation which can only be conceived as taking place among fallen beings—tainted with a curse. It springs not the nature of man as man, or from the nature of society as such, but from the nature of man as sinful, and the nature of society as disordered. . . .

It is a natural evil which God has visited upon society, because man kept not his first estate, but fell, and, under the Gospel, is turned, like all natural evils, into the means of an effective spiritual discipline. . . .

Slaves are not to escape slavery, however, and whites are not to end it. Instead:

The slave is to show reverence for God—the freedom of his inward man—by a cheerful obedience to the lawful commands of his master;—the master, his regard for one who is his master in heaven, by rendering to the slave that which is just and equal. The character of both is determined, in the sight of God, by the spirit which pervades their single acts, however the acts may differ in themselves....

Our Savior directs us to do unto others what, in their situations, it would be right and reasonable in us to expect from them....

The rule then simply requires, in the case of slavery, that we should treat our slaves as we should feel that we had a right to be treated if we were slaves ourselves—it is only enforcing by benevolence the apostolic injunction—Masters give unto your servants, that which is just and equal. Do right, in other words, as you would claim right....

In short, the Golden Rule does not ask a white Christian to question whether slavery is right, it merely asks whites to treat slaves nicely within the confines of the institution.

* * *

Resolves of the Southern Convention at Nashville, June 10–11, 1850.[12]

In June 1850, Southern leaders held a convention in Nashville to form a plan of action for the South. Secession seemed a likely outcome. By June, however, the Compromises of 1850, including the Fugitive Slave Act, were in the works. The prospect of their passage satisfied proslavery moderates, so secession did not really get onto the agenda. Instead, the convention passed a series of resolutions. The first six require the federal government to guarantee slaveowners the right to enter all U.S. territories with their slaves. Moreover, Resolution 7 threatens secession and war if the government does not do so. Thus what had been an extremist position about slavery in the territories becomes the majority position in Nashville. Resolution 8 then offers an olive branch, however. It veers toward Northern Democrats' position of popular sovereignty, letting the residents of a territory set up "institutions fitted to them," though it leaves the details vague. It stands in some conflict with its predecessors, since presumably the federal government would not guarantee slavery if a territory's residents did not so desire. Resolution 11 suggests a different fallback position: extend the Missouri Compromise line westward to the Pacific. Resolution 24 then returns to an absolutist position. It grants Congress "no power under the Constitution to create or destroy [slavery] anywhere." Such a view makes the Missouri Compromise and any extension of it westward unconstitutional.[13] Final resolutions treat slavery petitions and fugitive slaves and promise another convention if Congress does not meet slaveowners' demands.

1. *Resolved,* That the territories of the United States belong to the people of the several States of this Union as their common property. That the citizens of the several States have equal rights to migrate with their property to these territories, and are equally entitled to the protection of the federal government in the enjoyment of that property so long as the territories remain under the charge of that government.

2. *Resolved*, That Congress has no power to exclude from the territory of the United States any property lawfully held in the States of the Union, and any acts which may be passed by Congress to effect this result is a plain violation of the Constitution of the United States.

3. *Resolved*, That it is the duty of Congress to provide governments for the territories, since the spirit of American Institutions forbids the maintenance of military governments in time of peace, and as all laws heretofore existing in territories once belonging to foreign powers which interfere with the full enjoyment of religion, the freedom of the press, the trial by jury, and all other rights of persons and property as secured or recognized in the Constitution of the United States, are necessarily void so soon as such territories become American territories, it is the duty of the federal government to make early provision for the enactment of those laws which may be expedient and necessary to secure to the inhabitants of and emigrants to such territories the full benefit of the constitutional rights we assert.

4. *Resolved*, That to protect property existing in the several States of the Union the people of these States invested the federal government with the powers of war and negotiation and of sustaining armies and navies, and prohibited to State authorities the exercise of the same powers. They made no discrimination in the protection to be afforded or the description of the property to be defended, nor was it allowed to the federal government to determine what should be held as property. Whatever the States deal with as property the federal government is bound to recognize and defend as such. Therefore it is the sense of this Convention that all acts of the federal government which tend to denationalize property of any description recognized in the Constitution and laws of the States, or that discriminate in the degree and efficiency of the protection to be afforded to it, or which weaken or destroy the title of any citizen upon American territories, are plain and palpable violations of the fundamental law under which it exists.

5. *Resolved*, That the slaveholding States cannot and will not submit to the enactment by Congress of any law imposing onerous conditions or restraints upon the rights of masters to remove with their property into the territories of the United States, or to any law making discrimination in favor of the proprietors of other property against them.

6. *Resolved*, That it is the duty of the federal government plainly to recognize and firmly to maintain the equal rights of the citizens of the several States in the territories of the United States, and to repudiate the power to make a discrimination between the proprietors of different species of property in the federal legislation. The fulfillment of this duty by the federal government would greatly tend to restore the peace of the country and to allay the exasperation and excitement which now exists between the different sections of the Union.

For it is the deliberate opinion of this Convention that the tolerance Congress has given to the notion that federal authority might be employed incidentally and indirectly to subvert or weaken the institution existing in the States confessedly beyond federal jurisdiction and control, is a main cause of the discord which menaces the existence of the Union, and which has well nigh destroyed the efficient action of the federal government itself.

7. *Resolved*, That the performance of this duty is required by the fundamental law of the Union. The equality of the people of the several States composing the Union cannot be disturbed without disturbing the frame of American institutions. This principle is violated in the denial to the citizens of the slaveholding States of power to enter into the territories with the property lawfully acquired in the States. The warfare against this right is a war upon the Constitution. The defenders of this right are the defenders of the Constitution. Those who deny or impair its exercise, are unfaithful to the Constitution, and if disunion follows the destruction of the right they are the disunionists.

8. *Resolved*, That the performance of its duties, upon the principle we declare, would enable Congress to remove the embarrassments in which the country is now involved. The vacant territories of the United States, no longer regarded as prizes for sectional rapacity and ambition, would be gradually occupied by inhabitants drawn to them by their interests and feelings. The institutions fitted to them would be naturally applied by governments formed on American ideas, and approved by the deliberate choice of their constituents. The community would be educated and disciplined under a republican administration in habits of self government, and fitted for an association as a State, and to the enjoyment of a place in the confederacy. A community so formed and organized might well claim admission to the Union and none would dispute the validity of the claim.

9. *Resolved*, That a recognition of this principle would deprive the questions between Texas and the United States of their sectional character, and would leave them for adjustment without disturbance from sectional prejudices and passions, upon considerations of magnanimity and justice.

10. *Resolved*, That a recognition of this principle would infuse a spirit of conciliation in the discussion and adjustment of all subjects of sectional dispute, which would afford a guarantee of an early and satisfactory determination.

11. *Resolved*, That in the event a dominant majority shall refuse to recognize the great constitutional rights we assert, and shall continue to deny the obligations of the Federal Government to maintain them, it is the sense of this convention that the territories should be treated as property, and divided between the sections of the Union, so that the rights of both sections be adequately secured in their respective shares. That we are aware this course is open to grave objections, but we are ready to acquiesce in the adoption of the line of 36 deg.

30 min. north latitude, extending to the Pacific ocean, as an extreme concession, upon considerations of what is due to the stability of our institutions.

12. *Resolved*, That it is the opinion of this Convention that this controversy should be ended, either by a recognition of the constitutional rights of the Southern people, or by an equitable partition of the territories. That the spectacle of a confederacy of States, involved in quarrels over the fruits of a war in which the American arms were crowned with glory, is humiliating. That the incorporation of the Wilmot Proviso in the offer of settlement, a proposition which fourteen States regard as disparaging and dishonorable, is degrading to the country. A termination to this controversy by the disruption of the confederacy or by the abandonment of the territories to prevent such a result, would be a climax to the shame which attaches to the controversy which it is the paramount duty of Congress to avoid.

13. *Resolved*, That this Convention will not conclude that Congress will adjourn without making an adjustment of this controversy, and in the condition in which the Convention finds the question before Congress, it does not feel at liberty to discuss the methods suitable for a resistance to measures not yet adopted, which might involve a dishonor to the Southern States.

Resolutions 14–18 support the claims of Texas to a much larger portion of the land ceded by Mexico than Texas wound up getting and require the admission of four new slaveholding states, in addition to Texas, out of the remaining territory. Resolutions 19–23 mostly argue that Mexican laws governing the territory are null and void. Mexico had abolished slavery, and Southerners did not want this prohibition continued, now that the United States governed the land.

24. *Resolved*, That slavery exists in the United States independent of the Constitution. That it is recognized by the Constitution in a three-fold aspect, first as property, second as a domestic relation of service or labor under the law of a State, and lastly as a basis of political power. And viewed in any or all of these lights, Congress has no power under the Constitution to create or destroy it anywhere; nor can such power be derived from foreign laws, conquest, cession, treaty or the laws of nations, nor from any other source but an amendment of the Constitution itself.

25. *Resolved*, That the Constitution confers no power upon Congress to regulate or prohibit the sale and transfer of slaves between the States.

26. *Resolved*, That the reception or consideration by Congress of resolutions, memorials or petitions, from the States in which domestic slavery does not exist, or from the people of the said States, in relation to the institution of slavery where it does exist, with a view of effecting its abolition, or to impair the

rights of those interested in it, to its peaceful and secure enjoyment, is a gross abuse and an entire perversion of the right of petition as secured by the federal Constitution, and if persisted in must and will lead to the most dangerous and lamentable consequences; that the right of petition for a redress of grievances as provided for by the Constitution was designed to enable the citizens of the United States to manifest and make known to Congress the existence of evils under which they were suffering, whether affecting them personally, locally or generally, and to cause such evils to be redressed by the people and competent authority, but was never designed or intended as a means of inflicting injury on others or jeopardizing the peaceful and secure enjoyment of their rights, whether existing under the Constitution or under the sovereignty and authority of the several States.

27. *Resolved*, That it is the duty of Congress to provide effectual means of executing the 2d section of the 4th article of the Constitution, relating to the restoration of fugitives from service or labor.

28. *Resolved*, That when this Convention adjourn, it adjourn to meet at Nashville, in the State of Tennessee, the 6th Monday after the adjournment of the present session of Congress, and that the Southern States be recommended to fill their delegations forthwith.

* * *

JOURNAL, RESOLUTION, AND ORDINANCE,
STATE CONVENTION OF SOUTH CAROLINA,
APRIL 26–30, 1852.[14]

South Carolina's state convention finally met in December 1851. The next April, it passed a resolution declaring that South Carolina had the right to secede and had ample cause, owing to "the frequent violations of the Constitution of the United States by the Federal Government, and its encroachments upon the reserved rights of the sovereign States of this Union, especially in relation to slavery." The state gives no examples of these "violations." South Carolina would remain in the United States for "considerations of expediency only," the main consideration being that no other state was willing to secede at that point.

Pursuant to an act of the Legislature, of the State of South Carolina, entitled "An Act to provide for the appointment of Deputies to a Southern Congress, and to call a Convention of the People of this State,"* [*See Addenda at the end of the Journal.] ratified on the 20th day of December, 1850; and also "An Act to fix the time for the meeting of the Convention elected under the authority of an Act entitled 'An Act to provide for the appointment of Delegates to a Southern Congress, and to call a Convention of the People of this State,'" passed in the year of our Lord one thousand eight hundred and fifty, ratified on the 16th December, 1851, the Delegates of the several election districts and parishes of this State assembled in the Hall of the House of Representatives, in the Capitol, at Columbia, in the State of South Carolina, on this day, at 12 o'clock, meridian.

The journal then describes the organizing of the convention, the election of John H. Means, governor of South Carolina, as the president, and the resolution and ordinance recommended by the Select Committee of Twenty-one, which are as follows:

Resolved by the people of South Carolina in Convention assembled, That the frequent violations of the Constitution of the United States by the Federal Government, and its encroachments upon the reserved rights of the sovereign States of this Union, especially in relation to slavery, amply justify this State, so far as any duty or obligation to her confederates is involved, in dissolving at once all political connection with her co-States; and that she forbears the exercise of this manifest right of self government from considerations of expediency only.

AN ORDINANCE to declare the right of this State to secede from the Federal Union.

We the People of the State of South Carolina, in Convention assembled, do declare and ordain, and it is hereby declared and ordained, That South Carolina, in the exercise of her sovereign will, as an independent State, acceded to the Federal Union, known as the United States of America; and that in the exercise of the same sovereign will, it is her right, without let, hindrance, or molestation from any power whatsoever, to secede from the said Federal Union; and that for the sufficiency of the causes which may impel her to such separation, she is responsible alone, under God, to the tribunal of public opinion among the nations of the earth.

The convention adopted the resolution and ordinance, 136 to 19.

*   *   *

Two Images of Slavery:
Confederate $100 Bill (1862) and Obelisk, Fort Mill, South Carolina (1895).

Figure 1: Above is a Confederate $100 bill. Its illustrations include John C. Calhoun, advocate of slavery and secession, and a goddess figure, perhaps Columbia, but the dominant image is slaves "chopping" (weeding with a hoe) cotton.

Before the Civil War, plantation owners were happy to state that slaves worked and worked strenuously. Several images on Confederate paper currency show slavery's importance to the economy, social structure, and self-image of the South.[15] After the War, white Southerners airbrushed images of slavery to remove any unpleasantness. In 1895, Samuel White, "with approval of the Jefferson Davis Memorial Association," put up an obelisk to "the faithful slaves" who "toiled for the support of the [Confederate] army" and "with sterling fidelity guarded our defenceless homes." The 1862 image was more accurate. Slavery was first and last a labor system, not a paternalist program to educate and Christianize Africans. Historians have identified four key woes of the enslaved: the lack of independence intrinsic to the institution, the sense of racial inferiority conferred by the stunning gap between the lifestyles of planter and field hand, slaves' inability to control their own occupational and familial lives, and the violence to which they were subjected.

Figure 2: On the left, the Fort Mill obelisk shows a field hand resting comfortably; in another image, a black woman holds a white infant. The rear side lists ten of the "faithful" by name; eight have the surname "White"!

During the war, according to historian William Barney, "Southern whites were shocked to discover that the average domestic slave would be far more likely to lead Union soldiers to the family silver rather than to hide and guard it." African Americans also helped the Union in more important ways. During Grant's operations around Vicksburg and Sherman's "march to the sea" in Georgia and then northward through the Carolinas, African Americans told Union forces where the Confederates were, showed them the best places to ford streams, gave them food and water, and cheered them on their way. From the area around Fort Mill eastward to the Atlantic, thousands escaped to U.S. forces when they could, where they dug fortifications, did laundry, and otherwise made themselves useful. More than 5,000 from South Carolina fought in the United States armed forces. On the Confederate side, General Joseph E. Johnston wrote in early 1864, "The impressment of Negroes has been practiced ever since the war commenced, but we never have been able to keep the impressed Negroes with an army near the enemy. They desert." Historian Stephen Ash notes, "many whites were profoundly shaken by the revelation that slaves hated slavery and resented their masters." He quotes a white Confederate who overgeneralized in despair: "There is not *one Negro* in *all the South*, who will remain faithful *from attachment to their master & mistress*—not one." Commemorations of slave loyalty on the landscape embody a dishonest effort, decades later, to mystify that point.[16]

* * *

Samuel A. Cartwright (1793–1863), "Diseases and Peculiarities of the Negro Race," 1851.[17]

While the politicians moved toward separation, slavery also polarized other parts of American culture. This 1851 article drew many readers when it first came out, immediately being reprinted in *DeBow's Review*, the South's most important periodical. Both its genetic and biblical claims remained staples of traditional Southern white rhetoric well into the civil rights era.

Born in Virginia, Samuel Cartwright studied medicine under the famous Benjamin Rush in Philadelphia. He moved to Natchez and eventually New Orleans. In 1851, he submitted this report to the Louisiana Medical Association. To today's readers, his thinking seems spectacularly implausible. He postulates that African Americans are "unable to care for themselves," owing in part to "atmospherization of the blood." Supposedly blacks like to sleep with bedclothes over their faces, so their brains don't get enough oxygen to develop right. For that reason (and others), slavery is best for them. Any black people who do not agree—indeed, who foolishly try to escape bondage—suffer from a disease, "Drapetomania," or "runaway madness." People who engage in what historians now call "day-to-day resistance" to slavery—doing chores poorly, breaking tools, following orders literally even when they make little sense—he again considers victims of a disease, "dysaesthesia Ethiopia," daydreaming and idleness. That such acts might be rational responses to the demand for unrewarded toil never occurs to Cartwright.

Cartwright also supplies an example of the most common use of the Bible to justify African slavery, the story of Noah's drunkenness in Genesis. Noah had three sons. One, Ham, made the mistake of seeing his father naked, passed out on his bed, drunk. The other two covered their father. To punish Ham's bad behavior, God pronounces a curse upon one of his sons, Canaan: "A servant of servants shall he be unto his brethren." Increasingly after 1830, slaveowners converted this story into a rationale for black bondage. It shouldn't have worked; the Bible never says that "Hamites" were black or lived in Africa. Nor were the Hamites cursed—it was the Canaanites—ancestors of the non-Jewish people who today inhabit Lebanon, Palestine, Israel, and Jordan. Moreover, the most explicit treatment of race in the Bible flatly contradicts white supremacy. Numbers 12: 1–15 tells that Moses took a black wife (often translated "Ethiopian woman"). "And Miriam and Aaron spake against Moses because of the Ethiopian woman whom he had married." Such talk displeased the Lord, so he called Moses, Miriam, and Aaron out in front of the tabernacle tent. "You have been bad-mouthing my servant Moses!" he exclaimed, and turned Miriam white as snow—often translated "leprous." Immediately Miriam and Aaron saw that whiteness was not so important and cried out for relief. Moses too asked God to mitigate the punishment, so God left her leprous for just a week; then she was cured. Somehow this passage never caught on in the white South.[18] The "races of Ham" myth did; Loewen encountered it frequently in Mississippi during the 1960s as a rationale for continued segregation and discrimination.

[Atmospherization of the blood] is the true cause of that debasement of mind, which has rendered the people of Africa unable to take care of themselves. It is the true cause of their indolence and apathy, and why they have chosen, through countless ages, idleness, misery and barbarism, to industry and frugality,—why social industry, or associated labor, so essential to all progress in civilisation and improvement, has never made any progress among them, or the arts and sciences taken root on any portion of African soil inhabited by them; as is proved by the fact that no letters, or even hieroglyphics—no buildings, roads or improvements, or monuments of any kind, are any where found, to indicate that they have ever been awakened from their apathy and sleepy indolence, to physical or mental exertion. To the same physiological causes, deeply rooted in the organization, we must look for an explanation of the strange facts, why none of the languages of the native tribes of Africa, as proved by ethnographical researches, have risen above common names, standing for things and actions, to abstract terms or generalizations;—why no form of government on abstract principles, with divisions of power into separate departments, has ever been instituted by them;—why they have always preferred, as more congenial to their nature, a government combining the legislative, judicial and executive powers in the same individual, in the person of a petty king, a chieftain or master;— why, in America, if let alone, they always prefer the same kind of government, which we call slavery, but which is actually an improvement on the government of their forefathers. . . .

Cartwright then writes several paragraphs comparing African Americans to children. Then he turns to religion.

I have thus hastily and imperfectly noticed some of the more striking anatomical and physiological peculiarities of the Negro race. The question may be asked, Does he belong to the same race as the white man? Is he a son of Adam? Does his peculiar physical conformation stand in opposition to the Bible, or does it prove its truth? These are important questions, both in a medical, historical and theological point of view. They can better be answered by a comparison of the facts derived from anatomy, physiology, history and theology, to see if they sustain one another. We learn from the Book of Genesis, that Noah had three sons, Shem, Ham and Japheth, and that Canaan, the son of Ham, was doomed to be servant of servants unto his brethren. From history, we learn that the descendants of Canaan settled in Africa, and are the present Ethiopians, or black race of men; that Shem occupied Asia, and Japheth the north of Europe. In the 9th chapter and the 27th verse of Genesis, one of the most authentic books of the Bible, is the remarkable prophecy: God shall enlarge Japheth and he shall dwell in the tents of Shem, and Canaan shall be his servant. Japheth has been greatly enlarged by the discovery of a new world, the continent of America. He found in it the Indians, whom natural history declares to be of Asiatic origin, in other words, the descendants of Shem: he drove out Shem, and occupied his tents: and now the remaining part of the prophecy is in the process of fulfillment, from the facts every where before us, of Canaan having become his servant. The question arises, is the Canaanite, or Ethiopian, qualified for the trying duties of servitude, and unfitted for the enjoyment of freedom? If he be, there is both wisdom, mercy and justice in the decree dooming him to be servant of servants, as the decree is in conformity to his nature. Anatomy and physiology have been interrogated, and the response is, that the Ethiopian, or Canaanite, is unfitted, from his organization and physiological laws predicated on that organization, for the responsible duties of a free man, but, like the child, is only fitted for a state of dependence and subordination. When history is interrogated, the response is, that the only government under which the negro has made any improvement in mind, morals, religion, and the only government under which he has led a happy, quiet and contented life, is that under which he is subjected to the arbitrary power of Japheth in obedience to the Divine decree. When the original Hebrew of the Bible is interrogated, we find, in the significant meaning of the original name of the negro, the identical fact set forth, which the knife of the anatomist at the dissecting table has made appear; as if the revelations of anatomy, physiology and history, were a mere re-writing of what Moses wrote. In the Hebrew word "Canaan," the original name of the Ethiopian, the word *slave by nature*, or language to the same effect, is written by the inspired penman. Hence, there is no conflict between the revelations of the science of medicine, history, and the inductions drawn from the Baconian philosophy, and the authority of the Bible; one supports the other.

Cartwright then has a section titled "Negro Consumption," which he blames on "erythism of mind," or "sulkiness and dissatisfaction."

Drapetomania, or the Disease Causing Slaves to Run Away

Drapetomania is from [*drapeto*, transliterated from the Greek] a runaway slave, and [*mania*], *mad or crazy*. It is unknown to our medical authorities, although its diagnostic symptoms, the absconding from service, is well known to our planters and overseers, as it was to the ancient Greeks, who expressed by the single word [*drapeto*] the fact of the absconding, and the relation that the fugitive held to the person he fled from. I have added to the word meaning runaway slave, another Greek term, to express the disease of the mind causing him to abscond. In noticing a disease not heretofore classed among the long list of maladies that man is subject to, it was necessary to have a new term to express it. The cause, in the most of cases, that induces the negro to run away from service, is as much a disease of the mind as any other species of mental alienation, and much more curable, as a general rule. With the advantages of proper medical advice, strictly followed, this troublesome practice that many negroes have of running away, can be almost entirely prevented, although the slaves be located on the borders of a free State, within a stone's throw of the abolitionists. I was born in Virginia, east of the Blue Ridge, where negroes are numerous, and studied medicine some years in Maryland, a slave State, separated from Pennsylvania, a free State, by Mason & Dixon's line—a mere air line, without wall or guard. I long ago observed that some persons, considered as very good, and others as very bad masters, often lost their negroes by their absconding from service; while the slaves of another class of persons, remarkable for order and good discipline, but not praised or blamed as either good or bad masters, never ran away, although no guard or forcible means were used to prevent them. The same management which prevented them from walking over a mere nominal, unguarded line, will prevent them from running away anywhere.

To ascertain the true method of governing negroes, so as to cure and prevent the disease under consideration, we must go back to the Pentateuch, and learn the true meaning of the untranslated term that represents the negro race. In the name there given to that race, is locked up the true art of governing negroes in such a manner that they cannot run away. The correct translation of that term declares the Creator's will in regard to the negro; it declares him to be the submissive knee-bender. In the anatomical conformation of his knees, we see "*genu flexit*" written in the physical structure of his knees, being more flexed or bent, than any other kind of man. If the white man attempts to oppose the Deity's will, by trying to make the negro anything else than "*the submissive knee-bender*" (which the Almighty declared he should be,) by trying to raise him to a level with himself, or by putting himself on an equality with the negro; or if he abuses the power which God has given him over his fellow-man, by being cruel to him or punishing him in anger, or by neglecting to protect him from the wanton abuses of his fellow-servants and all others, or by denying him the usual comforts and necessaries of life, the negro will run away: but if he keeps him in the position that we learn from the Scriptures he was intended to occupy, that is, the position of submission, and if his master or overseer be kind and gracious in his bearing towards him, without condescension, and at the same time ministers to his physical wants and protects him from abuses, the negro is spellbound, and cannot run away. "*He shall serve Japheth*; he shall be his servant of servants;"—on the conditions above mentioned—conditions that are clearly implied, though not directly expressed. According to my experience, the "genu flexit"—the awe and reverence, must be exacted from them, or they will despise their masters, become rude and ungovernable and run away. On Mason and Dixon's line, two classes of persons were apt to lose their negroes; those who made themselves too familiar with them, treating them as equals, and making little or no distinction in regard to color; and, on the other hand, those who treated them cruelly, denied them the common necessaries of life, neglected to protect them against the abuses of others, or frightened them by a blustering manner of approach, when about to punish them for misdemeanors. Before negroes run away, unless they are frightened or panic-struck, they become sulky and dissatisfied. The cause of this sulkiness and dissatisfaction should be inquired into and removed, or they are apt to run away or fall into the negro consumption. When sulky and dissatisfied without cause, the experience of those on the line and elsewhere was decidedly in favor of whipping them out of it, as a preventive measure against absconding or other bad conduct. It was called whipping the devil out of them.

If treated kindly, well fed and clothed, with fuel enough to keep a small fire burning all night, separated into families, each family having its own house—not permitted to run about at night, or to visit their neighbors, or to receive visits, or to use intoxicating liquors, and not overworked or exposed too much to the weather, they are very easily governed—more so than any other people in the world. When all this is done, if any one or more of them, at any time, are inclined to raise their heads to a level with their master or overseer, humanity and their own good require that they should be punished until they fall into that submissive state which it was intended for them to occupy in all after time, when their progenitor received the name of Canaan, or "submissive kneebender." They have only to be kept in that state, and treated like children, with care, kindness, attention and humanity, to prevent and cure them from running away.

Dysesthesia Ethiopis, or Hebetude of Mind and Obtuse Sensibility of Body
A DISEASE PECULIAR TO NEGROES CALLED BY OVERSEERS,
"RASCALITY"

Dysaesthesia Aethiopis is a disease peculiar to negroes, affecting both mind and body, in a manner as well expressed by dysaesthesia, the name I have given it, as could be by a single term. There is both mind and sensibility, but both seem to be difficult to reach by impressions from without. There is partial insensibility of the skin, and so great a hebetude of the intellectual faculties as to be like a person half asleep, that is with difficulty aroused and kept awake. It differs from every other species of mental disease, as it is accompanied with physical signs or lesions of the body, discoverable to the medical observer, which are always present and sufficient to account for the symptoms. It is much more prevalent among free negroes living in clusters by themselves, than among slaves on our plantations, and attacks only such slaves as live like free negroes in regard to diet, drinks, exercise, etc. It is not my purpose to treat of the complaint as it prevails among free negroes, nearly all of whom are more or less afflicted with it, that have not got some white person to direct and to take care of them. To narrate its symptoms and effects among them would be to write a history of the ruins and dilapidation of Hayti and every spot of earth they have ever had uncontrolled possession over for any length of time. I propose only to describe its symptoms among slaves.

From the careless movements of the individuals affected with the complaint, they are apt to do much mischief, which appears as if intentional, but is mostly owing to the stupidness of mind and insensibility of the nerves induced by the disease. Thus, they break, waste and destroy everything they handle,—abuse horses and cattle,—tear, burn or rend their own clothing, and paying no attention to the rights of property, they steal other's to replace what they have destroyed.

. . . The northern physicians and people have noticed the symptoms, but not the disease from which they spring. They ignorantly attribute the symptoms to the debasing influence of slavery on the mind, without considering that those who have never been in slavery, or their fathers before them, are the most afflicted, and the latest from the slave-holding South the least. The disease is the natural offspring of negro liberty—the liberty to be idle, to wallow in filth, and to indulge in improper food and drinks.

The best treatment, according to Cartwright, is to "put the patient to some hard kind of work in the open air and sunshine, that will compel him to expand his lungs, as chopping wood, splitting rails or sawing with the cross-cut or whip saw." After discussing other allegedly physiological maladies, Cartwright claims, "According to unalterable physiological laws, negroes, as a general rule, to which there are but few exceptions, can only have their intellectual faculties awakened in a sufficient degree to receive moral culture, and to profit by religious or other instruction, when under the compulsatory authority of the white man." He concludes:

Our Declaration of Independence, which was drawn up at a time when negroes were scarcely considered as human beings, *"That all men are by nature free and equal,"* and only intended to apply to white men, is often quoted in support of the false dogma that all mankind possess the same mental, physiological and anatomical organization, and that the liberty, free institutions, and whatever else would be a blessing to one portion, would, under the same external circumstances, be to all, without regard to any original or internal differences, inherent in the organization. Although England preaches this doctrine, she practises in opposition to it every where. Instance, her treatment of the Gypsies in England, the Hindoos in India, the Hottentots at her Cape Colony, and the aboriginal inhabitants of New Holland. The dysaesthesia ethiopis adds another to the many ten thousand evidences of the fallacy of the dogma that abolitionism is built on; for here, in a country where two races of men dwell together, both born on the same soil, breathing the same air, and surrounded by the same external agents—liberty, which is elevating the one race of people above all other nations, sinks the other into beastly sloth and torpidity; and the slavery, which the one would prefer death rather than endure, improves the other in body, mind and morals; thus proving the dogma false, and establishing the truth that there is a radical, internal, or physical difference between the two races, so great in kind, as to make what is wholesome and beneficial for the white man, as liberty, republican or free institutions, etc., not only unsuitable to the negro race, but actually poisonous to its happiness.

* * *

Slave Jail, Alexandria, c. 1859.

Figure 3: This slave jail behind Franklin and Armfield, slave traders in Alexandria, Virginia, provided "safe keeping at 25¢ per day."

Among other things, slavery was a penal system. On the plantation, few enslaved people had to be kept under lock and key. There they had family ties, friendships, and routines that were hard to break. Moreover, rural life afforded few options for escape. Owners could mobilize their neighbors, and any African American traveling without a pass would be challenged as a potential runaway. In cities, the situation was different. The anonymity of urban life made it harder for whites to know whether a black person was free, rented out, or absent from their owner without leave. Whites could hardly challenge every African American they saw. Nevertheless, plantation owners would often bring along a valet or coachman when visiting the city. Some hotels had rooms with barred windows and externally locked doors to draw such trade; owners could lock in their slaves for the night, then retire to their quarters secure in the knowledge that none could run away. As well, slave dealers often rented cells for this purpose to travelers whose hotel had no such facility. Dealers had particular reason to fear escape, for their slaves' ties to family, friends, and locale had already been torn apart.

* * *

Jefferson Davis (1808–89), "Endorsement"; T. L. Clingman (1812–97), "Endorsement"; and J. H. Van Evrie (1814–96), "Negroes and Negro 'Slavery,' The First an Inferior Race— The Latter, Its Normal Condition," 1853.[19]

Not just medicine and religion, but also science was pressed into the cause of defending slavery. When ichthyologist Louis Agassiz came to the United States in 1847, he championed scientific racism. Agassiz was an expert on fossil fishes, but his first encounters with African Americans—waiters in a Philadelphia hotel—filled him with a visceral disgust. Thereafter he wrote extensively about race. He claimed (incorrectly of course) that the different racial groups (as then defined) formed at different times, in different places, owing to divine intervention. Apologists for slavery bought into this kind of thinking, beginning with Dr. J. H. Van Evrie. Historian George Frederickson calls Van Evrie "perhaps the first professional racist in American history." With Rushmore G. Horton, another pro-Confederate New Yorker, he published a newspaper and various books on race. "Negroes and Negro 'Slavery,' The First an Inferior Race—The Latter, Its Normal Condition," a pamphlet in 1853, grew into a book by 1861. In 1868, it was retitled *White Supremacy and Negro Subordination* to reflect the demise of slavery. Jefferson Davis (1808–89), North Carolina congressman T. L. Clingman (1812–97), and J. D. B. DeBow (1820–67), who published *DeBow's Review*, the most influential magazine in the South, wrote blurbs for the inside cover of the pamphlet. Davis hoped that Van Evrie's arguments would help the South prevail in the ongoing national crisis by exposing the "fallacy" of racial equality.[20]

During the Civil War, Confederates used Van Evrie's arguments to try to win public support for slavery in the United States and Europe. At the time, Van Evrie lived in London. In 1864, proslavery Democrats in New York City published a notorious pamphlet that purported to be written by abolitionist Republicans. It professed to favor racial intermixture, which it called by a new word, "miscegenation." When it came out in London, Van Evrie responded with a revised edition of his book, retitled *Subgenation: The Theory of the Normal Relation of the Races—An Answer to "Miscegenation."* In it he wrote, "The equality of all whom God has created equal (white men) and the inequality of those He has made unequal (Negroes and other inferior races) are the corner-stone of American democracy, and the vital principle of American civilization and of human progress." He urged Peace Democrats to defeat Lincoln in 1864 and adopt the Confederate Constitution in the North.[21]

After the war, Confederates used these arguments about black inferiority to argue for ending Reconstruction. Van Evrie extended his "divine biology is destiny" analysis to sex, suggesting it would be "an outrage" for women to study law or captain a steamboat. During the Women's Suffrage Movement, neo-Confederates used these arguments to persuade every Southern state except Tennessee to reject the Nineteenth Amendment. During the Civil Rights Movement, they used similar assertions to oppose school desegregation and voting rights for African Americans. As late as the 1970s, the campaign for an Equal Rights Amendment for women failed to win approval from any Southern state except Tennessee.

From Hon. Jefferson Davis, Secretary of War.

WASHINGTON, 3*d* June, 1853.

Dr. Van Evrie:

Dear Sir, I have read the enclosed pages with great interest, and not as a Southern man merely, but as an American, I thank you for your able and manly exposure of a fallacy which more than any or all other causes has disturbed the tranquility of our people and endangered the perpetuity of our constitutional union. With high regard I am your obedient servant,

JEFFE'N DAVIS.

From Hon. T. L. Clingman, U.S. House of Representatives.

HOUSE REPRESENTATIVES, Dec. 18*th*, 1853

Dear Sir, I have read with much interest your chapter on "Negroes and Negro Slavery." Its propositions are strikingly and powerfully stated. Your blows against a popular delusion are given with dexterity, rapidity, and the force of a sledge-hammer. . . . A wide circulation of your pamphlet will be equally serviceable to the Northern and Southern sections of the Union.

Respectfully yours, &c.,

T. L. CLINGMAN

Van Evrie begins with five paragraphs we omit, arguing that abolitionists
like Harriet Beecher Stowe commit the key error of assuming "that the
Negro is a black white man."

The author of this publication has devoted several years to this enquiry, especially to that portion of the general subject, embracing the *specific* character of
the negro, and the natural relations of whites and negroes: the results of which
he is now prepared to lay before the public.

Stripping off the skin of the negro, he proposes to demonstrate to the senses,
as well as the reason, that he is not a black white man, or a man merely with a
black skin, but a DIFFERENT AND INFERIOR SPECIES OF MAN;—that this
difference is radical, and total, and relatively, as great in the primordial arrangement of elementary particles, or the single globule of blood, as in the color of
the skin, or the grosser facts, palpable to the senses;—that it is original, invari-
able, and indestructible, as long as the present order of creation itself lasts;—
that the physical structure of the race is necessarily and perpetually linked with
corresponding faculties, capabilities, wants, necessities, in short, with a *specific*
nature, and is thus designed by the Almighty Creator for corresponding purposes, or a social position harmonizing with those wants, etc.;—that therefore
all the charges against the social system of the South, being based on false as-
sumptions, are themselves necessarily false;—that so-called slavery is neither
a "wrong" nor an "evil," nor is its extension dangerous, but that it is a normal
condition, a natural relation, based upon the "higher law," in harmony with the
order, progress, and general well-being of the superior one, and absolutely essential to the very existence of the inferior race.

Van Evrie includes several paragraphs about the relationship of this pamphlet to his larger planned book, which was eventually published. He then
writes five paragraphs suggesting that science now knows that mankind
evolved in several different places, leading to several different races.
Whether true or not, he continues, what is more important is the "specific
character" of each race.

Commencing with the simpler forms of organized existence, and ascending
in the scale till reaching the Caucasian man, (the most elaborate in his structure, and therefore the highest endowed in his faculties,) all intermediates in
the series, whether human or brute, Mongolian or Negro, Ouran-Outan, or
Chimpanzee, are alike subject to classification, as well as the lowest and sim-
plest forms of organic life. Indeed a classification founded upon positive facts,
and a true knowledge of the *specific* differences in human races, is a work of
less difficulty than it is in the simple forms; for the superadded moral nature of

the former furnishes additional facts for our guidance. Throughout the whole world of organic existence there is a perfect adaptation of means and ends, and the structural arrangement of each *species*, or each original and permanent creation, is in perfect harmony with its faculties and the purposes assigned to it by the Creator. This is a truth equally palpable in the organization of the individual; those organs, most elaborate and complex in their structure, are those performing the most important functions. Thus the heart, the centre of the vital functions, is comparatively simple in its structure; while the brain, the centre of the animal, as well as the intellectual functions, is wonderfully complex. Thus, too, the sense of sight is performed through an exceedingly complex and exquisitely delicate apparatus, while the organism of locomotion is comparatively simple.

This great and fundamental law of organized life pervades the whole world of animated being, and serves as a positive and unmistakable test or admeasurement of the character and relations of all the innumerable series that compose it. In precise proportion to the complexity of an organ in the human body is the importance of function; precisely too as is the complexity of structural arrangement in any *species*, whether human or animal, so, too, if the superiority of faculties in such *species*, and elevation of purposes assigned to it by the Creator. In nothing, perhaps, is this truth more palpable than in the case of woman; who, with a far more elaborate and exquisitely organized nervous system than man, has also finer moral perceptions, as well as more delicate sensibilities, while her muscular system and organs of locomotion, necessary alone to mere physical power, are infinitely inferior to the other sex. The facts of organic life, its laws of development, its necessities, and in the more elevated forms of the human races, its rights, as well as the duties that attach to it, that are indeed inseparable from it, are so little studied or understood even by educated persons, that nothing is more common than for such to lecture the public on the duty, of forcing their civilization or modes of action on other *races*. Thus an American Secretary of State will talk learnedly about some races who, amalgamating with others, beget a mongrel breed, utterly good for nothing, while others with an aptitude for amalgamation, beget a more vigorous and progressive race, than either of the originals. How near a truth, and yet what an immense distance from it! Had the orator of the Colonization Society said that amalgamation with separate *races* of men, as ourselves and the Negro, is followed by a mongrel brood, however superior mentally to the Negro, yet vastly inferior to the white, and as certain to perish as the mule, or any other hybrid generation; but that amalgamation with the Irishman or German, or any other variety of our own *species* or *race*, would be followed by a more vigorous stock than either of the originals, he would have declared an *eternal truth*. But we may also say, had he known this truth, he would not have been the orator of the

Colonization Society, or if so, his lecture would have been very different indeed from that absurd effort to convince his audience that they were bound to go to work, and compel the different and *inferiorly* organized Negro to perform the functions of the Caucasian; that two widely separated organizations, differently endowed and differently designed by Almighty power, should be compelled by *human force* to exercise the same faculties, and perform the same purposes; a supposition about as rational, and as much dependent on fact, as that a watch and saw-mill are equally designed to measure time, or that elephants and mice should catch their prey, or supply themselves with food in exactly the same manner....

Van Evrie then has a long paragraph about how women differ from men. He continues:

Each *specific* organization or form of existence, with its distinct physical structure, is also endowed with specific or distinct faculties, and designed by the Creator for *specific* purposes. To disregard this, to demand the same rights, and compel the same duties, to say that the *inferiorly* organized and *inferiorly* endowed Negro shall be a member of Congress, while the *superiorly* organized white man shall black boots; or the former a professor in college, while the latter hoes cotton; or that a system shall be brought to bear upon them to force an equality, when nature has made none, and permits none, is a contradiction of all the laws of organic existence, and as entirely beyond the power of man to effect, as the attempt to do so is repugnant to reason.

So too with woman: with a distinct organization, endowed with distinct and peculiar faculties, and designed for distinct and peculiar purposes, those who would seek to force her out of, or beyond her sphere—to compel her to study law, or command a steamboat, as well as nurse a baby, or cook a dinner—would equally violate nature, and inflict an outrage upon her....

To violate these laws—to say because the Negro has certain general resemblances to the white man, or that the female has some qualities resembling the other sex, that the same rules shall apply to them universally; is not only to fight against progress and the nature of things, but would be a rapid stride towards barbarism. Indeed, in such an absurd application of inherent right or "*equality*" there is no stopping place in the whole organism of nature. If women must exercise the "rights," and perform the duties of men, (for the two things are inseparable,) why not children? Certainly a boy of twelve or fourteen years of age has as strong muscles, and is as capable of manual labor and has a capacity to perform the duties of men, as well as most females. As a physiological fact, there is no *positive* boundary between men and animals; and though the Negro is further separated from the "Ouran Outan" than he is from the white or

Caucasian man, the actual difference between the latter is as distinct, or rather it is a *fact*, as well as the former. Again; the white, or Caucasian man, as well as the Negro, has some qualities in common, not only with the Simiadae, but with the whole Mammalia, and remotely even with still lower forms of organized life. Thus the whole world of organism is bound together in one continuous chain; though the links in that chain are distinct and *specific*, and as plain and comprehensible to human reason as they are wisely and beneficently designed by the Creator.

Where, with these facts before us, can we or should we stop? The Negro has not only more in common with us than he has with the Ouran-Outan, but really has nothing in common with the latter that we ourselves have not, except that he has these common qualities more prominently; but should we therefore attempt, in all respects, to make the Negro our equal, and deny to the Ouran-Outan everything? Or rather, should we not, in conformity with the eternal and immutable facts of nature, grant to the Negro all that he possesses in common with us, and no more; and to the Ouran-Outan, and still inferiour creatures, what belong to them, or have consideration for them to the extent that they approximate to us? Unfortunately, the distinctions that separate, yet bind closely together, all the *species* of men, have not been investigated or understood, and a few general resemblances have been confounded and mistaken, so that a very large portion of mankind are entirely ignorant of their true character....

If the Creator had designed the horse for food, he would have created him differently, and, instead of the tough and stringy muscles so appropriate to strength and swiftness, would have constructed him with reference to human digestion. And if he had designed the Negro for the same purpose as the white or Caucasian man, he would have given him the same faculties—or rather we should say, he would not have been created at all, for the single fact that he exists is decisive of the will and intention of the Creator. In Europe, where women are placed at the head of nations and rule over millions of men, and where their husbands, whom *nature* places at the head of the household, stand behind their chairs, to receive their orders, thus outraging common sense as much as nature herself, and where fathers kiss the hands of their own off-spring, as their slaves or subjects, "women's rights" should flourish in such congenial soil: for the more the laws of nature are violated and reason trampled under foot, the longer such a "system" may be continued. Or, when the millions in profound ignorance of their rights, are not permitted to enjoy the tenth part of the proceeds of their labor, while a mere fraction (men like themselves) live in idle and extravagant luxury at their expense, it may be expected that "human rights" or "negro rights," or the elevation of the Negro to that same level which the millions occupy, would be actively advocated; for here too, as in the case of family relations, the more the laws of nature are trampled upon, the longer those who profit by such a condition of things may hope to retain them.

But in the United States, among a people almost universally educated, and where the fact of "equality" is almost universally understood, and acted on personally as well as politically, the advocacy of woman's "equality" in the sense that they argue it, or "equality" of the Negro to the white man in any sense whatever, is inexcusable on the ground of ignorance; and those thus warring against the laws of nature and the progress of society deserve to be treated as its enemies—or as absolute maniacs, and irresponsible for the evils they seek to inflict upon it.

Van Evrie then ends with a section asserting that abolition is a conspiracy of British aristocrats against American democracy.

* * *

GEORGE FITZHUGH (1806–81), *CANNIBALS ALL!*
OR SLAVES WITHOUT MASTERS, 1857.[22]

George Fitzhugh wrote two famous apologetics for slavery, *A Sociology for the South* and *Cannibals All!* This excerpt from the latter's first chapter makes a point that Southern defenders of slavery used repeatedly: capitalists treated their workers much worse than did planters, who felt a paternalist responsibility for the well-being of their slaves. A simple thought experiment suffices to show the fallacy in this argument: no one, North or South, found "wage slavery" so unpleasant that they voluntarily submitted to the real kind. Conversely, slavery was a penal system, with passes, patrols, and bars on hotel room windows.

We are, all, North and South, engaged in the White Slave Trade, and he who succeeds best, is esteemed most respectable. It is far more cruel than the Black Slave Trade, because it exacts more of its slaves, and neither protects nor governs them. We boast, that it exacts more, when we say, "that the *profits* made from employing free labor are greater than those from slave labor." The profits, made from free labor, are the amount of the products of such labor, which the employer, by means of the command which capital or skill gives him, takes away, exacts or "exploitates" from the free laborer. The profits of slave labor are that portion of the products of such labor which the power of the master enables him to appropriate. These profits are less, because the master allows the slave to retain a larger share of the results of his own labor, than do the employers of free labor. But we not only boast that the White Slave Trade is more exacting and fraudulent (in fact, though not in intention,) than Black Slavery; but we also boast, that it is more cruel, in leaving the laborer to take care of himself and family out of the pittance which skill or capital have allowed him to retain. When the day's labor is ended, he is free, but is overburdened with the cares of family and household, which make his freedom an empty and delusive mockery. But his employer is really free, and may enjoy the profits made by others' labor, without a care, or a trouble, as to their well-being. The negro slave is free, too, when the labors of the day are over, and free in mind as well as body; for the master provides food, raiment, house, fuel, and everything else necessary to the physical well-being of himself and family. The master's labors commence just when the slave's end. No wonder men should prefer white slavery to capital, to negro slavery, since it is more profitable, and is free from all the cares and labors of black slave-holding.

... [A]ll good and respectable people are "Cannibals all," who do not labor, or who are successfully trying to live without labor, on the unrequited labor of other people:—Whilst low, bad, and disreputable people, are those who labor to support themselves, and to support said respectable people besides. Throwing the negro slaves out of the account, and society is divided in Christendom into four classes: The rich, or independent respectable people, who live well and labor not at all; the professional and skillful respectable people, who do a little light work, for enormous wages; the poor hard-working people, who support every body, and starve themselves; and the poor thieves, swindlers and sturdy beggars, who live like gentlemen, without labor, on the labor of other people. The gentlemen exploitate, which being done on a large scale, and requiring a great many victims, is highly respectable—whilst the rogues and beggars take so little from others, that they fare little better than those who labor.

... The negro slaves of the South are the happiest, and, in some sense, the freest people in the world. The children and the aged and infirm work not at all, and yet have all the comforts and necessaries of life provided for them. They enjoy liberty, because they are oppressed neither by care nor labor.

The women do little hard work, and are protected from the despotism of their husbands by their masters.[23] The negro men and stout boys work, on the average, in good weather, not more than nine hours a day. The balance of their time is spent in perfect abandon. Besides, they have their Sabbaths and holidays. White men, with so much of license and liberty, would die of ennui; but negroes luxuriate in corporeal and mental repose. . . .

The free laborer must work or starve. He is more of a slave than the negro, because he works longer and harder for less allowance than the slave, and has no holiday, because the cares of life with him begin when its labors end. He has no liberty, and not a single right. . . .

Free laborers have not a thousandth part of the rights and liberties of negro slaves. Indeed, they have not a single right or a single liberty, unless it be the right or liberty to die. But the reader may think that he and other capitalists and employers are freer than negro slaves. Your capital would soon vanish, if you dared indulge in the liberty and abandon of negroes. You hold your wealth and position by the tenure of constant watchfulness, care and circumspection. You never labor; but you are never free. . . .

* * *

ALEXANDER H. STEPHENS (1812–83), "SPEECH ON THE BILL TO ADMIT KANSAS AS A STATE UNDER THE TOPEKA CONSTITUTION," HOUSE OF REPRESENTATIVES, JUNE 28, 1856.[24]

Claiming that slavery was a blessing to slaves, Southerners worked during the 1850s to extend slavery's reach. Under the Kansas-Nebraska Act, citizens in Kansas were to determine whether Kansas should become a free or slave state. "Border Ruffians" crossed from Missouri into Kansas to vote for a proslavery constitution, prompting "Free Soilers" to enact a constitution of their own. Here Georgia congressman Alexander Stephens, soon to be vice president of the Confederacy, argues against accepting Kansas as a free state. He begins with lengthy comments about parliamentary matters, defends the Kansas-Nebraska Act, claims Free Soilers were trying to take Kansas by violence, and then proposes new elections for a new territorial constitutional convention. He closes with the following general arguments about slavery as the "natural place" for African Americans, also justified in the Bible.

Are we, Mr. Speaker, to remain a united people? Are we to go on in that high career of achievement in science, in art, and in civilization, which we have so conspicuously entered upon? Or are we to be arrested in our upward course long before reaching the half-way point toward ultimate culmination. Are our deeds of glory all numbered? Are the memories of the past to be forgotten, and the benefits and blessings of the present to be derided and rejected? Is the radiant orb of day brightening the morning of our existence to be darkened and obscured, and with it the light of the world extinguished forever? And all this because Congress, in its wisdom, has thought proper to permit the free white men of Kansas to determine for themselves whether the negro in that territory shall be the same nondescript outcast, neither citizen nor slave, amongst them, that he is in sixteen States of the Union, or whether he shall occupy the same condition there in relation to them which a Christian philanthropy has assigned him in the other fifteen States. I say Christian philanthropy, notwithstanding the remarks of the gentleman from Indiana, [Mr. DUNN,] and the gentleman from Ohio, [Mr. GIDDINGS,] the other day, denouncing slavery as a violation of the laws of nature and of God! To those remarks, though my time is short, I wish very briefly to reply before I close.

Even, however, if slavery be sinful, as they affirm, or their language implies, permit me here to ask, is not the sin the same whether the slave be held in Georgia, Carolina, or in Kansas? Is it any more sinful in one place than another? But are these gentlemen correct? Is African slavery, as it exists in the South, either a violation of the laws of nature, the laws of nations, or the laws of God? I maintain that it is not. It has been recognized by the laws of nations from time immemorial. The highest court in this country, the Supreme Court of the United States, has so decided the laws of nations to be. And where do we get the laws of nature but in nature's works about us? Those general rules and principles by which all things in nature, according to their kinds respectively, seem to be regulated, and to which they seem to conform, we call laws; and in the handiwork of creation nothing is more striking to the philosophic observer than that order is nature's first great law.

Gradation, too, is stamped upon every thing animate as well as inanimate— if, indeed, there be any thing inanimate. A scale, from the lowest degree of inferiority to the highest degree of superiority, runs through all animal life. We see it in the insect tribes—we see it in the fishes of the sea, the fowls of the air, in the beasts of the earth, and we see it in the races of men. We see the same principle pervading the heavenly bodies above us. One star differs from another star in magnitude and lustre some are larger, others are smaller—but the greater and superior uniformly influences and controls the lesser and inferior within its sphere. If there is any fixed principle or law of nature it is this. In the races of men we find like differences in capacity and development. The negro is inferior to the white man; nature has made him so; observation and history, from the remotest times, establish the fact; and all attempts to make the inferior equal to the superior is but an effort to reverse the decrees of the Creator, who has made all things as we find them, according to the counsels of his own will. The Ethiopian can no more change his nature or his skin than the leopard his spots. Do what you will, a negro is a negro, and he will remain a negro still. In the social and political system of the South the negro is assigned to that subordinate position for which he is fitted by the laws of nature. Our system of civilization is founded in strict conformity to these laws. Order and subordination, according to the natural fitness of things, is the principle upon which the whole fabric of our southern institutions rests.

Then as to the law of God—that law we read not only in his works about us, around us, and over us, but in that inspired Book wherein he has revealed his will to man. When we differ as to the voice of nature, or the language of God, as spoken in nature's works, we go to that great Book, the Book of books, which is the fountain of all truth. To that Book I now appeal. God, in the days of old, made a covenant with the human family for the redemption of fallen man: that covenant is the corner-stone of the whole Christian system. Abram, afterwards called Abraham, was the man with whom that covenant was made. He was the great first head of an organized visible church here below. He believed God, and it was accounted to him for righteousness. He was in deed and in truth the father of the faithful. Abraham, sir, was a slaveholder. Nay, more, he was required to have the sign of that covenant administered to the slaves of his household.

Mr. CAMPBELL. Page, bring me a Bible.

Mr. STEPHENS. I have one here which the gentleman can consult if he wishes. Here is the passage, Genesis xvii. 13. God said to Abraham:

"13. He that is *born in thy house* and he that is *bought with thy money* must needs be circumcised; and my covenant shall be in your flesh for an everlasting covenant."

Yes, sir, Abraham was not only a slaveholder, but a slave dealer it seems, for he bought men with his money, and yet it was with him the covenant was made by which the world was to be redeemed from the dominion of sin. And it was into his bosom in heaven that the poor man who died at the rich man's gate was borne by angels, according to the parable of the Saviour. In the 20th chapter of Exodus, the great moral law is found—that law that defines sin—the ten commandments, written by the finger of God himself upon tables of stone. In two of these commandments, the 4th and 10th, verses 10th and 17th, slavery is expressly recognized, and in none of them is there any thing against it—this is the moral law. In Leviticus we have the civil law on this subject, as given by God to Moses for the government of his chosen people in their municipal affairs. In chapter xxv, verses 44, 45, and 46, I read as follows:

"44. Both thy bondmen and thy bondmaids which thou shalt have, shall be of the heathen that are round about you; of them ye shall buy bond men and bondmaids.

"45. Moreover, of the children of the strangers that do sojourn among you, of them ye shalt buy, and of their families that are with you which they begat in your land: and they shall be your possession.

"46. And ye shall take them as an inheritance for your children after you, to inherit them for a possession; they shall be your bondmen forever; but over your brethren, the children of Israel, ye shall not rule one over another, with rigor."

This was the law given to the Jews soon after they left Egypt, for their government when they should reach the land of promise. They could have had no slaves then. It authorized the introduction of slavery amongst them when they should become established in Canaan. And it is to be noted that their bondmen and bondmaids to be bought, and held for *a possession and an inheritance* for their children after them, were to be of the heathen round about them. Over their brethren they were not to rule with rigor. Our southern system is in strict conformity with this injunction. Men of our own blood and our own race, wherever born, or from whatever clime they come, are free and equal. We have no castes or classes amongst white men—no "upper tendoms" or "lower tendom." All are equals. Our slaves were taken from the heathen tribes the barbarians of Africa. In our households they are brought within the pale of the covenant, under Christian teaching and influence; and more of them are partakers of the benefits of the gospel than ever were rendered so by missionary enterprise. The wisdom of man is foolishness—the ways of Providence are mysterious. Nor does the negro feel any sense of degradation in his condition—he is not *degraded*. He occupies and fills the same *grade* or rank in society and the State that he does in the scale of being; it is his natural place; and all things fit when nature's great first law of order is conformed to.

Again: Job was certainly one of the best men of whom we read in the Bible. He was a large slaveholder. So, too, were Isaac and Jacob, and all the patriarchs. But, it is said, this was under the Jewish dispensation. Granted. Has any change been made since? Is any thing to be found in the New Testament against it? Nothing—not a word. Slavery existed when the gospel, was preached by Christ and his Apostles, and where they preached: it was all around them. And though the Scribes and Pharisees were denounced by our Saviour for their hypocrisy and robbing "widows' houses," yet not a word did He utter against slaveholding. On one occasion He was sought for by a centurion, who asked him to heal his slave, who was sick. Jesus said he would go but the centurion objected, saying: "Lord, I am not worthy that thou shouldst come under my roof; but speak the word only, and my servant shall be healed. For I am a man under authority, having soldiers under me; and I say to this man, go, and he goeth and to another come, and he cometh; and to my *slave*, do this, and he doeth it." Matthew viii. 9. The word rendered here "servant," in our translation, means *slave*. It means just such a servant as all our slaves at the South are. I have the original Greek. . . .

We omit four paragraphs in which Stephens argues the New Testament accepts the existence of slavery. He concludes:

. . . In no place in the New Testament, sir, is slavery held up as sinful. Several of the Apostles alluded to it, but none of them—not one of them, mentions or condemns it as a relation sinful in itself, or violative of the laws of God, or even Christian duty. They enjoin the relative duties of both master and slave. . . .

Let no man, then, say that African slavery as it exists in the South, incorporated in, and sanctioned by the constitution of the United States, is in violation of either the laws of nations, the laws of nature, or the laws of God!

And if it "must needs be" that such an offence shall come from this source, as shall sever the ties that now unite these States together in fraternal bonds, and involve the land in civil war, then "woe be unto them from whom the offence cometh!"

* * *

Jefferson Davis (1808–89), Speech at State Fair, Augusta, Maine, September 29, 1858.[25]

In Maine's capital, Jefferson Davis lauds New England's experiments in cattle breeding and also commends New Englanders because "[t]hey kept pure the Caucasian blood which flowed in their veins." He also elides our Indian wars, saying we Americans got our territory fairly, unlike other nations.

The stars on our flag, recording the number of the States united, have already been more than doubled; and I hopefully look forward to the day when the constellation shall become a galaxy covering the stripes, which record the original number of our political family, and shall shed over the nations of the earth the light of regeneration to mankind. It has sometimes been said to be our manifest destiny that we should possess the whole of this continent. Whether it shall ever all be part of the United States is doubtful, and may never be desirable; but that in some form or other, it should come under the protectorate or control of the United states, is a result which seems to me, in the remote future, certain. It waits as the consequence upon intellectual vigor, upon physical energy, upon the capacity to govern, and can only be defeated by a suicidal madness, of which it does not belong to the occasion to treat.

I would not be understood to advocate what is called filibustering. Our country has never obtained territory except fairly, honorably and peaceably. We have conquered territory, but have asserted not titled as the right of conquest, returning to Mexico all except the part she agreed to sell and for which we paid a liberal price. England having filibustered around the world, has reproached us for aggrandizement, and we point to history and invite a comparison. There is no stain upon our escutcheon, no smoke upon our garments, and thus may they remain pure forever! The acquisitions of which I spoke, the protectorate which was contemplated, were such as the necessities of the future should demand, and the good of others as much as our own require, and this step by step, faster or slower, will I believe, finally embrace the continent of America and its adjacent islands.

I am not among those who desire to incorporate into our Union, countries densely populated with a different race. Deserts, 'tis the province of our people to subdue. A mere handful of inhabitants, such as existed in Louisiana, are soon enveloped in the tide of immigration; of this character of acquisition I have no fear; but the mingling of races is a different thing. I have looked with interest and pleasure upon the crosses of your cattle and horses, and saw in it the evidence of improvement. Let your Messengers, your Morgans, your Drews, and your Eastons be mingled with each other and with new importations so with your Durhams, Devons, Ayershires and your Jerseys. The limit to these experiments will be where experience shows deterioration. There is one cross which it is to be hoped you will avoid: 'tis that which your Puritan fathers would not adopt or even entertain. They kept pure the Caucasian blood which flowed in their veins, and therein is the cause of your present high civilization, your progress, your dignity and your strength. We are one, let us remain unmixed. In our neighbors of Southern and Central America we have a sufficient warning; and may it never be our ill-fortune to learn by experience the lessons taught by their example.

* * *

John B. Gordon (1832–1904), "An Address Delivered Before the Thalian & Phi Delta Societies of Oglethorpe University," June 18, 1860.[26]

During the Civil War, Gordon, a Georgia lawyer, would become a general in Lee's army. During Reconstruction, he led the Ku Klux Klan in Georgia.[27] Here he begins with seventeen paragraphs in flowery language vaguely comparing the U.S. government and Constitution to those of other countries, notably ancient Greece, France, and Great Britain. He sees the United States as superior. Then, in the paragraphs included here, he argues for "constitutional liberty," by which he means the rights of slaveowners to enter any territory with their slaves and be protected by the federal government, regardless of the wishes of the citizens or legislators of the territory. He then suggests "dismemberment of this Union" if the Republicans win. Like most other proslavery Southerners soon to become Confederates, he foresees and advocates taking land to the south, all the way to Panama. And he argues "negro slavery . . . is morally, socially, and politically *right.*"

But time fails me to speak further, of those peculiarities, which make us the happiest, the freest and most prosperous people on the face of the globe; and are strongly indicative of our future. Of the perfect equality, upon which all new acquisitions of territory are admitted—thus preventing that jealous discontent which was so formidable an enemy, to the prosperity of Greece and Rome—or of Religious Liberty, the child which was born among us, and is the guardian angel of civil liberty. But, notwithstanding these facts, there is but one policy, which we can pursue, that will guarantee our continuance, as a free and united people. It is this—a strict and unwavering fidelity to the provisions of our Magna Charta.

Does it conflict with our prejudices or personal preferences? These must all be sacrificed. Equal burthens from and equal protection to each and every member of this Confederacy, is a position from which no emergency whatever should drive us. Can you love, can you venerate that Government for the support of which you pay your money and your blood, and yet from which you cannot receive, for your person and property, protection from any and all enemies on the common domain? You, Southerner, embark with your property, on the high seas, and as you read the statute book of your country and wrap yourself in the Stars and Stripes, you glory in this shield which shall ward off the shaft of foreign or domestic foe; but do you seek a home on the territory of the country—on the wide and fertile prairie of the Great Northwest—on soil purchased by the common treasure and common blood—regulated by the laws of the common government, And over which waves the common flag? Be not deceived! You go without recognition, without protection; you are there "a heathen man, and a stranger"—your rights disregarded, your property a prey to the spoiler, and your complaints the derision of those who wantonly despoil you.

But, we are told that this idea of protection leads to dis-union. Far from it. It is the only position which can save the Union—the only one, surely, which can make the Union worth the saving. A sacrifice of principles may destroy us—a strict adherence to it, never. A people who, for principle's sake, fought, in infancy and weakness, seven years, and who, in maintaining their principles of equality, have, in little more than three quarters of a century, arrived at a position which England, with her boasted constitution, has been unable to reach in seventeen hundred years, has, in my humble judgment, the guarantee of Heaven that in defence of those principles she shall never lose supremacy. Let us still hope and pray for the continuance of constitutional liberty among us. Let us hope that when the present political troubles shall end, the decision of the American people will be for the maintenance of those principles of equality which alone can perpetuate the Union of these States. But if our hopes are to be blasted—if, when these political batteries shall be silenced, and the smoke is lifted from the field, the sad truth will be realized, that the conflict has resulted in the elevation to power of that horde who cry out against our rights and peculiar institutions, "crucify them! crucify them!" then let there be no hesitation on the part of the Southern people as to a dismemberment of this Union, rather than the more dreaded alternative of submission to fanatical dictation and Abolition rule. Let us not fear the consequences. The spirit of RESISTANCE is the spirit of LIBERTY; and He who holds in His own hands the destinies of nations, and is the Friend and Protector of constitutional liberty everywhere, is also the Friend and Protector of the institutions of the South: for, to-day, African slavery is the Mightiest Engine in the universe for the civilization, elevation and refinement of mankind—the surest guarantee of the continuance of liberty among ourselves. Then let us do our duty, protect our liberties, and leave the consequences with God, who alone can control them. Do this, and we shall secure to OURSELVES, at least, the principles of our great constitution, and the blessings consequent on the maintenance of these principles. Do this, and the day is not far distant when the Southern Flag shall be omnipotent from the Gulf of Panama to the coast of Delaware; when Cuba shall be ours; when the western breeze shall kiss our flag, as it floats in triumph from the gilded turrets of Mexico's capital; when the well clad, well fed, Southern, Christian slave shall nightly beat his Tambourine and Banjo, amid the orange-bowered groves of Central America; and when a pro-slavery Legislature shall meet in council in the Halls of Montezumas. And our foreign population, too, shall be encouraged by a successful resistance, on our part, to the aggressions of these Northern tyrants. The brave and generous "Sons of Erin," in whose veins mingles the blood of Curran and of Phillips, of O'Connell and the lamented Emmett, shall return to the house of their childhood, with the lessons we have taught them; and, pointing to us, as a people too chivalrous to submit to oppression, shall encourage their countrymen to free themselves of those burdens which eloquently tell of England's *gratitude (?)* to Ireland. And borne by wind and steam, on sea and railroad, and trembling along our telegraphic wires, shall come to those who have found homes among us, the glad tidings, from their kindred in every land under the heavens, that the influence of the Southern Confederacy is working the emancipation of the world.

Young Gentlemen of the Phi Delta Society: Allow me now to return to you my grateful acknowledgements for this invitation to address you, and to assure you of my sincere appreciation of the honor it confers. Permit me, in conclusion, to suggest to you, and to all the young gentlemen whom I have the honor to address, that when you have left these pleasant scenes and associations, to take your positions politically among your fellow men, you make it your first great duty to thoroughly understand the position of our constitution. Be ready to render to every section of the Union its rights, under that instrument. Ask no more for the South—submit to nothing less. And so far from admitting that negro slavery is an evil and an institution of tyranny, take the position, everywhere, that it is morally, socially, and politically *right*—and that it is, in truth, the hand-maid of civil liberty. Let these ideas become, as they will, universal among the Southern people and the powers of the world cannot remove from its firm basis, or prevent the progress of this Heaven-blessed institution. Who shall be able to check it? Can you change the laws of Nature, or annul the decrees of Jehovah? How high must you build a barrier to check the beautiful Oconee in its onward course to the seas? You must build it as high as its source—as high as the snow flake that melts on the mountain side, or the pearly dew-drop that trembles on the mountain's brow; so, to check the progress of this institution, you must erect your barrier as high as Heaven itself; for it has its origin in the edict of the King of Kings and Lord of Lords.

CHAPTER 2

SECESSION (1859–1861)

As the 1850s wore on, Southern politicians made ever more extreme demands on behalf of slavery. In 1820–21, Congress had passed the Missouri Compromise, which admitted Missouri as a slave state but otherwise forbade slavery north of the latitude of Missouri's border with Arkansas. Almost every Southerner in Congress had voted yes. In 1854, the Kansas-Nebraska Act allowed slavery north of Arkansas, indeed, north of Missouri, so long as the citizens in a territory wanted it. Southern politicians cheered. By 1860–61, any compromise on guaranteeing slavery's expansion into the territories had become untenable to most politicians in the Deep South. Slaves made up an investment greater than the total investment in all manufacturing companies and railroads in the United States. With such an immense interest to protect, proslavery extremists favored disunion, even if it meant war. According to Jefferson Davis, on the eve of the Civil War the South produced almost three-fourths of all U.S. exports.[1] Southern cotton provided the raw material for the largest single industry in Great Britain, perhaps ensuring a loyal ally. For these and other reasons, including the South's military tradition, many Southern leaders thought secession would not lead to war and the South would triumph if it did.

The South Carolina legislature issued a call on December 22, 1859, included here, for a Southern Convention to consider secession. Then the Democratic Party tore itself in two over the issue of slavery in the territories; we include its majority and minority platform planks. But it took the November election to build sufficient secession sentiment in other states. After Lincoln won, clerics and other ideological leaders rushed to justify such a move; we include Benjamin Palmer's "Thanksgiving Sermon" as an example.

In 1850, the Nashville Convention had disappointed South Carolina's secessionists, who failed to win Southwide support for secession. This time, they acted on their own, believing that other slave states, at least in the Deep South, would follow suit. One after another, South Carolina, Mississippi, Florida,

Alabama, Georgia, Louisiana, Texas, Virginia, Arkansas, Tennessee, and North Carolina left the United States.[2] As they left, all but the last provided statements telling why, which we include in the order in which they seceded. We also include the remarks of two ambassadors sent by early-seceding states to persuade others to join them. South Carolina's "Declaration of the Immediate Causes Which Induce and Justify the Secession of South Carolina from the Federal Union" is the most important of all these pieces. It came first and influenced the content and even the language of several other declarations. Slavery provides the common thread among these items, tied to concern over the election of a president with stated opposition to slavery.

The South was not just seceding over slavery, but also white supremacy, in which most whites, North and South, sincerely believed. Many white Southerners had come to see the 4,000,000 African Americans in their midst as a menace, were slavery ever to end. Several items in this chapter—"The Address of the People of South Carolina . . . To the People of the Slaveholding States," Henry Benning's address to Virginia, and the secession documents of Georgia and Texas—predict calamity, even race war, if slavery is not protected. This facet of Confederate ideology helps explain why white Southerners—even many who owned no slaves and had no prospects of owning any—mobilized so swiftly and effectively to protect their key institution. As John Marshall, a leading Texas secessionist, put it, "It is essential to the honor and safety of every poor white man to keep the negro in his present state of subordination and discipline."[3]

* * *

South Carolina General Assembly, "Resolutions for a Southern Convention," December 22, 1859.[4]

John Brown's raiders at Harpers Ferry, October 16–18, 1859, were quickly subdued. Nevertheless, they further polarized Southern opinion against the North, especially after Brown's eloquent words at trial prompted some Northerners to mourn his execution. In late 1859, citing "assaults upon the institution of slavery," Governor William Gist called for South Carolina to act. Its legislature responded with these four resolutions, bringing that state to the edge of secession and inviting other states to join. South Carolina acted before Republicans had even nominated Lincoln and before Democrats had split.

Whereas, The State of South Carolina, by her ordinance of A.D. 1852, affirmed her right to secede from the confederacy whenever the occasion should arise justifying her in her own judgment in taking that step, and in the resolutions adopted by her Convention declared that she forbore the immediate exercise of that right from considerations of expediency only; and,

Whereas, More than seven years have elapsed since that Convention adjourned, and in the intervening time the assaults upon the institution of slavery and upon the rights and equality of the Southern States have unceasingly continued with increasing violence and in new and more alarming forms; be it therefore

1. *Resolved unanimously*, That the State of South Carolina, still deferring to her Southern sisters, nevertheless respectfully announces to them that it is the deliberate judgment of this General Assembly that the slave-holding States should immediately meet together to concert measures for united action.

2. *Resolved unanimously*, That the foregoing preamble and resolutions be communicated by the Governor to all the slave-holding States, with the earnest request of this State that they will appoint deputies and adopt such measures as in their judgment will promote the said meeting.

3. *Resolved unanimously,* That a special Commissioner be appointed by his Excellency the Governor to communicate the foregoing preamble and resolutions to the State of Virginia, and to express to the authorities of that State the cordial sympathy of the people of South Carolina with the people of Virginia, and their earnest desire to unite with them in measures of common defence.

4. *Resolved unanimously,* That the State of South Carolina owes it to her own citizens to protect them and their property from every enemy, and that, for the purpose of military preparations for any emergency, the sum of one hundred thousand dollars ($100,000) be appropriated for military contingencies.

* * *

JEFFERSON DAVIS,
CONGRESSIONAL RESOLUTIONS ON
"RELATIONS OF STATES," U.S. SENATE,
MARCH 1, 1860.[5]

Pushing ever further toward a guarantee of slavery in all lands controlled by the federal government, Senator Davis submitted these resolutions seeking the Senate's approval. All seven treat slavery, four explicitly. The Buchanan administration supported Davis, the Senate approved all seven, and they became the blueprint for the majority platform at the 1860 Democratic convention. However, the resolutions placed Northern Democrats like Stephen A. Douglas in a very difficult position, since Resolution 5 requires Congress to guarantee slavery in a territory regardless of the wishes of its inhabitants. The stage was set for a rupture of the Democratic Party.

1. *Resolved*, That, in the adoption of the Federal Constitution, the States adopting the same acted severally as free and independent sovereignties, delegating a portion of their powers to be exercised by the Federal Government for the increased security of each against dangers, *domestic* as well as foreign; and that any intermeddling by any one or more States, or by a combination of their citizens, with the domestic institutions of the others, on any pretext whatever, political, moral, or religious, with a view to their disturbance or subversion, is in violation of the Constitution, insulating to the States so interfered with, endangers their domestic peace and tranquility—objects for which the Constitution was formed—and, by necessary consequence, tends to weaken and destroy the Union itself.

2. *Resolved*, That negro slavery, as it exists in fifteen States of this Union, composes an important portion of their domestic institutions, inherited from their ancestors, and existing at the adoption of the Constitution, by which it is recognized as constituting an important element in the apportionment of powers among the States; and that no change of opinion or feeling on the part of the non-slaveholding States of the Union in relation to this institution can justify

them or their citizens in open or covert attacks thereon, with a view to its over-throw; and that all such attacks are in manifest violation of the mutual and solemn pledge to protect and defend each other, given by the States, respectively, on entering into the constitutional compact which formed the Union, and are a manifest breach of faith and violation of the most solemn obligations.

3. *Resolved,* That the Union of these States rests on the equality of rights and privileges among its members, and that it is especially the duty of the Senate, which represents the States in their sovereign capacity, to resist all attempts to discriminate either in relation to persons or property in the Territories, which are the common possessions of the United States, so as to give advantages to the citizens of one State which are not equally assured to those of every other State.

4. *Resolved,* That neither Congress nor a Territorial Legislature, whether by direct legislation or legislation of an indirect and unfriendly character, possesses power to annul or impair the constitutional right of any citizen of the United States to take his slave property into the common Territories, and there hold and enjoy the same while the territorial condition remains.

5. *Resolved,* That if experience should at any time prove that the judiciary and executive authority do not possess the means to insure adequate protection to constitutional rights in a Territory, and if the territorial government shall fail or refuse to provide the necessary remedies for that purpose it will be the duty of Congress to supply such deficiency.

6. *Resolved,* That the inhabitants of a Territory of the United States, when they rightfully form a constitution to be admitted as a State into the Union, may then, for the first time, like the people of a State, when forming a new constitution, decide for themselves whether slavery as a domestic institution shall be maintained or prohibited within their jurisdiction; and they shall be received into the Union with or without slavery, as their constitution may prescribe at the time of their admission.

7. *Resolved,* That the provision of the Constitution for the rendition of fugitives from service or labor, "without the adoption of which the Union could not have been formed," and that the laws of 1793 and 1850, which were enacted to secure its execution, and the main features of which, being similar, bear the impress of nearly seventy years of sanction by the highest judicial authority, should be honestly and faithfully observed and maintained by all who enjoy the benefits of our compact of Union; and that all acts of individuals or of State Legislatures to defeat the purpose or nullify the requirements of that provision, and the laws made in pursuance of it, are hostile in character, subversive of the Constitution, and revolutionary in their effect.

* * *

OFFICIAL PROCEEDINGS OF THE DEMOCRATIC CONVENTION, APRIL 28–MAY 1, 1860.[6]

In 1860, meeting in Charleston, South Carolina, the Democratic Party split over the issue of slavery in the territories, presaging the breakup of the United States. Southerners controlled the Committee on Resolutions. Its majority report advocates acquiring Cuba and denounces Northern states' half-hearted attempts to enforce the Fugitive Slave Law. It takes an extreme proslavery position on the territory question, requiring the government to use "all its departments"—presumably including the military—to protect the right of owners to bring in slaves (although the resolutions avoid the "s-word"), regardless of whatever laws the territorial legislature or Congress might pass. As historian Harry Jaffa put it, writing for the conservative think tank The Claremont Institute, this was "a demand for an unprecedented extension of *federal* power."[7] It does concede that a territory might, at the point of becoming a state, choose to become a free state.[8] According to historians Eric Foner and Olivia Mahoney, few Southern extremists thought Democrats would adopt this platform; on the contrary, "many hoped the demand would split both the party and the country and produce an independent Southern Confederacy."[9]

The main minority report proposes to "abide by the decision of the Supreme Court" regarding slavery in the territories. That court in *Dred Scott* had held that Congress had no right to interfere with slavery in the territories; the federal government must indeed "protect" it. Either report makes the United States a proslavery nation except in those states that have rejected slavery within their borders. However, Northern Democrats, led by Stephen A. Douglas, claimed that *Dred Scott* left room for local control: if a territorial government did not actively support slavery by passing the laws needed to hold people in bondage, then slavery would be hard to sustain. In fact, *Dred Scott* suggests that the Supreme Court under Chief Justice Roger Taney would have required federal protection for slave property.[10] By 1860, however, the "correct" proslavery position had shifted. Now Southern leaders insisted that the party stand for a federal guarantee for slavery in every territory and would not wait for a Supreme Court decision on the matter. When the convention adopted the minority report, Southern delegations walked out.

Ellipses replace discussions that have nothing to do with Confederate matters.

Evening Session, April 28, 1860.

The Convention re-assembled at four o'clock P. M., and was called to order by the President.

Mr. AVERY, of North Carolina on behalf of the Committee on Resolutions, ... [introduced the majority report]

Resolved, That the platform adopted by the Democratic party at Cincinnati be affirmed, with the following explanatory resolutions.

1. That the government of a Territory organized by an act of Congress, is provisional and temporary; and, during its existence, all citizens of the United States have an equal right to settle with their property in the Territory without their rights, either of person or property, being destroyed or impaired by Congressional or Territorial legislation.

2. That it is the duty of the Federal Government, in all its departments, to protect, when necessary, the rights of persons and property in the Territories, and wherever else its constitutional authority extends.

3. That when the settlers in a Territory having an adequate population form a State Constitution, the right of sovereignty commences, and, being consummated by admission into the Union, they stand on an equal footing with the people of other States; and the State thus organized ought to be admitted into the Federal Union, whether its Constitution prohibits or recognizes the institution of slavery.

4. That the Democratic party are in favor of the acquisition of the Island of Cuba, on such terms as shall be honorable to ourselves and just to Spain, at the earliest practicable moment.

5. That the enactments of State Legislatures to defeat the faithful execution of the Fugitive Slave Law, are hostile in character, subversive of the Constitution, and revolutionary in their effect.

6. That the Democracy of the United States recognize it as the imperative duty of this Government to protect the naturalized citizen in all his rights, whether at home or in foreign lands, to the same extent as its native-born citizens.

Whereas, one of the greatest necessities of the age, in a political, commercial, postal and military point of view, is a speedy communication between the Atlantic and Pacific coasts; therefore, be it

Resolved, That the Democratic party do hereby pledge themselves to use every means in their power to secure the passage of some bill, to the extent of the constitutional authority of Congress, for the construction of a Pacific Railroad, from the Mississippi River to the Pacific Ocean, at the earliest practicable moment....

Mr. SAMUELS, of Iowa, submitted a report from a minority of the Committee, which he offered as a substitute for, and an amendment to, the majority report made by Mr. Avery.

Its primary point of difference with the majority report was the following:

2. Inasmuch as difference of opinion exists in the Democratic party as to the nature and extent of the powers of a Territorial Legislature, and as to the powers and duties of Congress, under the Constitution of the United States, over the institution of slavery within the Territories,

Resolved, That the Democratic party will abide by the decision of the Supreme Court of the United States upon these questions of Constitutional law.

Mr. BUTLER, of Massachusetts, then submitted a report from a minority of the Committee, which he offered as a substitute for both of the reports already submitted.

Butler's minority report contained no resolution about slavery in the territories, nothing about getting Cuba, and nothing about a transcontinental railroad. After some debate, the convention adopted the minority resolutions introduced by Samuels. Then they decided to vote on each resolution individually and rejected the second, adopting the rest. This prompted the delegations of at least seven slave states to walk out after telling the convention their reasons. Mr. Walker of Alabama presented a written communication to the Convention that referred to twelve resolutions his state party had passed the previous January. Like the Alabama Resolutions of 1848 (pages 36–39), they all concerned slavery, including these points:

1. *Resolved by the Democracy of the State of Alabama, in Convention assembled,* That holding all issues and principles upon which they have heretofore affiliated and acted with the National Democratic party to be inferior in dignity and importance to the great question of slavery, they content themselves with a general re-affirmance of the Cincinnati Platform as to such issues, and also indorse said Platform as to slavery, together with the following resolutions:

2. *Resolved further,* ... The unqualified right of the people of the slaveholding States to the protection of their property in the States, in the

Territories, and in the wilderness, in which Territorial Governments are as yet unorganized.

6. *Resolved further*, That the Congress of the United States has no power to abolish slavery in the Territories, or to prohibit its introduction into any of them.

7. *Resolved further*, That the Territorial Legislatures, created by the legislation of Congress, have no power to abolish slavery, or to prohibit the introduction of the same, or to impair by unfriendly legislation, the security and full enjoyment of the same within the Territories....

Walker's report continued:

But it has been the pleasure of this Convention, by an almost exclusive sectional vote, not representing a majority of the States, nor a majority of the Democratic electoral votes, to adopt a Platform which does not, in our opinion, nor in the opinion of those who urge it, embody in substance the principles of the Alabama resolutions.

[Therefore,] it becomes our duty to withdraw from this Convention.

Mr. BARRY, of Mississippi, rose and stated that they would retire from the Convention with the delegation from Alabama, and would have no further connection with the Convention....

Mr. MOUTON, of Louisiana, rose in behalf of the delegation from that State, and stated that the majority of the delegation would no longer take a part in the proceedings of the Convention. That two delegates still determined to remain in the Convention....

Mr. SIMMONS, of South Carolina, presented to the Convention a statement in writing, as follows:

We, the undersigned, delegates appointed by the Democratic State Convention of South Carolina, beg leave respectfully to state, that according to the principles enunciated in their platform at Columbia, the power, either of the Federal Government, or of its agent, the Territorial Government, to abolish or legislate against property in slaves, by either direct or indirect legislation, is explicitly denied; and as the platform adopted by this Convention palpably and intentionally pretermits any expression affirming the incapacity of the Territorial Government so to legislate, they do not believe they would be acting in good faith to their principles, or in accordance with the wishes of their constituents, longer to remain in this Convention; and they hereby therefrom respectfully announce their withdrawal.

A Mississippi delegate then read a statement explaining his delegation's withdrawal.

Mr. Milton of Florida, addressed the Convention, and presented a communication, as follows:

The undersigned, Democratic Delegates from the State of Florida, enter this, their solemn protest, against the action of the Convention in voting down the platform of the majority.

Florida, with her Southern sisters, is entitled to a clear and unambiguous recognition of her rights in the Territories.

Mr. BRYAN, of Texas, addressed the Convention, and presented a protest, in writing, as follows:

The undersigned, Delegates from the State of Texas, would respectfully protest against the late action of this Convention, in refusing to adopt the report of the majority of the Committee on Resolutions, which operates as the virtual adoption of principles affirming doctrines in opposition to the decision of the Supreme Court in the Dred Scott case, and in conflict with the Federal Constitution, and especially opposed to the Platform of the Democratic party of Texas, which declares:

... That it is the right of every citizen to take his property of any kind, including slaves, into the common territory belonging equally to all the States of the Confederacy, and to have it protected there under the Federal Constitution. Neither Congress nor a Territorial Legislature, nor any human power, has any authority, either directly or indirectly, to impair these sacred rights; and they, having been affirmed by the Supreme Court in the decision of the Dred Scott case, we declare that it is the duty of the Federal Government, the common agent of all the States, to establish such government and enact such laws for the Territories, and so change the same from time to time as may be necessary to insure protection and preservation of these rights, and prevent every infringement of the same....

Mr. BURROWS, of Arkansas, rose and addressed the Convention, and presented a communication, as follows:

... We re-affirm ... that neither Congress nor a Territorial Legislature, whether by direct legislation or by legislation of an indirect and unfriendly character, possesses the power to annul or impair the Constitutional rights of any citizen of the United States to take his slave property into the common Territories, and there hold and enjoy the same, and that if experience should at any time prove that the judiciary and executive power do not possess the means to insure protection to Constitutional rights in a Territory, and if the Territorial Government should fail or refuse to provide the necessary remedies for that purpose, it will be the duty of Congress to supply the deficiency....

The next day Louisiana's last two delegates similarly withdrew, leaving a written explanation:

SIR: The undersigned, delegates from the State of Louisiana, in withdrawing from the Convention, beg leave to make the following statement of facts:

On the 5th day of March, 1860, the Democracy of Louisiana assembled in State Convention at Baton Rouge, and unanimously adopted the following declaration of their principles:

Resolved, That the Territories of the United States belong to the several States as their common property, and not to individual citizens thereof; that the Federal Constitution recognizes property in slaves; and as such, the owner thereof is entitled to carry his slaves into any Territory in the United States; to hold them there as property; and in case the people of the Territories, by inaction, unfriendly legislation or otherwise, should endanger the tenure of such property, or discriminate against it by withholding that protection given to other species of property in the Territories, it is the duty of the General Government to interpose, by the active exertion of its constitutional power, to secure the rights of the slaveholder.

The principles enunciated in the foregoing resolution are guaranteed to us by the Constitution of the United States, and their unequivocal recognition by the Democracy of the Union we regard as essential, not only to the integrity of the party, but to the safety of the States whose interests are directly involved. They have been embodied in both of the series of resolutions presented to the Convention by a majority of the States of the Union, and have been rejected by a numerical vote of the delegates.

The Convention has, by this vote, refused to recognize the fundamental principles of the Democracy of the State we have the honor to represent, and we feel constrained, in obedience to a high sense of duty, to withdraw from its deliberations, and unanimously to enter our solemn protest against its action....

* * *

Benjamin Palmer (1818–1902),
"Thanksgiving Sermon," November 29, 1860.[11]

Partly because the Democrats split and ran two candidates, Abraham Lincoln won the presidency in November 1860. Benjamin Palmer, minister of the First Presbyterian Church of New Orleans and first head of the Presbyterian Church of the Confederacy, hailed from South Carolina. In 1869, he became the first president of the Southern Historical Society, formed to collect Confederate records and perpetuate pro-Confederate interpretations of the Civil War. Palmer is a hero to the modern Confederate Christian movement.[12] In this sermon, delivered shortly after Lincoln's victory, Palmer endorses secession on behalf of slavery. He sees defending slavery as the South's religious duty and identifies antislavery as the side of radicalism and godlessness. The extract we include is also paternalist, averring that slaveowners are guardians of their chattel while abolitionists are "the worst foes of the black race." We omit several opening paragraphs about why he doesn't normally comment on public affairs but feels compelled to do so.[13]

In determining our duty in this emergency it is necessary that we should first ascertain the nature of the trust providentially committed to us. A nation often has a character as well defined and intense as that of an individual. This depends, of course upon a variety of causes operating through a long period of time. It is due largely to the original traits which distinguish the stock from which it springs, and to the providential training which has formed its education. But, however derived, this individuality of character alone makes any people truly historic, competent to work out its specific mission, and to become a factor in the world's progress. The particular trust assigned to such a people becomes the pledge of the divine protection; and their fidelity to it determines the fate by which it is finally overtaken. What that trust is must be ascertained from the necessities of their position, the institutions which are the outgrowth of their principles and the conflicts through which they preserve their identity and independence. If then the South is such a people, what, at this juncture, is their providential trust? I answer, that it is to conserve and to perpetuate the institution of domestic slavery as now existing. . . . With this institution assigned to our keeping, what reply shall we make to those who say that its days are numbered? My own conviction is, that we should at once lift ourselves, intelligently, to the highest moral ground and proclaim to all the world that we hold this trust from God, and in its occupancy we are prepared to stand or fall as God may appoint. If the critical moment has arrived at which the great issue is joined, let us say that, in the sight of all perils, we will stand by our trust; and God be with the right!

The argument which enforces the solemnity of this providential trust is simple and condensed. It is bound upon us, then, by the principle of self-preservation, that "first law" which is continually asserting its supremacy over all others. Need I pause to show how this system of servitude underlies and supports our material interests; that our wealth consists in our lands and in the serfs who till them; that from the nature of our products they can only be cultivated by labor which must be controlled in order to be certain; that any other than a tropical race must faint and wither beneath a tropical sun? Need I pause to show how this system is interwoven with our entire social fabric; that these slaves form parts of our households, even as our children; and that, too, through a relationship recognized and sanctioned in the Scriptures of God even as the other? Must I pause to show how it has fashioned our modes of life, and determined all our habits of thought and feeling, and moulded the very type of our civilization? How then can the hand of violence be laid upon it without involving our existence? The so-called free States of this country are working out the social problem under conditions peculiar to themselves. These conditions are sufficiently hard, and their success is too uncertain to excite in us the least jealousy of their lot. With a teeming population, which the soil cannot support; with their wealth depending upon arts, created by artificial wants; with an external friction between the grades of their society; with their labor and their capital grinding against each other like the upper and nether millstones; with labor cheapened and displaced by new mechanical inventions, bursting more asunder the bonds of brotherhood—amid these intricate perils we have ever given them our sympathy and our prayers, and have never sought to weaken the foundations of their social order. God grant them complete success in the solution of all their perplexities! We, too, have our responsibilities and trials; but they are all bound up in this one institution, which has been the object of such unrighteous assault through five and twenty years. If we are true to ourselves we shall, at this critical juncture, stand by it and work out our destiny.

This duty is bound upon us again as the constituted guardians of the slaves themselves. Our lot is not more implicated in theirs, than their lot in ours; in our mutual relations we survive or perish together. The worst foes of the black race are those who have intermeddled on their behalf. We know better than others that every attribute of their character fits them for dependence and servitude. By nature the most affectionate and loyal of all races beneath the sun, they are also the most helpless; and no calamity can befall them greater than the loss of that protection they enjoy under this patriarchal system. Indeed, the experiment has been grandly tried of precipitating them upon freedom which they know not how to enjoy; and the dismal results are before us in statistics that astonish the world. With the fairest portions of the earth in their possession and with the advantage of a long discipline as cultivators of the soil, their constitutional indolence has converted the most beautiful islands of the sea into a howling waste. It is not too much to say that if the South should, at this moment, surrender every slave, the wisdom of the entire world, united in solemn council, could not solve the question of their disposal. Their transportation to Africa, even if it were feasible, would be but the most refined cruelty; they must perish with starvation before they could have time to relapse into their primitive barbarism. Their residence here, in the presence of the vigorous Saxon race, would be but the signal for their rapid extermination before they had time to waste away through listlessness, filth and vice. Freedom would be their doom; and equally from both they call upon us, their providential guardians, to be protected. I know this argument will be scoffed abroad as the hypocritical cover thrown over our own cupidity and selfishness; but every Southern master knows its truth and feels its power. My servant, whether born in my house or bought with my money, stands to me in the relation of a child. Though providentially owing me service, which, providentially, I am bound to exact, he is, nevertheless, my brother and my friend, and I am to him a guardian and a father. He leans upon me for protection, for counsel, and for blessing; and so long as the relation continues, no power but the power of Almighty God shall come between him and me. Were there no argument but this, it binds upon us the providential duty of preserving the relation that we may save him from a doom worse than death.

It is a duty which we owe, further, to the civilized world. It is a remarkable fact that during these thirty years of unceasing warfare against slavery, and while a lying spirit has inflamed the world against us, that world has grown more and more dependent upon it for sustenance and wealth. Every tyro knows that all branches of industry fall back upon the soil. We must come, every one of us, to the bosom of this great mother for nourishment. In the happy partnership which has grown up in providence between the tribes of this confederacy, our industry has been concentrated upon agriculture. To the North we have cheerfully resigned all the profits arising from manufacture and commerce. Those profits they have, for the most part, fairly earned, and we have never begrudged them. We have sent them our sugar and bought it back when refined; we have sent them our cotton and bought it back when spun into thread or woven into cloth. Almost every article we use, from the shoe lachet to the most elaborate and costly article of luxury, they have made and we have bought; and both sections have thriven by the partnership, as no people ever thrive before since the first shining of the sun. So literally true are the words of the text, addressed by Obadiah to Edom, "All the men of our confederacy, the men that were at peace with us, have eaten our bread at the very time they have deceived and laid a wound under us." Even beyond this the enriching commerce which has built the splendid cities and marble palaces of England, as well as of America, has been largely established upon the products of our soil; and the bloom; upon Southern fields gathered by black hands have fed the spindle: and looms of Manchester and Birmingham not less than of Lawrence and Lowell. Strike now a blow at this system of labor and the world itself totters at the stroke. Shall we permit that blow to fall? Do we not owe it to civilized man to stand in the breach and stay the uplifted arm? If the blind Samson lays hold of the pillars which support the arch of the world's industry, how many more will be buried beneath its ruins than the lords of the Philistines? "Who knoweth whether we are not come to the kingdom for such a time as this."

Last of all, in this great struggle, we defend the cause of God and religion. The abolition spirit is undeniably atheistic....

Here Palmer spends half a page comparing abolitionists to the Jacobins who promoted the Reign of Terror during the French Revolution. Later this comparison became a favorite of neo-Confederate writers.

This spirit of atheism, which knows no God who tolerates evil, no Bible which sanctions law, and no conscience that can be bound by oaths and covenants, has selected us for its victims, and slavery for its issue. Its banner-cry rings out already upon the air—"liberty, equality, fraternity," which simply interpreted mean bondage, confiscation and massacre. With its tricolor waving in the breeze,—it waits to inaugurate its reign of terror. To the South the high position is assigned of defending, before all nations, the cause of all religion and of all truth. In this trust, we are resisting the power which wars against constitutions and laws and compacts, against Sabbaths and sanctuaries, against the family, the State, and the Church; which blasphemously invades the prerogatives of God, and rebukes the Most High for the errors of his administration; which, if it cannot snatch the reign of empire from his grasp, will lay the universe in ruins at his feet. Is it possible that we shall decline the onset?

This argument, then, which sweeps over the entire circle of our relations, touches the four cardinal points of duty to ourselves, to our slaves, to the world, and to Almighty God. It establishes the nature and solemnity of our present trust, to preserve and transmit our existing system of domestic servitude, with the right, unchallenged by man, to go and root itself wherever Providence and nature may carry it. This trust we will discharge in the face of the worst possible peril. Though war be the aggregation of all evils, yet should the madness of the hour appeal to the arbitration of the sword, we will not shrink even from the baptism of fire. If modern crusaders stand in serried ranks upon some plain of Esdraelon, there shall we be in defence of our trust. Not till the last man has fallen behind the last rampart, shall it drop from our hands; and then only in surrender to the God who gave it.

Palmer closes with several paragraphs arguing for secession, even though, he admits, Lincoln was elected fairly and promises not to disturb slavery in the South. Why? Without a doubt, he notes accurately, the new president is "against the extension of slavery into the new territories of the Union, and the re-opening of the African slave trade." Ultimately, Lincoln seeks to end slavery everywhere. Palmer asks his audience, "What say you to this, to whom this great providential trust of conserving slavery is assigned?" The South must secede to maintain slavery, else "within five and twenty years the history of St. Domingo will be the record of Louisiana."[14]

* * *

CHRISTIANA BANNER, 1994 (1911, 1851).

Figure 4: As its banners make clear, Christiana still takes pride in this incident. The image shows a U.S. flag from 1851 with an obelisk superimposed over it. Residents put up this obelisk in 1911, a surprising time for such a monument, in the midst of the Nadir of race relations. The quote on the banner is by Frederick Douglass.

This banner in Christiana, a small town in southern Pennsylvania, illustrates one of the reasons South Carolina (and other states) gave for seceding. In 1851, Edward Gorsuch, a Maryland slaveowner, heard that four people whom he formerly owned were living near Christiana. (Actually, one was already safe in Canada.) Gorsuch, his son, a cousin, and two neighbors obtained the services of a U.S. marshal in Philadelphia. At dawn on September 11, they approached a farmhouse near Christiana where they understood the fugitives were living and demanded them. In the words of the nearby Pennsylvania state historical marker, "Neighbors gathered, fighting ensued, and Gorsuch was killed." The visitors retreated, while Parker and the other fugitives escaped by train to Rochester, New York, and Canada.

The governor of Maryland demanded swift punishment for everyone involved. The United States indicted 36 blacks and 5 whites, not just for violating the new Fugitive Slave Law but, at the request of President Millard Fillmore, for treason. (The idea was, since the Fugitive Slave Law was an enabling act to carry out the fugitive slave clause of the Constitution, violators were somehow guilty of trying to overthrow the Constitution, hence the nation.) A miller, Castner Hanway, who lived nearby, had been the first white neighbor to arrive. The Southerners inferred, wrongly, that he must be the leader of the resistance. He was the first person tried, in Independence Hall; Thaddeus Stevens was one of his lawyers. The jury found him innocent; indeed, no one was ever convicted for the death of Edward Gorsuch. This outraged slaveowners.[15]

* * *

South Carolina Secession Convention, "Declaration of the Immediate Causes Which Induce and Justify the Secession of South Carolina from the Federal Union," December 24, 1860.[16]

Triggered by Lincoln's election, Deep South states held conventions that issued short ordinances stating they were seceding and longer statements telling why. The ordinances have little substance. We include the longer statements in the order in which the states seceded, South Carolina's first. Its "Declaration" served as a model for several other states as they left the Union. It begins by citing South Carolina's 1852 threat to secede, which gave as reasons "the frequent violations of the Constitution of the United States by the Federal Government, and its encroachments upon the reserved rights of the sovereign States of this Union, especially in relation to slavery." That sentence does refer to states' rights, but the Declaration then takes quite a different turn. First, it provides an eleven-paragraph history lesson emphasizing the independence of each state before and during the period when the United States operated under the Articles of Confederation. This lesson fails to note that South Carolina was one of the states that decried the looseness of this arrangement and called for a constitutional convention to set up a more powerful central government.

The last paragraph of this lesson provides an unusual view of "the law of compact," claiming that each party can decide on "his own judgment" whether the other has lived up to its terms; if not, then the individual (or state) can do as it wants. Such a holding at law would end commerce, marriage, indeed civil society. As historian William C. Davis notes, "There are very few ways to legally break a contract unilaterally," and none of them applied in 1860. At the time of secession, the federal government was not guilty of *any* noncompliance with the Constitution, even from an extreme proslavery viewpoint. Notwithstanding the weakness of this reasoning, however, many political leaders, including some Unionists, believed secession was legal. Others did not, including Robert E. Lee, who called it "nothing but revolution."[17]

The rest of the document declares the "immediate causes" that have led South Carolina to secede. Various states, listed by name, have interfered with federal efforts to enforce the fugitive slave clause of the Constitution. South Carolina is further upset with New York, because it no longer allows "the right of transit for a slave." In past years, some slaveowners had gone west via the Erie Canal and Great Lakes. Others had brought enslaved servants along when visiting New York City or Long Island. No longer, because New York's judges now decreed that since the state does not recognize slavery, these people can go free. As well, South Carolina takes offense because Northern states allow citizens to denounce "as sinful the institution of Slavery"; some even let African Americans be voting citizens.[18] However, until the Fifteenth Amendment, passed during Reconstruction after the Civil War, setting qualifications for voting was a state's right. In sum, every grievance that South Carolina lists refers to acts by states and individuals in the North. South Carolina has no quarrel with the federal government, controlled by proslavery Democrats in the Buchanan administration. After the first paragraph, South Carolina makes no claim on behalf of the right of any state to do anything that the federal government was forbidding, other than secession itself. On the contrary: South Carolina *opposes* states' rights when claimed by free states. It is also infuriated that Northern states "have united in the election of a man to the high office of President of the United States whose opinions and purposes are hostile to Slavery."

The people of the State of South Carolina in Convention assembled, on the 2d day of April, A.D. 1852, declared that the frequent violations of the Constitution of the United States by the Federal Government, and its encroachments upon the reserved rights of the States, fully justified this State in, their withdrawal from the Federal Union; but in deference to the opinions and wishes of the other Slaveholding States, she forbore at that time to exercise this right. Since that time these encroachments have continued to increase, and further forbearance ceases to be a virtue.

And now the State of South Carolina, having resumed her separate and equal place among nations, deems it due to herself, to the remaining United States of America, and to the nations of the world, that she should declare the immediate causes which have led to this act.

In the year 1765, that portion of the British Empire embracing Great Britain undertook to make laws for the Government of that portion composed of the thirteen American Colonies. A struggle for the right of self-government ensued, which resulted, on the 4th of July, 1776, in a Declaration, by the Colonies, "that they are, and of right ought to be, FREE AND INDEPENDENT STATES; and that, as free and independent States, they have full power to levy war, conclude peace, contract alliances, establish commerce, and to do all other acts and things which independent States may of right do."

They further solemnly declared that whenever any "form of government becomes destructive of the ends for which it was established, it is the right of the people to alter or abolish it, and to institute a new government." Deeming the Government of Great Britain to have become destructive of these ends, they declared that the Colonies "are absolved from all allegiance to the British Crown, and that all political connection between them and the State of Great Britain is, and ought to be, totally dissolved."

In pursuance of this Declaration of Independence, each of the thirteen States proceeded to exercise its separate sovereignty; adopted for itself a Constitution, and appointed officers for the administration of government in all its departments—Legislative, Executive and Judicial. For purposes of defence they united their arms and their counsels; and, in 1778, they entered into a League known as the Articles of Confederation, whereby they agreed to intrust the administration of their external relations to a common agent, known as the Congress of the United States, expressly declaring, in the first article, "that each State retains its sovereignty, freedom and independence, and every power, jurisdiction and right which is not, by this Confederation, expressly delegated to the United States in Congress assembled."

Under this Confederation the War of the Revolution was carried on; and on the 3d of September, 1783, the contest ended, and a definite Treaty was signed by Great Britain, in which she acknowledged the Independence of the Colonies in the following terms:

"ARTICLE 1. His Britannic Majesty acknowledges the said United States, viz.: New Hampshire; Massachusetts Bay, Rhode Island and Providence Plantations, Connecticut, New York, New Jersey, Pennsylvania, Delaware, Maryland, Virginia, North Carolina, South Carolina and Georgia, to be FREE, SOVEREIGN, AND INDEPENDENT STATES; that he treats with them as such; and, for himself, his heirs and successors, relinquishes all claims to the government, propriety, and territorial rights of the same and every part thereof."

Thus were established the two great principles asserted by the Colonies, namely, the right of a State to govern itself; and the right of a people to abolish a Government when it becomes destructive of the ends for which it was instituted. And concurrent with the establishment of these principles, was the fact that each Colony became and was recognized by the mother country as a FREE, SOVEREIGN, AND INDEPENDENT STATE.

In 1787, Deputies were appointed by the States to revise the articles of Confederation; and on 17th September, 1787, these Deputies recommended, for the adoption of the States, the Articles of Union, known as the Constitution of the United States.

The parties to whom this constitution was submitted were the several sovereign States; they were to agree or disagree, and when nine of them agreed, the compact was to take effect among those concurring; and the General Government, as the common agent, was then to be invested with their authority.

If only nine of the thirteen States had concurred, the other four would have remained as they then were—separate, sovereign States, independent of any of the provisions of the Constitution. In fact, two of the States did not accede to the Constitution until long after it had gone into operation among the other eleven; and during that interval, they each exercised the functions of an independent nation.

By this Constitution, certain duties were imposed upon the several States, and the exercise of certain of their powers was restrained, which necessarily impelled their continued existence as sovereign states. But, to remove all doubt, an amendment was added, which declared that the powers not delegated to the United States by the Constitution, nor prohibited by it to the States, are reserved to the States respectively, or to the people. On the 23d May, 1788, South Carolina, by a Convention of her people, passed an ordinance assenting to this Constitution, and afterwards altered her own Constitution to conform herself to the obligation she had undertaken.

Thus was established, by compact between the States, a Government with defined objects and powers, limited to the express words of the grant. This limitation left the whole remaining mass of power subject to the clause reserving it to the States or the people, and rendered unnecessary any specification of reserved rights. We hold that the Government thus established is subject to the two great principles asserted in the Declaration of independence; and we hold further that the mode of its formation subjects it to a third fundamental principle, namely, the law of compact. We maintain that in every compact between two or more parties, the obligation is mutual; that the failure of one of the contracting parties to perform a material part of the agreement, entirely releases the obligation of the other; and that where no arbiter is provided, each party is remitted to his own judgment to determine the fact of failure, with all its consequences.

In the present case, that fact is established with certainty. We assert that fourteen of the States have deliberately refused for years past to fulfill their constitutional obligations, and we refer to their own statutes for the proof.

The Constitution of the United States, in its fourth Article, provides as follows: "No person held to service or labor in one State under the laws thereof, escaping into another, shall, in consequence of any law or regulation therein, be discharged from such service or labor, but shall be delivered up, on claim of the party to whom such service or labor may be due."

This stipulation was so material to the compact that without it that compact would not have been made. The greater number of the contracting parties held slaves, and they had previously evinced their estimate of the value of such a stipulation by making it a condition in the Ordinance for the government of the territory ceded by Virginia, which now composes the states north of the Ohio river.

The general government, as the common agent, passed laws to carry into effect these stipulations of the states. For many years these laws were executed. But an increasing hostility on the part of the non-slaveholding states to the institution of slavery has led to a disregard of their obligations, and the laws of the General Government, have ceased to effect the objects of the Constitution. The States of Maine, New Hampshire, Vermont, Massachusetts, Connecticut, Rhode Island, New York, Pennsylvania, Illinois, Indiana, Michigan, Wisconsin, and Iowa, have enacted laws which either nullify the acts of Congress, or render useless any attempt to execute them. In many of these States the fugitive is discharged from the service or labor claimed, and in none of them has the State Government complied with the stipulation made in the Constitution. The State of New Jersey, at an early day, passed a law in conformity with her constitutional obligation; but the current of Anti-Slavery feeling has led her more recently to enact laws which render inoperative the remedies provided by her own laws and by the laws of Congress. In the State of New York even the right of transit for a slave has been denied by her tribunals; and the States of Ohio and Iowa have refused to surrender to justice fugitives charged with murder, and with inciting servile insurrection in the State of Virginia. Thus the constitutional compact has been deliberately broken and disregarded by the non-slaveholding States; and the consequence follows that South Carolina is released from her obligation.

The ends for which this Constitution was framed are declared by itself to be "to form a more perfect union, to establish justice, insure domestic tranquillity, provide for the common defence, promote the general welfare, and secure the blessings of liberty to ourselves and our posterity."

These ends it endeavored to accomplish by a Federal Government, in which each State was recognized as an equal, and had separate control over its own institutions. The right of property in slaves was recognized by giving to free persons distinct political rights; by giving them the right to represent, and burdening them with direct taxes for, three-fifths of their slaves; by authorizing the importation of slaves for twenty years; and by stipulating for the rendition of fugitives from labor.

We affirm that these ends for which this Government was instituted have been defeated, and the Government itself has been destructive of them by the action of the non-slaveholding States. Those States have assumed the right of deciding upon the propriety of our domestic institutions; and have denied the rights of property established in fifteen of the States and recognized by the Constitution; they have denounced as sinful the institution of Slavery; they have permitted the open establishment among them of societies, whose avowed object is to disturb the peace of and eloign the property of the citizens of other States. They have encouraged and assisted thousands of our slaves to leave their homes; and those who remain, have been incited by emissaries, books, and pictures, to servile insurrection.

For twenty-five years this agitation has been steadily increasing, until it has now secured to its aid the power of the common Government. Observing the *forms* of the Constitution, a sectional party has found within that article establishing the Executive Department, the means of subverting the Constitution itself. A geographical line has been drawn across the Union, and all the States north of that line have united in the election of a man to the high office of President of the United States whose opinions and purposes are hostile to Slavery. He is to be intrusted with the administration of the common Government, because he has declared that "Government cannot endure permanently half slave, half free," and that the public mind must rest in the belief that Slavery is in the course of ultimate extinction.

This sectional combination for the subversion of the Constitution has been aided, in some of the States, by elevating to citizenship persons who, by the supreme law of the land, are incapable of becoming citizens; and their votes have been used to inaugurate a new policy, hostile to the South, and destructive of its peace and safety.

On the 4th of March next this party will take possession of the Government. It has announced that the South shall be excluded from the common territory, that the Judicial tribunal shall be made sectional, and that a war must be waged against Slavery until it shall cease throughout the United States.

The guarantees of the Constitution will then no longer exist; the equal rights of the States will be lost. The Slaveholding States will no longer have the power of self-government, or self-protection, and the Federal Government will have become their enemy.

Sectional interest and animosity will deepen the irritation; and all hope of remedy is rendered vain, by the fact that the public opinion at the North has invested a great political error with the sanctions of a more erroneous religious belief.

We, therefore, the people of South Carolina, by our Delegates in Convention assembled, appealing to the Supreme Judge of the world for the rectitude of our intentions, have solemnly declared that the Union heretofore existing between this State and the other States of North America is dissolved, and that the State of South Carolina has resumed her position among the nations of the world, as a separate and independent state, with full power to levy war, conclude peace, contract alliances, establish commerce, and to do all other acts and things which independent States may of right do.

* * *

South Carolina Secession Convention, "The Address of the People of South Carolina, Assembled in Convention, To the People of the Slaveholding States of the United States 1861," December 24, 1860.[19]

On the same day that it ratified the "Declaration of the Immediate Causes," the South Carolina convention produced this second document aimed at a narrower audience. Perhaps for this reason, it uses more flamboyant terms like "despotism," and it was written by the notorious fire eater Robert Barnwell Rhett. He begins by claiming that South Carolina is seceding for constitutional reasons, with no specificity as to what that means. Several paragraphs decry tyranny through taxation, by which is meant the tariff. This is remarkable, because South Carolina's representatives had unanimously supported the existing tariff in 1857.[20] Next, Rhett attacks the unequal spending of federal funds for general improvements, blaming Yankee favoritism for the backward conditions of Southern cities and ports. Then he moves to more defensible grounds. "The Union of the Constitution was a Union of slaveholding States," he claims, accurately. "If it is right to preclude or abolish slavery in a Territory, why should it be allowed to remain in the States?" The document then predicts that the North will run roughshod over the South, eventually emancipating its slaves, leading to ruin. Perhaps because it was more vague, rhetorical, and disputable, this "Address" never drew as much attention as the "Declaration of the Immediate Causes." Other states don't quote it, and emissaries from seceding states don't use its arguments when trying to persuade other slaveholding states to follow them.

It is seventy-three years since the Union between the United States was made by the Constitution of the United States. During this time, their advances in wealth, prosperity and power has been with scarcely a parallel in the history of the world. The great object of their Union was defence against external aggression; which object is now attained, from their mere progress in power. Thirty-one millions of people, with a commerce and navigation which explore every sea, and with agricultural productions which are necessary to every civilized people, command the friendship of the world. But unfortunately, our internal peace has not grown with our external prosperity. Discontent and contention have moved in the bosom of the Confederacy for the last thirty-five years. During this time, South Carolina has twice called her people together in solemn Convention, to take into consideration the aggressions and unconstitutional wrongs perpetrated by the people of the North on the people of the South. These wrongs were submitted to by the people of the South, under the hope and expectation that they would be final. But such hope and expectation have proved to be vain. Instead of producing forbearance, our acquiescence has only instigated to new forms of aggression and outrage; and South Carolina, having again assembled her people in Convention, has this day dissolved her connection with the States constituting the United States.

The one great evil, from which all other evils have flowed, is the overthrow of the Constitution of the United States. The government of the United States is no longer the Government of the Confederated Republics, but of a consolidated Democracy. It is no longer a free Government, but a despotism. It is, in fact, such a Government as Great Britain attempted to set over our fathers; and which was resisted and defeated by a seven years' struggle for independence.

The Revolution of 1776 turned upon one great principle, self-government— and self-taxation, the criterion of self-government. Where the interests of two people united together under one Government, are different, each must have the power to protect its interest by the organization of the Government, or they cannot be free. The interests of Great Britain and of the Colonies were different and antagonistic. Great Britain was desirous of carrying out the policy of all nations towards their Colonies, of making them tributary to her wealth and power. She had vast and complicated relations with the whole world. Her policy toward her North American Colonies was to identify them with her in all those complicated relations; and to make them bear, in common with the rest of the Empire, the full burden of her obligations and necessities. She had a vast public debt; she had an European policy and an Asiatic policy, which had occasioned the accumulation of her public debt; and which kept her in continual wars. The North American Colonies saw their interests, political and commercial sacrificed by such a policy. Their interests required that they should not be identified with the burdens and wars of the mother country. They had been settled under charters, which gave them self-government; at least so far as their property was concerned. They had taxed themselves, and had never been taxed by the Government of Great Britain. To make them a part of a consolidated Empire, the Parliament of Great Britain determined to assume the power of legislating for the Colonies in all cases whatsoever. Our ancestors resisted the pretension. They refused to be a part of the consolidated Government of Great Britain.

The Southern States now stand exactly in the same position toward the Northern States that the Colonies did toward Great Britain. The Northern States, having the majority in Congress, claim the same power of omnipotence in legislation as the British Parliament. "The General Welfare," is the only limit to the legislation of either; and the majority in Congress, as in the British Parliament, are the sole judges of the expediency of the legislation this "General Welfare" requires. Thus, the government of the United States has become a consolidated Government; and the people of the Southern States are compelled to meet the very despotism their fathers threw off in the Revolution of 1776.

The consolidation of the Government of Great Britain over the Colonies, was attempted to be carried out by the taxes. The British Parliament undertook to tax the Colonies, to promote British interests. Our fathers resisted this pretension. They claimed the right of self-taxation *through their Colonial Legislatures.* They were not represented in the British Parliament, and, therefore, could not rightly be taxed by its legislation. The British Government however, offered them a representation in Parliament; but it was not sufficient to enable them to protect themselves from the majority, and they refused the offer. Between taxation without any representation, and taxation without a representation adequate to protection, there was no difference. In neither case would the Colonies tax themselves. Hence, they refused to pay the taxes by the British Parliament.

And so with the Southern States, towards the Northern States, in the vital matter of taxation. They are in a minority in Congress. Their representation in Congress is useless to protect them against unjust taxation; and they are taxed by the people of the North *for their benefit*, exactly as the people of Great Britain taxed our ancestors in the British Parliament for their benefit. For the last forty years, the taxes laid by the Congress of the United States, have been laid with a view of subserving the interests of the North. The people of the South have been taxed by duties on imports, not for revenue, but for an object inconsistent with revenue—to promote, by prohibitions, Northern interests in the production of their mines and manufactures.

There is another evil, in the condition of the Southern towards the Northern States, which our ancestors not only taxed themselves, but all the taxes collected from them, were expended amongst them. Had they submitted to the pretensions of the British Government, the taxes collected from them would have been expended in other parts of the British Empire. They were fully aware of the effect of such a policy in impoverishing the people from whom taxes were collected, and in enriching those who receive the benefit of their expenditure. To prevent the evils of such a policy, was one of the motives which drove them on to revolution. Yet this British policy has been fully realized towards the Southern States by the Northern States. The people of the Southern States are not only taxed for the benefit of the Northern States, but after the taxes are collected, three-fourths of them are expended at the North. This cause, with others, connected with the operation of the General Government, has made the cities of the south provincial. There growth is paralyzed; they are mere suburbs of Northern cities. The agricultural productions of the South are the basis of the foreign commerce of the United States; yet Southern cities do not carry it on. Our foreign trade is almost annihilated. In 1740, there were five ship-yards in South Carolina, to build ships to carry on our direct trade with Europe. Between 1740 and 1779, there were built in these yards, twenty-five square-rigged vessels, besides a great number of sloops and schooners, to carry on our coast and West India trade. In the half century immediately preceding the Revolution from 1726 to 1775, the population of South Carolina increased sevenfold.

No man can, for a moment, believe that our ancestors intended to establish over their posterity, exactly the same sort of Government they had overthrown. The great object of the Constitution of the United States, in its internal opera-tion, was, doubtless, to secure the great end of the Revolution—a limited free Government—a Government limited to those maters only, which were general and common to all portions of the United States. All sectional or local inter-ests were to be left to the States. By no other arrangement would they obtain free Government, by a Constitution common to so vast a Confederacy. Yet, by gradual and steady encroachments on the part of the people of the North, and acquiescence on the part of the South, the limitations in the Constitution have been swept away; and the Government of the United States has become con-solidated, with a claim of limitless powers in its operation.

It is not at all surprising, such being the character of the Government of the United States, that it should assume to possess power over all the institutions of the country. The agitations on the subject of slavery are the natural results of the consolidation of the Government. Responsibility follows power; and if the people of the North have the power by Congress "to promote the general welfare of the United States," by any means they deem expedient—why should they not assail and overthrow the institution of slavery in the South? They are responsible for its continuance or existence, in proportion to their power. A majority in Congress, according to their interested and perverted views, is om-nipotent. The inducements to act upon the subject of slavery, under such cir-cumstances, were so imperious, as to amount almost to a moral necessity. To make, however, their numerical power to rule the Union, the North must con-solidate their power. It would be united, on any matter common to the whole Union—in other words, on any constitutional subject—for on such subjects divisions are as likely to exist in the North as in the South. Slavery was strictly a sectional interest. If this could be made the criterion of parties at the North, the North could be united in its power; and thus carry out its measures of sectional ambition, encroaching and aggrandizement. To build up their sectional predominance in the Union, the Constitution must be first abolished by constructions; but that being done, the consolidation of the North, to rule the South, by the tariff and slavery issues, was in the obvious course of things.

The Constitution of the United States was an experiment. The experiment consisted in uniting under one Government, peoples living in different climates, and having different pursuits and institutions. It matters not how carefully the limitations of such a Government be laid down in the Constitution—its success must, at least, depend upon the good faith of the parties to the constitutional compact, in enforcing them. It is not in the power of human language to exclude false inferences, constructions and perversions, in any Constitution; and when vast sectional interests are to be subserved, involving the appropriation of countless millions of money, it has not been the usual experience of mankind, that words on parchments can arrest power. The Constitution of the United States, rested on the assumption that power would yield to faith—that integrity would be stronger than interest; and that thus, the limitations of the Constitution would be observed. The experiment has been fairly made. The Southern States, from the commencement of the Government, have striven to keep it within the orbit prescribed by the Constitution. The experiment has failed. The whole Constitution, by the constructions of the Northern people, has been absorbed by its preamble. In their reckless lust for power, they seem unable to comprehend that seeming paradox—that the more power is given to the General Government, the weaker it becomes. Its strength consists in the limitation of its agency to objects of common interests to all sections. To extend the scope of its power over sectional or local interests, is to raise up against it opposition and resistance. In all such matters, the General Government must necessarily be a despotism, because all sectional or local interests must ever be represented by a minority in the councils of the General Government—having no power to protect itself against the rule of the majority. The majority, constituted from those who do not represent these sectional or local interests, will control and govern them. A free people cannot submit to such a Government. And the more it enlarges the sphere of its power, the greater must be the dissatisfaction it must produce, and the weaker it must become. On the contrary, the more it abstains from usurped powers, and the more faithfully it adheres to the limitations of the Constitution, the stronger it is made. The Northern people have had neither the wisdom nor the faith to perceive, that to observe the limitations of the Constitution was the only way to its perpetuity.

Under such a Government, there must, of course, be many and endless "irrepressible conflicts," between the two great sections of the Union. The same faithlessness which has abolished the Constitution of the United States, will not fail to carry out the sectional purposes for which it has been abolished. There must be conflict; and the weaker section of the Union can only find peace and liberty in an independence of the North. The repeated efforts made by South Carolina, in a wise conservatism, to arrest the progress of the General Government in its fatal progress to consolidation, have been unsupported and she has been denounced as faithless to the obligations of the Constitution, by the very men and States, who were destroying it by their usurpations. It is now too late to reform or restore the government of the United States. All confidence in the North is lost by the South. The faithlessness of the North for half a century, has opened a gulf of separation between the North and the South which no promises nor engagements can fill.

It cannot be believed, that our ancestors would have assented to any union whatever with the people of the North, if the feelings and opinions now existing amongst them, had existed when the Constitution was framed. There was then no tariff—no fanaticism concerning negroes. It was the delegates from New England who proposed in the Convention which framed the Constitution, to the delegates from South Carolina and Georgia, that if they would agree to give Congress the power of regulating commerce *by a majority*, that they would support the extension of the African Slave Trade for twenty years. African slavery existed in all the States but one. The idea that the Southern States would be made to pay that tribute to their northern confederates which they had refused to pay to Great Britain; or that the institutions of African slavery would be made the grand basis of a sectional organization of the North to rule the South, never crossed the imaginations of our ancestors. The Union of the Constitution was a Union of slaveholding States. It rests on slavery, by prescribing a representation in Congress for three-fifths of our slaves. There is nothing in the proceedings of the Convention which framed the Constitution, to show that the Southern States would have formed any other Union; and still less, that they would have formed a Union with more powerful non-slaveholding States, having a majority in both branches of the Legislature of the Government. They were guilty of no such folly. Time and the progress of things have totally altered the relations between the Northern and Southern States, since the Union was established. That identity of feelings, interests and institutions which once existed, is gone. They are now divided, between agricultural and manufacturing, and commercial States; between slaveholding and non-slaveholding States. Their institutions and industrial pursuits have made them totally different peoples. That equality in the Government between the two sections of the Union which once existed, no longer exists. We but imitate the policy of our fathers in dissolving a union with non-slaveholding confederates, and seeking a confederation with slaveholding States.

Experience has proved that slaveholding States cannot be safe in subjection to non-slaveholding States. Indeed, no people can ever expect to preserve its rights and liberties, unless these be in its own custody. To plunder and oppress, where plunder and oppression can be practiced with impunity, seemed to be the natural order of things. The fairest portions of the world elsewhere, have been turned into wildernesses, and the most civilized and prosperous communities have been impoverished and ruined by anti-slavery fanaticism. The people of the North have not left us in doubt as to their designs and policy. United as a section in the late Presidential election, they have elected as the exponent of their policy, one who has openly declared that all the States of the United States must be made *free States or slave States*. It is true, that amongst those who aided in his election, there are various shades of anti-slavery hostility. But if African slavery in the Southern States be the evil their political combination affirms it to be, the requisitions of an inexorable logic must lead them to emancipation. If it is right to preclude or abolish slavery in a Territory, why should it be allowed to remain in the States? The one is not at all more unconstitutional than the other, according to the decisions of the Supreme Court of the United States. And when it is considered that the Northern States will soon have the power to make that Court what they please, and that the Constitution never has been any barrier whatever to their exercise of power, what check can there be, in the unrestrained counsels of the North to emancipation? There is sympathy in association, which carries men along without principle; but when there is principle, and that principle is fortified by long existing prejudices and feelings, association is omnipotent in party influences. In spite of all disclaimers and professions, there can be but one end by the submission of the South to the rule of a sectional anti-slavery government at Washington; and that end, directly or indirectly, must be—the emancipation of the slaves of the South. The hypocrisy of thirty years—the faithlessness of their whole course from the commencement of our union with them, show that the people of the non-slaveholding North are not and cannot be safe associates of the slaveholding South, under a common Government. Not only their fanaticism, but their erroneous views of the principles of free Governments, render it doubtful whether, if separated from the South, they can maintain a free Government amongst themselves. Numbers, with them, is the great element of free Government. A majority is infallible and omnipotent. "The right divine to rule in kings," is only transferred to their majority. The very object of all Constitutions, in free popular Government, is to restrain the majority. Constitutions, therefore, according to their theory, must be most unrighteous inventions, restricting liberty. None ought to exist; but the body politic ought simply to have a political organization, to bring out and enforce the will of the majority. This theory may be harmless in a small community, having identity of interests and pursuits; but over a vast State—still more, over a vast Confederacy, having various and conflicting interests and pursuits, it is a remorseless despotism. In resisting it, as applicable to ourselves, we are vindicating the great cause of free Government, more important, perhaps, to the world, than the existence of all the United States. Nor in resisting it, do we intend to depart from the safe instrumentality, the system of Government we have established with them, requires. In separating from them, we invade no rights—no interest of theirs. We violate no obligation or duty to them. As separate, independent States in Convention, we made the Constitution of the United States with them; and as separate and independent States, each State acting for itself, we adopted it. South Carolina, acting in her sovereign capacity, now thinks proper to secede from the Union. She did not part with her Sovereignty in adopting the Constitution. The last thing a State can be presumed to have surrendered, is her Sovereignty. Her Sovereignty is her life. Nothing but a clear express grant can alienate it. Inference is inadmissible. Yet it is not at all surprising that those who have construed away all the limitations of the Constitution, should also by construction, claim the annihilation of the Sovereignty of the States. Having abolished all barriers to their omnipotence, by their faithless constructions in the operations of the General Government, it is most natural that they should endeavor to do the same towards us in the States. The truth is, they having violated the express provisions of the Constitution, it is at an end, as a compact. It is morally obligatory only on those who choose to accept its perverted terms. South Carolina, deeming the compact not only violated in particular features, but virtually abolished by her Northern confederates, withdraws herself as a party from its obligations. The right to do so is denied by her Northern confederates. They desire to establish a sectional despotism, not only omnipotent in Congress, but omnipotent over the States; and as if to manifest the imperious necessity of our secession, they threaten us with the sword, to coerce submission to their rule.

Citizens of the slaveholding States of the United States! Circumstances beyond our control have placed us in the van of the great controversy between the Northern and Southern States. We would have preferred that other States should have assumed the position we now occupy. Independent ourselves, we disclaim any design or desire to lead the counsels of the other Southern States. Providence has cast our lot together, by extending over us an identity of pursuits, interests and institutions. South Carolina desires no destiny separated from yours. To be one of a great Slaveholding Confederacy, stretching its arms over a territory larger than any over in Europe possesses—with productions which make our existence more important to the world than that of any other people inhabiting it—with common institutions to defend, and common dangers to encounter—we ask your sympathy and confederation. Whilst constituting a portion of the United States, it has been *your* statesmanship which has guided it, in its mighty strides to power and expansion. In the field, as in the cabinet, *you* have led the way to its renown and grandeur. You have loved the Union, in whose service your great statesmen have labored, and your great soldiers have fought and conquered—not for the material benefits it conferred, but with the faith of a generous and devoted chivalry. You have long lingered in hope over the shattered remains of a broken Constitution. Compromise after compromise, formed by our concessions, has been trampled under foot by your Northern confederates. All fraternity of feeling between the North and the South is lost, or has been converted to hate; and we, of the South, are at last driven together by the stern destiny which controls the existence of nations. Your bitter experience of the faithlessness and rapacity of your Northern confederates may have been necessary to evolve those great principles of free Government, upon which the liberties of the world depend, and to prepare you for the grand mission of vindicating and reestablishing them. We rejoice that other nations should be satisfied with their institutions. Contentment is a great element of happiness, with nations as with individuals. We are satisfied with ours. If they prefer a system of industry, in which capital and labor are in perpetual conflict—and chronic starvation keeps down the natural increase of population—and a man is worked out in eight years—and the law ordains that children shall be worked only *ten hours a day*—and the sabre and the bayonet are the instruments of order—be it so. It is their affair, not ours. We prefer, however, our system of industry, by which labor and capital are identified in interest, and capital, therefore, protects labor—by which our population doubles every twenty years—by which starvation is unknown, and abundance crowns the land—by which order is preserved by an unpaid police, and many fertile regions of the world, where the white man cannot labor, are brought into usefulness by the labor of the African, and the whole world is blessed by our productions. All we demand of other peoples is to be left alone, to work out our own high destinies. United together, and we must be the most independent, as we are among the most important, of the nations of the world. United together, and we require no other instrument to conquer peace, than our beneficent productions. United together, and we must be a great, free and prosperous people, whose renown must spread throughout the civilized world, and pass down, we trust to the remotest ages. We ask you to join us in forming a Confederacy of Slaveholding States.

* * *

Mississippi Secession Convention, "A Declaration of the Immediate Causes Which Induce and Justify the Secession of the State of Mississippi from the Federal Union," January 26, 1861.[21]

Mississippi seceded on January 9, 1861. Its declaration, passed later, copies South Carolina's title and is even more forthright as to why it quits the Union: "Our position is thoroughly identified with the institution of slavery." Mississippi's declaration consists mostly of a series of "It" statements, parallel to the "He" statements (referring to King George) in the U.S. Declaration of Independence. "It" here refers to hostility to slavery. Like South Carolina, Mississippi complains that most Northern states have "nullified the Fugitive Slave Act." Mississippi is also outraged by abolitionist preaching and publications and by John Brown's raid. Paradoxically, the state attacks "It" for advocating "negro equality" while not seeking "to elevate or to support the slave."

In the momentous step which our State has taken of dissolving its connection with the government of which we so long formed a part, it is but just that we should declare the prominent reasons which have induced our course.

Our position is thoroughly identified with the institution of slavery the greatest material interest of the world. Its labor supplies the product which constitutes by far the largest and most important portions of the commerce of the earth. These products are peculiar to the climate verging on the tropical regions, and by an imperious law of nature none but the black race can bear exposure to the tropical sun. These products have become necessities of the world, and a blow at slavery is a blow at commerce and civilization. That blow has been long aimed at the institution, and was at the point of reaching its consummation. There was no choice left us but submission to the mandates of abolition, or a dissolution of the Union, whose principles had been subverted to work out our ruin.

That we do not overstate the dangers to our institution, a reference to a few facts will sufficiently prove.

The hostility to this institution commenced before the adoption of the Constitution, and was manifested in the well-known Ordinance of 1787, in regard to the Northwestern Territory.

The feeling increased, until, in 1819–20, it deprived the South of more than half the vast territory acquired from France.

The same hostility dismembered Texas and seized upon all the territory acquired from Mexico.

It has grown until it denies the right of property in slaves, and refuses protection to that right on the high seas, in the Territories, and wherever the government of the United States had jurisdiction.

It refuses the admission of new slave States into the Union, and seeks to extinguish it by confining it within its present limits, denying the power of expansion.

It tramples the original equality of the South under foot.

It has nullified the Fugitive Slave Law in almost every free State in the Union, and has utterly broken the compact which our fathers pledged their faith to maintain.

It advocates negro equality, socially and politically, and promotes insurrection and incendiarism in our midst.

It has enlisted its press, its pulpit and its schools against us, until the whole popular mind of the North is excited and inflamed with prejudice.

It has made combinations and formed associations to carry out its schemes of emancipation in the States and wherever else slavery exists.

It seeks not to elevate or to support the slave, but to destroy his present condition without providing a better.

It has invaded a State, and invested with the honors of martyrdom the wretch whose purpose was to apply flames to our dwellings, and the weapons of destruction to our lives.

It has broken every compact into which it has entered for our security.

It has given indubitable evidence of its design to ruin our agriculture, to prostrate our industrial pursuits and to destroy our social system.

It knows no relenting or hesitation in its purposes; it stops not in its march of aggression, and leaves us no room to hope for cessation or for pause.

It has recently obtained control of the Government, by the prosecution of its unhallowed schemes, and destroyed the last expectation of living together in friendship and brotherhood.

Utter subjugation awaits us in the Union, if we should consent longer to remain in it. It is not a matter of choice, but of necessity. We must either submit to degradation, and to the loss of property worth four billions of money, or we must secede from the Union framed by our fathers, to secure this as well as every other species of property. For far less cause than this, our fathers separated from the Crown of England.

Our decision is made. We follow their footsteps. We embrace the alternative of separation; and for the reasons here stated, we resolve to maintain our rights with the full consciousness of the justice of our course, and the undoubting belief of our ability to maintain it.

* * *

Florida Secession Convention, "Cause for Secession," January 7, 1861.[22]

Florida did not secede until January 10, but this terse document tells why. It expresses dismay about the "strength of the anti-slavery sentiment of the free States." Its second paragraph also claims secession as an "undoubted right."

WHEREAS, All hope of the preservation of the Federal Union, upon terms consistent with the safety and honor of the slave-holding States, has finally dissipated by the recent indications of the strength of the anti-slavery sentiment of the free States. Therefore,

Be it resolved by the People of the State of Florida in Convention assembled, That, as it is the undoubted right of the several States of the Federal Union, known as the United States of America, to withdraw from the said Union at such time and for such cause or causes as in the opinion of the people of each State, acting in their sovereign capacity, may be just and proper, in the opinion of this Convention, the existing causes are such to compel the State of Florida to proceed to exercise that right.

* * *

Alabama Secession Convention, "Resolution of Resistance," January 7, 1861, and "Ordinance of Secession," January 11, 1861.[23]

The longest paragraph of Alabama's short resolution says that Alabama secedes because "the Black Republican Party" won, and on the platform that slavery should not be extended into the territories and should eventually be ended within the existing states, an accurate statement of the Republican position.

Whereas, the only bond of union between the several States is the Constitution of the United States; and Whereas, that Constitution has been *violated*, both by the Government of the United States, and by a majority of the Northern States, in their separate legislative action, *denying* to the people of the Southern States their Constitutional rights;

And Whereas, a sectional party, known as the Black Republican Party, has, in the recent election, elected Abraham Lincoln to the office of President, and Hannibal Hamlin to the office of Vice-President of these United States, upon the avowed *principle* that the Constitution of the United States *does not recognise property in slaves*, and that the Government should prevent its extension into the common Territories of the United States, and that the power of the Government should be so exercised that slavery in time, should be exterminated:

Resolved, By the people of Alabama, in Convention assembled That the State of Alabama cannot, and will not, submit to the Administration of Lincoln and Hamlin as President and Vice President of the United States, upon the principles referred to in the preamble.

The first paragraph of Alabama's Ordinance of Secession also tells why. Like South Carolina and other states, Alabama cites the election of Lincoln and actions by Northern states.

Whereas, the election of Abraham Lincoln and Hannibal Hamlin to the offices of President and Vice President of the United States of America, by a sectional party, avowedly hostile to the domestic institutions and to the peace and security of the people of the State of Alabama, preceded by many and dangerous infractions of the Constitution of the United States by many of the States and people of the Northern section, is a political wrong of so insulting and menacing a character as to justify the people of the State of Alabama in the adoption of prompt and decided measures for their future peace and security; ..

* * *

Georgia Committee of Seventeen, "Report on Causes for Secession," January 29, 1861.[24]

Georgia seceded on January 19, 1861. This report tells why. Like other seceding states, Georgia complains about the actions of "our non-slaveholding confederate States, with reference to the subject of African slavery," not about the federal government. Georgia also refers to "Lincoln," leader of a party "admitted to be an anti-slavery party." Georgia also resurrects the South's old complaint about protective tariffs before admitting that the tariff of 1846 remedied the problem. Then the document focuses at length on the North's hostility to slavery and promotion of "negro equality," eventually prophesying catastrophe if such policies prevail.

The people of Georgia have dissolved their political connection with the Government of the United States of America, present to their confederates, and the world, the causes which have led to the separation. For the last ten years we have had numerous and serious causes of complaint against our non-slaveholding confederate States, with reference to the subject of African slavery. They have endeavored to weaken our security, to disturb our domestic peace and tranquility, and persistently refused to comply with their express constitutional obligations to us in reference to that property, and by the use of their power in the Federal Government, have striven to deprive us of an equal enjoyment of the common Territories of the Republic. This hostile policy of our confederates has been pursued with every circumstance of aggravation which could arouse the passions and excite the hatred of our people, and has placed the two sections of the Union, for many years past, in the condition of virtual civil war. Our people, still attached to the Union, from habit and National traditions, and averse to change, hoped that time, reason and argument, would bring, if not redress, at least exemption from farther insults, injuries and dangers. Recent events have fully dissipated all such hopes, and demonstrated the necessity of separation. Our Northern confederates, after a full and calm hearing of all the facts, after a fair warning of our purpose not to submit to the rule of the authors of all these wrongs and injuries, have, by a large majority, committed the

Government of the United States into their hands. The people of Georgia, after an equally full and fair and deliberate hearing of the case, have declared with equal firmness, that they shall not rule over them. A brief history of the rise, progress and policy of anti-slavery, and of the political organization into whose hands the administration of the Federal Government has been committed, will fully justify the pronounced verdict of the people of Georgia. The party of Lincoln, called the Republican party, under its present name and organization is of recent origin. It is admitted to be an anti-slavery party, while it attracts to itself by its creed, the scattered advocates of exploded political heresies, of condemned theories in political economy, the advocates of commercial restrictions, of protection, of special privileges, of waste and corruption in the administration of Government; anti-slavery is its mission and its purpose. By anti-slavery it is made a power in the State. The question of slavery was the great difficulty in the way of the formation of the Constitution. While the subordination and the political and social inequality of the African race were fully conceded by all, it was plainly apparent that slavery would soon disappear from what are now the non-slaveholding States of the original thirteen; the opposition to slavery was then, as now, general in those States, and the Constitution was made with direct reference to that fact. But a distinct abolition party was not formed in the United States, for more than half a century after the Government went into operation. The main reason was, that the North, even if united, could not control both branches of the Legislature during any portion of that time. Therefore, such an organization must have resulted, either in utter failure, or in the total overthrow of the Government. The material prosperity of the North was greatly dependent on the Federal Government; that of the South not at all. In the first years of the Republic, the navigating, commercial and manufacturing interests of the North, began to seek profit and aggrandizement at the expense of the agricultural interests. Even the owners of fishing smacks, sought and obtained bounties for pursuing their own business, which yet continue and half a million of dollars are now paid them annually out of the Treasury. The navigating interests begged for protection against foreign ship builders, and against competition in the coasting trade; Congress granted both requests, and by prohibitory acts, gave an absolute monopoly of this business to each of their interests, which they enjoy without diminution to this day. Not content with these great and unjust advantages, they have sought to throw the legitimate burthens of their business as much as possible upon the public; they have succeeded in throwing the cost of light-houses, buoys, and the maintenance of their seamen, upon the Treasury, and the Government now pays above two millions annually for the support of these objects. These interests in connection with the commercial and manufacturing classes, have also succeeded, by means of subventions to mail steamers, and the reduction of postage, in relieving their business from the payment of about seven millions of dollars annually, throwing it upon the public Treasury, under the name of postal deficiency. The manufacturing interest entered into the same struggle early, and has clamored steadily for Government bounties and special favors. This interest was confined mainly to the Eastern and Middle non-slaveholding States. Wielding these great States, it held great power and influence, and its demands were in full proportion to its power. The manufacturers and miners wisely based their demands upon special facts and reasons, rather than upon general principles, and thereby mollified much of the opposition of the opposing interest. They pleaded in their favor, the infancy of their business in this country, the scarcity of labor and capital, the hostile legislation of other countries towards them, the great necessity of their fabrics in the time of war, and the necessity of high duties to pay the debt incurred in our war for independence; these reasons prevailed, and they received for many years enormous bounties by the general acquiescence of the whole country.

But when these reasons ceased, they were no less clamorous for government protection; but their clamors were less heeded, the country had put the principle of protection upon trial, and condemned it. After having enjoyed protection to the extent of from fifteen to two hundred per cent, upon their entire business, for above thirty years, the Act of 1846 was passed. It avoided sudden change, but the principle was settled, and free-trade, low duties, and economy in public expenditures was the verdict of the American people. The South, and the Northwestern States sustained this policy. There was but small hope of its reversal, upon the direct issue, none at all.

All these classes saw this, and felt it, and cast about for new allies. The anti-slavery sentiment of the North offered the best chance for success. An anti-slavery party must necessarily look to the North alone for support; but a united North was now strong enough to control the government in all of its departments, and a sectional party was therefore determined upon. Time, and issues upon slavery were necessary to its completion and final triumph. The feeling of anti-slavery, which it was well known was very general among the people of the North, had been long dormant or passive, it needed only a question to arouse it into aggressive activity. This question was before us: we had acquired a large territory by successful war with Mexico; Congress had to govern it, how in relation to slavery was the question, then demanding solution. This state of facts gave form and shape to the anti-slavery sentiment throughout the North, and the conflict began. Northern anti-slavery men of all parties asserted the right to exclude slavery from the territory by Congressional legislation, and demanded the prompt and efficient exercise of this power to that end. This insulting and unconstitutional demand was met with great moderation and firmness by the South. We had shed our blood and paid our money for its acquisition; we demanded a division of it, on the line of the Missouri restriction, or an equal participation in the whole of it. These propositions were refused, the agitation became general, and the public danger great. The case of the South was impregnable. The price of the acquisition was the blood and treasure of both sections of all; and therefore it belonged to all, upon the principles of equity and justice.

The Constitution delegated no power to Congress to exclude either party from its free enjoyment; therefore, our right was good, under the Constitution. Our rights were further fortified by the practice of the government from the beginning. Slavery was forbidden in the country north-west of the Ohio river, by what is called the Ordinance of 1787. That Ordinance was adopted under the old confederation, and by the assent of Virginia, who owned and ceded the country; and, therefore, this case must stand on its own special circumstances. The government of the United States claimed territory by virtue of the treaty of 1783 with Great Britain; acquired territory by cession from Georgia and North Carolina; by treaty from France, and by treaty from Spain. These acquisitions largely exceeded the original limits of the Republic. In all of these acquisitions the policy of the government was uniform. It opened them to the settlement of all the citizens of all the States of the Union. They emigrated thither with their property of every kind (including slaves), all were equally protected by public authority in their persons and property, until the inhabitants became sufficiently numerous, and otherwise capable of bearing the burthens and performing the duties of self-government, when they were admitted into the Union, upon equal terms with the other States, with whatever republican constitution they might adopt for themselves.

Under this equally just and beneficent policy, law and order, stability and progress, peace and prosperity marked every step of the progress of these new communities, until they entered as great and prosperous commonwealths into the sisterhood of American States. In 1820, the North endeavored to overturn this wise and successful policy, and demanded that the State of Missouri should not be admitted into the Union, unless she first prohibited slavery within her limits, by her Constitution. After a bitter and protracted struggle, the North was defeated in her special object; but her policy and position led to the adoption of a section in the law, for the admission of Missouri, prohibiting slavery in all that portion of the territory acquired from France, lying North of 36 deg. 30 min. North latitude, and outside of Missouri. The venerable Madison, at the time of its adoption, declared it unconstitutional; Mr. Jefferson condemned the restriction, and foresaw its consequences, and predicted that it would result in the dissolution of the Union. His prediction is now history. The North demanded the application of the principle of prohibition of slavery to all of the territory acquired from Mexico, and all other parts of the public domain, then and in all future time. It was the announcement of her purpose to appropriate to herself all the public domain then owned and thereafter to be acquired by the United States. The claim itself was less arrogant and insulting than the reason with which she supported it. That reason was her fixed purpose to limit, restrain and finally to abolish slavery in the States where it exists. The South, with great unanimity, declared her purpose to resist the principle of prohibition to the last extremity. This particular question, in connection with a series of questions affecting the same subject, was finally disposed of by the defeat of prohibitory legislation.

The Presidential election of 1852, resulted in the total overthrow of the advocates of restriction and their party friends. Immediately after this result, the anti-slavery portion of the defeated party, resolved to unite all the elements in the North, opposed to slavery, and to stake their future political fortunes upon their hostility to slavery everywhere. This is the party to whom the people of the North have committed the government. They raised their standard in 1856, and were barely defeated; they entered the Presidential contest again, in 1860, and succeeded.

The prohibition of slavery in the territories, hostility to it everywhere, the equality of the black and white races, disregard of all constitutional guarantees in its favor, were boldly proclaimed by its leaders, and applauded by its followers.

With these principles on their banners and these utterances on their lips, the majority of the people of the North demand, that we shall receive them as our rulers.

The prohibition of slavery in the territories is the cardinal principle of this organization.

For forty years this question had been considered, and debated in the halls of Congress, before the people, by the press, and before the tribunals of justice. The majority of the people of the North in 1860, decided it in their own favor. We refuse to submit to that judgment, and in vindication of our refusal, we offer the constitution of our country, and point to the total absence of any express power to exclude us; we offer the practice of our government, for the first thirty years of its existence, in complete refutation of the position that any such power is either necessary or proper to the execution of any other power in relation to the territories. We offer the judgment of a large minority of the people of the North, amounting to more than one-third who united with the unanimous voice of the South against this usurpation; and finally, we offer the judgment of the Supreme Court of the United States, the highest judicial tribunal of our country in our favor. This evidence ought to be conclusive, that we have never surrendered this right; the conduct of our adversaries admonishes us that if we had surrendered it, it is time to resume it.

The faithless conduct of our adversaries, is not confined to such acts as might aggrandize themselves or their section of the Union; they are content, if they can only injure us. The constitution declares, that persons charged with crimes in one State and fleeing to another, shall be delivered up on the demand of the Executive authority of the State from which they may flee, to be tried in the jurisdiction where the crime was committed. It would appear difficult to employ language freer from ambiguity; yet, for above twenty years, the non-slaveholding States, generally, have wholly refused to deliver up to us persons charged with crimes affecting slave property; our confederates, with punic faith, shield and give sanctuary to all criminals, who seek to deprive us of this property, or who use it to destroy us. This clause of the constitution has no other sanction than their good faith; that is withheld from us; we are remediless in the Union; out of it, we are remitted to the laws of nations.

A similar provision of the Constitution requires them to surrender fugitives from labor. This provision and the one last referred to, were our main inducements for confederating with the Northern States; without them, it is historically true, that we would have rejected the Constitution. In the fourth year of the Republic, Congress passed a law to give full vigor and efficiency to this important provision. This Act depended to a considerable degree upon the local magistrates of the several States for its efficiency; the non-slaveholding States generally repealed all laws intended to aid the execution of that Act, and imposed penalties upon those citizens whose loyalty to the Constitution, and their oaths, might induce them to discharge their duty. Congress then passed the act of 1850, providing for the complete execution of this duty by Federal Officers. This law which their own bad faith rendered absolutely indispensable for the protection of constitutional rights, was instantly met with ferocious revilings, and all conceivable modes of hostility. The Supreme Court unanimously, and their own local Courts, with equal unanimity, (with the single and temporary exception of the Supreme Court of Wisconsin,) sustained its constitutionality in all of its provisions. Yet it stands today a dead letter, for all practicable purposes, in every non-slaveholding State in the Union. We have their covenants, we have their oaths, to keep and observe it, but the unfortunate claimant, even accompanied by a Federal Officer, with the mandate of the highest judicial authority in his hands, is everywhere met, with fraud, with force, and with legislative enactments, to elude, to resist and defeat him; claimants are murdered with impunity; officers of the law are beaten by frantic mobs, instigated by inflammatory appeals from persons holding the highest public employment in these States, and supported by legislation in conflict with the clearest provisions of the Constitution, and even the ordinary principles of humanity. In several of our confederate States, a citizen can not travel the highway with his servant, who may voluntarily accompany him, without being declared by law a felon, and being subjected to infamous punishments. It is difficult to perceive how we could suffer more by the hostility, than by the fraternity of such brethren.

The public law of civilized nations requires every State to restrain its citizens or subjects from committing acts injurious to the peace and safety of any other State, and from attempting to excite insurrection, or to lessen the security, or to disturb the tranquility of their neighbors, and our Constitution wisely gives Congress the power to punish all offences against the laws of nations.

These are sound and just principles which have received the approbation of just men in all countries, and all centuries. But they are wholly disregarded by the people of the Northern States, and the Federal Government is impotent to maintain them. For twenty years past, the Abolitionists and their allies in the Northern States, have been engaged in constant efforts to subvert our institutions, and to excite insurrection and servile war amongst us. They have sent emissaries among us, for the accomplishment of these purposes. Some of these efforts have received the public sanction of a majority of the leading men of the Republican party in the National Councils, the same men who are now proposed as our rulers. These efforts have in one instance led to the actual invasion of one of the slave-holding States, and those of the murderers and incendiaries, who escaped public justice by flight, have found fraternal protection among our Northern Confederates.

These are the men who say the Union shall be preserved. Such are the opinions and such are the practices of the Republican Party, who have been called by their own votes to administer the Federal Government under the Constitution of the United States; we know their treachery, we know the shallow pretences under which they daily disregard its plainest obligations; if we submit to them, it will be our fault and not theirs. The people of Georgia have ever been willing to stand by this bargain, this contract; they have never sought to evade any of its obligations; they have never hitherto sought to establish any new government, they have struggled to maintain the ancient right of themselves and the human race, through and by that Constitution. But they know the value of parchment rights, in treacherous hands, and therefore, they refuse to commit their own to the rulers whom the North offer us. Why? Because by their declared principles and policy, they have outlawed three thousand millions of our property in the common territories of the Union, put it under the ban of the Republic in the States where it exists, and out of the protection of Federal law everywhere; because they give sanctuary to thieves and incendiaries who assail it to the whole extent of their power, in spite of their most solemn obligations and covenants; because their avowed purpose is to subvert our society, and subject us, not only to the loss of our property but the destruction of ourselves, our wives and our children, and the desolation of our homes, our altars, and our firesides. To avoid these evils, we resume the powers which our fathers delegated to the Government of the United States, and henceforth will seek new safeguards for our liberty, equality, security and tranquility.

Texas Secession Convention, "A Declaration of the Causes Which Impel the State of Texas to Secede from the Federal Union," February 2, 1861.[25]

The Texas convention took Texas from the United States on February 1–2, 1861, further ratified by popular vote on February 23. In its Declaration, Texas notes that it was an independent entity between 1836 and 1845, when it voluntarily joined the United States. (Most seceding states were creations of the United States from their beginnings.) Texas also points out that Louisiana's secession and Arkansas's anticipated secession would leave it isolated if it did not secede. The rest of the Texas document models after South Carolina's "Declaration of Immediate Causes."[26] Texas castigates Northerners for "proclaiming the debasing doctrine of the equality of all men," and declares "that the governments of the various States, and of the confederacy itself, were established exclusively by the white race, for themselves and their posterity." The African race has no place other than as slaves.

A declaration of the causes which impel the State of Texas to secede from the Federal Union.

The government of the United States, by certain joint resolutions bearing date the 1st day of March, in the year A.D. 1845, proposed to the Republic of Texas, then *a free sovereign and independent nation*, the annexation of the latter to the former, as one of the co-equal States thereof,

The people of Texas, by deputies in convention assembled on the fourth day of July of the same year, assented to and accepted said proposals and formed a constitution for the proposed State, upon which on the 29th day of December in the same year, said State was formally admitted into the Confederated Union.

Texas abandoned her separate national existence and consented to become one of the Confederated States to promote her welfare, insure her domestic tranquility and secure more substantially the blessings of peace and liberty to her people. She was received into the confederacy with her own constitution, under the guarantee of the federal constitution and the compact of annexation, that she should enjoy these blessings. She was received as a commonwealth holding, maintaining and protecting the institution known as negro slavery the servitude of the African to the white race within her limits a relation that had existed from the first settlement of her wilderness by the white race, and which her people intended should exist in all future time. Her institutions and geographical position established the strongest ties between her and other slaveholding States of the confederacy. Those ties have been strengthened by association. But what has been the course of the government of the United States and of the people and authorities of the non-slave-holding States, since our connections with them?

The controlling majority of the Federal Government, under various pretences and disguises, has so administered the same as to exclude the citizens of the Southern States, unless under odious and unconstitutional restrictions, from all the immense territory owned in common by all the States on the Pacific Ocean, for the avowed purpose of acquiring sufficient power in the common government to use it as a means of destroying the institutions of Texas and her sister slaveholding States.

By the disloyalty of the Northern States and their citizens and the imbecility of the Federal Government, infamous combinations of incendiaries and outlaws have been permitted in those States and the common territory of Kansas to trample upon the federal laws, to war upon the lives and property of Southern citizens in that territory, and finally, by violence and mob law, to usurp the possession of the same as exclusively the property of the Northern States.

The Federal Government, while but partially under the control of these our unnatural and sectional enemies, has for years almost entirely failed to protect the lives and property of the people of Texas against the Indian savages on our border, and more recently against the murderous forays of banditti from the neighboring territory of Mexico; and when our State government has expended large amounts for such purpose, the Federal Government has refused reimbursement therefor, thus rendering our condition more insecure and harassing than it was during the existence of the Republic of Texas.

These and other wrongs we have patiently borne in the vain hope that a returning sense of justice and humanity would induce a different course of administration.

When we advert to the course of individual non-slave-holding States, and that a majority of their citizens, our grievances assume far greater magnitude. The States of Maine, Vermont, New Hampshire, Connecticut, Rhode Island, Massachusetts, New York, Pennsylvania, Ohio, Wisconsin, Michigan and Iowa, by solemn legislative enactments, have deliberately, directly or indirectly violated the 3rd clause of the 2nd section of the 4th article of the federal constitution, and laws passed in pursuance thereof; thereby annulling a material provision of the compact, designed by its framers to perpetuate amity between the members of the confederacy and to secure the rights of the slave-holding States in their domestic institutions—a provision founded in justice and wisdom, and without the enforcement of which the compact fails to accomplish the object of its creation. Some of those States have imposed high fines and degrading penalties upon any of their citizens or officers who may carry out in good faith that provision of the compact, or the federal laws enacted in accordance therewith.

In all the non-slave-holding States, in violation of that good faith and comity which should exist between entirely distinct nations, the people have formed themselves into a great sectional party, now strong enough in numbers to control the affairs of each of those States, based upon the unnatural feeling of hostility to these Southern States and their beneficent and patriarchal system of African slavery, proclaiming the debasing doctrine of the equality of all men, irrespective of race or color—a doctrine at war with nature, in opposition to the experience of mankind, and in violation of the plainest revelations of the Divine Law. They demand the abolition of negro slavery throughout the confederacy, the recognition of political equality between the white and the negro races, and avow their determination to press on their crusade against us, so long as a negro slave remains in these States.

For years past this abolition organization has been actively sowing the seeds of discord through the Union, and has rendered the federal congress the arena for spreading firebrands and hatred between the slave-holding and non-slave-holding States.

By consolidating their strength, they have placed the slave-holding States in a hopeless minority in the federal congress, and rendered representation of no avail in protecting Southern rights against their exactions and encroachments.

They have proclaimed, and at the ballot box sustained, the revolutionary doctrine that there is a "higher law" than the constitution and laws of our Federal Union, and virtually that they will disregard their oaths and trample upon our rights.

They have for years past encouraged and sustained lawless organizations to steal our slaves and prevent their recapture, and have repeatedly murdered Southern citizens while lawfully seeking their rendition.

They have invaded Southern soil and murdered unoffending citizens, and through the press their leading men and a fanatical pulpit have bestowed praise upon the actors and assassins in these crimes, while the governors of several of their States have refused to deliver parties implicated and indicted for participation in such offenses, upon the legal demands of the States aggrieved.

They have, through the mails and hired emissaries, sent seditious pamphlets and papers among us to stir up servile insurrection and bring blood and carnage to our firesides.

They have sent hired emissaries among us to burn our towns and distribute arms and poison to our slaves for the same purpose.

They have impoverished the slave-holding States by unequal and partial legislation, thereby enriching themselves by draining our substance.

They have refused to vote appropriations for protecting Texas against ruthless savages, for the sole reason that she is a slave-holding State.

And, finally, by the combined sectional vote of the seventeen non-slave-holding States, they have elected as president and vice-president of the whole confederacy two men whose chief claims to such high positions are their approval of these long continued wrongs, and their pledges to continue them to the final consummation of these schemes for the ruin of the slave-holding States.

In view of these and many other facts, it is meet that our own views should be distinctly proclaimed.

We hold as undeniable truths that the governments of the various States, and of the confederacy itself, were established exclusively by the white race, for themselves and their posterity; that the African race had no agency in their establishment; that they were rightfully held and regarded as an inferior and dependent race, and in that condition only could their existence in this country be rendered beneficial or tolerable.

That in this free government all white men are and of right ought to be entitled to equal civil and political rights; that the servitude of the African race, as existing in these States, is mutually beneficial to both bond and free, and is abundantly authorized and justified by the experience of mankind, and the revealed will of the Almighty Creator, as recognized by all Christian nations; while the destruction of the existing relations between the two races, as advocated by our sectional enemies, would bring inevitable calamities upon both and desolation upon the fifteen slave-holding States.

By the secession of six of the slave-holding States, and the certainty that others will speedily do likewise, Texas has no alternative but to remain in an isolated connection with the North, or unite her destinies with the South.

For these and other reasons, solemnly asserting that the federal constitution has been violated and virtually abrogated by the several States named, seeing that the federal government is now passing under the control of our enemies to be diverted from the exalted objects of its creation to those of oppression and wrong, and realizing that our own State can no longer look for protection, but to God and her own sons—We the delegates of the people of Texas, in Convention assembled, have passed an ordinance dissolving all political connection with the government of the United States of America and the people thereof and confidently appeal to the intelligence and patriotism of the freemen of Texas to ratify the same at the ballot box, on the 23rd day of the present month.

Adopted in Convention on the 2nd day of Feby, in the year of our Lord one thousand eight hundred and sixty-one and of the independence of Texas the twenty-fifth.

* * *

George Williamson (1829–82), Louisiana Secession Commissioner, "Letter to President and Gentlemen of the Convention of the People of Texas," February 11, 1861.[27]

Louisiana seceded on January 26, 1861, but the convention that took Louisiana out of the Union never passed a statement telling why. When Louisiana sent a "Secession Commissioner" to neighboring Texas, however, he explains his state's reasons. It is all about Lincoln and slavery: "[A] stalwart fanatic of the Northwest" is about to take office. "Louisiana looks to the formation of a Southern confederacy to preserve the blessings of African slavery." If Texas does not join, that would be "a most fatal blow to African slavery." The secession commissioners drew lots of press attention, North and South. Across the South, they numbered 52.[28]

To the Hon. O. M. Roberts, President of the convention of the people of Texas.
Mr. President and Gentlemen of the Convention of the people of Texas.

I have the honor to address you as the commissioner of the people of Louisiana, accredited to your honorable body. With this communication, by the favor of your presiding officer, will be laid before you my credentials, the ordinance of secession, a resolution in regard to the Mississippi river and the ordinance to provide for the appointment of delegates to a convention to form a Southern Confederacy. These ordinances and the resolution were adopted at their respective dates by the people of Louisiana in convention assembled, after serious debate and calm reflection.

Being desirous of obtaining the concurrence of the people of Texas in what she has done, Louisiana invites you to a candid consideration of her acts in resuming the powers delegated to the government of the late United States, and in providing for the formation of a confederacy of "The States which have seceded and may secede." The archives of the Federal Government bear ample testimony to the loyalty of Louisiana to the American Union. Her conservatism has been proverbial in political circles. The character and pursuits of her people, her immense agricultural wealth, her large banking capital, her possession of the great commercial metropolis of the South, whose varied trade almost rivals that of the city of "ten thousand masts" present facts sufficient to make "assurance doubly sure" she did not take these grave steps for light or transient causes. She was impelled to this action to preserve her honor, her safety, her property and the free institutions so sacred to her people. She believed the federal agent had betrayed her trust, had become the facile instrument of a hostile people, and was usurping despotic powers. She considered that the present vacillating executive, on the 4th of March next, would be supplanted by a stalwart fanatic of the Northwest, whose energetic will, backed by the frenzied bigotry of unpatriotic masses, would cause him to establish the military despotism already inaugurated.

The people of Louisiana were unwilling to endanger their liberties and property by submission to the despotism of a single tyrant, or the canting tyranny of pharisaical majorities. Insulted by the denial of her constitutional equality by the non-slave-holding States, outraged by their contemptuous rejection of proffered compromises, and convinced that she was illustrating the capacity of her people for self-government by withdrawing from a union that had failed, without fault of hers, to accomplish its purposes, she declared herself a free and independent State on the 26th day of January last. History affords no example of a people who changed their government for more just or substantial reasons. Louisiana looks to the formation of a Southern confederacy to preserve the blessings of African slavery, and of the free institutions of the founders of the Federal Union, bequeathed to their posterity. As her neighbor and sister State, she desires the hearty co-operation of Texas in the formation of a Southern Confederacy. She congratulates herself on the recent disposition evinced by your honorable body to meet this wish, by the election of delegates to the Montgomery convention. Louisiana and Texas have the same language, laws and institutions. They grow the same great staples—sugar and cotton. Between the citizens of each exists the most cordial social and commercial intercourse. The Red river and the Sabine form common highways for the transportation of their produce to the markets of the world. Texas affords to the commerce of Louisiana a large portion of her products, and in exchange the banks of New Orleans furnish Texas with her only paper circulating medium. Louisiana supplies to Texas a market for her surplus wheat, grain and stock; both States have large areas of fertile, uncultivated lands, peculiarly adapted to slave labor; and they are both so deeply interested in African slavery that it may be said to be absolutely necessary to their existence, and is the keystone to the arch of their prosperity. Each of the States has an extended Gulf coast, and must look with equal solicitude to its protection now, and the acquisition of the entire control of the Gulf of Mexico in due time. No two States of this confederacy are so identified in interest, and whose destinies are so closely interwoven with each other. Nature, sympathy and unity of interest make them almost one. Recognizing these facts, but still confident in her own powers to maintain a separate existence, Louisiana regards with great concern the vote of the people of Texas on the ratification of the ordinance of secession, adopted by your honorable body on the 1st of the present month. She is confident a people who so nobly and gallantly achieved their liberties under such unparalleled difficulties will not falter in maintaining them now. The Mexican yoke could not have been more galling to "the army of heroes" of '36 than the Black republican rule would be to the survivors and sons of that army at the present day.

The people of Louisiana would consider it a most fatal blow to African slavery, if Texas either did not secede or having seceded should not join her destinies to theirs in a Southern Confederacy. If she remains in the union the abolitionists would continue their work of incendiarism and murder. Emigrant aid societies would arm with Sharp's rifles predatory bands to infest her northern borders. The Federal Government would mock at her calamity in accepting the recent bribes in the army bill and Pacific railroad bill, and with abolition treachery would leave her unprotected frontier to the murderous inroads of hostile savages. Experience justifies these expectations. A professedly friendly federal administration gave Texas no substantial protection against the Indians or abolitionists, and what must she look for from an administration avowedly inimical and supported by no vote within her borders. Promises won from the timid and faithless are poor hostages of good faith. As a separate republic, Louisiana remembers too well the whisperings of European diplomacy for the abolition of slavery in the times of annexation not to be apprehensive of bolder demonstrations from the same quarter and the North in this country. The people of the slave-holding States are bound together by the same necessity and determination to preserve African slavery. The isolation of any one of them from the others would make her the theatre for abolition emissaries from the North and from Europe. Her existence would be one of constant peril to herself and of imminent danger to other neighboring slave-holding communities. A decent respect for the opinions and interests of the Gulf States seems to indicate that Texas should co-operate with them. I am authorized to say to your honorable body that Louisiana does not expect any beneficial result from the peace conference now assembled at Washington. She is unwilling that her action should depend on the border States. Her interests are identical with Texas and the seceding States. With them she will at present co-operate, hoping and believing in his own good time God will awaken the people of the border States to the vanity of asking for; or depending upon, guarantees or compromises wrung from a people whose consciences are too sublimated to be bound by that sacred compact, the constitution the of the late United States. That constitution the Southern States have never violated, and taking it as the basis of our new government we hope to form a slave-holding confederacy that will secure to us and our remotest posterity the great blessings its authors designed in the Federal Union. With the social balance wheel of slavery to regulate its machinery, we may fondly indulge the hope that our Southern government will be perpetual. Geo. Williamson, Commissioner of the State of Louisiana, City of Austin Feby 11th 1861

* * *

Henry L. Benning (1814–75), "Address Delivered Before the Virginia State Convention," February 18, 1861.[29]

In mid-February, Virginia was not ready to quit the United States. Georgia sent Henry Benning, a justice of its supreme court, as a "secession commissioner" to convince Virginia to secede. Other states did likewise, sending representatives to Texas, Missouri, Kentucky, even Delaware. Their arguments parallel the "causes for secession" adopted by the states as they left the Union. Always, slavery is their focus. As Benning emphasizes to Virginia, Georgia has concluded that "separation from the North was the only thing that could prevent the abolition of her slavery." He reasons that the Republicans are becoming a permanent majority in the North, centered on eventually ending slavery. He also worries that slaves are waning as a proportion of total population in the border states and deems this due, again, to antislavery feeling in the North. As states like Virginia continue to sell their slaves south, the Cotton States will become two-to-one slave in population. Then, when Republicans end slavery, blacks will win political power there, whereupon whites will unleash race war, with lurid consequences: "our men will be all exterminated," and the land will "become a howling wilderness." Finally, Northerners will exterminate African Americans and take the land for themselves!

Mr. President and Gentlemen of the Convention:

I have been appointed by the Convention of the State of Georgia, to present to you the ordinance of secession of Georgia, and further, to invite Virginia, through you, to join Georgia and the other seceded States in the formation of a Southern Confederacy. This, sir, is the whole extent of my mission. I have no power to make promises, none to receive promises; no power to bind at all in any respect. But still, sir, it has seemed to me that a proper respect for this Convention requires that I should with some fullness and particularity, exhibit to the Convention the reasons which have induced Georgia to take that important step of secession, and then to lay before the Convention some facts and considerations in favor of the acceptance of the invitation by Virginia. With your permission, then, sir, I will pursue this course.

What was the reason that induced Georgia to take the step of secession? That reason may be summed up in one single proposition. It was a conviction; a deep conviction on the part of Georgia, that a separation from the North was the only thing that could prevent the abolition of her slavery. This conviction was the main cause. It is true that the effect of this conviction was strengthened by a further conviction that such a separation would be the best remedy for the fugitive slave evil, and also the best, if not the only remedy, for the territory evil. But, doubtless, if it had not been for the first conviction the step would not have been taken. It, therefore, becomes important to inquire whether this conviction was well founded.

Is it true, then, that but for the separation from the North, slavery would be abolished in Georgia? I address myself to the proofs of that proposition.

In the first place, I say that the North hates slavery. And I use the expression, the North hates slavery, designedly. Hate is the feeling, and it is the whole North that bears it. That this is true of the Black Republican party at the North will, I suppose, be admitted. If there is a doubt upon it in the mind of any one who listens to me, a few of the proofs which could fill this room, will, I think, be sufficient to satisfy him. I beg to refer to a few of the proofs; and the first that I shall adduce consists in two or three sentences from a speech of Mr. Lincoln's, made in October, 1858. They are as follows: "I have always hated slavery as much as any abolitionist; I have always been an old line Whig; I have always hated it, and I always believed it in the course of ultimate extinction, and if I were in Congress and a vote should come up on the question, whether slavery should be excluded from the territory, in spite of the Dred Scott decision, I would vote that it should."

These are pregnant sentences. They contain both a sentiment and a principle of political conduct. The former is that his hatred of slavery equals that of any abolitionist, and, therefore, that it equals that of Sumner or John Brown. The latter is that his action against slavery is not to be restrained by the Constitution of the United States, as interpreted by the Supreme Court of the United States. If you can find any degree of hatred greater than that, I should like to see it. This is the sentiment of the chosen leader of the Black Republican party; and can you doubt that it is not entertained by every member of that party? You cannot, I think. He is a representative man; his sentiments are the sentiments of his party; his principles of political action are the principles of political action of his party. I insist, then, that it is true that at least the Republican party of the North hates slavery.

My next proposition is, that the Republican party is the North. That party is in a permanent majority there.

Here follow four paragraphs arguing that the North is permanently Republican.[30]

Is it true, then, that the North hates slavery? My next proposition is that in the past the North has, at every instant, invariably exerted against slavery, all the power which it had at that instant. The question merely was what was the amount of power it had to exert against it. They abolished slavery in that magnificent empire which you presented to the North; they abolished slavery in every Northern State, one after another; they abolished slavery in all the territory above the line of 36° 30', which comprised about one million square miles. They have endeavored to put the Wilmot Proviso upon all the other territories of the Union, and they succeeded in putting it upon the territories of Oregon and Washington. They have taken from slavery all the conquests of the Mexican war, and appropriated them to anti-slavery; and if one of our fugitives escapes into the States, they do all they can to make a free man of him; they maltreat his pursuers, and sometimes murder them. They make raids into your States with a view to raise insurrection, to destroy and murder indiscriminately all classes, ages and sexes, and when the perpetrators are caught and brought to punishment, half the North go into mourning. If some of the perpetrators escape, they are shielded by the authorities of Northern States—not by an irrepressible mob, but by the regularly organized authorities.

My next proposition is, that we have a right to argue from the past to the future and to say, that if in the past the North has done this, it will in the future abolish slavery, if it shall acquire the power to do so.

My next proposition is that the North is in the course of acquiring this power. Is that true? I say, gentlemen, that the North is acquiring that power by two processes, one of which is operating with great rapidity—that process is by the admission of new States. The public territory is capable of forming from twenty to thirty States of larger size than the average of the States now in the Union. This territory has now become Northern territory, and every State that comes into the Union will be a free State. We may rest assured, sir, that that is a fixed fact. The events in Kansas should satisfy every one of the truth of this. The other process is that by which some of our own slave States are becoming free States. In some of the slave States the slave population is actually on the decrease, and, I believe that in all of them it is relatively to the white population on the decrease. The census shows that slaves are decreasing in Delaware and Maryland; and that in the other States in the same parallel, the relative state of the decrease and increase is against the slave population. It is not wonderful that this should be so. The anti-slavery feeling has become so great at the North that the owners of slave property in these States have a presentiment that it is a doomed institution, and the instincts of self-interest impel them to get rid of doomed property. The consequence is, that slavery will go down lower and lower—until it gets to the bottom—the Cotton States.

What else could be expected. It has upon it the weight of the half of a Continent—and under the pressure of such a weight as that, it must continue to sink until it reaches the bottom, and with an ever increasing rapidity, for as it sinks the weight on it will ever increase. When it shall have reached the bottom, the time will have come when the North will have the power to amend the Constitution. And then she will amend it and abolish slavery.

My proposition is, then, I insist, true that the North is acquiring the power to abolish slavery in the Cotton States. We have seen that as soon as she acquires the power she will exercise it.

The next question, therefore, is, what kind of thing will that abolition be?

By the time such abolition comes, the black race in those States will be double of the white. Consequently as the majority, it will then go into political power; and those States will have black governors, black judges, black legislators, black juries, black witnesses, everything black.

Is it to be supposed that the white race will stand that? It is not a supposable case. Although not half so numerous, we may readily assume that war will break out everywhere like hidden fire, and it is probable that the white race, being superior in every respect, may at first push the other back.

The latter consequence will then call upon the General Government for aid to put down domestic violence, and that Government will obey the call and come down upon us with overwhelming numbers.

The consequence will be that our men will be all exterminated or expelled to wander as vagabonds over a hostile earth, and as for our women, their fate will be too horrible to contemplate even in fancy.

This is the meaning of abolition as it concerns the white race in the Cotton States.

But this is not all. The white race having been exterminated the land will go into the exclusive possession of the black, and will, in consequence, rapidly pass into the condition of St. Domingo, and become a howling wilderness. The North, looking on, will say to itself, this ought not to be, and mindful of its ancient principle, it will declare that this goodly land and the fullness thereof are the Lord's, and he made it not for these black heathen, but for his saints—and we are his saints. And they will take possession of it and exterminate the blacks. This the end will be that the Yankee will walk our soil as sole lord, having exterminated both us and our slaves.

This is what abolition in the Cotton States would be. Sir, can you blame us for flying to any measure to prevent this?

* * *

Virginia Secession Convention, "Resolutions," March 28–April 5, 1861.[31]

Virginia's secession convention had a Committee on Federal Relations that proposed fourteen resolutions, all adopted by the convention. Like the statements made by other states, Virginia emphasizes slavery. These resolutions were more moderate than in most other seceding states, however, for Virginia is still not ready to secede. About the territories, a division along the Missouri Compromise line would have satisfied Virginia. On April 17, spurred by the conquest of Fort Sumter, Virginia finally seceded, a decision ratified by referendum on May 23, 1861.

Resolution 1: Be it resolved and declared by the people of the State of Virginia in Convention assembled, That the States which composed the United States of America, when the Federal Constitution was formed were independent sovereignties, and in adopting that instrument the people of each State agreed to associate with the people of the other States, upon a footing of exact equality. It is the duty therefore, of the common Government to respect the rights of the States and the equality of the people thereof, and, within the just limits of the Constitution, to protect, with equal care, the great interests that spring from the institutions of each.

Resolution 2: African slavery is a vital part of the social system of the States wherein it exists, and as that form of servitude existed when the Union was formed, and the jurisdiction of the several States over it within their respective limits, was recognized by the Constitution, any interference to its prejudice by the federal authority, or by the authorities of other States, or by the people thereof, is in derogation from plain right, contrary to the Constitution, offensive and dangerous.

Resolution 3: The choice of functionaries of a common Government established for the common good, for the reason that they entertain opinions and avow purposes hostile to the institutions of some of the States, necessarily excludes the people of one section from participation in the administration of Government, subjects the weaker to the domination of the stronger section, leads to abuse, and is incompatible with the safety of those whose interests are imperiled; the formation therefore, of geographical or sectional parties in respect to Federal politics is contrary to the principles on which our systems rests, and tends to its overthrow.

Resolution 4: The Territories of the United States constitute a trust to be administered by the General Government, for the common benefit of the people of the several States, and any policy in respect to such Territories calculated to confer greater benefits on the people of one part of the United States, than on the people of another part, is contrary to equality and prejudicial to the rights of some for whose equal benefits the trust was created. If the equal admission of slave labor and free labor into any Territory, excites unfriendly conflict between the systems, a fair partition of the Territories ought to be made between them, and each system ought to be protected within the limits assigned to it, by the laws necessary for its proper development.

Resolution 5: The sites of the federal forts, arsenals, &c., within the limits of the States of this Union, were acquired by the Federal Government, and jurisdiction over them ceded by the States, as trusts, for the common purposes of the Union during its continuance; and upon the separation of the States, such jurisdiction reverts of right to the States, respectively, by which the jurisdiction was ceded. Whilst a State remains in the Union, the legitimate use of such forts, &c., is to protect the country against foreign force. To use, or prepare them to be used to intimidate a State, or constrain its free action, is a perversion of the purposes for which they were obtained; they were not intended to be used against the States, in whose limits they are found, in the event of civil war. In a time of profound peace with foreign nations, and when no symptoms of domestic insurrection appear—but whilst irritating questions of the deepest importance are pending between the States—to accumulate within the limits of a State, interested in such questions, an unusual amount of troops and munitions of war, not required for any legitimate purpose, is unwise, impolitic and offensive.

Resolution 6: Deeply deploring the present distracted condition of the country, and lamenting the wrongs that have impelled some of the States to dissolve their connection with the Federal Government, but sensible of the blessings of the Union, and impressed with its importance to the peace, prosperity and progress of the people, we earnestly desire, that an adjustment may be reached by which the Union may be re-established in its integrity, and peace, prosperity and fraternal feelings be restored throughout the land.

Resolution 7: To remove the existing causes of complaint much may be accomplished by the Federal and State Governments; the laws for the rendition of fugitives from labor and of fugitives from justice shall be made more effectual, the expenditures of the Government may be reduced within more moderate limits and the abuses that have entered into the Administrative departments reformed. The State authorities may repeal their unfriendly and unconstitutional legislation, and substitute in its stead such as becomes the comity and is due to the rights of the States of the same Union. But to restore the Union and preserve confidence, the Federal Constitution should be amended in those particulars wherein experience has exhibited defects and discovered approaches dangerous to the institutions of some of the States.

Resolution 8: The people of Virginia recognize the American principle that government is founded in the consent of the governed, and the right of the people of the several States of this Union, for just causes, to withdraw from their association under the Federal Government with the people of the other States, and to erect new governments for their better security, and they will never consent that the Federal power, which is in part their power, shall be exerted for the purpose of subjugating the people of such States to the Federal authority.

Resolutions 9–14 implore the seceded states and the federal government to avoid military action. At this point, Virginia still hopes to negotiate a way out of this crisis. Meanwhile, it plans to meet with representatives from nonseceded slave states like Kentucky, Maryland, and Missouri. When Confederates opened fire on Fort Sumter on April 12, a wave of Southern nationalist sentiment in Virginia ended these initiatives.

* * *

Arkansas Secession Convention, "Resolutions," March 11, 1861.[32]

Like Virginia, Arkansas was not ready to secede when it passed a series of resolutions giving its reasons. In mid-March, its convention was still trying to entice the Deep South back into the Union by persuading Northern states to pass a series of constitutional amendments protecting slavery forever.[33] On May 6, a month after Sumter, the convention finally passed its ordinance of secession, referencing as causes these resolutions, as well as castigating Lincoln for calling up an army to prevent secession. Like South Carolina's "Declaration," Arkansas's resolutions attack free states for interfering with the recovery of fugitive slaves, disallowing slave transit, and letting African Americans vote, and cite the rise of a sectional Republican Party and its opposition to slavery in the territories.

We, the people of the State of Arkansas, in convention assembled, in view of the unfortunate and distracted condition of our once happy and prosperous country, and of the alarming dissentions existing between the northern and southern sections thereof; and desiring that a fair and equitable adjustment of the same may be made; do hereby declare the following to be just cause of complaint on the part of the people of the southern states, against their brethren of the northern, or non-slaveholding states:

1. People of the northern states have organized a political party, purely sectional in character, the central and controlling idea of which is, hostility to the institution of African slavery, as it exists in the southern states, and that party has elected a President and Vice President of the United States, pledged to administer the government upon principles inconsistent with the rights, and subversive of the interests of the people of the southern states.

2. They have denied to the people of the southern states the right to an equal participation in the benefits of the common territories of the Union, by refusing them the same protection to their slave property therein that is afforded to other property, and by declaring that no more slave states shall be admitted into the Union.

3. They have declared that Congress possesses, under the constitution, and ought to exercise, the power to abolish slavery in the territories, in the District of Columbia, and in the forts, arsenals and dock yards of the United States, within the limits of the slaveholding states.

4. They have, in disregard of their constitutional obligation, obstructed the faithful execution of the fugitive slave laws by enactments of their state legislatures.

5. They have denied the citizens of southern states the right of transit through non-slaveholding states with their slaves, and the right to hold them temporarily sojourning therein.

6. They have degraded American citizens by placing them upon an equality with negroes at the ballot box.

They have, by their prominent men and leaders, declared the doctrine of the irrepressible conflict, or the assertion of the principle that the institution of slavery is incompatible with freedom; that both cannot exist at once; that this continent must be wholly free, or wholly slave. They have in one or more instances refused to surrender negro thieves to the constitutional demand of the constituted authority of a sovereign state.

1. To redress the grievances hereinbefore complained of, and as a means of restoring harmony and fraternal good will between the people of all the states, the following amendments to the constitution of the United States are proposed:

2. The President and Vice President of the United States shall each be chosen alternatively from a slaveholding and non-slaveholding state—but, in no case, shall both be chosen from slaveholding or non-slaveholding states.

3. In all the territory of the United States now held, or which may hereafter be acquired, situated north of latitude 36 deg. 30 min., slavery or involuntary servitude, except as a punishment for crime is prohibited while such territory shall remain under territorial government. In all territory now held, or which may hereafter be acquired, south of said line of latitude, slavery of the African race is hereby recognized as existing and shall not be interfered with by Congress, but shall be protected as property by all the departments of the territorial government, during its continuance. And when any territory, north or south of said line, within such boundaries as Congress may prescribe, shall contain the population requisite for a member of Congress, according to the then federal ratio of representation of the people of the United States, it shall, if its form of government be republican, be admitted into the Union on an equal footing with the original states, with or without slavery, as the constitution of such new state may provide.

4. Congress shall have no power to legislate upon the subject of slavery, except to protect the citizen in his right of property in slaves.

5. That in addition to the provisions of third paragraph of the second section of the fourth article of the constitution of the United States, Congress shall have power to provide, by law, and it shall be its duty so to provide, that the United States shall pay to the owner, who shall apply for it, the full value of his fugitive slave, in all cases, when the marshal, or other officer, whose duty it was to arrest said fugitive, was prevented from doing so by violence; or when, after arrest, said fugitive was rescued by force, and the owner thereby prevented and obstructed in the pursuit of his remedy for the recovery of his fugitive slave under the same clause of the constitution and the laws made in pursuance thereof. And in all such cases, when the United States shall pay for such fugitive, she shall have the right, in their own name, to sue the county in which said violence, intimidation or rescue was committed, and to recover from it, with interests and damages, the amount paid by them for said fugitive slave. And the said county, after it has paid said amount to the United States, may, for its indemnity, sue and recover from the wrongdoers or rescuers, by whom the owner was prevented from the recovery of his fugitive slave, in like manner as the owner himself might have sued and recovered.

6. The third paragraph, of the second section of the fourth article of the constitution, shall not be construed to prevent any of the states from having concurrent jurisdiction with the United States, by appropriate legislation, and through the section of their judicial and ministerial officers, from enforcing the delivery of fugitives from labor to the person to whom the such service or labor is due.

7. Citizens of slaveholding states when traveling through, or temporarily sojourning with their slaves in non-slaveholding states, shall be protected in their right of property in such slaves.

8. The elective franchise, and the right to hold office, whether federal, state, territorial or municipal, shall not be exercised by persons of the African race, in whole or in part.

9. These amendments, and the third paragraph of the second section of the first article of the constitution, and the third paragraph of the second section of the fourth article thereof, shall not be amended or abolished, without the consent of all the states.

That the sense of the people of the United States may be taken upon the amendments above proposed;

1. Resolved by the people of Arkansas in Convention assembled, That we recommend the calling of a convention of the states of the Federal Union, at the earliest practicable day, in accordance with the provisions of the fifth article of the constitution of the United States.

2. Resolved further, That a committee of three delegates of this convention be appointed, whose duty it shall be to lay before the President and Congress of

the United States, and before governors and legislatures of the several states, a copy of these proceedings.

3. Resolved further, That looking to the call of a national convention, as recommended in the first resolution above, this convention elect five delegates to represent the State of Arkansas in such convention.

4. Resolved further, That a committee of five delegates of this convention be appointed to prepare an address to the people of the United States, urging upon them the importance of a united effort on the part of the patriotic citizens of all sections and parties to save the country from the dangers which impend it, and which threaten its destruction—and especially to arrest the reckless and fanatical spirit of sectionalism north and south, which, if not arrested, will inevitably involve us in a bloody civil war.

Mr. Grace moved that the resolutions be received, and that 200 copies be printed for the use of the convention; which motion prevailed.

* * *

ISHAM HARRIS (1818–97), GOVERNOR OF TENNESSEE, "MESSAGE TO THE LEGISLATURE," JANUARY 7, 1861.[34]

Tennessee governor Isham Harris sent a prosecession message to the legislature on December 8, 1860, calling on it to meet on January 7 to consider seceding. The legislature in turn authorized a referendum on whether to call a secession convention. In February, the state voted against the idea. Then came Sumter and Lincoln's call for troops. Noting the impact of the Confederate capture of Sumter on Southern opinion, one Tennessee historian wrote in 1898, "The bombardment of Fort Sumter was a deliberate move on [the part of Confederate leaders] for the purpose of strengthening their cause by the secession of the border states."[35] On May 6, the legislature approved a new ordinance calling for secession, not for a convention, and sent it to the voters. A month later, they passed it.[36] On May 9, while still awaiting the action of the people, the Tennessee legislature sent a "Legislative Address to the People of Tennessee," effectively seceding. It ended, "Tennessee has taken her position and has proudly determined to throw her banners to the breeze, and will give her strength to the sacred cause of freedom for the WHITE MAN OF THE SOUTH."[37]

Since Tennessee did not call a convention, it constructed no statement of causes, of course. Governor Harris's message to the legislature does tell why he is calling upon it to secede and thus constitutes such a statement. Harris is outraged by: "the systematic, wanton, and long continued agitation of the slavery question," the growth of a sectional party, and Northern states' "refusal to deliver up the fugitive," and agrees with *Dred Scott* that Congress cannot restrict slavery anywhere. But Harris also adds some unusual complaints:

• "It"—by which he refers to the abolitionist party—"excluded . . . the Southern people from California." This is a reach, since the Republican Party had not been born when California became a state and since pro-

Southern settlers in California at the time agreed that it should become a free state.
- Congress would not admit Kansas under its proslavery constitution. Yet the fraudulent vote for that constitution so upset Kansas's own territorial governor, Robert Walker, a slaveowner from Mississippi, that he resigned when the Buchanan administration accepted it.
- "It has burned the towns, poisoned the cattle, and conspired with the slaves to depopulate Northern Texas." This charge refers to a spate of fires in and around Dallas during the summer of 1860, which a Dallas newspaper editor blamed on abolitionist Northern preachers who had allegedly stirred up local slaves. Historian Donald Reynolds calls this a hoax designed to persuade white Southerners in wavering states to push for secession.[38]

The ninth section of the third article of the Constitution, provides that, on extraordinary occasions, the Governor may convene the General Assembly. Believing the emergency contemplated, to exist at this time, I have called you together. . . .

The systematic, wanton, and long continued agitation of the slavery question, with the actual and threatened aggressions of the Northern States and a portion of their people, upon the well-defined constitutional rights of the Southern citizen; the rapid growth and increase, in all the elements of power, of a purely sectional party, whose bond of union is uncompromising hostility to the rights and institutions of the fifteen Southern States, have produced a crisis in the affairs of the country. . . .

The Constitution distinctly recognises *property* in slaves—makes it the duty of the States to deliver the fugitive to his owner, but contains no grant of power to the Federal Government to interfere with this species of property, except "the power coupled with the duty," common to all civil Governments, to protect the rights of *property*, as well as those of *life* and *liberty*, of the citizen, which clearly appears from the exposition given to that instrument by the Supreme Court of the United States in the case of Dred Scott vs. Sandford. In delivering the opinion of the Court, Chief Justice Taney said:

"Now, as we have already said in an earlier part of this opinion, upon a different point, *the right of property in a slave is distinctly and expressly affirmed in the Constitution*."

"And no word can be found in the Constitution which gives Congress a greater power over slave property, or which entitles property of that kind to less protection than property of any other description. *The only power conferred, is the power coupled with the duty, of guarding and protecting the owner in his rights*."

. . . At first the anti-slavery cloud, which now overshadows the nation, was no larger than a man's hand. Most of you can remember, with vivid distinctness, those days of brotherhood, when throughout the whole North, the abolitionist was justly regarded as an enemy of his country. Weak, diminutive and contemptible as was this party in the purer days of the Republic, it has now grown to colossal proportions, and its recent rapid strides to power, have given it possession of the present House of Representatives, and elected one of its leaders to the Presidency of the United States; and in the progress of events, the Senate and Supreme Court must also soon pass into the hands of this party—a party upon whose revolutionary banner is inscribed, "No more slave States, no more slave Territory, no return of the fugitive to his master"—an "irrepressible conflict" between the Free and Slave States; "and whether it be long or short, peaceful or bloody, the struggle shall go on, until the sun shall not rise upon a master or set upon a slave."

Nor is this all; it seeks to appropriate to itself, and to exclude the slaveholder from the territory acquired by the common blood and treasure of all the States.

It has, through the instrumentality of Emigrant Aid Societies, under State patronage, flooded the Territories with its minions, armed with Sharp's rifles and bowie knives, seeking thus to accomplish, by intimidation, violence and murder, what it could not do by constitutional legislation.

It demanded, and from our love of peace and devotion to the Union, unfortunately extorted in 1819–20, a concession which excluded the South from about half the territory acquired from France.

It demanded, and again received, as a peace offering in 1845, all of that part of Texas, North of 36° 30' North latitude, if at any time the interest of the people thereof shall require a division of her territory.

It would submit to nothing less than a compromise in 1850, by which it dismembered that State, and remanded a territorial condition a considerable portion of its territory South of 36 30.

It excluded, by the same Compromise, the Southern people from California, whose mineral wealth, fertility of soil, and salubrity of climate, is not surpassed on earth; by prematurely forcing her into the Union under a Constitution, conceived in fraud by a set of adventurers, in the total absence of any law authorizing the formation of a Constitution, fixing the qualification of voters, regulating the time, place, or manner of electing delegates, or the time or place of the meeting of such Convention. Yet all these irregular and unauthorized proceedings were sanctified by the fact that the Constitution prohibited slavery, and forever closed the doors of that rich and desirable territory against the Southern people. And while the Southern mind was still burning under a humiliating sense of this wrong, it refused to admit Kansas into the Union upon a Constitution, framed by authority of Congress, and by delegates elected in conformity to law, upon the ground that slavery was recognized and protected.

It claims the constitutional right to abolish slavery in the District of Columbia, the forts, arsenals, dock-yards and other places ceded to the United States, within the limits of slaveholding States.

It proposes a prohibition of the slave trade between the States, thereby crowding the slaves together and preventing their exit South, until they become unprofitable to an extent that will force the owner finally to abandon them in self-defence.

It has, by the deliberate Legislative enactment of a large majority of the Northern States, openly and flagrantly nullified that clause of the Constitution which provides that:

"No person held to service or labor in one State under the laws thereof, escaping into another, shall, in consequence of any law or regulation therein, be discharged from such service or labor, but shall be delivered up on claim of the party to whom such service or labor may be due." . . .

He denounces Ohio for failing to comply with the fugitive slave clause. Then, again using "It" to refer to "the abolitionist party," he continues his list of complaints.[39]

It has, through the executive authority of other States, denied extradition of murderers and marauders.

It obtained its own compromise in the Constitution to continue the importation of slaves, and now sets up a law, higher than the Constitution, to destroy this property imported and sold to us by their fathers.

It has caused the murder of owners in pursuit of their fugitive slaves, and shielded the murderers from punishment.

It has, upon many occasions, sent its emissaries into the Southern States to corrupt our slaves; induce them to run off, or excite them to insurrection.

It has run off slave property by means of the "under-ground railroad," amounting in value to millions of dollars, and thus made the tenure by which slaves are held in the border States so precarious as to materially impair their value.

It has, by its John Brown and Montgomery raids, invaded sovereign States and murdered peaceable citizens.

It has justified and "exalted to the highest honors of admiration, the horrid murders, arsons, and rapine of the John Brown raid, and has canonized the felons as saints and martyrs."

It has burned the towns, poisoned the cattle, and conspired with the slaves to depopulate Northern Texas.

It has, through certain leaders, proclaimed to the slaves the terrible motto, "Alarm to the sleep, fire to the dwellings, poison to the food and water of slaveholders."

It has repudiated and denounced the decision of the Supreme Court.

It has assailed our rights as guaranteed by the plainest provisions of the Constitution, from the floor of each house of Congress, the pulpit, the hustings, the school room, their State Legislatures, and through the public press, dividing and disrupting churches, political parties, and civil governments.

It has, in the person of the President elect, asserted the equality of the *black* with the *white race*.

These are some of the wrongs against which we have remonstrated for more than a quarter of a century, hoping, but in vain, for their redress, until some of our sister States, in utter despair of obtaining justice at the hands of these lawless confederates, have resolved to sever the ties which have bound them together, and maintain those rights out of the Union, which have been the object of constant attack and encroachment within it. . . .

We omit five paragraphs about submitting to the people the question of whether to hold a convention to determine what to do and nine paragraphs proposing constitutional amendments that might save the Union by enshrining slavery forever.

With these amendments to the Constitution, I should feel that our rights were reasonably secure, not only in theory, but in fact, and should indulge the hope of living in the Union in peace. Without these, or some other amendments, which promise an equal amount and certainty of security, there is no hope of peace or security in the government.

If the non-slaveholding States refuse to comply with a demand, so just and reasonable; refuse to abandon at once and forever their unjust war upon us, our institutions and our rights; refuse, as they have heretofore done, to perform, in good faith, the obligations of the compact of union, much as we may appreciate the power, prosperity, greatness, and glory of this government; deeply as we deplore the existence of causes which have already driven one State from the Union; much as we may regret the imperative necessity which they have wantonly and wickedly forced upon us, every consideration of self preservation and self-respect require that we should assert and maintain our "equality in the Union, or independence out of it."

In my opinion, the only mode left us of perpetuating the Union upon the principles of justice and equality, upon which it was originally established, is by the Southern States, identified as they are, in interest, sentiment and feeling, and must, in the natural course of events, share a common destiny, uniting in the expression of a fixed and unalterable resolve, that the rights guaranteed by the Constitution must be *respected*, and *fully* and *perfectly* secured in the present Government, or asserted and maintained in a homogenous Confederacy of Southern States. . . .

Harris closes with several paragraphs that evoke possible alternatives, from compromise to war. He then reports on the number and readiness of the state militia for a possible military conflict and afterward discusses the problems of crop failures and the failure of banks in Tennessee.

* * *

John W. Ellis (1820–61), Governor of North Carolina, "Proclamation," April 17, 1861.[40]

The last state to secede, North Carolina, issued no statement of causes.[41] Its secession ordinance, passed on May 20, 1861, simply took the state out of the Union in response to war preparations by the federal government. The governor's proclamation calling the legislature into session terms Lincoln's call for troops a "high-handed act of tyrannical outrage."

WHEREAS: By Proclamation of Abraham Lincoln, President of the United States, followed by a requisition of Simon Cameron, Secretary of War, I am informed that the said Abraham Lincoln has made a call for 75,000 men to be employed for the invasion of the peaceful homes of the South, and for the violent subversions of the liberties of a free people, constituting a large part of the whole population of the late United States: And, whereas, this high-handed act of tyrannical outrage is not only in violation of all constitutional law, in utter disregard of every sentiment of humanity and Christian civilization, and conceived in a spirit of aggression unparalleled by any act of recorded history, but is a direct step towards the subjugation of the whole South, and the conversion of a free Republic, inherited from our fathers, into a military despotism, to be established by worse than foreign armies on the ruins of our once glorious Constitution of Equal Rights.

Now, therefore, I, John W. Ellis, Governor of the State of North-Carolina, for these extraordinary causes, do herby issue this, my Proclamation, notifying and requesting the Senators and Members of the House of Commons of the General Assembly of North-Carolina, to meet in Special Session at the Capitol, in the City of Raleigh, on Wednesday the first of May next. And I furthermore exhort all good citizens throughout the State to be mindful that their first allegiance is due to the Sovereignty which protects their homes and dearest interests, as their first service is due for the sacred defence of their hearths, and of the soil which holds the graves of our glorious dead.

United action in defence of the sovereignty of North-Carolina, and of the rights of the South, becomes now the duty of all.

CHAPTER 3

CIVIL WAR (1861–1865)

As the Confederacy got under way, like other representatives from seceded states, Jefferson Davis had to choose whether to stay in or resign from Congress. As he makes clear in his valedictory, his decision was easy, since he had advised his home state of Mississippi to secede. He then uses his farewell speech to woo those slave states—Missouri, Arkansas, Kentucky, Tennessee, Maryland, North Carolina, and above all Virginia—that had not yet joined. His "Message to the Confederate Congress about Ratification of the Constitution," two weeks after the Confederacy took Fort Sumter, similarly incorporates a prosecession summary of constitutional history, arguing that it is a state's right. Both speeches make crystal clear that secession was for slavery.

In some ways, the two governments were quite similar. Confederates modeled their constitution after the U.S. Constitution and did not materially alter the balance of power between state and federal governments. The new constitution does guarantee the right to own slaves in every state and territory, regardless of local sentiment, including territory to be gained in the future. Alexander Stephens, vice president of the Confederacy, spends the first paragraphs of his famous "Cornerstone Speech," included here, explaining the ways that he believes the Confederate Constitution is better than the U.S. Constitution. Then he reaches its key "improvement," to which he devotes the most attention: "Our new Government is founded upon . . . the great truth that the negro is not equal to the white man; that slavery—subordination to the superior race—is his natural and moral condition."

Another difference was in their treatment of dissent. Neo-Confederates today make much of Abraham Lincoln's crackdown on civil liberties during the war. Some even sell T-shirts of his image with a red "no parking" slash over it and the words "Sic semper tyrannis" (see page 370 for an example). The Ludwig von Mises Institute, a neo-Confederate think tank, characterizes Lincoln's leadership as "totalitarian methods of wartime governance." Lincoln indeed suspended habeas corpus, especially in Maryland, against people some of whom were "guilty of little more than southern sympathies," in the words of historian James McPherson. But the Confederacy proved more tyrannical. Historian John Majewski points out, "The Confederacy owned key industries, regulated prices and wages, and instituted the most far-reaching draft in North America." He calls the police power of the Confederate state "staggering." Every railroad passenger "needed a special government pass," for example. According to political scientist Richard Bensel, "a central state as well-organized and powerful as the Confederacy did not emerge until the New Deal and subsequent mobilization for World War II."[1]

Confederates severely curtailed civil liberties. On March 1, 1862, Jefferson Davis declared martial law in Richmond and some other cities. Confederate authorities rounded up hundreds of civilians suspected of disloyalty and locked them in two Richmond warehouses converted to prisons. Everywhere, Confederates treated dissenters much more harshly than did the Union. On occasion, Confederates rounded up and murdered citizens suspected of favoring the United States. In October 1862, for example, Confederate militia scattered through Cooke County and neighboring parts of North Texas, arresting more than 200 people. Without trial, they hanged at least 42 "for conspiring to commit treason and foment insurrection"—the largest mass hanging in American history. Nor was Texas unusual. In northwest Alabama, Robert Guttery recalled that it was common "for Union men to be arrested, put in the county jail, others sent to military prisons, some hung and others shot."[2] Nor were these isolated acts; we include instructions by Arkansas governor H. M. Rector to arrest citizens guilty of statements of loyalty to the United States and bring them to him, possibly to face execution.

The Confederate flag differed from the U.S. flag as well, of course, but initially they shared some elements. Most Americans think that the battle flag of Lee's Army of Northern Virginia, also adopted by some other units, was "the Confederate flag." It wasn't. The battle flag was not flown on ships, the capitol, or other government buildings. Confederates chose their first official flag, the "Stars and Bars," partly because it did *not* differ radically from the U.S. flag. They flew it atop forts and ships for two years, but its resemblance to the U.S. flag created confusion on the battlefield. Confederates adopted their second national flag, the "Stainless Banner," partly because it was so white, as editorials in the *Savannah Morning News* make clear.

The Confederacy also differed in its treatment of African Americans. U.S. enlistment of black troops set off a firestorm of criticism in Dixie. We include responses by Jefferson Davis, the Confederate Congress, General Edmund Kirby Smith, and a major Arkansas newspaper, all proclaiming death or enslavement to African American prisoners of war and death to their white officers. In practice, some Confederates committed the war crime of murdering black prisoners and their officers; others treated them like common POWs.[3]

Crucial to Confederate success would have been recognition by other nations, especially Great Britain and France. Diplomats reported that emphasizing slavery as the reason for secession won them no traction in Europe. Nor were Southern religious justifications for slavery likely to work; clerics had spearheaded England's abolition of slavery in 1833. Henry Hotze, Confederate agent in London, responded by invoking the new "scientific racism." This line of thinking would grow more important to neo-Confederates in decades to come.

The Confederacy never won recognition as a nation. By the end of 1864, its situation had become dire. Three months before his surrender to Grant, Robert E. Lee suggested giving up slavery if doing so would help the cause of independence. Neo-Confederates today often portray Lee as opposed to slavery, but in his letter to a member of the Virginia legislature, Lee begins by stating that slavery is the "best" relationship "that can exist between the white and black races while intermingled as at present in this country." He suggests emancipation only because it is happening anyway and will be less "pernicious" if done by the South.[4] In one of its last acts, the Confederacy allowed for black soldiers, while still trying to hold on to slavery for the mass of African Americans.

The Civil War transformed attitudes among many white citizens and leaders in the North. As they saw how black enlisted men performed and learned about the help black civilians gave Union armies and POWs, most members of U.S. armed forces came to favor abolition. Many went further and supported equal rights. The Emancipation Proclamation meant that soldiers and sailors were now fighting for black freedom as well as national unity; hence cognitive dissonance also worked to soften white Northern attitudes about black people. Nothing comparable took place in the Confederacy. To be sure, the prowess of black men of war impressed some Southern soldiers and officers, but other Southerners came to despise African Americans; they realized many slaves had only feigned love for their owners and had run off as soon as Union forces approached. At war's end, slavery was over, but conflict over white supremacy had only begun.

* * *

JEFFERSON DAVIS (1808–89), "FAREWELL TO THE U.S. SENATE," JANUARY 21, 1861.[5]

In the words of the Senate website, this speech is "one of the most dramatic events ever enacted in the chamber of the United States Senate." The galleries were packed; every senator was in his seat. Davis was the "acknowledged leader of the South in Congress." His position was well known; he had been one of the "fire eaters" advising his home state of Mississippi to secede. He aimed this speech not only at his Senate colleagues, to whom he voiced courteous words of parting, but also at Southern leaders like Robert E. Lee who were wavering about secession. To them, he argues that secession is clearly a state's right and that the Republican emphasis on the equality of all races makes it a necessity. He overstates both cases: the next selection discusses secession in more detail, and most Republicans were far from ready to grant African Americans equal rights.[6]

I rise, Mr. President, for the purpose of announcing to the Senate that I have satisfactory evidence that the State of Mississippi, by a solemn ordinance of her people, in convention assembled, has declared her separation from the United States. Under these circumstances, of course, my functions are terminated here. It has seemed to me proper, however, that I should appear in the Senate to announce that fact to my associates, and I will say but very little more. The occasion does not invite me to go into argument; and my physical condition would not permit me to do so, if it were otherwise; and yet it seems to become me to say something on the part of the State I here represent on an occasion as solemn as this.

It is known to Senators who have served with me here that I have for many years advocated, as an essential attribute of State sovereignty, the right of a State to secede from the Union. Therefore, if I had thought that Mississippi was acting without sufficient provocation, or without an existing necessity, I should still, under my theory of the Government, because of my allegiance to the State of which I am a citizen, have been bound by her action. I, however, may be permitted to say that I do think she has justifiable cause, and I approve of her act. I conferred with her people before that act was taken, counseled them then that, if the state of things which they apprehended should exist when their Convention met, they should take the action which they have now adopted.

I hope none who hear me will confound this expression of mine with the advocacy of the right of a State to remain in the Union, and to disregard its constitutional obligation by the nullification of the law. Such is not my theory. Nullification and secession, so often confounded, are, indeed, antagonistic principles. Nullification is a remedy which it is sought to apply within the Union, against the agent of the States. It is only to be justified when the agent has violated his constitutional obligations, and a State, assuming to judge for itself, denies the right of the agent thus to act, and appeals to the other states of the Union for a decision; but, when the States themselves and when the people of the States have so acted as to convince us that they will not regard our constitutional rights, then, and then for the first time, arises the doctrine of secession in its practical application.

A great man who now reposes with his fathers, and who has often been arraigned for want of fealty to the Union, advocated the doctrine of nullification because it preserved the Union. It was because of his deep-seated attachment to the Union—his determination to find some remedy for existing ills short of a severance of the ties which bound South Carolina to the other States—that Mr. Calhoun advocated the doctrine of nullification, which he proclaimed to be peaceful, to be within the limits of State power, not to disturb the Union, but only to be a means of bringing the agent before the tribunal of the States for their judgment.[7]

Secession belongs to a different class of remedies. It is to be justified upon the basis that the states are sovereign. There was a time when none denied it. I hope the time may come again when a better comprehension of the theory of our Government, and the inalienable rights of the people of the States, will prevent any one from denying that each State is a sovereign, and thus may reclaim the grants which it has made to any agent whomsoever.

I, therefore, say I concur in the action of the people of Mississippi, believing it to be necessary and proper, and should have been bound by their action if my belief had been otherwise; and this brings me to the important point which I wish, on this last occasion, to present to the Senate. It is by this confounding of nullification and secession that the name of a great man whose ashes now mingle with his mother earth has been invoked to justify coercion against a seceded State. The phrase, "to execute the laws," was an expression which General Jackson applied to the case of a State refusing to obey the laws while yet a member of the Union. That is not the case which is now presented. The laws are to be executed over the United States, and upon the people of the United States. They have no relation to any foreign country. It is a perversion of terms—at least, it is a great misapprehension of the case—which cites that expression for application to a State which has withdrawn from the Union.[8] You may make war on a foreign state. If it be the purpose of gentlemen, they may make war against a State which has withdrawn from the Union; but there are no laws of the United States to be executed within the limits of a seceded State. A State, finding herself in the condition in which Mississippi has judged she is—in which her safety requires that she should provide for the maintenance of her rights out of the Union—surrenders all the benefits (and they are known to be many), deprives herself of the advantages (and they are known to be great), severs all the ties of affection (and they are close and enduring), which have bound her to the Union; and thus divesting herself of every benefit—taking upon herself every burden—she claims to be exempt from any power to execute the laws of the United States within her limits.

I well remember an occasion when Massachusetts was arraigned before the bar of the Senate, and when the doctrine of coercion was rife, and to be applied against her, because of the rescue of a fugitive slave in Boston. My opinion then was the same that it is now. Not in a spirit of egotism, but to show that I am not influenced in my opinions because the case is my own, I refer to that time and that occasion as containing the opinion which I then entertained, and on which my present conduct is based. I then said that if Massachusetts—following her purpose through a stated line of conduct—chose to take the last step, which separates her from the Union, it is her right to go, and I will neither vote one dollar nor one man to coerce her back; but I will say to her, Godspeed, in memory of the kind associations which once existed between her and the other States.

It has been a conviction of pressing necessity—it has been a belief that we are to be deprived in the Union of the rights which our fathers bequeathed to us—which has brought Mississippi to her present decision. She has heard proclaimed the theory that all men are created free and equal, and this made the basis of an attack upon her social institutions; and the sacred Declaration of Independence has been invoked to maintain the position of the equality of the races. That Declaration is to be construed by the circumstances and purposes for which it was made. The communities were declaring their independence; the people of those communities were asserting that no man was born—to use the language of Mr. Jefferson—booted and spurred, to ride over the rest of mankind; that men were created equal—meaning the men of the political community; that there was no divine right to rule; that no man inherited the right to govern; that there were no classes by which power and place descended to families; but that all stations were equally within the grasp of each member of the body politic. These were the great principles they announced; these were the purposes for which they made their declaration; these were the ends to which their enunciation was directed. They have no reference to the slave; else, how happened it that among the items of arraignment against George III was that he endeavored to do just what the North has been endeavoring of late to do, to stir up insurrection among our slaves? Had the Declaration announced that the negroes were free and equal, how was the prince to be arraigned for raising up insurrection among them? And how was this to be enumerated among the high crimes which caused the colonies to sever their connection with the mother-country? When our Constitution was formed, the same idea was rendered more palpable; for there we find provision made for that very class of persons as property; they were not put upon the equality of footing with white men— not even upon that of paupers and convicts; but, so far as representation was concerned, were discriminated against as a lower caste, only to be represented in the numerical proportion of three-fifths. So stands the compact which binds us together.[9]

Then, Senators, we recur to the principles upon which our Government was founded; and when you deny them, and when you deny us the right to withdraw from a Government which, thus perverted, threatens to be destructive of our rights, we but tread in the path of our fathers when we proclaim our independence and take the hazard. This is done, not in hostility to others, not to injure any section of the country, not even for our own pecuniary benefit, but from the high and solemn motive of defending and protecting the rights we inherited, and which it is our duty to transmit unshorn to our children.

I find in myself perhaps a type of the general feeling of my constituents towards yours. I am sure I feel no hostility toward you, Senators from the North. I am sure there is not one of you, whatever sharp discussion there may have been between us, to whom I cannot now say, in the presence of my God, I wish you well; and such, I feel, is the feeling of the people whom I represent toward those whom you represent. I, therefore, feel that I but express their desire when I say I hope, and they hope, for peaceable relations with you, though we must part. They may be mutually beneficial to us in the future, as they have been in the past, if you so will it. The reverse may bring disaster on every portion of the country, and, if you will have it thus, we will invoke the God of our fathers, who delivered them from the power of the lion, to protect us from the ravages of the bear; and thus, putting our trust in God and in our firm hearts and strong arms, we will vindicate the right as best we may.

In the course of my service here, associated at different times with a variety of Senators, I see now around me some with whom I have served long; there have been points of collision, but, whatever of offense there has been to me, I leave here. I carry with me no hostile remembrance. Whatever offense I have given which has not been redressed, or for which satisfaction has not been demanded, I have, Senators, in this hour of our parting, to offer you my apology for any pain which, in the heat of discussion, I have inflicted. I go hence unencumbered by the remembrance of any injury received, and having discharged the duty of making the only reparation in my power for any injury offered.

Mr. President and Senators, having made the announcement which the occasion seemed to me to require, it only remains for me to bid you a final adieu.

* * *

JEFFERSON DAVIS (1808–89), "MESSAGE TO THE CONFEDERATE CONGRESS ABOUT RATIFICATION OF THE CONSTITUTION," APRIL 29, 1861.[10]

Davis directed this message not so much to the Confederate Congress as to the people and leaders of the slave states that had yet to secede. After a paragraph announcing ratification of the Confederate Constitution, he sets forth "a brief review of the relations heretofore existing between us and the States which now unite in warfare against us."[11] He then argues the compact theory: that each state entered into the compact voluntarily, hence has the right to leave voluntarily. In 1851, running for governor, Davis had "denied secession as a constitutional right, holding it rather to be revolutionary." Readers will form their own conclusion as to the validity of the "compact theory" of the national union, which was debated then and is still debated today; footnotes provide some of the arguments made on the other side.[12] Even if Davis is correct and states *did* have the right to secede, his argument would supply only the "how" of secession, not the "why." After all, a "state's right" to secede cannot itself be a reason to secede.

Davis then moves to the "why," claiming that Republicans have "perverted" the federal government "into a machine for their control in . . . *domestic* affairs," meaning slavery (italics in the original). To this point, of course, the federal government had done nothing about slavery; Abraham Lincoln had been in office less than two months. As in one or two of the state secession documents, Davis also brings up the tariff, even though the South had not had a tariff issue for years. Many of his points are accurate, however, such as his claim that "negro slavery existed" in all but one of the thirteen original states. He exaggerates the extent of abolitionist activity and the success of the Underground Rail Road to make the case that slavery was threatened and secession was required to preserve it. Paradoxically, he paints a blissful picture of slave life, contradicted by his own emphasis on slave escapes and unrest, as well as by such other sources as slave narratives and spirituals. He also claims that from its founding, the Democratic Party countenanced secession, which would have been news to Democratic president Andrew

Jackson, who promised war upon South Carolina when it nullified a tariff and threatened to secede in 1833.

Gentlemen of the Congress: It is my pleasing duty to announce to you that the Constitution framed for the establishment of a permanent Government for the Confederate States has been ratified by conventions in each of those States to which it was referred. To inaugurate the Government in its full proportions and upon its own substantial basis of the popular will, it only remains that elections should be held for the designation of the officers to administer it. There is every reason to believe that at no distant day other States, identified in political principles and community of interests with those which your represent, will join this Confederacy, giving to its typical constellation increased splendor, to its Government of free, equal, and sovereign States a wider sphere of usefulness, and to the friends of constitutional liberty a greater security for its harmonious and perpetual existence. It was not, however, for the purpose of making this announcement that I have deemed it my duty to convoke you at an earlier day than that fixed by yourselves for your meeting. The declaration of war made against this Confederacy by Abraham Lincoln, the President of the United States, in his proclamation issued on the 15th day of the present month, rendered it necessary, in my judgment, that you should convene at the earliest practicable moment to devise the measures necessary for the defense of the country. The occasion is indeed an extraordinary one. It justifies me in a brief review of the relations heretofore existing between us and the States which now unite in warfare against us and in a succinct statement of the events which have resulted in this warfare, to the end that mankind may pass intelligent and impartial judgment on its motives and objects. During the war waged against Great Britain by her colonies on this continent a common danger impelled them to a close alliance and to the formation of a Confederation, by the terms of which the colonies, styling themselves States, entered "*severally* into a firm league of friendship with each other for their common defense, the security of their liberties, and their mutual and general welfare, binding themselves to assist each other against all force offered to or attacks made upon them, or any of them, on account of religion, sovereignty, trade, or any other pretense whatever."[13] In order to guard against any misconstruction of their compact, the several States made explicit declaration in a distinct article that "*each* State *retains its* sovereignty, freedom, and independence, and every power, jurisdiction, and right which is not by this Confederation *expressly delegated* to the United States in Congress assembled."

Under this contract of alliance, the war of the Revolution was successfully waged, and resulted in the treaty of peace with Great Britain in 1783, by the terms of which the several States were *each by name* recognized to be independent. The Articles of Confederation contained a clause whereby all alterations were prohibited unless confirmed by the Legislatures of *every State* after being agreed to by Congress; and in obedience to this provision, under the resolution of Congress of the 21st of February, 1787, the several States appointed delegates who attended a convention "for the *sole and express purpose* of revising the Articles of Confederation and reporting to Congress and the several Legislatures such alterations and provisions therein as shall, when agreed to in Congress *and confirmed by the States*, render the Federal Constitution adequate to the exigencies of Government and the preservation of the Union." It was by the delegates chosen by the *several States* under the resolution just quoted that the Constitution of the United States was framed in 1787 and submitted to the *several States* for ratification, as shown by the seventh article, which is in these words: "The ratification of the *conventions of nine States* shall be sufficient for the establishment of this Constitution *between the States* so ratifying the same." I have italicized certain words in the quotations just made for the purpose of attracting attention to the singular and marked caution with which the States endeavored in every possible form to exclude the idea that the separate and independent sovereignty of each State was merged into one common government and nation, and the earnest desire they evinced to impress on the Constitution its true character that of a compact between independent States.

The Constitution of 1787, having, however, omitted the clause already recited from the Articles of Confederation, which provided in explicit terms that each State *retained* its sovereignty and independence, some alarm was felt in the States, lest this omission should be construed into an abandonment of their cherished principle, and they refused to be satisfied until amendments were added to the Constitution placing beyond any pretense of doubt the reservation by the States of all their sovereign rights and powers not expressly delegated to the United States by the Constitution.[14]

Strange, indeed, must it appear to the impartial observer, but it is none the less true that all these carefully worded clauses proved unavailing to prevent the rise and growth in the Northern States of a political school which has persistently claimed that the government thus formed was not a compact *between* States, but was in effect a national government, set up *above* and *over* the States. An organization created by the States to secure the blessings of liberty and independence against *foreign* aggression, has been gradually perverted into a machine for their control in their *domestic* affairs.[15] The *creature* has been exalted above its *creators*; the *principals* have been made subordinate to the *agent* appointed by themselves.

The people of the Southern States, whose almost exclusive occupation was agriculture, early perceived a tendency in the Northern States to render the common government subservient to their own purposes by imposing burdens on commerce as a protection to their manufacturing and shipping interests. Long and angry controversies grew out of these attempts, often successful, to benefit one section of the country at the expense of the other. And the danger of disruption arising from this cause was enhanced by the fact that the Northern population was increasing, by immigration and other causes, in a greater ratio than the population of the South. By degrees, as the Northern States gained preponderance in the National Congress, self-interest taught their people to yield ready assent to any plausible advocacy of their right as a majority to govern the minority without control. They learned to listen with impatience to the suggestion of any constitutional impediment to the exercise of their will, and so utterly have the principles of the Constitution have been corrupted in the Northern mind that, in the inaugural address delivered by President Lincoln in March last, he asserts as an axiom, which he plainly deems to be undeniable, that the theory of the Constitution requires in all cases the majority shall govern;[16] and in another memorable instance the same Chief Magistrate did not hesitate to liken the relations between a State and the United States to those which exist between a county and a State in which it is situated and by which it was created.[17] This is the lamentable and fundamental error on which rests the policy that has culminated in his declaration of war against these Confederate States.[18]

In addition to the long continued and deep-seated resentment felt by the Southern States at the persistent abuse of the powers they had delegated to the Congress, for the purpose of enriching the manufacturing and shipping classes of the North at the expense of the South, there has existed for nearly half a century another subject of discord, involving interests of such transcendent magnitude as at all times to create the apprehension in the minds of many devoted lovers of the Union that its permanence was impossible.

When the several States delegated certain powers to the United States Congress, a large portion of the laboring population consisted of African slaves imported into the colonies by the mother country. In twelve out of the thirteen States negro slavery existed, and the right of property in slaves was protected by law. This property was recognized in the Constitution, and provision was made against its loss by the escape of the slave. The increase in the number of slaves by further importation from Africa was also secured by a clause forbidding Congress to prohibit the slave trade anterior to a certain date, and in no clause can there be found any delegation of power to the Congress authorizing it in any manner to legislate to the prejudice, detriment, or discouragement of the owners of that species of property, or excluding it from the protection of the Government.

The climate and soil of the Northern States soon proved unpropitious to the continuance of slave labor, whilst the converse was the case at the South. Under the unrestricted free intercourse between the two sections, the Northern States consulted their own interests by selling their slaves to the South and prohibiting slavery within their limits.[19] The South were willing purchasers of a property suitable to their wants, and paid the price of the acquisition without harboring a suspicion that their quiet possession was to be disturbed by those who were inhibited not only by want of constitutional authority, but by good faith as vendors, from disquieting a title emanating from themselves.

As soon, however, as the Northern States that prohibited African slavery within their limits had reached a number sufficient to give their representation a controlling voice in the Congress, a persistent and organized system of hostile measures against the rights of the owners of slaves in the Southern States was inaugurated and gradually extended. A continuous series of measures was devised and prosecuted for the purpose of rendering insecure the tenure of property in slaves. Fanatical organizations, supplied with money by voluntary subscription, were assiduously engaged in exciting amongst the slaves a spirit of discontent and revolt; means were furnished for their escape from their owners, and agents secretly employed to entice them to abscond; the constitutional provision for their rendition to their owners was first evaded, then openly denounced as a violation of conscientious compact; owners of slaves were mobbed and even murdered in open day solely for applying to a magistrate for the arrest of a fugitive slave; the dogmas of these voluntary organizations soon obtained control of the Legislatures of many of the Northern States, and laws were passed providing for the punishment, by ruinous fines and long-continued imprisonment in jails and penitentiaries, of citizens of the Southern States who should dare to ask aid of the officers of the law for the recovery of their property. Emboldened by success, the theatre of agitation and aggression against the clearly expressed constitutional rights of the Southern States was transferred to the Congress. Senators and Representatives were sent to the common councils of the nation, whose chief title to this distinction consisted in the display of a spirit of ultra fanaticism, and whose business was not "to promote the general welfare or insure domestic tranquility," but to awaken the bitterest hatred against the citizens of sister States by violent denunciation of their institutions; the transaction of public affairs was impeded by repeated by efforts to usurp powers not delegated by the Constitution, for the purpose of impairing the security of property in slaves, and reducing those States which held slaves to a condition of inferiority. Finally a great party was organized for the purpose of obtaining the administration of the Government with the avowed object of using its power for the total exclusion of the slave States from all participation in the benefits of the public domain acquired by all the States in common, whether by conquest or purchase; of surrounding them entirely by States in which slavery should be prohibited; of those rendering the property in slaves so insecure as to be comparatively worthless, and thereby annihilating in effect property worth thousands of millions of dollars. This party, thus organized, succeeded in the month of November last in the election of its candidate for the Presidency of the United States.

In the meantime, under the mild and genial climate of the Southern States and the increasing care and attention for the well-being and comfort of the laboring classes, dictated alike by interest and humanity, the African slaves had augmented in number from about 600,000, at the date of the adoption of the constitutional compact to upward of 4,000,000. In moral and social condition they had been elevated from brutal savages into docile, intelligent, and civilized agricultural laborers, and supplied not only with bodily comforts but with careful religious instruction. Under the supervision of a superior race their labor had been so directed as not only to allow a gradual and marked amelioration of their own condition, but to convert hundreds of thousands of square miles of the wilderness into cultivated lands covered with a prosperous people; towns and cities had sprung into existence, and had rapidly increased in wealth and population under the social system of the South; the white population of the Southern slaveholding States had augmented from about 1,250,000 at the date of the adoption of the Constitution to more than 8,500,000, in 1860; and the productions in the South of cotton, rice, sugar, and tobacco, for the full development and continuance of which the labor of African slaves was and is indispensable, had swollen to an amount which formed nearly three-fourths of the exports of the whole United States and had become absolutely necessary to the wants of civilized man.

With interests of such overwhelming magnitude imperiled, the people of the Southern States were driven by the conduct of the North to the adoption of some course of action to avert the danger with which they were openly menaced. With this view the Legislatures of the several States invited the people to select delegates to conventions to be held for the purpose of determining for themselves what measures were best adapted to meet so alarming a crisis in their history.

Here it may be proper to observe that from a period as early as 1798 there had existed in *all* of the States of the Union a party almost uninterruptedly in the majority based upon the creed that each State was, in the last resort, the sole judge as well of its wrongs as of the mode and measure of redress. Indeed, it is obvious that under the law of nations this principle is an axiom as applied to the relations of independent sovereign States, such as those which had united themselves under the constitutional compact. The Democratic party of the United States repeated, in its successful canvass in 1856, the declaration made in numerous previous political contests, that it would "faithfully abide by and uphold the principles laid down in the Kentucky and Virginia resolutions of 1798, and in the report of Mr. Madison to the Virginia Legislature in 1799; and that it adopts those principles as constituting one of the main foundations of its political creed."

The principles thus emphatically announced embrace that to which I have already adverted the right of each State to judge of and redress the wrongs of which it complains. These principles were maintained by overwhelming majorities of the people of all the States of the Union at different elections, especially in the elections of Mr. Jefferson in 1805, Mr. Madison in 1809, and Mr. Pierce in 1852.

In the exercise of a right so ancient, so well-established, and so necessary for self-preservation, the people of the Confederate States, in their conventions, determined that the wrongs which they had suffered and the evils with which they were menaced required that they should revoke the delegation of powers to the Federal Government which they had ratified in their several conventions. They consequently passed ordinances resuming all their rights as sovereign and independent States and dissolved their connection with the other States of the Union.

Having done this, they proceeded to form a new compact amongst themselves by new articles of confederation, which have been also ratified by the conventions of the several States with an approach to unanimity far exceeding that of the conventions which adopted the Constitution of 1787. They have organized their new Government in all its departments; the functions of the executive, legislative, and judicial magistrates are performed in accordance with the will of the people, as displayed not merely in a cheerful acquiescence, but in the enthusiastic support of the Government thus established by themselves; and but for the interference of the Government of the United States in this legitimate exercise of the right of a people to self-government, peace, happiness, and prosperity would now smile on our land. . . .

Davis then tells of the commissioners he sent to treat with the Lincoln administration, which refused to meet with them, since doing so would imply recognition of the Confederacy as a nation. Then he gives a history of the events leading up to Sumter intended to convince his listeners and readers that the Confederacy was forced to fire on the fort. (This argument work poorly, for the fact of firing made Confederates the aggressors. Nevertheless, most Southerners, even in wavering states like Virginia and Arkansas, took pride in the quick capture of the fort, which moved them closer to secession.) The rest of Davis's speech concerned mechanics of secession—shipbuilding, organizing governmental departments, securing forts, and sending ambassadors abroad.

* * *

The Constitution of the Confederate States of America, March 11, 1861.[20]

The Confederate Constitution incorporates most of the U.S. Constitution. Here we include only the major differences between the two, which we place in boldface.[21] Confederates adopted some interesting innovations, including a limit of one six-year term for the chief executive, a line-item veto, and seats for cabinet members in the legislature to explain their policies. Taking the Democratic side of an earlier Democrat/Whig debate, they ban using federal revenue for internal improvements and prohibit protective tariffs.[22] The postal service must be self-supporting within two years.

About states' rights, the Confederate Constitution does not reflect very much concern. Its preamble does make an important gesture in that direction, adding the italicized words: "We, the people of the Confederate States, *each State acting in its sovereign and independent character*, in order to form a permanent federal government."[23] However, preambles to constitutions rarely carry much jurisprudential force. As well, to what is the Ninth Amendment to the U.S. Constitution, the Confederate version adds the italicized words: "The enumeration in the Constitution, of certain rights, shall not be construed to deny or disparage others retained by the people *of the several States*." This phrase does occur elsewhere in the U.S. Constitution, however. Also, Confederate states can impeach federal district court judges who serve within them. On the other hand, the Confederate Constitution introduces federal qualifications for voting; the U.S. Constitution left these to the states.

More important than these details is what Confederates do *not* do. They leave intact the clauses in the U.S. Constitution that grant the federal government power over the states. Consider three examples:

• Article 1, §8, ¶3 in both constitutions reads: "[Congress has power] To regulate Commerce . . . among the several States." Before secession, slaveowners had worried that the national government might use that clause to justify regulating or ending the internal slave trade.

• More basic yet is Article 6, §1, ¶3 in the Confederate Constitution: "This Constitution, and the laws of the Confederate States made in pursuance thereof . . . shall be the supreme law of the land; and the judges in every State shall be bound thereby, anything in the constitution or laws of any State to the contrary notwithstanding." Again, Confederates inserted this clause unchanged.[24]

• Article 4, §2, ¶1 of the Confederate Constitution does not allow states to abolish slavery. The Confederacy thus denies states the key right that later apologists say drove it to secede: the right to decide whether or not to have slavery. Clearly the new government cares more about slavery than states' rights.

• The new constitution also incorporates Article 1, §8, ¶15: "[Congress has power] To provide for calling forth the militia to execute the laws of the Confederate States, suppress insurrections." Thus the Confederacy preserves the same language to combat secession that Lincoln would use against it. Moreover, by adding to its first sentence "to form a *permanent* federal government," the new preamble implicitly denies secession as a state's right.[25]

The biggest changes in the new document treat slavery. The Confederate Constitution guarantees the rights of slaveowners in every state and territory, regardless of what that state or territory itself might desire. It guarantees the right of slave transit: even if the Confederacy some day were to include a free state, carrying slaves into that state still would not free them. And it uses the word "slaves"; the U.S. Constitution substituted euphemisms like "other persons." Most important, except by constitutional amendment, Article 1, §9, ¶4 protects slavery forever: "No bill of attainder, ex post facto law, or law denying or impairing the right of property in negro slaves shall be passed."

Interestingly, the new constitution bans the international slave trade except with the United States and grants Congress power to prohibit that trade as well. In the late 1850s, proslavery politicians had made noises about reopening the international trade, but now that they had the chance, they backed off. Two considerations precluded such a move. First, Confederate leaders sought recognition from European nations, which would never happen if the Confederacy reopened the Atlantic slave trade. Second, when it adopted its constitution, the Confederacy consisted of just the Deep South states. Its leaders desperately hoped to attract the Upper South, linked to the Deep South by their interest in selling slaves.[26] Here the Confederacy offers Virginia, Kentucky, and other slave states on the border a carrot and stick: if you join, your slaves will never face competition from other suppliers, but if you don't, we might cut you out of our market.

Article I, Section II

5. The House of Representatives shall choose their Speaker and other officers; and shall have the sole power of impeachment; except that **any judicial or other federal officer resident and acting solely within the limits of any State, may be impeached by a vote of two-thirds of both branches of the Legislature thereof.**

Section VI

2. . . . **Congress may, by law, grant to the principal officer in each of the Executive Departments a seat upon the floor of either House, with the privilege of discussing any measures appertaining to his department.**

Section VII

2. . . . **The President may approve any appropriation and disapprove any other appropriation in the same bill. In such case he shall, in signing the bill, designate the appropriations disapproved; and shall return a copy of such appropriations, with his objections, to the House in which the bill shall have originated; and the same proceedings shall then be had as in case of other bills disapproved by the President.**

Section VIII

The Congress shall have power

1. To lay and collect taxes . . . but **no bounties shall be granted from the treasury—nor shall any duties or taxes on importations from foreign nations be laid to promote or foster any branch of industry;** and all duties, imposts, and excises shall be uniform throughout the Confederate States. . . .

3. To regulate commerce with foreign nations . . . ; but **neither this, nor any other clause contained in the Constitution, shall ever be construed to delegate the power to Congress to appropriate money for any internal improvement intended to facilitate commerce; except for the purpose of furnishing lights, beacons, and buoys, and other aids to navigation upon the coasts, and the improvement of harbors and the removing of obstructions in river navigation, in all which cases, such duties shall be laid on the navigation facilitated thereby, as may be necessary to pay the costs and expenses thereof:**

Section IX

1. The importation of negroes of the African race, from any foreign country, other than the slaveholding States or Territories of the United States of America, is hereby forbidden; and Congress is required to pass such laws as shall effectually prevent the same.

2. Congress shall also have power to prohibit the introduction of slaves from any State not a member of, or Territory not belonging to, this Confederacy....

4. No bill of attainder, ex post facto law, or law denying or impairing the right of property in negro slaves shall be passed....

9. Congress shall appropriate no money from the treasury except by a vote of two-thirds of both Houses, taken by yeas and nays, unless it be asked and estimated for by some one of the heads of Department, and submitted to Congress by the President....

Article 11, Section I

1. The executive power shall be vested in a President of the Confederate States of America. **He and the Vice President shall hold their offices for the term of six years; but the President shall not be reeligible.** The President and Vice President shall be elected as follows: ...

Section II

3. **The principal officer in each of the Executive Departments, and all persons connected with the diplomatic service, may be removed from office at the pleasure of the President. All other civil officers of the Executive Department may be removed at any time by the President, or other appointing power, when their services are unnecessary, or for dishonesty, incapacity, inefficiency, misconduct, or neglect of duty; and when so removed, the removal shall be reported to the Senate, together with the reasons therefor.**

Article IV, Section II

1. The citizens of each State shall be entitled to all the privileges and immunities of citizens in the several States, **and shall have the right of transit and sojourn in any State of this Confederacy, with their slaves and other property; and the right of property in said slaves shall not be thereby impaired.**

Section III

3. The Confederate States may acquire new territory; and Congress shall have power to legislate and provide governments for the inhabitants of all territory belonging to the Confederate States, lying without the limits of the several States; and may permit them, at such times, and in such manner as it may by law provide, to form States to be admitted into the Confederacy. **In all such territory, the institution of negro slavery as it now exists in the Confederate States, shall be recognized and protected by Congress, and by**

the territorial government; and the inhabitants of the several Confederate States and Territories, shall have the right to take to such territory any slaves, lawfully held by them in any of the States or Territories of the Confederate States.

* * *

Alexander H. Stephens (1812–83), "African Slavery: The Corner-Stone of the Southern Confederacy," March 22, 1861.[27]

Alexander Stephens was an unusual choice for Confederate vice president. A former Whig, he had supported Stephen A. Douglas for president and argued against leaving the Union at Georgia's secession convention. After Georgia seceded, however, he declared allegiance to the Confederacy and was chosen vice president partly because he could appeal to others who had been reluctant to secede. He helped draft the Confederate Constitution; ten days after its adoption, he made the case for it before a huge crowd in Savannah. Much later, neo-Confederate apologists claimed that his statements regarding slavery and white supremacy were transcribed poorly or were somehow anomalous. However, this passage closely resembles other addresses by Stephens, such as in Atlanta before going to Savannah and to the Virginia secession convention a month later. There he said, "The great truth, I repeat, upon which our system rests, is the inferiority of the African."[28]

We omit several paragraphs telling small ways that Stephens believes the new constitution is better than the old and pick up when Stephens reaches the fundamental "improvement," to which he devotes the most attention.

But not to be tedious in enumerating the numerous changes for the better, allow me to allude to one other though last, not least: the new Constitution has put at rest *forever* all the agitating questions relating to our peculiar institutions—African slavery as it exists among us—the proper *status* of the negro in our form of civilization. This was the immediate cause of the late rupture and present revolution. Jefferson, in his forecast, had anticipated this, as the "rock upon which the old Union would split." He was right. What was conjecture with him, is now a realized fact. But whether he fully comprehended the great truth upon which that rock *stood* and *stands*, may be doubted. The prevailing ideas entertained by him and most of the leading statesmen at the time of the formation of the old Constitution were, that the enslavement of the African was in violation of the laws of nature; that it was wrong in *principle*, socially, morally and politically. It was an evil they knew not well how to deal with; but the general opinion of the men of that day was, that, somehow or other, in the order of Providence, the institution would be evanescent and pass away. This idea, though not incorporated in the Constitution, was the prevailing idea at the time. The Constitution, it is true, secured every essential guarantee to the institution while it should last, and hence no argument can be justly used against the constitutional guarantees thus secured, because of the common sentiment of the day. Those ideas, however, were fundamentally wrong. They rested upon the assumption of the equality of races. This was an error. It was a sandy foundation, and the idea of a Government built upon it; when the "storm came and wind blew, it *fell*."

Our new Government is founded upon exactly the opposite idea; its foundations are laid, its cornerstone rests, upon the great truth that the negro is not equal to the white man; that slavery—subordination to the superior race—is his natural and moral condition. (Applause.)

This, our new Government, is the first, in the history of the world, based upon this great physical, philosophical, and moral truth. This truth has been slow in the process of its development, like all other truths in the various departments of science. It is so even amongst us. Many who hear me, perhaps, can recollect well that this truth was not generally admitted, even within their day. The errors of the past generation still clung to many as late as twenty years ago. Those at the North who still cling to these errors with a zeal above knowledge, we justly denominate fanatics. All fanaticism springs from an aberration of the mind from a defect in reasoning. It is a species of insanity. One of the most striking characteristics of insanity, in many instances, is forming correct conclusions from fancied or erroneous premises; so with the anti_slavery fanatics; their conclusions are right if their premises are. They assume that the negro is equal, and hence conclude that he is entitled to equal privileges and rights, with the white man. If their premises were correct, their conclusions would be logical and just; but their premises being wrong, their whole argument fails. I recollect once of having heard a gentleman from one of the Northern States, of great power and ability, announce in the House of Representatives, with imposing effect, that we of the South would be compelled, ultimately, to yield upon this subject of slavery; that it was as impossible to war successfully against a principle in politics, as it was in physics or mechanics. That the principle would ultimately prevail. That we, in maintaining slavery as it exists with us, were warring against a principle, a principle founded in nature, the principle of the equality of man. The reply I made to him was, that upon his own grounds we should succeed, and that he and his associates in their crusade against our institutions would ultimately fail. The truth announced, that it was a impossible to war successfully against a principle in politics as well as in physics and mechanics, I admitted, but told him it was he and those acting with him who were warring against a principle. They were attempting to make things equal which the Creator had made unequal.

In the conflict thus far, success has been on our side, complete throughout the length and breadth of the Confederate States. It is upon this, as I have stated, our social fabric is firmly planted, and I cannot permit myself to doubt the ultimate success of a full recognition of this principle throughout the civilized and enlightened world.

As I have stated, the truth of this principle may be slow in development, as all truths are, and ever have been, in the various branches of science. It was so with the principles announced by Galileo; it was so with Adam Smith and his principles of political economy. It was so with Harvey, and his theory of the circulation of the blood. It is stated that not a single one of the medical profession, living at the time of the announcement of the truths made by him, admitted them. Now, they are universally acknowledged. May we not therefore look with confidence to the ultimate universal acknowledgment of the truths upon which our system rests? It is the first Government ever instituted upon principles in strict conformity to nature, and the ordination of Providence, in furnishing the material of human society. Many Governments have been founded upon the principles of certain classes; but the classes thus enslaved, were of the same race, and in violation of the laws of nature. Our system commits no such violation of nature's laws. The negro by nature, or by the curse against Canaan, is fitted for that condition which he occupies in our system. The architect, in the construction of buildings, lays the foundation with the proper material the granite then comes the brick or marble. The substratum of our society is made of the material fitted by nature for it, and by experience we know that it is the best not only for the superior, but for the inferior race, that it should be so. It is, indeed, in conformity with the Creator. It is not for us to inquire into the wisdom of His ordinances or to question them. For His own purposes He has made one race to differ from another, as He has made "one star to differ from another in glory."

The great objects of humanity are best attained, when conformed to His laws and decrees, in the formation of Governments as well as in all things else. Our Confederacy is founded upon principles in strict conformity with these laws. This stone which was rejected by the first builders "is become the chief stone of the corner" in our new edifice. (Applause.)

I have been asked, what of the future? It has been apprehended by some, that we would have arrayed against us the civilized world. I care not who or how many they may be, when we stand upon the eternal principles of truth we are obliged and must triumph.

Thousands of people, who begin to understand these truths, are not yet completely out of the shell. They do not see them in their length and breadth. We hear much of the civilization and Christianization of the barbarous tribes of Africa. In my judgment, those ends will never be obtained but by first teaching them the lesson taught to Adam, that "in the sweat of thy brow shalt thou eat bread," and teaching them to work, and feed, and clothe themselves.

* * *

GOVERNOR H. M. RECTOR (1816–99), LETTER TO COLONEL SAM LESLIE, NOVEMBER 28, 1861.[29]

Arkansas governor H. M. Rector orders Leslie "to arrest all men in your county who profess friendship for the Lincoln government" and implies that they will be executed as traitors: "[M]arch them to this place, where they will be dealt with, as enemies of their country whose peace and safety is being endangered by their disloyal and treasonable acts." Leslie arrested almost 80 Unionists from northwest Arkansas and marched them in logging-chains to Little Rock. Of the 117 Unionists arrested throughout the state, all but 15 chose enlistment in the Confederate army. The remaining 15 faced a grand jury, which found that they had committed no crimes and released them.[30] In 1874, Democrats selected Rector as president of the constitutional convention to write the new white supremacist constitution that formally overthrew Arkansas's interracial Reconstruction government.

Sir,

Your letter of the 26th Inst has just reached me by couriers Melton and Griffin. I regret *extremely* that any of our citizens should prove disloyal to their government. But if they so conduct themselves the power of those in authority must be exercised to preserve peace, and enforce obedience to the Constitution and the Laws.

The people of the State of Arkansas through their representatives in Convention have taken the State out of the Old Union and attached it to the Confederacy. And although there may be a minority against this action, yet ours is a government where a majority rules and the minority must submit.

I and my officers in the state are sworn to support and enforce the laws as they are and individuals, one or many, rebelling against those laws, must be looked after and if for the safety of the country it becomes necessary to arrest and imprison them or to *execute* them for *treason*, that must and will be done promptly and certainly, if it is necessary to call out every man in the State to accomplish it.

Still, I deeply regret the necessity, but will not be deterred from doing my whole duty let the blow fall where it may. You will therefore proceed to arrest all men in your county who profess friendship for the Lincoln government or who harbor or support others arousing hostility to the Confederate States or the State of Arkansas. And when so arrested you will march them to this place, where they will be dealt with, as enemies of their country whose peace and safety is being endangered by their disloyal and treasonable acts.

To enable you to enforce this order you will call out such of the Militia as may be necessary and you will be careful also to afford protection to the loyal citizens and their property in your county, as occurring events may seem to require your interposition for their security.

Confiding in your intelligence and devotion to your state, and to the Confederacy of which you are a citizen, I entertain no opinion other than that you will do your whole duty, as a man and an officer.

Respectfully, H. M. Rector Gov and Commander in Chief, A.M.

* * *

THREE NATIONAL FLAGS OF THE CONFEDERACY, 1861, 1863, 1865.[31]

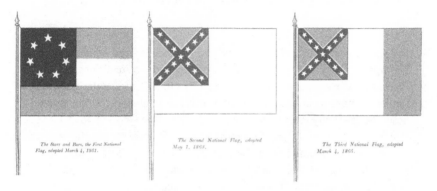

The Stars and Bars, the First National Flag, adopted March 4, 1861.

The Second National Flag, adopted May 1, 1863.

The Third National Flag, adopted March 4, 1865.

Figure 5, Figure 6, and Figure 7: To the left is the first Confederate flag, "the Stars and Bars," adopted March 4, 1861. Center is "the Stainless Banner," which flew for most of the next two years. At right is the third flag, but only a few copies were ever made before the Confederacy ceased to exist.

Although the new government chose its first flag, "the Stars and Bars," owing partly to its similarities with the U.S. flag, as feelings against the United States hardened, its resemblance to "Old Glory" aroused enmity. In the spring of 1863, partly for that reason, Confederates sought another emblem. On May 1, they adopted "the Stainless Banner," as editorials by William Thompson, reproduced below, carried the day. However, its resemblance to a flag of surrender caused confusion, so, late in the war a red strip was added, forming a third national flag. It flew only from March 4, 1865, to the final surrender in May.

According to historian Guy Lancaster, the first national flag was most often associated with the Confederacy before 1948. In that year, Strom Thurmond "made a point of displaying" the battle flag of the Army of Northern Virginia "during his campaign for the presidency on the platform of the racist States' Rights Democratic Party." Since then, the battle flag has been "the cornerstone of 'Confederate heritage' movements."[32]

* * *

William T. Thompson (1812–82),
"Proposed Designs for the 2nd National Confederate Flag," April–May 1863.

In editorials in the *Savannah Morning News*, founder and editor William Thompson proposed what became the second national flag of the Confederacy. He also got William Ross Postell, a Confederate blockade runner, to make a colored drawing of it. It is overwhelmingly white on purpose. George Henry Preble, the authority on American flags, noted in 1872 that Thompson's editorials, "republished with approval by the Richmond papers, about the time the vote was taken in the House on the flag," persuaded the Confederate Congress to adopt what came to be called "the Stainless Banner." After the war, Thompson became an extreme opponent of black voting and Republican politicians.[33]

April 23, 1863.

The Confederate Congress has at length adopted a great seal, which we think is both appropriate and in good taste. "An equestrian portrait of Washington (after the statue which surmounts his monument in the Capitol Square at Richmond), surrounded with a wreath composed of the principal agricultural products of the South (cotton, tobacco, sugar-cane, corn, wheat, and rice), having around its margin, 'THE CONFEDERATE STATES OF AMERICA,' With the motto, '*Deo Vindice*' ('With God for our leader we will conquer'), and under the feet of the horseman the date, 'Feb. 22, 1862.'"

This device and motto will be approved by the good taste and moral sentiment of our people, and now it only remains for Congress to adopt an appropriate flag for the Confederacy in order that we may present to the world the symbols as well as the power and substance of a great and glorious nationality. During the first session of the Provisional Congress, the subject of a flag occupied much of the attention of that body. Designs were invited, and numerous models flags were received from all portions of the confederacy, and submitted to the committee on the flag and seal; but for various reasons the committee was unable to adopt any of the designs presented, and Congress was on the eve of adjourning without a Confederate flag, when necessity compelled them, almost impromptu, to adopt our present flag [the Stars and Bars]. Since then the subject has been frequently discussed in Congress and by the press, but neither have been able to agree upon a substitute for the present flag, to which all object on account of its resemblance to that of the abolition despotism against which we are fighting. To avoid the evil consequences growing out of a confusion of flags on the battle-field, General Beauregard adopted the Southern Cross or battle-flag, which has so grown in favor with the army as to be universally substituted in the field for the stars and bars. This battle-flag has been consecrated by the best blood of the nation, it is hallowed by the memories of glorious victories, it is sanctified by the symbol of our religious faith, and illuminated by the constellated emblems of our Confederate States, but it is in some important respects unsuited for a national ensign. Extended to the proper dimensions, the symmetry of its design would be destroyed, and, having no reverse (no union down), it cannot be used as a signal-flag of distress. The objects to be attained in the adoption of a flag are simplicity, distinctness, significance, and beauty. To combine the liberty colors, red, white, and blue, so as to accomplish these ends, and yet to avoid too great resemblance to the flag of some other nation, is the difficulty to be overcome. By a very simple arrangement all these ends may be attained, and, to our taste, a very appropriate and beautiful flag formed. Our idea is simply to combine the present battle-flag with a pure white standard sheet; our Southern Cross, blue on a red field, to take the place on the white flag that is occupied by the blue union in the old United States flag, or the St. George's cross in the British flag. As a people, we are fighting to maintain the Heaven-ordained supremacy of the white man over the inferior or colored race; a white flag would thus be emblematical of our cause. Upon a red field would stand forth our Southern Cross, gemmed with the stars of our confederation, all combined, preserving in beautiful contrast the red, white, and blue. Such a flag would be chaste, beautiful, and significant, while it would be easily made of silk or bunting, and would be readily distinguished from the flags of other nations.

It may be objected that a flag in which white prevails might be mistaken for a flag of truce, that it could not be as distinctly seen as red or blue, that it would be easily soiled, &c. The first objection is not good, for the reason that the red field and blue cross would be a prominent feature of the flag, and from its position at the top against the staff could not be hidden by the folds of the flag. In the smoke of battle, or at sea against the blue sky, the white would stand as vividly, as either the stars or stripes of abolitiondom, the tricolor of France, or the red flag of England; as for the other objections, we have always observed that the white stripes have stood the battle and the breeze as well and looked as fresh and bright as the red.[34]

Thompson then received a telegram announcing "that the Senate had adopted the flag he had suggested, with the addition of a blue stripe to the
centre of the white field," in Preble's account.[35] In response, he penned
the following editorial lambasting this idea.

April 28, 1863.

It appears the House of Representatives have yet to act upon the new flag adopted by the Senate, and we learn from the Richmond papers that it is probable
that the House will amend it by striking out the blue bar in the centre of the
white field. It is to be hoped that they will do so, as the bar is objectionable on
several accounts, and is a deformity to what would otherwise be a significant,
and appropriate flag. Let any one make a drawing in colors, on paper, and they
will at once discover that the blue bar running up the centre of the white field
and joining with lower arm of the blue cross is in bad taste, and utterly destructive of the symmetry and harmony of the design. The broad, horizontal blue
bar, forming on the end of the smaller blue bar, belonging to this cross, and
which extends up to the upper corner of the red union at an angle of about forty-five degrees, presents to the eye a disproportioned, awkward, and unmean-
ing figure, not unlike a blue handled jackknife or razor with the blade not quite
the full extent. Another objection is the disproportion which the lower white
bar, extending the full length of the flag bears to the shorter blue and white bars
above. And still another objection that the large blue bar detracts from the conspicuousness of the blue cross. Still another objection is the resemblance which
the bars will still have to the Yankee flag. If for no other reason than this, we
should discard the bars, and every thing that resembles or is suggestive of the
old stripes. While we consider the flag which has been adopted by the Senate
as a very decided improvement of the old United States flag we still think the
battle-flag on a pure white field was appropriate and handsome. Such a flag
would be a suitable emblem of our young confederacy, and, sustained by the
brave strong arms of the South, it would soon take rank among ensigns of the
nations, and be hailed by the civilized world "THE WHITE MAN'S FLAG."

After learning that his design had prevailed, Thompson exulted.

May 4, 1863.

We are pleased to learn by our dispatch from Richmond that Congress has
had the good taste to adopt for the flag of the confederacy the battle-flag on a
plain white field, in lieu of the blue and white bars proposed by the Senate. The
flag, as adopted, is precisely the same as that suggested by us a short time since,
and is, in our opinion, much more beautiful and appropriate than either the red
and white bars or the white field and blue bar as first adopted by the Senate. As

a national emblem, it is significant of our higher cause, the cause of a superior race, and a higher civilization contending against ignorance, infidelity, and barbarism. Another merit in the new flag is, that it bears no resemblance to the now infamous banner of the Yankee vandals.

* * *

Jefferson Davis (1808–89), "Message to the Confederate Congress," January 12, 1863.[36]

The Confederate president minces no words in decrying Lincoln's Emancipation Proclamation. He calls it "the most execrable measure recorded in the history of guilty man." It will doom African Americans "to extermination." More important than words is his reaction in the form of policy: henceforth the Confederate army will no longer treat captured U.S. officers as prisoners of war. Instead, it will turn them over to state authorities, who will treat them as "criminals engaged in exciting servile insurrection"—meaning the death penalty.[37]

The public journals of the North have been received, containing a proclamation, dated on the 1st day of the present month, signed by the President of the United states, in which he orders and declares all slaves within ten of the States of the Confederacy to be free, except such as are found within certain districts now occupied in part by the armed forces of the enemy. We may well leave it to the instincts of that common humanity which a beneficent Creator has implanted in the breasts of our fellowmen of all countries to pass judgment on a measure by which several millions of human beings of an inferior race, peaceful and contented laborers in their sphere, are doomed to extermination, while at the same time they are encouraged to a general assassination of their masters by the insidious recommendation "to abstain from violence unless in necessary self-defense." Our own detestation of those who have attempted the most execrable measure recorded in the history of guilty man is tempered by profound contempt for the impotent rage which it discloses. So far as regards the action of this Government on such criminals as may attempt its execution, I confine myself to informing you that I shall, unless in your wisdom you deem some other course more expedient, deliver to the several State authorities all commissioned officers of the United States that may hereafter be captured by our forces in any of the States embraced in the proclamation, that they may be dealt with in accordance with the laws of those States providing for the punishment of criminals engaged in exciting servile insurrection.[38] The enlisted soldiers I shall continue to treat as unwilling instruments in the commission of these crimes, and shall direct their discharge and return to their homes on the proper and usual parole.

In this political aspect this measure possesses great significance, and to it in this light I invite your attention. It affords to our whole people the complete and crowning proof of the true nature of the designs of the party which elevated to power the present occupant of the Presidential chair at Washington and which sought to conceal its purpose by every variety of artful device and by the perfidious use of the most solemn and repeated pledges on every possible occasion. I extract in this connection as a single example of the following declaration, made by President Lincoln under the solemnity of his oath as Chief Magistrate of the United States, on the 4th of March, 1861:

Apprehension seems to exist among the people of the Southern States that by the accession of a Republican Administration their property and their peace and personal security are to be endangered. There has never been any reasonable cause for such apprehension. Indeed, the most ample evidence to the contrary has all the while existed and been open to their inspection. It is found in nearly all the published speeches of him who now addresses you. I do but quote from one of those speeches when I declare that I have no purpose directly or indirectly, to interfere with the institution of slavery in the States where it exists. I believe I have no lawful right to do so; and I have no inclination to do so. Those who nominated and elected me did so with full knowledge that I had made this and many similar declarations and had never recanted them; and more than this, they placed in the platform for my acceptance and as law to themselves and to me the clear and emphatic resolution which I now read:

"*Resolved*, That the maintenance inviolate of the rights of the States, and especially the right of each state to order and control its own domestic institutions according to its own judgment exclusively, is essential to that balance of power on which the perfection and endurance of our political fabric depend; and we denounce the lawless invasion by armed force of the soil of any State or Territory, no matter under what pretext, as the gravest of crimes."

Nor was this declaration of the want of power or disposition to interfere with our social system confined to a state of peace. Both before and after the actual commencement of hostilities the President of the United States repeated in formal official communication to the Cabinets of Great Britain and France that he was utterly without constitutional power to do the act which he has just committed, and that in no possible event, whether secession of these States resulted in the establishment of a separate Confederacy or in the restoration of the Union, was there any authority by virtue of which he could either restore a disaffected State to the Union by force of arms or make any change in any of its institutions. I refer especially for the verification of this assertion to the dispatches addressed by the Secretary of the State of the United States, under direction of the President, to the Ministers of the United States at London and Paris, under date of 10th and 22d of April, 1861.

The people of this Confederacy, then, cannot fail to receive this proclamation as the fullest vindication of their own sagacity in foreseeing the uses to which the dominant party in the United States intended from the beginning to apply their power, nor can they cease to remember with devout thankfulness that it is to their own vigilance in resisting the first stealthy progress of approaching despotism that they owe their escape from consequences now apparent to the most skeptical. This proclamation will have another salutary effect in calming the fears of those who have constantly evinced the apprehension that this war might end by some reconstruction of the old Union or some renewal of close political relations with the United States. These fears have never been shared by me, nor have I ever been able to perceive on what basis they could rest. But the proclamation affords the fullest guarantee of the impossibility of such a result; it has established a state of things which can lead to but one of three possible consequences the extermination of the slaves, the exile of the whole white population from the Confederacy, or absolute and total separation of these States from the United States.

This proclamation is also an authentic statement of the United States of its inability to subjugate the South by force of arms, and as such must be accepted by neutral nations, which can no longer find any justification in withholding our just claims to formal recognition. It is also in effect an intimation to the people of the North that they must prepare to submit to a separation, now become inevitable, for that people are too acute not to understand a restoration of the Union has been rendered forever impossible by the adoption of a measure which from its very nature neither admits of retraction nor can coexist with union.

* * *

Confederate Congress, "Response of the Confederate Congress to Message from Jefferson Davis on the Emancipation Proclamation," May 1, 1863.[39]

The Confederate Congress changed Davis's policy to declare that the Confederate government shall retain custody of white POWs, including officers, except those who command or aid black soldiers. These shall be "put to death, or be otherwise punished." Black POWs shall be turned over to state authorities, to face probable enslavement and possible death. Both documents are in harmony with the ruthless actions of Confederate leaders when white supremacy was at issue, policies that had taken effect with the start of hostilities. In November 1862, for example, Confederate raiders seized four African Americans in U.S. uniforms on a South Carolina island and asked Richmond what to do with them. President Davis and his secretary of war approved their "summary execution."[40]

That they recommend that the Senate agree to the amendment of the House of Representatives, amended so as to read as follows:

"[1.] *Resolved by the Congress of the Confederate States of America*, in response to the message of the President transmitted to Congress at the commencement of the present session, That, in the opinion of Congress, the commissioned officers of the enemy ought not be delivered to the authorities of the respective states, as suggested in the said message; but all captives taken by the Confederate forces ought to be dealt with and disposed of by the Confederate Government.

"2. That, in the judgment of Congress, the proclamations of the President of the United States, dated, respectively, September 22, 1862, and January 1, 1863, and the other measures of the Government of the United States and of its authorities, commanders, and forces, designed or tending to emancipate slaves in the Confederate States, or to abduct such slaves, or to incite them to insurrection, or to employ negroes in war against the Confederate States, or to overthrow the institution of African slavery and bring on a servile war in these States, would, if successful, produce atrocious consequences, and they are inconsistent with the spirit of those usages which in modern warfare prevail among civilized nations. They may, therefore, be properly and lawfully repressed by retaliation.

"3. That in every case wherein, during the present war, any violation of the laws or usages of war among the civilized nations shall be or has been done and perpetrated by those acting under the authority of the Government of the United States, on the persons or property of citizens of the Confederate States, or of those under the protection on in the land or naval service of the Confederate States, or of any State of the Confederacy, the President of the Confederate States is hereby authorized to cause full and ample retaliation to be made for every such violation in such manner and to such extent as he may think proper.

"4. That every white person, being a commissioned officer, or acting as such, who during the present war shall command negroes or mulattoes in arms against the Confederate States, or who shall arm, train, organize, or prepare negroes or mulattoes for military service against the Confederate States, or who shall voluntarily aid negroes or mulattoes in any military enterprise, attack, or conflict in such service, shall be deemed as inciting servile insurrection, and shall, if captured, be put to death, or be otherwise punished, at the discretion of the court.

"5. Every person being a commissioned officer or acting as such in the service of the enemy who shall, during the present war, excite, attempt to excite, or cause to be excited a servile insurrection or who shall incite or cause to be incited a slave to rebel, shall, if captured, be put to death or be otherwise punished, at the discretion of the court.

"6. Every person charged with an offense punishable under the preceding resolutions shall, during the present war, be tried before the military court attached to the army or corps by the troops of which he shall have been captured, be put to death or be otherwise punished, at the discretion of the court.

"7. All negroes and mulattoes who shall be engaged in war or be taken in arms against the Confederate States or shall give aid or comfort to the enemies of the Confederate States shall, when captured in the Confederate States, be delivered to the authorities of the State or States in which they shall be captured, to be dealt with according to the present or future laws of such State or States."

And that the title of the resolution be amended so as to read "Joint resolution on the subject of retaliation."

* * *

RICHARD TAYLOR (1826–79), EDMUND KIRBY SMITH (1824–93), "TREATMENT OF AFRICAN AMERICAN PRISONERS OF WAR," JUNE 8, 13, 16, 1863.

From January 1863 to war's end, General Edmund Kirby Smith was in charge of all Confederate forces west of the Mississippi River. After taking Vicksburg, Mississippi, on July 4, 1863, and Port Hudson, Louisiana, five days later, the United States controlled the river. After that, Smith operated largely on his own. His forces comprised the national Confederate government in the trans-Mississippi. In this correspondence, Smith sets policy about the treatment of African American prisoners of war after learning that his subaltern, General Richard Taylor, has captured fifty black soldiers at Milliken's Bend, Louisiana. Smith hopes "this may not be so," because he wants all black POWs killed at once. "If they are taken, however," they are to be turned over to civilian authorities "to be tried for crimes against the State," a sure death sentence. S. S. Anderson, assistant adjutant-general for the Confederacy, notes that doing so will avoid retaliation by the United States upon Confederate POWs.

"Letter from Richard Taylor to Gen. Smith," June 8, 1863.[41]

This report by General Taylor to General Smith discusses the capture of African American troops in the battle of Milliken's Bend.

DISTRICT OF WEST LOUISIANA, *Richmond, June 8, 1863*

GENERAL: I have the honor to report the events of the past few days. As soon as I learned of the capture of Richmond by Captain McLean, of Harrison's battalion, viz, on the night of 3d ultimo [instant], I ordered General [J. G.] Walker to push on a force of 200 infantry to insure holding the bridge, adding to it two guns of Harrison's artillery. This force crossed the Tensas in a flat, which I had secured the day before, and reached Richmond at sunset on the 4th.[42] On the same day General Walker encamped 3 miles from Dunlap's, on Tensas. I had succeeded in collecting material for a bridge (there being but one flat, the one above mentioned, on the river), and on the morning of the 5th commenced the work, superintending it in person. At 4 p.m. a substantial bridge was completed, when I pushed on to this point, sending notice to General Walker of the completion of the bridge. Arriving at dusk, I soon met Major [Isaac F.] Harrison from below. He reported the parish of Tensas and Lower Madison clear of the enemy. One of his companies, under Captain McCall, attacked on the morning of the 4th a negro camp on Lake Saint Joseph. He found them some 90 strong. Killed the captain (white), 12 negroes, and captured the remainder. Some 60 women and children in the camp were also secured. Captain McCall led 60 men. Major Harrison brought off some few arms, medicines, &c., from Perkins', Surget's, Casin, and Carthage, all of which points he found abandoned by the enemy. At several places much property had been burned. . . .

McCulloch's brigade lost some 20 killed and perhaps 80 wounded. A very large number of the negroes were killed and wounded, and, unfortunately, some 50, with 2 of their white officers, captured. I respectfully ask instructions as to the disposition of these prisoners. A number of horses and mules, some few small arms, and commissary stores were also taken. In this affair General McCulloch appears to have shown great personal bravery, but no capacity for handling masses.—R. Taylor, Major-General, Commanding; Brig. Gen. W. R. Boggs, Chief of Staff.

Letter from General Smith to General Cooper in Richmond, Virginia, enclosing a report from General Taylor regarding the capture of African American troops and a memo from Assistant Adjutant-General Anderson.[43]

Headquarters Department Trans-Mississippi, *Shreveport, La., June 16, 1863*
General S. Cooper, Adjutant and Inspector General, Richmond, Va.
GENERAL: I have the honor to inclose you two letters, addressed to Major-General Taylor, in regard to the disposition to be made of negroes and their officers captured in arms. Unfortunately such captures were made by some of Major-General Taylor's subordinates.

I have heard unofficially that the last Congress did not adopt any retaliatory legislation on the subject of armed negroes and their officers, but left the President to dispose of this delicate and important question. In the absence of any legislation and of any orders except those referred to in the inclosed letters, I saw no other proper and legal course for me to pursue except the one I adopted.

I have the honor to be, general, your obedient servant, E. Kirby Smith
[Inclosure No. 1]
Headquarters Department Trans-Mississippi, Shreveport, La., June 13, 1863.
Maj. Gen. R. Taylor, Commanding District of Louisiana:

GENERAL: I have been unofficially informed that some of your troops have captured negroes in arms. I hope this may not be so, and that your subordinates who may have been in command of capturing parties may have recognized the propriety of giving no quarter to armed negroes and their officers. If they are taken, however, you will turn them over to the State authorities to be tried for crimes against the State, and you will afford such facilities in obtaining witnesses as the interests of the public service will permit. I am told that negroes found in a state of insurrection may be tried by a court of the parish in which the crime is committed, composed of two justices of the peace and a certain number of slave-holders. Governor Moore has called on me and stated that if the report is true that any armed negroes have been captured he will send the attorney-general to conduct the prosecution as soon as you notify of the capture.

I have the honor to be, general, your obedient servant, E. Kirby Smith, *Lieutenant-General, Commanding.*

[Inclosure No. 2]
Headquarters Department Trans-Mississippi, *Shreveport, La., June 13, 1863.*

GENERAL: In answer to the communication of Brigadier-General Hébert, of the 6th instant, asking what disposition should be made of negro slaves taken in arms, I am directed by Lieutenant-General Smith to say no quarter should be shown to them. If taken prisoners, however, they should be turned over to the executive authorities of the States in which they may be captured, in obedience to the proclamation of the President of the Confederate States, sections 3 and 4, published to the Army in General Orders, No. 111, Adjutant and Inspector General's Office, series of 1862. Should negroes thus taken be executed by the military authorities capturing them it would certainly provoke retaliation. By turning them over to the civil authorities to be tried by the laws of the State no exceptions can be taken.

I am, general, very respectfully, your obedient servant, S. S. Anderson, *Assistant Adjutant-General.*

* * *

FORT PILLOW MASSACRE, APRIL 12, 1864.[44]

Figure 8: This illustration of the massacre in *Frank Leslie's Illustrated Newspaper*, a month afterward, surely based on verbal accounts, helped Northern readers visualize and remember Fort Pillow.

On April 12, 1864, Confederate cavalry leader Nathan Bedford Forrest attacked Fort Pillow, 40 miles north of Memphis. The United States had occupied the fort with a mix of black troops and white Tennessee volunteers, all recently recruited. Built to overlook the Mississippi River, the fort's low earthen walls offered little protection from attack from the east. Forrest's 1,500 men overwhelmed its 550 Union defenders in about twenty minutes. A letter by a Union soldier after the battle tells what happened next: "Our boys when they saw they were overpowered threw down their arms and held up, some their handkerchiefs and some their hands in token of surrender, but no sooner were they seen than they were shot down, and if one shot failed to kill them, the bayonet or revolver did not." Forrest despised its defenders, the whites as traitors and the blacks as slaves in rebellion. According to a Confederate newspaper correspondent, however, "[T]he whites received quarter, but the Negroes were shown no mercy." A Confederate sergeant wrote to his sisters seven days after the battle:

The slaughter was awful—words cannot describe the scene. The poor deluded Negroes would run up to our men, fall upon their knees, and with uplifted hands scream for mercy, but they were ordered to their feet and then shot down. The white men fared but little better. Their fort turned out to be a great slaughter pen—blood, human blood stood about in pools and brains could have been gathered up in any quantity. I with several others tried to stop the butchery and at one time had partially succeeded, but General Forrest ordered them shot down like dogs and the carnage continued. Finally our men became sick of blood and the firing ceased.

Soldiers testified before the resulting congressional inquiry that Confederates buried some wounded soldiers alive and crucified others by nailing them onto tent frames and then setting the tents afire. Forrest's men took Major Bradford, the Union commander, in custody and killed him too, a day or so after the battle. As one result, to the end of the war a year later, black U.S. regiments charged into battle with the cry of vengeance, "Remember Fort Pillow!"

At first, Confederates exulted in the slaughter. In his initial report, Forrest claimed that his force killed more than 70% of the Union troops. "The river was dyed with the blood of the slaughtered for 200 yards," he boasted, and "hoped" Fort Pillow would "demonstrate to the Northern people that Negro soldiers cannot cope with Southerners." James Chalmers, his second-in-command, bragged that his troops had "taught the mongrel garrison of blacks and renegades a lesson long to be remembered." However, such statements, reported proudly across the South, led to an outcry in the North. Death or capture removes a person as a fighting force. Therefore captured soldiers are not supposed to be killed. The actions of Forrest's men at Fort Pillow violated the rules of war.[45] Forrest became something of a scapegoat in the North for acts that took place in many Confederate commands, including at Milliken's Bend and Jackson, Louisiana; Poison Spring, Arkansas; Flat Rock Creek in Indian Territory; Brice's Cross Roads, Mississippi; Olustee, Florida; and various other places, including the Crater during the siege of Petersburg, Virginia. The Confederacy never charged anyone with any wrongdoing as a result of any of these events. The selections just above—Davis's message to the Confederate Congress on January

12, 1863, Congress's reply, and the correspondence among Confederate generals Taylor, Smith, and Cooper—show that such acts were in line with Confederate policy. In the long run, this policy worked against the Confederacy: when word spread of what happened at Fort Pillow, Americans fought with particular fury and on occasion took no prisoners. Confederate soldiers sometimes shrank from opposing them.[46]

* * *

John R. Eakin (1822–55),
"The Slave Soldiers," June 8, 1864.[47]

Eakin was born in Tennessee, where he became a lawyer. In 1857, he moved to Washington, an important town in antebellum Arkansas, and soon became its mayor. Under his editorship, the *Washington Telegraph*, the most important newspaper in the trans-Mississippi Confederacy, became a propaganda organ for the Confederacy. After Reconstruction, Eakin became a justice on the Arkansas Supreme Court. This editorial seethes at U.S. policy of recruiting African Americans into its armed forces. Probably referring to Confederate soldiers who killed black POWs after the Battle of Poison Springs, Arkansas, in late April 1864,[48] Eakin approves: "They have cut the Gordian knot with the sword. They did right." He argues further, "[W]e cannot treat negroes taken in arms as prisoners of war without a destruction of the social system for which we contend."

The Slave Soldiers.—Amongst there stupendous wrongs against humanity, shocking to the moral sense of the world, like Herod's massacre of the Innocents, or the eve of St. Bartholomew, the crime of Lincoln in seducing our slaves into the ranks of his army will occupy a prominent position. All minor and local massacres pale before it. It would, if accomplished as intended, consign four millions of human beings to sure extermination.

Loathsome as the character of Lincoln appears in other respects, in this it is pre-eminently hideous.

The world has had its Neros, and great conquerors delighting in human blood. Never one has before times dared the bloody height of wheedling millions of harmless, happy and innocent people to destruction by bloody death, or sure starvation, and laughed at their calamities. It towers aloft the acme of crime.

The work is in process, and has been partly accomplished. Thousands of souls of this unhappy race, have already been flown from the crowded Lazar houses of the North, from bodies starved and frozen in their inhospitable clime, from carcasses weltering in their gore upon battle fields, where they have been coldly and heartlessly exposed to slaughter, and stand at Heaven's chancery with the black and damning accusation against the author of their ruin. Will it not be.

> "When they do meet at court.
> This look of theirs will hurl his soul from heaven,
> And fiends will snatch at it."

God knows! We must not judge lest we be judged. But on earth he is most foul and horrible.

It is the curse of evil that its effects are not confined to authors and victims. We too are drawn unwillingly into the vortex of its consequences, and may be compelled to courses which may wring our hearts with pity. A great problem is forced upon us. The most important ever presented in the history of international law. We cannot shut our eyes and pass it by. It cries aloud for solution, and that at once. No delay is possible, or worse and more terrible complications will surely follow.

How shall we treat our slaves arrayed under the banners of the invader, and marching to desolate our homes and firesides? Who can answer that flippantly? We do not envy such a man. It is a case in which it well becomes our rulers to pray most earnestly for Divine guidance. May they have it soon! Meanwhile the problem has met our soldiers in the heat of battle, where there has been no time for discussion. They have cut the Gordian knot with the sword. They did right. It was not theirs to untangle its knotty folds. It is far better for the deluded victims, and for us, that the fate which may perhaps be considered inevitable, should come upon them in hot blood, and the excitement of the battle field.

But it is nevertheless of the most pressing importance that our Government should adopt some system in the treatment of these unfortunates, well defined to ourselves, and made known to the enemy in order to be prepared to meet its consequences. That we may make no retractions, nor betray fatal vascillation, it is indispensable to be right. Without firmness we cannot succeed. To be firm we must be conscientiously right. Let us calmly examine the principles which apply, and as far as may be, reconcile humanity with the safety of those institutions upon which our Government rests. All the time remembering, that the loftiest humanity dictates the preservation of our Government, and the happiness and welfare of its citizens, at any cost however terrible.

Independently of the fact, that slavery under our Constitution is the normal and proper condition of the African races, we could not, under the law of nations, object to the enlistment of free blacks in the enemy's ranks, or refuse to treat them as prisoners of war. No nation generally, has the right to dictate to a hostile power the race or color of its soldiers. But the existence of slavery with us, fixes the status of the African as inferior and subordinate, and precludes us from extending to the free negro any consideration above what is paid to our slaves. We have the right to require of all belligerents of every nation such consideration of our peculiar institution as not to force upon us, as soldiers and equals, persons of a race whom we cannot recognize as such without an abandonment of principle. The whole foundation of our social system rests upon the subordination and respect of our slaves, which can never be preserved if their fellows, persons of the same race and color, are allowed the haughty privilege of entering our houses, arresting, and commanding us as prisoners of war. It is an intentional insult upon the part of any belligerent, to send such amongst us. The case of the freed negro must rest upon the same basis as that of the slave, and he must share his fate, whatever that may be.

It is equally well settled by the universal sentiment of mankind in all ages, and by the practice of military nations since the dawn of civilization, ancient and modern, that it is disgraceful and inhuman to excite servile insurrection in the communities of the enemy. No belligerent could concede that right and live. It has no sanction is the law of nations. No power has the right to receive into its ranks the soldiers even of another and throw over them the aegis of its protection against the penalties of treason in case of capture. Much less its slaves. The duty of subordination and obedience in the slave is more fixed and determinate than that of the soldier. Hostile powers have ever been considered bound to respect the reciprocal relations which subsist between different classes of society in the enemy's country, and have never claimed the right to alter them by edicts or proclamations to such an extent as to enforce those changes by retaliation. Whilst a government stands it has the right to regulate the status of its subjects. Hostile powers may seduce or take away by force a portion of those subjects and protect them whilst under their power, but have never the right to return them to the government to which they belonged, with the haughty mandate that they should be absolved from the laws of that government, and placed in a condition dictated by the hostile powers. The statement of the proposition carries along its own absurdity. Had Napoleon sent to the Emperor Alexander a Russian serf after the invasion, with a mandate that he should be considered free, and treated as a freeman, it would have brought on him the derision of Europe. Nor would sending a number of them, with arms in their hands, have altered the case. When captured in Russian territory they would become subject to Russian laws.

When Lincoln's emancipation proclamation was published to the world, it excited a smile. It was derided as a magnificent piece of "brutem fulmen."[49] The wags advised him to issue a bull to the moon. How would the world be astonished to learn that we ourselves give full efficacy to this impudent assumption, and admit every slave who may have joined the Federal army, to be entitled to the rights of a freeman should he fall again into our hands.

It follows irresistibly that we cannot treat negroes taken in arms as prisoners of war without a destruction of the social system for which we contend. In this we must be firm, uncompromising and unfaltering. We must claim the full control of all negroes who may fall into our hands, to punish with death, or any other penalty, or remand them to their owners. If the enemy retaliate, we *must* do likewise; and if the *black flag* follows, the blood be upon their heads.

Meanwhile, until the fate of all such is determined by some definite action of our government, our soldiers are not bound to *receive* their surrender, and perhaps will note. By our laws any slave resisting a white man in lawful efforts to capture or control him, may be killed without crime. Any slave seeking the life of a white citizen may also be destroyed. What our soldiers do in fight has the sanction of law.

But it is to be hoped that the safety of our cause may be found consistent with a more humane course. Perhaps it may be found sufficient to punish the most guilty and dangerous with death, to condemn others to hard labor on public works under guards, and perhaps to pardon some who have been forced into ranks, and restore them again to their masters. These points we are for the present willing to submit to the wisdom of our government. Our present object is to remove all idea that the negro is entitled to the privileges of war. Space will not admit of the discussion of the policy to be observed towards them when taken toward white men commanding. They are both grave and anxious questions, and may be touched hereafter.

* * *

Henry Hotze (1833–87),
"The Negro's Place in Nature,"
December 10, 1863.[50]

According to historian Robert Bonner, Henry Hotze was "the most important Confederate propagandist in Europe."[51] Born in Switzerland, he moved
to Alabama and became a U.S. citizen in 1855. He served briefly in the
Confederate army and was then sent as an emissary to London. There he
mingled with members of the Anthropological Society, a new organization that had split from the established Ethnological Society over the issue of race. Hoping to win European support, the Confederacy subsidized
his London newspaper, the *Index*, subtitled "A Weekly Journal of Politics,
Literature, and News Devoted to the Exposition of the Mutual Interests,
Political and Commercial, of Great Britain and the Confederate States
of America."[52] Hotze's earlier editorials include defenses of Confederate
policy treating captured black soldiers as slaves and executing their white
officers. James Hunt, a founder of the Anthropological Society, believed in
polygenesis, the now-discredited doctrine that humans appeared on earth
in several places and times. This theory makes it easier to claim "[t]he
negro's place in nature is in subordination to the white race," thus justifying Confederate policy.

The very able, learned, and truly philosophic paper lately read by Dr. Hunt before the Anthropological Society, and which was published in the last two numbers of THE INDEX, cannot fail to command the critical attention of the scientific world, and the consequent discussion thereon will, it is to be hoped, do
much toward solving the problem on which it treats. But it will be unfortunate
if only those who are professed anthropologists should give heed to this valuable contribution to a hitherto greatly neglected, but highly important, subject.
. . . The golden rule for the individual, for the nation, for all the peoples of the
globe, is, that happiness and progress depend upon the right man being in the
right place. Dr. Hunt justly deplores the misery that has arisen from ignorance
and neglect of this law, and from this cause the negro has suffered more than

any other race. Instead, then, of using the negro as a political shuttlecock, it is the bounden duty of all those who desire to promote his welfare to first find out his proper place in nature, and then to employ all legitimate means to see that he is where he should be. . . .

The leading facts about the Negro are few in number, but they are sufficient to enable us to discern clearly his place in nature. The anatomist points out the differences between the conformation of the negro and the white races, and tells us that the brain of the negro is of smaller capacity. This class of evidence, though very important, is principally useful as an explanation of other phenomena. If anatomists had been silent we should still have known that the negro is inferior to the white man, though we should not have been aware of the immediate organic cause. If the negro race had been equal or nearly equal to other races, it would, like them, have had an independent history; but the negro has no history. When we trace his existence out of Africa in all ages we find him occupying a servile position, and at home his existence has been a blank. The negroes have never done anything in literature or science, not even to the extent of inventing a grammar. How is this? The negro has increased and multiplied as fast as other races and has had the same extraneous advantages. There is no other explanation than that the negro is undebatably inferior in intellect.

The next fact which we have to look at is the condition of the race in Africa. It is utterly impossible to exaggerate the savage barbarity and the utter degradation of the negro at home. . . .

What in modern times has been the condition of the negro abroad? In the West Indies the experiment has been tried of giving the negro full independence, and the result has been that a garden has become a wilderness, because the negro, except under compulsion, will not labour. In the Confederate States the negro race has been in subordination to the white race, and the result is, that it has made wonderful progress—that the savage has become a docile labourer, and that the heathen has become a Christian.

What, then, is the conclusion from these facts? Not, perhaps, that the negro should remain in perpetual slavery, but surely that the guidance and the intellect and the will of the white man are indispensable to him.

Illustrations are however hardly necessary, because we have the negro in the Confederate States in subordination to the white race, and we can see how he fares under such circumstances. In Africa, as we have already observed, the negro is a savage and a heathen, and in a state of inconceivable degradation. In the West Indies he is idle and dissolute. In the Southern States he is, so every traveler avers, industrious, thriving and Christianised; there is not on the face of the earth a class of labourers so happy. All his wants are supplied, and he enjoys the comforts of religion. What more can the Christian or the philanthropist desire for him? Do we want the negro to continue as he is in Africa, a savage and a heathen? Do we want him to be as he is in the West Indies, a curse and an encumbrance? The philanthropist and the Christian must reply that it is better that he should be as he is in the Southern states, blest and a blessing. We may admit then, whether we are or are not emancipationists, fully and without hesitation, the conclusions that are suggested by Dr. Hunt's painstaking and clever essay. The negro's place in nature is in subordination to the white race; but let us be glad, that subordination, the result of intellectual inferiority, does not preclude happiness in this world, and thank God that no intellectual qualification is necessary for eternal Salvation.

* * *

ROBERT E. LEE (1807–70), LETTER TO
HON. ANDREW HUNTER, JANUARY 11, 1865.[53]

On January 2, 1864, Confederate General Patrick Cleburne floated a proposal to arm slaves to fight for the Confederacy. It went nowhere. Other
generals called it "revolting," "incendiary," even "treasonous."[54] A year
later, desperate for troops, Robert E. Lee wrote Andrew Hunter, Virginia
state senator, pushing the same idea. Although Lee would "prefer to rely
upon our white population," that has become impossible. His letter antici-
pates that U.S. forces are likely to "penetrate our country and get access
to a large part of our negro population" and use them to tilt the balance of
power in the field. Rather than letting U.S. forces end slavery, Lee proposes
that Confederates do so themselves, gradually. The Black Codes passed by
Southern state legislatures after the end of the war, modeled after their
antebellum slave codes and restrictions on free blacks, suggest what this
"emancipation" would be like at best. On March 13, 1865, with their
backs against the wall, the Confederate Congress finally approved recruiting African Americans into its army. This was too late to do Lee any good;
he abandoned Richmond less than three weeks later.

Headquarters Army North Virginia, 11th January, 1865.
Hon. Andrew Hunter, Richmond, Va.

DEAR SIR: I have received your letter of the 7th inst., and, without confining
myself to the order of your interrogatories, will endeavor to answer them by a
statement of my views on the subject. I shall be most happy if I can contribute
to the solution of a question in which I feel an interest commensurate with
my desire for the happiness of our people. Considering the relation of master
and slave, controlled by humane laws and influenced by Christianity and an
enlightened public sentiment, as the best that can exist between the white and
black races while intermingled as at present in this country, I would deprecate
any sudden disturbance of that relation unless it be necessary to avert a greater
calamity to both. I should therefore prefer to rely upon our white population to
preserve the ratio between our forces and those of the enemy which experience

has shown to be safe. But in view of the preparations of our enemies it is our duty to provide for continued war, and not for a battle or campaign, and I fear that we cannot accomplish this without overtaxing the capacity of our white population. Should the war continue under existing circumstances, the enemy may in course of time penetrate our country and get access to a large part of our negro population. It is his avowed policy to convert the able-bodied men among them into soldiers, and to emancipate all.

The success of the Federal arms in the South was followed by a proclamation of President Lincoln for 280,000 men, the effect of which will be to stimulate the Northern States to procure as substitutes for their own people the negroes thus brought within their reach. Many have already been obtained in Virginia, and should the fortune of war expose more of her territory, the enemy would gain a large accession to his strength.

His progress will thus add to his numbers, and at the same time destroy slavery in a manner most pernicious to the welfare of our people. Their negroes will be used to hold them in subjection, leaving the remaining force of the enemy free to extend his conquest. Whatever may be the effect of our employing negro troops, it cannot be as mischievous as this. If it end in subverting slavery it will be accomplished by ourselves, and we can devise the means of alleviating the evil consequences to both races. I think, therefore we must decide whether slavery shall be extinguished by our enemies and the slaves be used against us, or use them ourselves at the risk of the effects which may be produced upon our social institutions. I believe that with proper regulations they can be made efficient soldiers. They possess the physical qualifications in an eminent degree. Long habits of obedience and subordination, coupled with the moral influence which in our country the white man possess over the black, furnish an excellent foundation for that discipline which is the best guarantee of military efficiency. Our chief aim should be to secure their fidelity.

There have been formidable armies composed of men having no interest in the cause for which they fought beyond their pay or hope of plunder. But it is certain that the surest foundation upon which the fidelity of an army can rest, especially in a service which imposes peculiar hardships and privations, is the personal interest of the soldier in the issue of the contest. Such an interest we can give our negroes by giving immediate freedom to all who enlist, and freedom at the end of the war to the families of those who discharge their duties faithfully (whether they survive or not,) together with the privilege of residing at the South. To this might be added a bounty for faithful service.

We should not expect slaves to fight for prospective freedom when they can secure it by going to the enemy, in whose service they will incur no greater risk than in ours. The reasons that induce me to recommend the employment of negro troops at all render the effects of the measures I have suggested upon slavery immaterial, and in my opinion the best means of securing the efficiency and fidelity of this auxiliary force would be to accompany the measure with a well-digested plan of gradual and general emancipation. As that will be the result of the continuance of the war, and will certainly occur if the enemy succeeds, it seems to be advisable to adopt it at once, and thereby secure all the benefits that will accrue to our cause.

The employment of negro troops under regulations similar in principle to those above indicated would, in my opinion, greatly increase our military strength, and enable us to relieve our white population to some extent. I think we could dispense with our reserve forces except in cases of necessity.

It would disappoint the hopes which our enemies base upon our exhaustion, deprive them in a great measure of the aid they now derive from black troops, and thus throw the burden of the war upon their own people. In addition to the great political advantages that would result to our cause from the adoption of a system of emancipation, it would exercise a salutary influence upon our whole negro population, by rendering more secure the fidelity of those who become soldiers and diminishing the inducements to the rest to abscond.

I can only say in conclusion, that whatever measures are to be adopted should be adopted at once. Every day's delay increases the difficulty. Much time will be required to organize and discipline the men, and action may be deferred until it is too late.

Very respectfully, your obedient servant—R. E. Lee, General.

* * *

MACON TELEGRAPH, EDITORIAL OPPOSING ENLISTMENT OF AFRICAN AMERICANS, JANUARY 6, 1865.[55]

During the desperate winter of 1864–65, with Sherman moving north from Savannah and Lee cooped up around Petersburg, several Confederate leaders joined Lee and proposed to arm slaves and accept them into the army. The result was a firestorm of protest. An example is this editorial in the *Macon Telegraph*, an important Georgia newspaper that still publishes today.

Amid the storm of revolution, governments are apt to forget the principles to secure which they were instituted, and by which they should be controlled. All history admonishes us of this truth. . . . It would be constantly kept in view, though all the bloody phases and terrible epochs of this relentless war, that slavery was the casus belli—that the principle of State Sovereignty, and its sequence, the right of secession, were important to the South principally, or solely as the armor that encased her peculiar institution—and that every life that has been lost in this struggle was an offering on the altar of African Slavery. In the light of this great and solemn truth, is it not a matter of wonder and astonishment, that Southern men should gravely propose to arm, and as a necessary consequence, emancipate all the able-bodied slaves in the Confederacy, or a large portion of them, thereby striking an irretrievable and fatal blow at the institution. The adoption of this policy would be foul wrong to our departed heroes who have fallen in its defense. The compulsory adoption of such a policy would be tantamount to defeat; for what else is the forced assimilation of our institutions to those of the North but the abandonment of the whole object of the war?

. . . The advocates of this measure surely have not considered well the consequences likely to result from arming our slaves. Evidences are not wanting to illustrate the ill-suppressed discontent of many of our slaves in the past. The people seem to have grown over secure because of the unexpected subordination of our slaves during the war. They should remember that the whole white population being under arms, any uprising of the negroes was more than ever impracticable. How different might be the state of things, if they too were armed. They would be equal, perhaps superior, in numbers to our effective white force. What horrors might result from a general revolt? Yankees without and negroes within! At best it is not to be expected that they would be more true than our white veterans, and if two-thirds of them should desert and disperse themselves over the country, co-operating with and led by bad men and deserters of long standing, how appalling would be our condition!

Upon the whole, the proposition under consideration seems to be opposed by principle, consistency, self-respect, honor and safety.

* * *

Howell Cobb (1815–68), Letter to James A. Seddon, Secretary of War, January 8, 1865.[56]

Another Georgia voice against arming slaves was Howell Cobb. He had been Speaker of the U.S. House of Representatives and governor of Georgia. As Speaker of the provisional legislature when the Confederacy formed, he was for two weeks head of the government and guided the writing of the Confederate Constitution. One phrase from this letter—"*If slaves will make good soldiers our whole theory of slavery is wrong*"—has been much quoted. In context, Cobb goes on to say, "but they won't make soldiers." To come to this conclusion, he willfully refuses to accept the accounts of sterling performance by black U.S. troops that emanated from observers on both sides. Italics are in the original.

HDQRS. GEORGIA RESERVES AND MIL. DIST. OF GEORGIA.
Macon, Ga., January 8, 1865
Hon. JAMES A. SEDDON,
Secretary of War, Richmond, Va.:
SIR: . . .

. . . *I think that the proposition to make soldiers of our slaves is the most pernicious idea that has been suggested since the war began.* It is to me a source of deep mortification and regret to see the name of that good and great man and soldier, General R. E. Lee, given as authority for such a policy. My first hour of despondency will be the one in which that policy shall be adopted. You cannot make soldiers of slaves, nor slaves of soldiers. The moment you resort to negro soldiers your white soldiers will be lost to you; and one secret of the favor with which the proposition is received in portions of the Army is the hope that when negroes go into the Army they will be permitted to retire. It is simply a proposition to fight the balance of the war with negro troops. You can't keep white and black troops together, and you can't trust negroes by themselves. It is difficult to get negroes enough for the purpose indicated in the President's message, much less enough for an Army. *Use all the negroes you can get, for all the purposes for which you need them, but don't arm them. The day you make soldiers of them is the beginning of the end of the revolution. If slaves will make good soldiers our whole theory of slavery is wrong*—but they won't make soldiers. As a class they are wanting in every qualification of a soldier. Better by far to yield to the demands of England and France and abolish slavery, and thereby purchase their aid, than resort to this policy, which leads as certainly to ruin and subjugation as it is adopted; you want more soldiers, and hence the proposition to take negroes into the Army. Before resorting to it, at least try every reasonable mode of getting white soldiers.... For heaven's sake try it before you fill with gloom and despondency the hearts of many of our truest and most devoted men by resorting to the suicidal policy of arming our slaves.

Sincerely, yours,

HOWELL COBB, *Major-general.*

* * *

J. H. STRINGFELLOW (1819–1905), LETTER TO PRESIDENT JEFFERSON DAVIS, FEBRUARY 8, 1865.[57]

John H. Stringfellow was born in Virginia and took a medical degree in Pennsylvania. He moved to Missouri around 1845. In 1854, he moved to Kansas and helped found the *Atchison Squatter Sovereign*, a proslavery newspaper, and the town of Atchison itself. He became Speaker of the House under the proslavery territorial government. In 1856, he led the sack of Lawrence, an attempt to drive out settlers who opposed slavery. In 1858, aware that free-soil settlers so outnumbered proslavery settlers that Kansas could not become a slave state, he returned to Virginia. During the Civil War, he served as a doctor in the Confederate army. Late in the war, he wrote Jefferson Davis, exploring the issue of arming slaves to do battle for the South. "We have not one soldier" from our slave population "in our ranks," he complains, while the United States has 200,000 and will soon have 100,000 more.[58] Like Lee, he suggests that Confederate emancipation would leave African Americans subservient, while enemy emancipation would not.[59]

GLEN ALLEN, HENRICO, February 8, 1865
[President Davis:]
MY DEAR SIR:

Impelled by the perils of our country and the thousand conflicting theories as to the cause and cure to continually have these things before me, I have been amazed to see that no one thus far have conceived, or if conceived had the boldness to present, in my judgment, the only solution of all these perils and difficulties. I address you because you have taken a long stride in the right direction, and because I believe your mind has already reached the true solution, but owing to peculiar circumstances has hesitated to enunciate it. The history of this war demonstrates the wonderful fact that the Confederate States mainly subsists both of the immense armies engaged in the conflict, and actually, after furnishing all the soldiers to one army, contributes about one-half of those making the army of its enemies, and should the war continue for another year the South will probably furnish two-thirds of the army of her foes. These facts which cannot be controverted, show certainly anything but weakness or inferiority on the part of the South; but it does show that a change of policy in relation to the conduct of the war, and that a radical one, must be adopted or we shall be destroyed. Let us look at a few facts: The Yankees must now have in their service 200,000 of our ex-slaves, and under their next draft will probably have half as many more. We have not one soldier from that source in our ranks. It is held by us that slaves will not make soldiers, therefore we refuse to put them in the service, and I think we are correct in so doing; but while we thus think and thus act our enemies are creating. In addition to their white force (which we have found to our cost in the last year to be quite as large as we could manage), an auxiliary army of own escaped slaves of 300,000 or 400,000 men. Now, however, we may decry the negro as a soldier, every one knows that if the white troops of the Yankees are numerous enough to hold all ours in check, then this negro army can at will ravage and destroy our whole country and we will be absolutely conquered by our own slaves. We allege that slaves will not fight in our armies. Escaped slaves fight and fight bravely for our enemies; therefore a freed slave will fight. If at the beginning of this war all our negroes had been free does any one believe the Yankees would have been able to recruit an army amongst them? Does any know of a solitary free negro escaping to them and joining their Army?[60] If our slaves were now to be freed would the Yankees be able to raise another recruit amongst them? If freedom and amnesty were declared in favor of those already in the Yankee lines would they not almost to a man desert to their old homes? Would not our freed negroes make us as good soldiers as they make for our enemies? Again, suppose we free a portion of our slaves and put them in the Army, we leave all the rest as a recruiting field for the enemy, from which we cannot get a single soldier, and thus we see one-half of our entire population of no avail to us, but on the contrary ready at every opportunity to join the ranks of our enemies.

Now, sir, Southern soldiers are the best that ever drew a blade in the cause of liberty, but there are some things which they cannot do; they cannot fight our battles against overwhelming numbers, and raise the necessary supplies for the Army and the women and children at home; and yet, sir, this is what they will be called upon to do if this war is protracted for two years longer. I ask, sir, then, in view of these facts, if the prompt abolition of slavery will not prove a remedy sufficient to arrest this tide of disaster? The Yankee Army will be diminished by it, our own Army can be increased by it, and our labor retained by it. Without it, if the war continues, we shall in the end by subjugated, our negroes emancipated, our lands parceled out amongst them, and if any of it be left to us, only an equal portion with our own negroes, and ourselves given only equal (if any) social and political rights and privileges. If we emancipate, our independence is secured, the white man only will have any and all political rights, retain all his real and personal property, exclusive of his property in his slave; make the laws to control the freed negro, who having no land, must labor for the landowner, and being an adequate supply of labor must work for the landowner on terms about as economical as though owned by him. . . .

We omit a lengthy passage detailing possible ways to pay for emancipation via tariffs.

By emancipation I think we would not only render our triumph secure, as I have attempted to prove, in and of itself, but in all future time the negro, in place of being useless in time of war as a soldier, and really dangerous, as we have seen to our cost, continues to be an element of strength; and I think we may reasonably hope that the nations of the earth would no longer be unwilling to recognize us, for surely no people ever before struggled so long and under so many difficulties and endure so many privations so uncomplainingly as we have without finding some friendly hand outstretched to encourage or to help; and there can be no other reason than that we are exclusively and peculiarly a nation of slave holders. I think that even amongst our enemies numbers would be added to those who are already willing to let us go in peace, for we should thus give the lie at once and forever to the charge that we are waging a war only for negro slavery, and the heart of every honest lover of human liberty through-out the world would sympathize with the men who for their cherished rights of freemen would wage such an unequal contest as we have waged and besides sacrificing all their earnest convictions as to the humanity and righteousness of slavery, were willing to sacrifice their property interest of $4,000,000,000 to se-cure their independence, which might all be saved, so far as the promises of our enemies are concerned by reconstruction. In my judgment the only question for us to decide is whether we shall gain our independence by freeing the negro, we retaining all the power to regulate them by law when so freed, or permit our enemies through our own slaves to compel us to submit to emancipation with equal or superior political rights for our negroes, and partial or complete con-fiscation of our property for the use and benefit of the negro. And, sir, if the war continues as it is now waged, and we are forced, by the overwhelming odds of the Yankees and our own slaves in arms against us, into submission, it would be but an act of simple justice for the Yankee Government to see to it that their ne-gro allies are at least as well provided for in the way of homes as those who have been arrayed in arms against them. I have always believed, and still believe, that slavery is an institution sanctioned, if not established, by the Almighty, and the most humane and beneficial relation that can exist between labor and capital; still I think that this contest has proven that in a military sense it is an element of weakness, and the teachings of Providence as exhibited in this war dictate conclusively and imperatively that to secure and perpetuate our independence we must emancipate the negro.

P. S.—We should then get rid of the only impediment in the way of an exchange of prisoners, thus getting 30,000 or 40,000 more men in the field.

I have given you what I conceive to be the only solution to our difficulties. How to effect this is a serious difficulty. Men are reluctant—in fact it might be imprudent to discuss this thing publicly, but we know that in great crisis men think and act rapidly or at least should do so. If Congress would be convinced of the correctness of this course they could, in convention with the Governors of the States, devise some method by which conventions of the States could be held and the necessary measures adopted; first by law of Congress, if necessary, provide for paying the owners for them. I have not found a single slave-holder with who I have conversed but is willing to submit to the measure if deemed necessary by the proper authorities. Indeed, I have no doubts of the power of Congress as a military necessity to impress all of the able-bodied male negros and pay for them, giving them their freedom, and providing for paying for the rest upon the condition of manumission, but the other course would be less objectionable. We burn an individual's cotton, corn, or meat to keep it from the enemy, so we can take his negro man and set him free to keep him from recruiting the enemy's Army.

I have written you this much hoping it may aid you in some way. I have shown what I have written to no one, nor communicated my intentions to any one. If you think what I have written worth anything, make what use of it you choose. If not, just stick it between the bars of your grate. What I have written is with an honest endeavor to aid you in guiding our ship through the perils and darkness which surround her, and from no feeling of dissatisfaction or distrust as to yourself, for you have all my sympathies and all of my trust and confidence.

With difficulties and the warmest admiration and respect, I remain your friend.

J. H. STRINGFELLOW

P. S.—Written very hurriedly and with no effort at arrangement but only as "food for thought."

J. H. S.

I opened the envelope to say that my communication was written before I heard of the return of our commissioners, and that I am more than sustained by their report and the action of the Yankee Congress on the slavery question, and now we have only to decide on or between emancipation for our independence or subjugation and emancipation, coupled with negro equality or superiority, as our enemies may elect.

J. H. S.

* * *

General Orders, No. 14, An Act to Increase the Military Force of the Confederate States, Approved March 13, 1865.[61]

Even faced with imminent defeat, Confederates could not bring themselves to act quickly, as Lee pleaded. Governors and national leaders pointed out that the guarantee of slavery in the Confederate Constitution made it unconstitutional to enlist slaves, let alone promise general emancipation. In mid-March, the Confederate Congress finally passed a bill allowing black recruitment by the narrowest of margins (9 to 8 in the Senate; 40 to 37 in the House). Despite Lee's suggestions, the bill offers neither "gradual and general emancipation" nor "freedom at the end of the war to the families" of soldiers. It does not even free the men themselves, except with "consent of the owners and of the States in which they may reside." Notwithstanding these defects, the army recruited two companies of African Americans in Richmond, but, according to McPherson, they saw no action before the war ended.[62]

AN ACT to increase the military force of the Confederate States.

The Congress of the Confederate States of America do enact, That, in order to provide additional forces to repel invasion, maintain the rightful possession of the Confederate States, secure their independence, and preserve their institutions, the President be, and he is hereby, authorized to ask for and accept from the owners of slaves, the services of such number of able-bodied negro men as he may deem expedient, for and during the war, to perform military service in whatever capacity he may direct.

SEC 2. That the General-in-Chief be authorized to organize the said slaves into companies, battalions, regiments, and brigades, under such rules and regulations as the Secretary of War may prescribe, and to be commanded by such officers as the President may appoint.

SEC 3. That while employed in the service the said troops shall receive the same rations, clothing, and compensation as are allowed to other troops in the same branch of the service.

SEC 4. That if, under the previous sections of this act, the President shall not be able to raise a sufficient number of troops to prosecute the war successfully and maintain the sovereignty of the States and the independence of the Confederate States, then he is hereby authorized to call on each State, whenever he thinks it expedient, for her quota of 300,000 troops, in addition to those subject to military service under existing laws, or so many thereof as the President may deem necessary to be raised from such classes of the population, irrespective of color, in each State, as the proper authorities thereof may determine: Provided, That not more than twenty-five per cent. of the male slaves between the ages of eighteen and forty-five, in any State, shall be called for under the provisions of this act.

SEC 5. That nothing in this act shall be construed to authorize a change in the relation which the said slaves shall bear toward their owners, except by consent of the owners and of the States in which they may reside, and in pursuance of the laws thereof.

* * *

CHAPTER 4

RECONSTRUCTION AND FUSION (1866–1890)

To Confederates and neo-Confederates, Reconstruction and Fusion[1] were a continuation of the struggle to maintain white supremacy by means other than war.[2] Reconstruction refers to the political reconstitution of the former Confederate states. Historians divide the period into two phases, Presidential or Confederate Reconstruction, lasting through 1867 as Congress struggled to influence President Andrew Johnson's policies, and Congressional Reconstruction, beginning in 1868. Reconstruction then ended in different years in different states (1869–77), as white supremacist Democratic politicians overthrew interracial Republican administrations. Nationally, Reconstruction formally ended in 1877, when the incoming Hayes administration ordered troops in Southern states to return to their barracks. No longer would they help interracial Republican state administrations stay in power by enforcing election laws or protecting state capitols.

Historians call the next period the "Fusion" era. African Americans continued to vote and serve on juries, albeit not always freely. Often ballots featured "fusion tickets" listing white Democrats for the more important offices like governor and sheriff, but including African Americans and white Republicans for minor offices like justice of the peace or coroner. Like Reconstruction, Fusion ended in different years in different states, when Democrats passed new state constitutions that removed African Americans from voting. Throughout Reconstruction and Fusion, at least until the 1890s, Americans argued over the role African Americans would play in society. Nationally, Republicans continued to show considerable concern for the rights of African Americans until 1891.

Soon after the war ended, most former Confederates recognized that the Civil War had resolved the issue of slavery. Slavery now seemed an idea whose time had passed. All other Western nations had already abolished the practice when the United States did so in 1865, except Brazil.[3] No major political leaders suggested undoing the Thirteenth Amendment.

With slavery over, some former owners were initially ambivalent about their former workers. Asked by a congressional committee on Reconstruction what Virginia should do with its African Americans, Robert E. Lee says, in testimony we include, "I think it would be better for Virginia if she could get rid of them." He explains to his son, "You will never prosper with the blacks, and it is abhorrent to a reflecting mind to be supporting and cherishing those who are plotting and working for your injury." Following Lee's counsel, Southern planters repeatedly tried to recruit German, Dutch, Chinese, Italian, and other nonblack workers. Their efforts met with little success, partly because few outsiders could be persuaded to immigrate to the hard work and low pay that was sharecroppers' usual lot.[4]

Most planters concluded that their interests lay in reemploying their ex-slaves, preferably under terms as close to slavery as possible. As soon as the war ended, state governments, dominated by former Confederates, passed Black Codes designed to keep African Americans subservient. In October 1865, at his inauguration as Mississippi's new governor, Benjamin Humphreys stated, "The planter cannot venture upon the cultivation of the great staple unless the laborer is compelled to comply with his contract, remaining and performing his proper amount of labor, day after day, and week after week, through the year; and if he attempts to escape, he should be returned to his employer, and forced to work until the time for which he has contracted has expired." The author of the 1876 article from which we excerpt Mississippi's Black Codes noted, "By oversight or otherwise the Governor forgot to say anything about compensation for the forced labor he proposes."

In 1868, in the introduction to his important book, *The Lost Cause Regained*, secessionist Edward A. Pollard makes clear the continuity between the Confederate cause and what Southern Democrats worked for during Reconstruction: "the true question which the war involved, and which it merely liberated for greater breadth of controversy, was the supremacy of the White race, and along with it the preservation of the political traditions of the country." If white supremacy could be reestablished, Pollard writes, then the South "really triumphs in the true cause of the war, with respect to all its fundamental and vital issues."

Some former Confederates did not want to acknowledge that they had seceded to perpetuate such an ill-fated cause. In *A Youth's History of the Great Civil War in the United States from 1861 to 1865*, excerpted here, R. G. Horton is unwilling even to use the word "slavery." First, he claims that Southern leaders seceded "to get away from the North," "from people who would not keep their compacts," but soon he agrees with Pollard that white supremacy was key. Alexander Stephens, former vice president of the Confederacy, similarly subsumes slavery under white supremacy as a cause. The South seceded to protect its right to determine "the proper status of the African" in a biracial society. "Over these questions," Stephens maintains in his 1868 book, "the Federal Government had no rightful control whatever." Stephens also renames the war.

Partly in response to the Black Codes, in 1868 the Republican majority in the U.S. Congress took over the political reconstruction of the seceded states, except Tennessee, which had already rejoined the Union. During Congressional Reconstruction, by passing the Fourteenth and Fifteenth amendments, the federal government was indeed trying to influence "the proper status of the African" in American society. Likewise, Pollard, Horton, and Stephens were not only writing to try to explain secession and war, they were also trying to alter contemporary national policy on race relations. Chapters 5 and 6 will show that neo-Confederate thinking continued to center around that issue to a considerable extent. Slavery was gone, but what Howell Cobb called "*our whole theory of slavery*"—that blacks are inherently inferior to whites —lasted through Reconstruction and Fusion, dominated the Nadir, and indeed, survives down to now.

Despite white racism, during Congressional Reconstruction African Americans participated fully in political and civic life. Some ex-Confederates came to believe that this was right, including James Longstreet, Lee's second-in-command at Gettysburg, and William Mahone, hero of the Crater outside Petersburg. Most did not, instead striving during and after Reconstruction to remove political and social rights from African Americans. Ex-Confederates formed the core of the Ku Klux Klan and related terrorist organizations, such as the Red Shirts in South Carolina and the Knights of the White Camellia in Louisiana. John B. Gordon headed the Klan in Georgia. His 1868 speech to African Americans, then enjoying full political rights, threatens his audience with extermination if they conflict with whites. Five years later, Jubal Early, also an unrepentant white supremacist, stresses the importance of history in the continuing Confederate cause. In 1881, during the Fusion era, Jefferson Davis undertook to distort the history of his cause. In his two-volume apologia for secession, he writes, "[To] whatever extent the question of slavery may have served as an *occasion*, it was far from the *cause* of the conflict."[5] Sources in Chapters 2 and 3 show that Davis is obfuscating: Lincoln's election was the occasion, while slavery was indeed the underlying cause.

Confederate and neo-Confederate thinking was not limited to race, however. In the North, the cause of women's rights became intertwined to a degree with black rights. Many abolitionists also championed women's rights, and some suffragists championed black rights. In the South, opposition to women's rights similarly became intertwined with opposition to black rights. Rev. R. L. Dabney, who assisted Stonewall Jackson during the war, uses sarcasm and hyperbole to lampoon suffrage and other rights for women in an included article.

Even late in the Fusion era, interracial coalitions won elections or almost won elections statewide in Virginia, North Carolina, Alabama, and other states. As late as 1890, African Americans still had a chance. In that year, Republicans failed to pass a "Federal Elections Act" designed to alleviate the violent resistance black voting aroused in the South. After this failure, Republicans moved on to new issues. Now the white South was free to institutionalize white supremacy. Confederates (and neo-Confederates) had won the long struggle they had lost, briefly, during the Civil War and Reconstruction.

* * *

Edmund Rhett Jr., "Letter to
Armistead Burt," October 14, 1865.[6]

Edmund Rhett Jr. was scion of a South Carolina family so famously prose-cession that the house in which he grew up is still known as the "Secession House." He was an officer in the Confederate infantry and an editor, with his brother, of the *Charleston Mercury* when he wrote this letter. Armistead Burt was a former U.S. representative from South Carolina. Rhett's pro-posals obviously would keep African Americans in perpetual subservience to whites, which is why he suggests lying low "until we are back in the Union." Not only South Carolina but Mississippi and other seceded states quickly took Rhett's advice, which is why the period 1865–68 is sometimes called "Confederate Reconstruction"; since President Andrew Johnson ap-proved, it is more often called "Presidential Reconstruction."[7]

Dear Sir:

With great diffidence and some hesitation I venture to enclose you certain propositions relative to the negro-discipline and negro-labor questions, which have occurred to me, and impressed me as essential to the preservation of our labor system, and, indeed, of our social system. As one of the Commission appointed to suggest such laws as are advisable for the regulation and for the protection of the negro, I venture to submit these propositions to your consideration.

... [T]he sudden entire overthrow of that system which has taken place is unwise, injurious, and dangerous to our whole system, pecuniary and social. ... [I]t must follow as a natural sequence, it appears to me, that, sudden and abrupt abolition having taken place by the force of arms, it should be to the utmost extent practicable be limited, controlled, and surrounded with such safeguards, as will make the change as slight as possible both to the white man and to the negro, the planter and the workman, the capitalist and the laborer. In other words, that the general interest both of the white man and the negro requires that he should be kept as near to his former condition as Law can keep him and that he should be kept as near to the condition of slavery as possible, and as far from the condition of the white man as practicable.

If you agree with me in these premises, I trust we shall not differ much in the conclusion—namely, as to what Laws are necessary to effect this end.

I know that there are those who look to getting rid of the negro entirely, and of resorting to white labor. I regard this idea as the mere infatuation of men who are at their wits' end. For in all of the cotton states all of the *good* lands are so malarious in the fall of the year as to render it impracticable for white men to labor under our suns. We must face the question—negroes must be made to work, or else cotton and rice must cease to be raised for export.

Your obt. Sevt.

Edmund Rhett

Enclosure—

1st An Act prohibiting all *Freedmen* . . . from ever holding, or owning *Real Estate* in South Carolina, or their posterity after them. An act of this sort is essential in order to uproot the idea which has now run the negroes crazy all over this state—namely that they are all to have 40 acre lots of their own. Let the idea of their ever owning land pervade amongst them, and they will never work for the white man, or upon any land but their own. The Act is essential because it will at once cut off all competition between the white and the black man. The black man must then forever labor upon the capital of the white man, and the white man must take care of him, or else he will soon have no labor. I regard it as the most vital Law that can be made for our future prospering.

2nd a stringent Act against vagrancy on the part of the Freedmen of African descent. A Law requiring each negro, in each district to have a recorded domicile which it shall be unlawful for him to leave without due notice given to some appointed magistrate; or without twelve months notice of the fact, and the place to which he intends to move; or some other restriction as to the method of his movements. Also requiring him to show that he is the lawful employ of some white man. For the violation of such restrictions as these, or such other restrictions as may be deemed expedient, let the vagrant negro be taken up and put to hard labor upon public works in chain gangs, such as the repairing and building high roads, and the paving and cleaning of streets, for not less than 60 days at one time; and then to be returned to his locality.

The object of this Law would be to give fixedness to this population and to prevent their eternal wanderings and floating about the state from one point to another, lazy, lawless, thieving and vagrandizing.

3rd An Act to enforce the fulfillment of contracts between the employer and the employee of freedmen—an Act by which the negro will be held both as a vagrant and a criminal should he leave the service of his employer until the term of the contract is fulfilled—by which he may be seized and put to hard labor for vagrancy, and 2) also be made to pay the planter the value of his wages for all the time of his contract not yet expired. The Law should be as stringent as words can make it to force the negro to work, and as penal as humanity would permit.

4th an act to regulate discipline. It is essential that there should be some system of discipline on larger plantations. Both under the apprentice system, and under the coolie system, some corporal punishment is found necessary on the part of the employer. . . .

Here, under these four propositions, we have the negro, first, put upon the footing of denizen. He can own no Real Estate—the soil is out of his reach. Then we have him located, and prevented from vagrandizing. Then we compel him to keep his contracts. Then we control him, and keep him under good discipline. Under these Laws, he must labor faithfully according to the laws of demand and supply, or else he must leave the state.

I do not conceive it impracticable to pass such Laws. Of course this is no time to do it. The question should not be broached until we are back in the Union. If it is now broached, it will only strengthen the Black Republican Party, and render the admission of the State difficult. After we are admitted, I believe there will be little difficulty. The [Andrew Johnson] Administration will support us.

* * *

MISSISSIPPI'S BLACK CODE,
NOVEMBER 24–29, 1865.[8]

At war's end, Confederates still ran state governments across most of the South. They had no intention of conferring citizenship upon their newly freed slaves. As the leading newspaper in Mississippi put it, "We must keep the ex-slave in a position of inferiority. We must pass such laws as will make him *feel* his inferiority."[9] That autumn, the Mississippi legislature hastened to comply by passing a series of acts collectively known as the "Black Codes," beginning with the vagrancy act on November 24, 1865. Section 2 provides for the arrest of any adult African American who could not show proof of employment. Interestingly, whites who associate with African Americans face even stiffer penalties. The next day, the legislature passed an ironically titled "Act to Confer Civil Rights on Freedmen, and for Other Purposes." Sections 5, 6, and 7 were key: laborers apparently do not get paid as they work and cannot quit without losing any pay they might receive at the end of their term of employment. Other parts of the Black Code forbid African Americans from owning land except in incorporated towns, so they could never farm on their own. Racial intermarriage carries the penalty of life imprisonment. Children younger than eighteen can be apprenticed to whites as indentured servants, and "the former owner of said minors shall have the preference." Those masters can also "inflict such moderate corporeal chastisement as a father or guardian is allowed to inflict." Finally, the legislature passed a bill "To Punish Certain Offenses." It forbids gun ownership by African Americans, except those "in the military service of the United States government" or licensed by the local jurisdiction. (Whites faced no such requirement.) Its second section, reprinted below, was so vague as to enable the arrest of any African American whom the civil authorities did not like. And like the other laws, persons who cannot pay their fines are to be hired out "to any white person who will pay said fine and costs, and take such convict for the shortest time."

Other Southern states rushed to pass Black Codes of their own. To be fair, some of their provisions were similar to Black Codes in such northern states as Oregon and Illinois. Across the North, however, antiracist sentiments aroused by the Civil War were prompting Republicans to ease these restrictions. Moreover, the Black Codes made it look like Mississippi had abolished slavery in name only. Republicans were outraged. The *Chicago Tribune*, the leading Republican organ in the Midwest, bellowed, "We tell the white men of Mississippi that the men of the North will convert the state of Mississippi into a frog pond before they will allow any such laws to disgrace one foot of soil in which the bones of our soldiers sleep and over which the flag of freedom waves."[10] Such reactions led to Congressional Reconstruction.

An Act to Amend the Vagrant Laws of Mississippi.

Sec. 2. That all freedmen, free Negroes, and mulattoes in this state over the age of eighteen years found on the second Monday in January, 1866, or thereafter, with no lawful employment or business, or found unlawfully assembling themselves together either in the day or night time, and all white persons so assembling with freedmen, free Negroes, or mulattoes, or usually associating with freedmen, free Negroes, or mulattoes on terms of equality, or living in adultery or fornication with a freedwoman, free Negro, or mulatto, shall be deemed vagrants; and, on conviction thereof, shall be fined in the sum of not exceeding, in the case of a freedman, free Negro, or mulatto, $50, and a white man, $200, and imprisoned at the discretion of the court, the free Negro not exceeding ten days, and the white man not exceeding six months. . . .

Sec. 5. . . . [I]n case any freedman, free Negro, or mulatto shall fail for five days after the imposition of any fine or forfeiture upon him or her for violation of any of the provisions of this act to pay the same, that it shall be, and is hereby made, the duty of the sheriff of the proper county to hire out said freedman, free Negro, or mulatto to any person who will, for the shortest period of service, pay said fine or forfeiture and all costs:

Provided, a preference shall be given to the employer, if there be one, in which case the employer shall be entitled to deduct and retain the amount so paid from the wages of such freedman, free Negro, or mulatto then due or to become due; and in case such freedman, free Negro, or mulatto cannot be hired out he or she may be dealt with as a pauper.

An Act to Confer Civil Rights on Freedmen, and for Other Purposes.

Sec. 5. That every freedman, free Negro, or mulatto shall, on the second Monday in January, 1866, and annually thereafter, have a lawful home or employment, and shall have written evidence thereof. . . .

Sec. 6. That if the laborer shall quit the service of the employer before expiration of his term of service without good cause he shall forfeit his wages for that year up to the time of quitting.

Sec. 7. That every civil officer shall, and every person may arrest and carry back to his legal employer any freedman, free Negro, or mulatto, who shall have quit the service of his or her employer before the expiration of his or her term of service without good cause, and such officer and person shall be entitled to receive ... the sum of five dollars and ten cents per mile[11] from the place of arrest to the place of delivery, and the same shall be paid by the employer, and held as a setoff for so much against the wages of said deserting employee.

An Act to Punish Certain Offenses ...

Section 2. *Be it further enacted,* that any freedman, free Negro, or mulatto committing riots, routs, affrays, trespasses, malicious mischief, cruel treatment to animals, seditious speeches, insulting gestures, language, or acts, or assaults on any person, disturbance of the peace, exercising the function of a minister of the Gospel without a license from some regularly organized church, vending spirituous or intoxicating liquors, or committing any other misdemeanor the punishment of which is not specifically provided for by law shall, upon conviction thereof in the county court, be fined not less than $10 and not more than $100,[12] and may be imprisoned, at the discretion of the court, not exceeding thirty days.

* * *

Robert E. Lee (1807–70), Testimony before the Congressional Joint Committee on Reconstruction, February 17, 1866.[13]

The Joint Congressional Committee on Reconstruction set up a subcommittee to inquire into conditions in the Southern states and make recommendations about Reconstruction policies. It subpoenaed various Confederate leaders, including Robert E. Lee. Henry T. Blow, Republican congressman from Missouri, asks the questions; Lee gives the answers. Lee expresses his opinion that Virginia would be better off without African Americans; Blow seems to be of like mind.

Question. Has there been any considerable change in the number of the negro population?

Answer. I suppose it has diminished, but I do not know.

Question. Diminished in consequences of more negroes going south than was made up by the natural increase?

Answer. My general opinion is that the number has diminished and for the reason you give.

Question. I suppose that the mass of the negroes in Virginia, at the present time, are able to work; that there are not many helpless ones among them?

Answer. There are helpless ones, certainly, but I do not know to what extent.

Question. What is your opinion about its being an advantage to Virginia to keep them there at all. Do you not think that Virginia would be better off if the colored population were to go to Alabama, Louisiana, and the other southern States?

Answer. I think it would be better for Virginia if she could get rid of them. That is no new opinion with me. I have always thought so, and have always been in favor of emancipation—gradual emancipation.

Question. As a matter of labor alone, do you not think that the labor which would flow into Virginia, if the negroes left it for the cotton States, would be far more advantageous to the State and to its future prosperity?

Answer. I think it would be for the benefit of Virginia, and I believe that everybody there would be willing to aid it.

Question. And do you not think it is peculiarly adapted to the quality of labor which would flow into it, from its great natural resources, in case it was made more attractive by the absence of the colored race?

Answer. I do.

* * *

Rushmore G. Horton (1826–68),
"A Youth's History of the Great Civil War in
the United States from 1861 to 1865," 1867.[14]

During the Civil War, Rushmore G. Horton co-edited the *Day-Book*, a newspaper in New York City that called itself "The White Man's Paper" and was notorious for its support of the Confederacy. During the 1864 presidential election campaign, it advertised political caricatures showing Republican leaders paired with ugly black women as part of a strategy that introduced the word "miscegenation" into the language. Probably Horton was involved in the failed Confederate plot of November 1864 to burn much of the city. After the war, he wrote and published probably the first history of the conflict from the Confederate side. In this excerpt, the reasons he gives to explain secession shift about. At one point Horton even writes that the "object was to preserve and perpetuate the sacred principles of liberty and self-government," but soon he reverses field: Southern leaders wanted to preserve self-government to "save themselves from the horrible consequences of amalgamation and social death." He then spends several paragraphs denouncing the "horror of negro equality" and racial amalgamation. At the time, this was mainstream neo-Confederate thought; the Mississippi Democratic Convention, for example, resolved in January 1868 "that the nefarious design of the Republican Party in Congress to place the white men of the Southern states under the governmental control of their late slaves, and degrade the Caucasian race as the inferior of the African negro, is a crime against the civilization of the age, which need only to be mentioned to be scorned by every intelligent mind." Horton's book was republished by Mary D. Carter of the United Daughters of the Confederacy and Lloyd T. Everett, a historian of the Confederacy, in 1925 and was promoted repeatedly in *Confederate Veteran*.[15]

Chapter VIII: The Policy and Objects of Secession.

WHILE very little, if any, difference of opinion existed at the South as to the *right* of secession, there were many people who doubted the *policy* of the movement. Prominent among these was the Hon. Alexander H. Stephens, of

Georgia, who advised against the step. It was felt by such men that it was going to place great power in the hands of the Abolition party, who might then set themselves up as in favor of the Union, and use the very prestige and power of the Government, which southern statesmen had mainly created, to make war upon them. They distrusted the peaceful professions of the Black Republican leaders, who were talking against coercion, and who were announcing themselves as willing "to let the South go."

As it has turned out, it would seem that these men were right; for the Abolition party did raise large armies in the name of the Union, actually to overthrow it—to subvert its form of government, and to bring a doom on the southern people which words cannot describe. However, the overwhelming impulse of the great majority of the Southern people at the time of which we are writing was to get away from the North. They did not wish to be associated any longer with a people the majority of whom could deliberately elect a man President on a platform of avowed hostility to their States. They desired to get away from people who would not keep their compacts.

Yet they wished the North no harm. The debates of the great leaders in Congress at the time of withdrawing, prove that they went more in sorrow than in anger. They evinced indeed a great reluctance to go; but they felt that the North had already sundered the political bands made by our forefathers, and that there was nothing left for them but to go, or stay and acquiesce in the overthrow of their Government. They chose to go, declaring that their object was to preserve and perpetuate the sacred principles of liberty and self-government which our forefathers established.

General Robert E. Lee, in a letter written since the war, dated January 6th, 1866, says, "All the South has ever asked or desired is, that the Union founded by our forefathers should be preserved, and that the Government as it was originally organized should be administered in purity and truth." Now the Abolitionists could not say this. They desired the Government, as it was formed, overthrown. General Lee desired the Government to remain just as it was. Mr. Seward said "No, Slavery must and shall be abolished." Mr. Lincoln stood on the same platform.

The great and overwhelming object the South had was to preserve to themselves the right of self-government, and thus save themselves from the horrible consequences of amalgamation and social death. They knew from their practical knowledge of the negro that he belonged to a distinct species of man; that his brain, his bones, his shape, his nerves, in fact that every part of his body was different from the white man's. They knew that he was liable to different diseases from the white man; that he required the care and protection of the superior race. They knew that to equalize the races was simply to follow the fate of Mexico and Central America.

What a splendid country was Mexico while under the control of the white blood of the pure Spanish race! Now what is it, after the white blood has all become mixed and diluted by amalgamation with the black race? When the black race held its natural position of subordination to the white race, Mexico was one of the richest and most prosperous countries on the globe; but now it is one of the meanest and most contemptible. The white man's proud and glorious civilization has faded out on the dead plain of amalgamation and negro equality. The white blood has become so muddy and polluted by admixture with the inferior race, that no lapse of time can ever redeem that population from the utter degradation and uncivilization into which it has fallen. So of all those once rich and flourishing countries to the south of the United States—since the abolition of negro subordination to the white race, they have all fallen back in civilization, and sunken down in a slough of social, political, and moral filth, and wretchedness! It makes the heart sick to contemplate them.

The West India Islands which, under negro servitude, or when the white man was sole master, were among the richest and most flourishing spots on the globe, now, under negro equality, are the poorest and most detested sinks of sorrow and pollution that oppress the imagination of man.

To save the most beautiful and productive portion of our country from a similar terrible fate, was the great motive which made the Southern States desire separation from the abolitionized States of the North. To save our country from the terrible scourge of negro amalgamation and negro equality, which the Black Republicans are now forcing upon us, was a patriotic and sacred thought in the minds of those who wished no further union with the madmen who were determined to force the shame and horror of negro equality upon us.

God only can tell what the consequences of this amalgamation policy may be to the cause of liberty and civilization! Unless the people arise and put a stop to the further progress of the disgusting and brutalizing notions of negro equality, we shall inevitably land at last where Mexico, the Central American States, and the West India Islands have gone already. Negro emancipation and negro equality are driving us on that fatal shore with alarming rapidity. A mongrel nation, or a nation of mixed races, never yet remained free and prosperous.

The English, Irish, French, Spanish or Germans may amalgamate without detriment, because they are only different families of the same, or the white race; but the negro being of a different and lower race, the offspring of such a union are *hybrids* or *mongrels*, and are always a weak, degraded, and wretched class of beings—as inferior to the white race as the mule is to the horse.

Such, then, were the points involved in the *policy* and *objects* of secession. If the Northern people could have understood the great wrong they were forcing upon the South, they never would have blamed her for seeking to save herself from the degradation of amalgamation. But they had, unfortunately, been made to believe that it was wicked to hold negroes as inferiors of white people. They did not understand the horrible sin and crime, disease and death involved in equalizing races. Hence they thought that the South acted "without good cause."

They were made to believe that she resisted Lincoln's election from mere spite, and from a long cherished desire to break up the Union. While the real truth was, that the great mass of the people of the South loved and cherished the Union, and only withdrew from it when they felt themselves not only compelled to do so, but actually driven out by the abolition party, who came into possession of the Government, threatening to use it to bring upon them and their children the most horrible doom that can possibly be inflicted upon any people.

In the North, where there are but few negroes, it is difficult to understand this subject, but if our population were one half blacks, we would very soon begin to comprehend what it meant to give the negro the same rights as the white man. Every child can see that in such a society only two things are possible. Either one race or the other would be master, or else they would be compelled to fraternize—to mingle, and with that comes all the horrible consequences we have just depicted.

In the light of subsequent events, nearly all will now allow that the South made a mistake when they demanded unconditional separation. True, they had many reasons to lose faith in the North, and to believe they would stand by no agreements if made. But if they had said all the time, "we stand ready to resume our places in the Union, when you of the North give us plain and distinct pledges and guarantees that you will abide by the Constitution and Union as they were formed," they would have deprived Mr. Lincoln and his party of nine-tenths of their capital. They could not then have set themselves up as "the Union party," while in fact they were the real *disunion* party, and always had been. Nor could they have made such a hue and cry about "the flag," which they had denounced as a "flaunting lie."

Perhaps you never saw the verses on the American flag which the Black Republicans circulated in 1854, just about the time they organized their party. I will give you two of them.

> All hail the flaunting lie
> The stars grow pale and dim,
> The stripes are bloody scars—
> A lie the vaunting hymn.
> Tear down the flaunting lie,
> Half-mast the starry flag,
> Insult no sunny sky
> With hate's polluted rag.

Now it does not look reasonable that a political party which endorsed such poetry could have been at all sincere in love for the American flag.

They simply put forth the cry of "the Union," and "the flag," to get the war started. After which they believed they could use it to accomplish their *real* purposes, which were the overthrow of our form of government, and its revolution from a White Man's government to that of a *mongrel* nation, in which negroes should have the same rights as white people.

This is now plainly apparent, if it never was before; and however mistaken the South may have been as to the *means* used to avert this calamity, no one not deluded with negro equality will deny that they were justified in taking any step which would save them and their children from such horrible consequences.

* * *

Jack Kershaw (1913–2010),
Statue of Nathan Bedford Forrest, 1998.

Figure 9: In July 1998, the League of the South dedicated this huge new statue of Nathan Bedford Forrest, made of plastic resin painted gold and silver, on private property bordering Interstate 65 near Nashville. Also participating were the Sons of Confederate Veterans, United Daughters of the Confederacy, and the Council of Conservative Citizens, the descendant organization of the [White] Citizens' Councils, the Mississippi-based organization that tried to destroy the civil rights movement. At this time, monuments to Forrest on public property were beginning to encounter turbulence. African Americans and others who favor racial equality argued that such gestures of veneration are inappropriate. Courtesy of James B. Jones Jr.

Tennessee has more historical markers and monuments to Nathan Bedford Forrest than Virginia boasts for George Washington, Illinois for Abraham Lincoln, or any other state for anybody. This adulation reflects Forrest's continuing popularity among neo-Confederates during and after the Nadir. At the time this statue went up, T-shirt companies were reporting that they sold five shirts with Forrest's image for every shirt with Robert E. Lee's. Although Forrest was a colorful and successful cavalry leader, he was a minor general. His surge in popularity in the 1990s and 2000s among neo-Confederates surely owed more to the civil rights movement of the 1960s and 1970s and to Forrest's role during Reconstruction as the first national head of the Ku Klux Klan. Sculptor Jack Kershaw is an unreconstructed white supremacist who worked with Vanderbilt professor Donald Davidson to get Dixiecrat Strom Thurmond on the ballot for president in 1948. Later Davidson and Kershaw tried unsuccessfully to stop the racial desegregation of public schools in Tennessee. In 1977, Kershaw volunteered to be the attorney for James Earl Ray, who had pled guilty to murdering Martin Luther King Jr. In 1994, Kershaw helped found the League of the South, a neo-Confederate organization described in Chapter 6 that still supports Southern secession.[16]

* * *

Edward A. Pollard (1831–72), "The Lost Cause Regained," 1868.[17]

During the Civil War, Pollard edited the *Richmond Examiner*, an important newspaper, and was very critical of the leadership of Jefferson Davis. Even before the war ended, and throughout Reconstruction, he wrote accounts of the war and edited a compilation of Confederate documents. In 1866, he wrote *The Lost Cause: A New Southern History of the War of the Confederates*, which popularized the term "Lost Cause" for generations of white Southerners. We include the introduction to his next book, *The Lost Cause Regained*, published in 1868, which explains that white Southerners seceded not exactly for slavery, but for white supremacy. During Reconstruction, white supremacy still seemed realizable; indeed, Reconstruction ended with the overthrow of interracial Republican state and local governments and the eventual passage, after 1890, of new state constitutions placing all power in white hands.

The author of the present work wrote a history of the recent war under the title of "The Lost Cause." The fitness of the title was singularly complimented, and the Words have since been permanently incorporated in the common language of the people. The author now proposes a title yet more fit and happy for the continuation of his historical Work: "The Lost Cause Regained." He does not hesitate to confess that a prolonged and mature reflection has given him larger and perhaps better views of the true nature of the recent War, and especially of its consequences; and he has risen from that reflection profoundly convinced that the true cause fought for in the late war has not been "lost" immeasurably or irrevocably, but is yet in a condition to be "regained" by the South on ultimate issues of the political contest.

It is scarcely possible in any introduction to recite the whole design of a literary Work. But the meaning of a title, which perhaps piques curiosity, may be fixed at once in the mind of the reader by the following brief summary of propositions:

That the late War was much misunderstood in the South, and its true inspiration thereby lost or diminished, through the fallacy that Slavery was defended as a property tenure, or as a peculiar institution of labour; when the true ground of defence was as of a barrier against a contention and War of races.

That the greatest value of Slavery was such a barrier.

That the War has done nothing more than destroy this barrier, and liberate and throw upon the country the ultimate question of the negro.

That the question of the Negro practically couples or associates a revolutionary design upon the Constitution; and that the true question which the war involved, and which it merely liberated for greater breath of controversy was the supremacy of the White race, and along with it the preservation of the political traditions of the country.

That in contesting the cause the South is far stronger than in any former contest, and is supplied with new aids and inspirations.

That if she succeeds to the extent of securing the supremacy of the White man, and the traditional liberties of the country—in short, to the extent of defeating the Radical party—she really triumphs in the true cause of the war, with respect to all its fundamental and vital issues.

That the triumph is at the loss of so many dollars and cents in the property tenure of Slavery—the South still retaining the Negro as a labourer, and keeping him in a condition where his political influence is as indifferent as when he was a slave;—and that the pecuniary loss is utterly insignificant, as the price of the "lost cause regained."

These propositions, we believe, sum a novel, and even sublime philosophy on the political questions of the day. They contain the true hope of the South; they suggest a new animation of a contest which lingers too much on mere partial and contracted issues.

* * *

Alexander H. Stephens (1812–83), "Conclusion," *A Constitutional View of the Late War Between the States*, 1868.[18]

Shortly after war's end, Alexander H. Stephens, former vice president of the Confederacy, is clear that the South seceded to protect its right to determine "the proper status of the African." Like Horton, Stephens hopes to unify the postwar white South to maintain white supremacy. This book marks an early use of "War Between the States." Actually, no one called it the "War Between the States" while it was going on.[19] While the conflict raged, it was called "the Civil War," "the Great Rebellion," or "the War of the Rebellion"—hence "Rebel." As the next chapter shows, however, Stephens sets a powerful precedent here: between 1890 and 1940 "War Between the States" became the preferred term in the South and achieved wide currency in the North as well.[20] "This great principle" referred to at the beginning of this excerpt is secession, "the right of any member to withdraw," which Stephens has just argued is the only real check to keep a government from becoming a "centralized despotic Empire." After Reconstruction, Georgia sent Stephens back to the U.S. House of Representatives and then elected him governor; he died in office in 1883.

The matter of Slavery, so-called, which was the proximate cause of these irregular movements on both sides, and which ended in the general collision of war, as we have seen, was of infinitely less importance to the Seceding States, than the recognition of this great principle. I say Slavery, so-called, because there was with us no such thing as Slavery in the full and proper sense of that word. No people ever lived more devoted to the principles of liberty, secured by free democratic institutions, than were the people of the South. None had ever given stronger proofs of this than they had done, from the day that Virginia moved in behalf of the assailed rights of Massachusetts, in 1774, to the firing of the first gun in Charleston Harbor, in 1861. What was called Slavery amongst us, was but a legal subordination of the African to Caucasian race. This relation was so regulated by law as to promote, according to the intent and design of the system, the best interests of both races, the Black as well as the White, the Inferior as well as the Superior. Both had rights secured, and both had duties imposed. It was a system of reciprocal service, and mutual bonds. But even the two thousand million dollars invested in the relation thus established, between private capital and the labor of this class of population, under the system, was but as the dust in the balance, compared with the vital attributes of the rights of Independence and Sovereignty on the part of the several States. For with these whatever changes and modifications, or improvements in this domestic institution, founded itself upon laws of nature, time, and experience, might have shown to be proper in the advancing progress of civilization, for the promotion of the great ends of society in all good Governments that is the best interest of all classes, without wrong or injury to any could, and would have been made by the superior race in these States, under the guidance of that reason, justice, and philanthropy, and statesmanship, which had ever marked their course, without the violent disruption of the entire social fabric, with all its attendant ills, and inconceivable wrongs, mischiefs, and sufferings; and especially without those terrible evils and consequences which must almost necessarily result from such disruptions and reorganizations as make a sudden and complete transfer of political power from the hands of the superior to the inferior race, in their present condition, intellectually and morally, in at least six States of the Union!

The system, as it existed, it is true, was not perfect. All admit this. No human systems are perfect. But great changes had been made in it, as this class of persons were gradually rising from their original barbarism, in their subordinate sphere, under the operation of the system, and from their contact, in this way, with the civilization of the superior race. . . .

Stephens suggests that slavery was the best arrangement for both races, and he would not support it unless he believed it was beneficial to African Americans.

This whole question of Slavery, so-called, was but one relating to the proper *status* of the African as an element of a society composed of the Caucasian and African races, and the *status* which was best, not for the one race or the other, but best, upon the whole, for both.

Over these questions, the Federal Government had no rightful control whatever.

They were expressly excluded, in the Compact of the Union, from its jurisdiction or authority. Any, such assumed control was a palpable violation of the Compact, which released all the parties to the Compact, affected by such action, from their obligation under the Compact. On this point there can be no shadow of doubt.

After three grandiose but muddled paragraphs extolling secession, Stephens ends his book with this sentence:

With this principle recognized, I looked upon it hereafter, and at no distant day, to become, by the natural law of political affinity "mutual convenience and reciprocal advantage" the great Continental Regulator of the Grand Federal Republic of "the United States of America," to whatever limits their boundaries might go, or to whatever extent their numbers might swell.

* * *

ROBERT E. LEE (1807–70),
"THE WHITE SULPHUR MANIFESTO,"
AUGUST 26, 1868.[21]

In the upcoming elections of 1868, William S. Rosecrans, U.S. Civil War general and now Democratic Party campaigner, sought to counter the Republican Party by getting a statement from former Confederate leaders. He prevailed upon Robert E. Lee to write such a letter, also known as "The White Sulphur Manifesto." After Lee signed, he suggested recruiting other ex-Confederate leaders who might sign and encouraged others to collect additional signatures. The purpose of the letter is to undermine and oppose the civil rights policies of the Republican Party during Reconstruction. Through this letter, Robert E. Lee plays a significant role in defeating civil rights and condemning African Americans to a century of discrimination and violence. The letter is addressed to Rosecrans.

General:

I have the honor to receive your letter of this date, and, in accordance with your suggestion, I have conferred with a number of gentlemen from the South, in whose judgment I have confidence, and who are well acquainted with the public sentiment of their respective States.

They have kindly consented to unite with me in replying to your communication, and their names will be found, with my own, appended to this answer.

With this explanation, we proceed to give you a candid statement of what we believe to be the sentiment of the Southern people in regard to the subjects to which you refer.

Whatever opinions may have prevailed in the past with regard to African slavery or the right of a State to secede from the Union, we believe we express the almost unanimous judgment of the Southern people when we declare that they consider these questions were decided by the war, and that it is their intention in good faith to abide by that decision. At the close of the war, the Southern people laid down their arms and sought to resume their former relations to the

government of the United States. Through their State conventions, they abolished slavery and annulled their ordinances of secession; and they returned to their peaceful pursuits with a sincere purpose to fulfill all their duties under the Constitution of the United States which they had sworn to support. If their action in these particulars had been met in a spirit of frankness and cordiality, we believe that, ere this, old irritations would have passed away, and the wounds inflicted by the war would have been, in a large measure, healed. As far as we are advised, the people of the South entertain no unfriendly feeling towards the government of the United States, but they complain that their rights under the Constitution are withheld from them in the administration thereof. The idea that the Southern people are hostile to the negroes and would oppress them, if it were in their power to do so, is entirely unfounded. They have grown up in our midst, and we have been accustomed from childhood to look upon them with kindness. The change in the relations of the two races has brought no change in our feelings towards them. They still continue an important part of our laboring population. Without their labor, the lands of the South would be comparatively unproductive; without the employment which Southern agriculture affords, they would be destitute of the means of subsistence and become paupers, dependent upon public bounty. Self-interest, if there were no higher motive, would therefore prompt the whites of the South to extend to the negro care and protection.

The important fact that the two races are, under existing circumstances, necessary to each other is gradually becoming apparent to both, and we believe that but for malign influences exerted to stir up the passions of the negroes, the relations of the two races would soon adjust themselves on a basis of mutual kindness and advantage.

It is true that the people of the South, in common with a large majority of the people of the North and West, are, for obvious reasons, inflexibly opposed to any system of laws that would place the political power of the country in the hands of the negro race. But this opposition springs from no feeling of enmity, but from a deep-seated conviction that, at present, the negroes have neither the intelligence nor the other qualifications which are necessary to make them safe depositories of political power. They would inevitably become the victims of demagogues, who, for selfish purposes, would mislead them to the serious injury of the public.

The great want of the South is peace. The people earnestly desire tranquility and restoration of the Union. They deplore disorder and excitement as the most serious obstacle to their prosperity. They ask a restoration of their rights under the Constitution. They desire relief from oppressive misrule. Above all, they would appeal to their countrymen for the re-establishment, in the Southern States, of that which has been justly regarded as the birth-right of every American, the right of self-government. Establish these on a firm basis, and we can safely promise, on behalf of the Southern people, that they will faithfully obey the Constitution and laws of the United States, treat the negro populations with kindness and humanity and fulfill every duty incumbent and peaceful citizens, loyal to the Constitution of their country.

* * *

John B. Gordon (1832–1904),
"To the Colored People," address in Charleston,
South Carolina, September 11, 1868.[22]

During Reconstruction, John Gordon led the Ku Klux Klan in Georgia. After its overthrow, Gordon was later elected senator and governor. He was also commander in chief of the United Confederate Veterans from its founding until his death in 1904.[23]

White Democrats used "carpetbaggers" to slur Republicans who had moved to the state from elsewhere; the term was meant to imply that they came in with their belongings in a carpetbag, hence were corrupt, looking to make their fortune off the postwar South. Although newcomers included Yankee schoolteachers and former Union soldiers who had developed friendships in the South, and although the postwar South was hardly a likely place to find easy money, the term has stuck. H. R. Helper, to whom Gordon alludes, wrote a famous prewar book, *The Impending Crisis of the South*, in which he argued slavery had hurt the South. Here, however, Gordon refers to a new work by Helper, *War of Races*, written when Helper had become rabidly antiblack.

In the course of a speech delivered in Charleston, on the 11th inst., by Gen. John B. Gordon, of Georgia, he addressed the colored portion of his audience in the following plain and simple language. We commend the advice given to the colored people of this section. Gen. Gordon said:

In the few words I shall say to you, my friends, if you will listen to me, I hope to deal with you candidly and honestly. The Radicals have told you that the Southern people were your enemies. But believe me, this is not so. I was opposed to your freedom. We were all opposed to your freedom. Now that's honest, isn't it? And why was this so? I'll tell you. We did not do this because we were your enemies but because we had bought you and paid our money for you. You belonged to the Northern people once, and some people think you belong to them now, in the Loyal League. It was the Northern States that sent to the shores of Africa and captured and brought your fathers to the North. And when your labor became unprofitable they sold you to the Southern people. The carpet-baggers will tell you that the North brought on the war to free you. Let me ask, why didn't they free you when they owned you? You might have been born free, and might now have owned the forty acres which the lying rascals promised you. I say they did not wage the war to free you, and no honest soldier who participated in it will say so. The idea was never entertained. Gen. Grant himself at one time threatened to quit the service if you were freed. They set you free because they wanted to use you, not from any love they bore you. And now they tell you that we are your enemies. Have we not been born on the same soil? Are not our interests identical? Have we not grown up together, and have not our fathers been buried under the same sod? Why, then are we your enemies?

You have been told to array yourselves against the whites. What would be the result of arraying the two races? A contest will come, which will be a war of races; then which race must triumph? My friends, let me tell you, the moment the war of races is inaugurated that moment the death warrant of the black man on this continent is signed. There are three millions of your race and forty millions of white men. Now, I ask you in all reason, which race must go down?

The speaker then alluded to the assertions of Helper, the Radical, who said that before the year 1872 no black man will have a habitation on this continent. In quoting this the speaker said: He says so because of speculation. Lands are scarce in the North, they have a surplus of labor, and they desire to blot out your race in order that they might come here, take possession of the place and cultivate the land. The Indian once lived where you now live, but where is he now? He couldn't live in peace with the white men, and he went to war. The few scattering mounds that are left in the State speak the result. Now, this is what Helper says must be your fate, and most singular to relate, a large majority of the Radical members of Congress are subscribers to his book and are giving it circulation.

Now I speak plainly. If you are disposed to live in peace with the white people they extend to you the hand of friendship. But if you attempt to inaugurate a war of races you will be exterminated. The Saxon race was never created by Almighty God to be ruled by the African. These are truths. We want peace with you. We cannot live as enemies. One or the other must go down.

* * *

Ku Klux Klan Postcard, c. 1937.

BANNER USED BY THE KU-KLUX.
Original now in North Carolina Room, Confederate Museum, Richmond, Virginia.

Figure 10: The sender's choice of a Lee-Jackson stamp shows his or her perception of the Ku Klux Klan as part of the Confederate heritage.

The Guilford Chapter of the North Carolina Division of the United Daughters of the Confederacy, proud of a Ku Klux Klan banner in the North Carolina Room of the Museum of the Confederacy, published this postcard, post-marked March 24, 1937, to commemorate it. This was in keeping of the UDC's celebration of the Ku Klux Klan as a heroic effort of ex-Confederate soldiers in maintaining white supremacy in the South.

R. L. Dabney (1820–98),
"Women's Rights Women," 1871.[24]

Of course, one need not be a Confederate to hold backward views about women's rights in 1871. But the two are related. Southern states were reluctant to enfranchise women. Even after Congress passed the Nineteenth Amendment, neo-Confederates influenced legislatures in Southern states, most of which refused to ratify it. This opposition lingered at least into the 1970s, when only Texas, among all former Confederate states, ratified the Equal Rights Amendment.[25] Robert Lewis Dabney was a chaplain in the Confederate army and an important Presbyterian minister after the war and remains an important figure to modern neo-Confederates and Christian Reconstructionists.

In our day, innovations march with so rapid a stride that they quite take away one's breath. The fantastical project of yesterday, which was mentioned only to be ridiculed, is to-day the audacious reform, and will be to-morrow the accomplished fact. Such has been the history, of the agitation for "women's rights," as they are sophistically called in this country. A few years ago this movement was the especial hobby of a few old women of both sexes, who made themselves the laughing-stock of all sane people by the annual ventilation of their crotchet. Their only recruits were a few of the unfortunates whom nature or fortune had debarred from those triumphs and enjoyments which are the natural ambition of the sex, and who adopted this agitation as the most feasible mode of expressing their spitefulness against the successful competitors. Today the movement has assumed such dimensions that it challenges the attention of every thoughtful mind.

If we understand the claims of the Women's Rights women, they are in substance two: that the legislation, at least, of society shall disregard all the natural distinctions of the sexes, and award the same specific rights and franchises to both in every respect; and that woman while in the married state shall be released from every species of conjugal subordination. The assimilation of the garments of the two sexes, their competition in the same industries and professions, and their common access to the same amusements and recreations, are social changes which the "strong-minded" expect to work, each one for herself, when once the obstructions of law are removed from the other points.

One result of the reflection which we have been able to give this movement, is the conviction that it will prevail in the so-called "United States." This is foreshadowed by the frantic lust for innovation which has seized the body of the people like an epidemic. It is enough with them to condemn any institution, that it was bequeathed us by our forefathers; because it is not the invention of this age, it is wrong, of course. In their eyes no experience proves anything, save the experience which they have had themselves. They do not suppose that our fathers were wise enough to interpret and record the lessons of former experiences. That certain things did not succeed in our forefathers' hands is no proof that they will not succeed in our hands; for we are "cute," we live in an enlightened age, and understand how to manage things successfully. The philosophy of the Yankee mind is precisely that of the Yankee girl who, when she asked for leave to marry at seventeen, was dissuaded by her mother that she "had married very early and had seen the folly of it." "Yes; but, Mamma," replied the daughter, "I want to see the folly of it for myself." Your Yankee philosopher is too self-sufficient to be cautioned from the past. He does not know history; he would not believe its conclusions if he did; he has no use for its lights, having enough "subjective" light of his own. To such a people the fact that a given experiment is too absurd to have been ever tried before, is an irresistible fascination: it is a chance not to be neglected.

The symptoms of approaching success which already exist are such as may well cheer the advocates of the new revolution. They who a few years ago counted their adherents by scores, now have tens of thousands. They are represented by their own press. They have received the support of at least one religious journal, which presumes to call itself Christian and is the organ of a numerous denomination—the *New York Independent*. They receive the obsequious homage of the demagogues of the day. They have already engrafted a part of their ideas upon some State constitutions. Their apostles are invited to lecture before "Christian Associations" (of that peculiar kind which enumerate billiard and card-tables among the means of grace), and before the United States Congress. And last, a kindred cause, that of indiscriminate divorces, is making such progress in many of the States that it will soon be able to lend a strong helping-hand to its sister. Now it is by just such steps that Radicalism grew from its despised infancy in this country. It was just thus that Abolitionism grew. It is thus that all things grow on the American soil which ripen their harvests of evil.

The advocates of these "women's rights" may be expected to win the day, because the premises from which they argue their revolution have been irrevocably admitted by the bulk of the people. Now this popular mind may not be

consciously or intentionally consistent and logical. It may jump to many conclusions without much analysis of the steps by which they are reached. It may
deliberately harbor the most express purpose to be guilty of any logical inconsistency, however outrageous, in pursuing its supposed interests; and may have
its mind ever so clearly made up to eat its own words and principles whenever
its convenience prompts that measure. But still the Creator has made man, in
spite of himself, a logical animal; and consequences will work themselves out,
whether he designs it or not, to those results which the premises dictate. History
will write out the corollaries of the theorems whether the projectors wish to stop
for them or not. Now, false principles are already firmly planted from which
the whole "Women's Rights" claim must follow. If we look at the coarser, more
concrete, and popular form in which the consequence is drawn, we find the argument for the popular, Radical mind perfectly unanswerable. "It has been decided that all negro men have a right to vote: is not a Yankee white woman with
her smartness and education as good as a stupid, ignorant, Southern black?" We
should like to see the answer to that logic from that premise which a Northern
Radical mind could be made to appreciate. An unanswerable point thus perpetually made upon the mind of the public, will impinge at last.

Or if we examine the argument in its more exact and logical form, we shall
find it, after the established (false) premises are granted, equally conclusive for
the educated. The very axioms of American politics now are, that "all men are
by nature equal," that all are inalienably "entitled to liberty and the pursuit of
happiness," and that "the only just foundation of government is in the consent
of the governed." There was a sense in which our fathers propounded these
statements; but it is not the one in which they are now held by Americans. Our
recent doctors of political science have retained these formularies of words as
convenient masks under which to circulate a set of totally different, and indeed
antagonistic notions; and they have succeeded perfectly. The new meanings of
which the "Whigs" of 1776 never dreamed are now the current ones. Those wise
statesmen meant to teach that all men are morally equal in the sense of the
Golden Rule: that while individual traits, rights, and duties vary widely in the
different orders of political society, these different rights all have some moral
basis; that the inferior has the same moral title (that of a common humanity
and common relation to a benignant Heavenly Father) to have his rights—the
rights of an inferior—duly respected, which the superior has to claim that his
very different rights shall be respected. The modern version is that there are
no superiors or inferiors in society; that there is a mechanical equality; that all
have specifically all the same rights; and that any other constitution is against
natural justice. Next: when our wise fathers said that liberty is an inalienable,
natural right, they meant by each one's liberty the privilege to do such things as

he, with his particular relations, ought to have a moral title to do; the particular things having righteous, natural limitations in every case, and much narrower limits in some cases than in others. Radical America now means by natural liberty each one's privilege to do what he chooses to do. By the consent of the governed our forefathers meant each Sovereign Commonwealth's consenting to the constitution under which it should be governed: they meant that it was unjust for Britain to govern America without America's consent. Which part of the human beings living in a given American State should constitute the State potentially, the populus whose franchise it was to express the will of the commonwealth for all—that was in their eyes wholly another question; to be wisely decided in different States according to the structure which Providence had given them. By "the consent of the governed" it would appeal that Radicalism means it is entirely just for Yankeedom to govern Virginia against Virginia's consent, and that it is not just to govern any individual human being without letting him vote for his governors. The utter inconsistency of the two parts of this creed is not ours to reconcile. It is certain that both parts (consistent or not) are firmly held as the American creed. The version given to the maxim as to individual rights is universally this: that natural justice requires that suffrage shall be coextensive with allegiance, except where the right has been forfeited by some crime (such as that which the men of 1861 committed in presuming to act on the principles of the men of 1776). To these errors the American people are too deeply committed to evade any of their logical applications. For the sake of these dogmas they have destroyed one Federal and eleven other State constitutions, have committed a half million of murders, and (dearest of all) have spent some seven thousand millions of dollars. Repudiate these maxims now! Never! This would be to dishonor the ghosts of all the slaughtered Union-Savers, to shame the sacrifices of all the "Trooly Lo'il" during the glorious four years, to dim the very crown of martyrdom upon the brow of the "late lamented," and worst of all, to outrage the manes of all those departed dollars.

Now then, when Mistress Amazona Narragansett steps forward, and having vindicated her claim to have belonged always to the true Israel of the "Unconditional Unionists," demands simple and obvious application of these honored maxims to her own case, how can she be gainsaid? Hitherto the State has governed her without asking her consent at the ballot-box. This is self-evidently against the immortal truth that "all just government is founded on the consent of the governed." The State has restrained her natural liberty of doing as she chose, compelling her to pay a great many dollars in taxes which she would rather have chosen to expend in crinoline, and forbidding her to do a great many other little acts, such as bigamy, etc., which might have been her preference (and therefore her natural right); and all this without even saving the State's credit and manners by asking her consent at the polls to the laws made for her. And last: the State has committed the crowning outrage and inconsistency of not letting her be a man because God made her a woman! What an outrage this to be committed on so frivolous a pretext! Be consoled, Mistress Amazona; it is simply impossible that such abuses can stand much longer in the full light of this reforming age. "The school-mistress is abroad." That mighty tide of progress which has already swept away the Constitution, and slavery, and State's rights, and the force of contracts public and private, with all such rubbish, will soon dissolve your grievance also. Has not the Radical version of the political gospel said, "All men are by nature mechanically equal?" And "man," Mistress Amazona (as you will know when you acquire the virile right of learning Latin) here means, not *vir*, but *homo*; the species irrespective of sex. It means that a woman has a natural right to do all the particular things that a man does (if she can), to sit on juries and shave her beard, to serve in the army and ride astraddle, to preach sermons and sing bass.

But seriously: a woman is a human being, and a grown woman is an adult. She is treated, and must be treated, by all governments as a citizen owing allegiance and subject to law. On those principles, which are the first principles of Radicalism, it is impossible to deny her right to vote and to participate in all the franchises of men. Her exclusion is a glaring instance of "class legislation"—that odious thing which Radicalism so strongly condemns as contrary to equality. To subject women to these disabilities is even a more glaring injustice than was the exclusion of the negro from American citizenship because he was "guilty of a skin"; for here the exclusion from natural rights is grounded on the sole fact that woman is "guilty of a sex." And especially are all those laws unnatural and inexcusable iniquities which subject the person or property of the wife to any marital authority. What is such marriage but a species of (white) domestic slavery? Nor is it any excuse to say that in America no woman enters the married state save at her own option; for to that state the most commanding instincts of woman's being impel her; and it is but a mocking tyranny to impose this slavery on the married state of woman, and tell her then that she need not submit to the yoke if she chooses to avoid it by sacrificing the chief instincts of her being. Why, it may be even said to the galley-slave: that he need not be a slave, provided he is willing to disregard that other primal instinct, the love of life: suicide will set him free!

Such is the logic of the Women's Rights party, from Radical premises. Its prospect of triumph is greatly increased by this, that its Northern opponents (the only ones who have any power to oppose) have disabled themselves from meeting it by their furious Abolitionism. The premises of that doctrine, to which they are so irrevocably committed, now shut their mouths. It is vain for the rabid negrophilist, Dr. Horace Bushnell, to write a book at this date against Women's Rights as the "Reform against Nature." He cannot consistently oppose it; he has himself naturalized the false principles from which that "reform" will flow. The true principles from which its folly might have been evinced, the principles held by us "Rebels," he has trampled down with the armed heel, and drowned in blood and buried under mountains of obloquy and odium and slander. He cannot resort to those sound premises. To meet the argument of these aspiring Amazons fairly, one must teach, with Moses, the Apostle Paul, John Hampden, Washington, George Mason, John C. Calhoun, and all that contemptible rabble of "old fogies," that political society is composed of "superiors, inferiors, and equals"; that while all these bear an equitable moral relation to each other, they have very different natural rights and duties; that just government is not founded on the consent of the individuals governed, but on the ordinance of God, and hence a share in the ruling franchise is not a natural right at all, but a privilege to be bestowed according to a wise discretion on a limited class having qualification to use it for the good of the whole; that the integers out of which the State is constituted are not individuals, but families represented in their parental heads; that every human being is born under authority (parental and civic) instead of being born "free" in the licentious sense that liberty is each one's privilege of doing what he chooses; that subordination, and not that license, is the natural state of all men; and that without such equitable distribution of different duties and rights among the classes naturally differing in condition, and subordination of some to others, and of all to the law, society is as impossible as is the existence of a house without distinction between the foundation-stone and the cap-stones. No words are needed to show hence that should either the voice of God or of sound experience require woman to be placed for the good of the whole society in a subordinate sphere, there can be no natural injustice in doing so. But these old truths, with their sound and beneficent applications, have been scornfully repudiated by Abolitionism and Radicalism. The North cannot, will not, avow and appeal to them, because that would be to confess that the injured South was all the time right in its opposition to Abolition; and the conquerors will rather let all perish than thus humble their pride to the poor conquered victims.

It may be inferred again that the present movement for women's rights will certainly prevail from the history of its only opponent, Northern conservatism. . . .

We omit three long paragraphs predicting victory for women's rights, owing to the "selfish timidity" of America's public men, especially its conservative leaders.

What then, in the next place, will be the effect of this fundamental change when it shall be established? The obvious answer is, that it will destroy Christianity and civilization in America.

Dabney then launches a long attack on women's rights in which he explains how it will destroy civilization and result in women being wretchedly oppressed and abused. He concludes his essay by returning to his general theme of how Radicalism and democracy are destroying America.

* * *

Jubal A. Early (1816–94),
"Speech to the Southern Historical Society,"
August 14, 1873.[26]

In 1873, the reorganized Southern Historical Society elected Jubal A. Early president. Early had commanded Confederate forces in the Shenandoah Valley and remained an unabashed and extreme white supremacist. When the Virginia Democratic Party (now renamed "Conservative Party"), home to most ex-Confederates, seated and applauded six African American delegates at its 1871 convention, Early "indignantly stormed out," according to historian Jack P. Maddex Jr. Later, after whites gunned down African Americans in the "Danville Massacre," leading to the reestablishing of Democratic rule, Early warned black Virginians in 1883 that, from now on, "the Negroes must know that they are to behave themselves and keep in their proper places."[27] His talk to the Southern Historical Society emphasizes that ex-Confederates and pro-Confederates must write history, or else their cause will be lost. He begins with some flowery remarks about history and then gets to the matter of Confederate history. Already, the process of mystifying the "Lost Cause" has begun: Early says the South seceded for "their sacred rights."

It is idle to talk about forgetting the past. We could not forget if we would, and I trust that there are many of us who would not forget if we could. When the captive Jews sat down by the rivers of Babylon, and wept for the desolation of their land, their captors and spoilers required of them mirth, saying, "Sing us one of the songs of Zion;" but they hanged their harps upon the willows; and the Psalmist has put into their mouths this indignant protest:

"How shall we sing the Lord's song in a strange land?

"If I forget thee, O Jerusalem, let my right hand forget her cunning.

"If I do not remember thee, let my tongue cleave to the roof of my mouth; if I prefer not Jerusalem above my chief joy."

Can it be expected that we shall prove less faithful than they?

In our day and generation we have witnessed more of devotion and heroism exhibited in a struggle for the right of self-government, than were ever exhibited in any previous struggle; and if we were to attempt to erase all traces of the contest through which we have gone, it would be a vain task, for the world will not permit the memory of such deeds as were performed on the battlefields of the Confederacy—nay, on this very soil of Virginia—to die. In this century the pyramids, the tombs, and the ruined temples and cities of ancient Egypt and Ethiopia have been explored, and long-forgotten hieroglyphics have been deciphered, at great cost and labor, for the purpose of ascertaining the true history of peoples long since supplanted by other and, conquering races. The ruins of Nineveh, of Babylon the Great, and of the other cities of ancient Assyria and Babylonia, including the supposed site of the Tower of Babel itself, have been excavated, in order to discover, on crumbling bricks and tablets, in inscriptions made in cuneiform characters, authentic traces of the history of peoples whose descendants no longer have a distinct or recognised existence on the face of the earth. And within this very year an enterprising German savant has been engaged in the effort to discover, on the classic banks of the Scamander, the site of ancient Troy, whose very existence has been regarded by many as a myth.

How, then, can it be imagined that the leading events of a struggle which, during its continuance, electrified the whole civilised world by the grandeur of the sacrifices endured and of the deeds performed by a people who were fighting for their sacred rights, against such odds and difficulties as had never been encountered in any previous struggle, will be permitted to fade from the memories of men? It is a vain delusion, an idle dream.

After more flowery language, now about ancient Greece and Troy, Early writes:

Let us take courage, and not despair because we have had another instance, in our own experience, of the fact that "might is often more powerful than right."

It has been incautiously said that "we submitted our rights to the arbitrament of arms, and the decision was against us; therefore it is our duty to accept the result as final and conclusive;" and it has even been declared that "the highest law that can exist is that established by force of arms." The first statement is not true in any sense. The people of the South asserted rights which had been secured by the valor of their ancestors, and which had descended to them by an indisputable title. When those rights were unconstitutionally assailed, and their homes and firesides were most wrongfully threatened and invaded, they rushed to arms to defend all that was dear to them, against the fire and sword of the invaders. It is a most gross perversion of language to call this a "submission of their rights to the arbitrament of arms." The other declaration embodies the sentiment of the red-handed conqueror, with his foot on the neck of his victims, as well as of the robber on the highway. When it comes from one who was overpowered by physical power in a manly struggle for the right, we can but weep over the frailty that is not proof against the temptations of adversity. We are bound to accept the miraculous conversion of the persecuting Saul on his way to Damascus, for that was a case of Divine interposition and revelation; but the thorough and radical conversion from the cherished sentiments of a lifetime, that could be produced only by four years of dreadful, though glorious, war in defence of those sentiments—and which conversion was not developed until all was lost and policy pointed the way to it—makes too great a demand on our faith. It is a most lamentable spectacle to behold one of the newly fledged proselytes attempting to keep step in the march to the tune of "John Brown's soul goes marching on."[28] It is very certain that there is no more truth now in the Latin phrase *Vox populi, vox Dei*, than there was when the people cried, "Crucify him! Crucify him!"

Some one has said that "Nations cannot commit great crimes with impunity, any more than can individuals;" and all history, sacred and profane, vindicates the truth of the remark. . . .

Rest assured that, sooner or later, a just retribution will overtake the commission of the foulest political crime the world has ever witnessed the utter annihilation of the autonomy of eleven free, sovereign States, and the subjection of the intelligent, virtuous populations of most of them to the rule of an ignorant and inferior race, utterly incapable of understanding the first principles of government, and in turn controlled and ruled for the very worst purposes by a vile herd of alien adventures, swindlers, and thieves.

Already, in the unrebuked corruption which stalks abroad, the accumulation of ill-gotten wealth, the prevalence of "rings" formed for the purposes of public plunder, the rage for luxury, and the stolid indifference manifested by the masses in regard to the monstrous wrongs which are now being committed, under the hardly colorable pretext of liberty and constitutional law, but really in utter contempt of both,—as for instance in Louisiana, South Carolina, and other Southern States,—may be discerned the evidences of that decay which precedes the end; and the thoughtful and observant cannot fail to perceive the indications of "the handwriting on the wall," though the knees of our Belshazzars—for we have many—may not smite the "one against the other," because they are drunk with their revelries or blinded by their passions.

After suggesting that bad things are brewing in the United States, Early says:

There is one thing which is very certain: we cannot escape the ordeal of history. Before its bar we must appear, either as criminals—rebels and traitors seeking to throw off the authority of a legitimate government to which we were bound by the ties of allegiance—or as patriots defending our rights and vindicating the true principles of the government founded by our fathers. In the former character our enemies are seeking to present us, not only by their historical records, but by their literature and by the whole scope and tendency of their legislation and governmental policy. Shall we permit the indictment to go forth to the world and to posterity without a vindication of our motives and our conduct? Are we willing that our enemies shall be the historians of our cause and our struggle? No! a thousand times no! The men who by their deeds caused so many of the battle-fields of the South to blaze with a glory unsurpassed in the annals of the world, cannot be so recreant to the principles for which they fought, the traditions of the past, and the memory of their comrades "dead upon the field of honor," as to abandon the tribunal of history to those before whose immense numbers and physical power alone they were finally compelled to yield from mere exhaustion. Nor can we trust our vindication to the pens of the non-combatants on our own side, who, if not workers of mischief in their spheres, were of no material assistance to us in the terrible conflict. It is a high and solemn duty which those who were part and parcel of it owe to their dead comrades, to themselves, and to posterity, to vindicate the honor and glory of our cause in the history of the struggle made in its defence.

Early then closes by attacking alleged errors in accounts of various Civil War battles recently published by non-Confederate authors.

* * *

JEFFERSON DAVIS (1808–89), "SLAVERY NOT THE CAUSE, BUT AN INCIDENT," 1881.[29]

After Appomattox, Jefferson Davis received heavy criticism from his Southern contemporaries for secession, which some Confederates now regretted, and for various aspects of his conduct of the war and the Confederate presidency. However, as former Confederates realized that the cause of white supremacy might not be lost, unlike slavery, Davis's star rose somewhat. It rose further with the publication of his two-volume defense of secession and the "Lost Cause," from which we take this excerpt.

... [T]o whatever extent the question of slavery may have served as an *occasion*, it was far from being the *cause* of the conflict.

I have not attempted, and shall not permit myself to be drawn into any discussion of the merits or demerits of slavery as an ethical or even as a political question. It would be foreign to my purpose, irrelevant to my subject, and would only serve—as it has invariably served, in the hands of its agitators—to "darken counsel" and divert attention from the genuine issues involved.

As a mere historical fact, we have seen that African servitude among us—confessedly the mildest and most humane of all institutions to which the name "slavery" has ever been applied—existed in all the original States, and that it was recognized and protected in the fourth article of the Constitution. Subsequently, for climatic, industrial, and economical—not moral or sentimental—reasons, it was abolished in the Northern, while it continued to exist in the Southern States. Men differed in their views as to the abstract question of its right or wrong, but for two generations after the Revolution there was no geographical line of demarkation for such differences. The African slave-trade was carried on almost exclusively by New England merchants and Northern ships. Mr. Jefferson—a Southern man, the founder of the Democratic party, and the vindicator of State rights—was in theory a consistent enemy to every form of slavery. The Southern States took the lead in prohibiting the slave-trade, and, as we have seen, one of them (Georgia) was the first State to incorporate such a prohibition in her organic Constitution. Eleven years after the agitation on the Missouri question, when the subject first took a sectional shape, the abolition of slavery was proposed and earnestly debated in the Virginia Legislature, and its advocates were so near the accomplishment of their purpose, that a declaration in its favor was defeated only by a small majority, and that on the ground of expediency. At a still later period, abolitionist lecturers and teachers were mobbed, assaulted, and threatened with tar and feathers in New York, Pennsylvania, Massachusetts, New Hampshire, Connecticut, and other States. One of them (Lovejoy) was actually killed by a mob in Illinois as late as 1837.

These facts prove incontestably that the sectional hostility which exhibited itself in 1820, on the application of Missouri for admission into the Union, which again broke out on the proposition for the annexation of Texas in 1844, and which reappeared after the Mexican war, never again to be suppressed until its fell results had been fully accomplished, was not the consequence of any difference on the abstract question of slavery. It was the offspring of sectional rivalry and political ambition. It would have manifested itself just as certainly if slavery had existed in all the States, or if there had not been a negro in America. No such pretension was made in 1803 or 1811, when the Louisiana purchase, and afterward the admission into the Union of the State of that name, elicited threats of disunion from the representatives of New England. The complaint was not of slavery, but of "the acquisition of more weight at the other extremity" of the Union. It was not slavery that threatened a rupture in 1832, but the unjust and unequal operation of a protective tariff.

It happened, however, on all these occasions, that the line of demarkation of sectional interests coincided exactly or very nearly with that dividing the States in which negro servitude existed from those in which it had been abolished. It corresponded with the prediction of Mr. Pickering, in 1803, that, in the separation certainly to come, "the white and black population would mark the boundary"—a prediction made without any reference to slavery as a source of dissension.

Of course, the diversity of institutions contributed, in some minor degree, to the conflict of interests. There is an action and reaction of cause and consequence, which limits and modifies any general statement of a political truth. I am stating general principles—not defining modifications and exceptions with the precision of a mathematical proposition or a bill in chancery. The truth remains intact and incontrovertible, that the existence of African servitude was in no wise the cause of the conflict, but only an incident. In the later controversies that arose, however, its effect in operating as a lever upon the passions, prejudices, or sympathies of mankind, was so potent that it has been spread, like a thick cloud, over the whole horizon of historic truth.

As for the institution of negro servitude, it was a matter entirely subject to the control of the States. No power was ever given to the General Government to interfere with it, but an obligation was imposed to protect it. Its existence and validity were distinctly recognized by the Constitution in at least three places:

First, in that part of the second section of the first article which prescribes that "representatives and direct taxes shall be apportioned among the several States which may be included within this Union, according to their respective members, which shall be determined by adding to the whole number of free persons, including those bound to service for a term of years, and, excluding Indians not taxed, three fifths of all other persons." "*Other* persons" than "*free* persons" and those "bound to service for a term of years" must, of course, have meant those permanently bound to service.

Secondly, it was recognized by the ninth section of the same article, which provided that "the migration or importation of such persons as any of the States now existing shall think proper to admit shall not be prohibited by Congress prior to the year one thousand eight hundred and eight." This was a provision inserted for the protection of the interests of the slave-trading New England States, forbidding any prohibition of the trade by Congress for twenty years, and thus virtually giving sanction to the legitimacy of the demand which that trade was prosecuted to supply, and which was its only object.

Again, and in the third place, it was specially recognized, and an obligation imposed upon every State, not only to refrain from interfering with it in any other State, but in certain cases to aid in its enforcement, by that clause, or paragraph, of the second section of the fourth article which provides as follows:

"No person held to service or labor in one State, under the laws thereof, escaping into another, shall, in consequence of any law or regulation therein, be discharged from such service or labor, but shall be delivered up on claim of the party to whom such service or labor may be due."

The President and Vice-President of the United States, every Senator and Representative in Congress, the members of every State Legislature, and "all executive and judicial officers, both of the United States and of the several States," were required to take an oath (or affirmation) to support the Constitution containing these provisions. It is easy to understand how those who considered them in conflict with the "higher law" of religion or morality might refuse to take such an oath or hold such an office—as the members of some religious sects refuse to take any oath at all or to bear arms in the service of their country—but it is impossible to reconcile with the obligations of honor or honesty the conduct of those who, having taken such an oath, made use of the powers and opportunities of the offices held under its sanctions to nullify its obligations and neutralize its guarantees. The halls of Congress afforded the vantage-ground from which assaults were made upon these guarantees. The Legislatures of various Northern States enacted laws to hinder the execution of the provisions made for the rendition of fugitives from service; State officials lent their aid to the work of thwarting them; and city mobs assailed the officers engaged in the duty of enforcing them.

With regard to the provision of the Constitution above quoted, for the restoration of fugitives from service or labor, my own view was, and is, that it was not a proper subject for legislation by the Federal Congress, but that its enforcement should have been left to the respective States, which, as parties to the compact of union, should have been held accountable for its fulfillment. Such was actually the case in the earlier and better days of the republic. No fugitive slave-law existed, or was required, for two years after the organization of the Federal Government, and, when one was then passed, it was merely as an incidental appendage to an act regulating the mode of rendition of fugitives from *justice*—not from service or labor.

In 1850 a more elaborate law was enacted as part of the celebrated compromise of that year. But the very fact that the Federal Government had taken the matter into its own hands, and provided for its execution by its own officers, afforded a sort of pretext to those States which had now become hostile to this provision of the Constitution, not only to stand aloof, but in some cases to adopt measures (generally known as "personal liberty laws") directly in conflict with the execution of the provisions of the Constitution.

The preamble to the Constitution declared the object of its founders to be, "to form a more perfect union, establish justice, insure domestic tranquility, provide for the common defense, promote the general welfare, and secure the blessings of liberty to ourselves and our posterity." Now, however (in 1860), the people of a portion of the States had assumed an attitude of avowed hostility, not only to the provisions of the Constitution itself, but to the "domestic tranquility" of the people of other States. Long before the formation of the Constitution, one of the charges preferred in the Declaration of Independence against the Government of Great Britain, as justifying the separation of the colonies from that country, was that of having "excited domestic insurrections among us." Now, the mails were burdened with incendiary publications, secret emissaries had been sent, and in one case an armed invasion of one of the States had taken place for the very purpose of exciting "domestic insurrection."

It was not the passage of the "personal liberty laws," it was not the circulation of incendiary documents, it was not the raid of John Brown, it was not the operation of unjust and unequal tariff laws, nor all combined, that constituted the intolerable grievance, but it was the systematic and persistent struggle to deprive the Southern States of equality in the Union—generally to discriminate in legislation against the interests of their people; culminating in their exclusion from the Territories, the common property of the States, as well as by the infraction of their compact to promote domestic tranquility.

The question with regard to the Territories has been discussed in the foregoing chapters, and the argument need not be repeated. There was, however, one feature of it which has not been specially noticed, although it occupied a large share of public attention at the time, and constituted an important element in the case. This was the action of the Federal judiciary thereon, and the manner in which it was received.

In 1854 a case (the well-known "Dred Scott case") came before the Supreme Court of the United States, involving the whole question of the *status* of the African race and the rights of citizens of the Southern States to migrate to the Territories, temporarily or permanently, with their slave property, on a footing of equality with the citizens of other States with *their* property of any sort. This question, as we have seen, had already been the subject of long and energetic discussion, without any satisfactory conclusion. All parties, however, had united in declaring, that a decision by the Supreme Court of the United States—the highest judicial tribunal in the land—would be accepted as final. After long and patient consideration of the case, in 1857, the decision of the Court was pronounced in an elaborate and exhaustive opinion, delivered by Chief-Justice Taney—a man eminent as a lawyer, great as a statesman, and stainless in his moral reputation—seven of the nine judges who composed the Court, concurring in it. The salient points established by this decision were:

1. That persons of the African race were not, and could not be, acknowledged as "part of the people," or citizens, under the Constitution of the United States;

2. That Congress had no right to exclude citizens of the South from taking their negro servants, as any other property, into any part of the common territory, and that they were entitled to claim its protection therein;

3. And, finally, as a consequence of the principle just above stated, that the Missouri Compromise of 1820, in so far as it prohibited the existence of African servitude north of a designated line, was unconstitutional and void. (It will be remembered that it had already been declared "inoperative and void" by the Kansas-Nebraska Bill of 1854.)

Instead of accepting the decision of this then august tribunal—the ultimate authority in the interpretation of constitutional questions—as conclusive of a controversy that had so long disturbed the peace and was threatening the perpetuity of the Union, it was flouted, denounced, and utterly disregarded by the Northern agitators, and served only to stimulate the intensity of their sectional hostility.

What resource for justice—what assurance of tranquility—what guarantee of safety—now remained for the South? Still forbearing, still hoping, still striving for peace and union, we waited until a sectional President, nominated by a sectional convention, elected by a sectional vote—and that the vote of a minority of the people—was about to be inducted into office, under the warning of his own distinct announcement that the Union could not permanently endure "half slave and half free"; meaning thereby that it could not continue to exist in the condition in which it was formed and its Constitution adopted. The leader of his party, who was to be the chief of his Cabinet, was the man who had first proclaimed an "irrepressible conflict" between the North and the South, and who had declared that abolitionism, having triumphed in the Territories, would proceed to the invasion of the States. Even then the Southern people did not finally despair until the temper of the triumphant party had been tested in Congress and found adverse to any terms of reconciliation consistent with the honor and safety of all parties. No alternative remained except to seek the security out of the Union which they had vainly tried to obtain within it. The hope of our people may be stated in a sentence. It was to escape from injury and strife in the Union, to find prosperity and peace out of it.

* * *

CHAPTER 5

THE NADIR OF RACE RELATIONS, 1890–1940

In 1890, Mississippi moved beyond Fusion politics. The state passed a new constitution with a key provision: "every elector shall . . . be able to read any section of the constitution of this State; or he shall be able to understand the same when read to him, or give a reasonable interpretation thereof." Local registrars—hangers-on of the white power structure—determined if would-be voters' interpretations were "reasonable." Many refused to register a single African American in their county, even those with degrees in political science. In practice, this law flagrantly violated the Fourteenth and Fifteenth amendments. Nevertheless, the United States did nothing. Noting the nonresponse, other Confederate states and even Oklahoma followed suit by 1907.[1] Also in 1890, the army destroyed the last important vestige of Native American independence in the Wounded Knee Massacre in South Dakota. As well, the Senate failed to pass, by the narrowest of margins, the "Federal Elections Act," a Republican measure intended to give the federal government authority to intervene against violence and fraud in Southern elections. After the failure, as was their custom, Democrats tarred Republicans as "nigger lovers." In the past, Republicans had replied by standing up for the rights of citizens to vote freely, without regard to race, but in 1891 they turned away from the subject. The Democrats had worn them down. Now African Americans were without political allies.

For these three reasons, 1890 is the appropriate starting date for what historians now call the Nadir of race relations in America. The idea that race relations actually grew worse has become well accepted by historians. Unfortunately, most Americans do not even know the term.[2] What caused race relations to deteriorate so badly? Of course, memories of the war had dimmed. In addition, three underlying causes explain why racism triumphed after 1890. First came the continuing Plains Indian Wars. Whites discovered gold on Indian land in Colorado, Dakota Territory, and elsewhere. If they had done so on white-owned land, or even black-owned land, they would have had to talk with the owner. Not so on American Indian land. Whites just moved in and took it, and when the Utes or Dakotas attacked, the army was called out to put them down. Second, immigrants posed a continuing problem for Republican antiracists. Try as they might, they could not win their votes, for two reasons. First, Republicans were beginning to flirt with prohibition. You do not win the Italian American vote by coming out against wine, or the Polish American vote by coming out against beer. Second, the Democrats' continued white supremacy appealed to new European immigrants who were competing with African Americans for jobs at the wharves, in the kitchens, on the railroads, and in the mines. Some Republicans converted to a more racist position to win these white ethnic votes. Others, including Henry Cabot Lodge, Massachusetts congressman who had sponsored the 1890 elections bill, grew disgusted with "ethnic Americans" and helped found the Immigration Restriction League. But if it is OK to keep out southern and eastern Europeans because they are considered inferior to WASPs, why isn't it OK to deny rights to African Americans? Third, imperialism as a modern ideology washed over our shores from Europe, and the United States bought into it, annexing Hawaii. Then, after winning the Spanish American War in 1898, the next year the United States turned on its ally, the Filipinos. The U.S. military governor, William Howard Taft, said "our little brown brothers" were not ready for democracy. Democrats responded, "What about our little brown brothers in Mississippi? in Alabama?" The McKinley administration had no cogent reply. The Nadir set in.

The first selection in this chapter, an 1899 essay by Stephen D. Lee, supplies a factual summary of the Nadir. Lee notes that "sentiment in [the Negro's] favor" is disappearing in the North, and "[h]e is being pushed aside as the white man needs work and tries to get it, to such an extent that at the North he has but few lines of employment now left." We also include Lee's famous 1906 "charge" to the Sons of Confederate Veterans, which emphasizes the importance of presenting "the true history of the South" to future generations.

The race riot in Wilmington, North Carolina, was another key moment in solidifying white supremacy. As in most other race riots prior to 1940, whites attacked blacks, overthrowing the elected interracial government of Wilmington by force. We include a photograph of some of the rioters. In an article we reprint from his magazine, *Confederate Veteran*, editor S. A. Cunningham defends the rioters. Again, the federal government did nothing. Two years later, North Carolina Democrats disfranchised African Americans statewide.

The government's failure to act left neo-Confederates free to govern the South as they wished. No longer could African Americans vote, and the new state governments immediately slashed the funds available for their education. Neo-Confederate organizations flourished: the United Confederate Veterans formed in 1889, the United Daughters of the Confederacy in 1894, and the Sons of Confederate Veterans in 1896.[3] These organizations, especially the UDC, transformed the landscape by erecting Confederate monuments everywhere, even in corners of the South that had been predominantly Unionist or uninhabited during the war.[4] Most U.S. monuments to the Civil War went up between 1864 and 1890; most Confederate monuments went up between 1890 and 1940.[5] The reason is simple: people put up monuments when they win.[6] In the 1890s, Confederates—or more accurately, neo-Confederates—won the Civil War. At least they won the objective for which they had seceded: freedom to subjugate African Americans without outside interference.

In turn, the new political landscape changed how these groups viewed and represented the past. Gradually, four key elements of neo-Confederate mythology emerged during the Nadir. First, slavery was good, and slaves liked it. (This was a throwback to arguments made in 1850.) Nevertheless, ending slavery was also good, because slavery was a burden on white planters. Second, the South seceded for states' rights, or perhaps over tariffs and taxes, not for slavery. Third, during the "War Between the States," Confederates displayed bravery and stainless conduct. They only lost owing to the brute size of the North. Conversely, slaves displayed loyalty to their "masters" during the war. Finally, and most important, during Reconstruction, vindictive Northern congressmen, childlike African Americans, and corrupt carpetbaggers and scalawags ravaged the prostrate South. We shall examine each element of the myth in turn.

During the Nadir, many Confederate and neo-Confederate writers returned to the idealized portrait of slavery that they had half-believed before the war. Forgotten was the outrage they had felt when "their" blacks abandoned the plantation and bolted for Union lines and freedom as soon as they could. Now *Confederate Veteran* published scores of stories of faithful slaves. As E. H. Hinton says in an essay we include, slaves loved slavery and their "childlike" position. After all, it civilized and Christianized "barbarous or at least semi-barbarous blacks only a few years removed from the utter savagery of African jungles." Not until Reconstruction, when "carpetbaggers" put vile thoughts of "social equality" into their minds, did African Americans become a problem, according to Hinton.[7]

Neo-Confederates also developed a new theory of secession in the Nadir years. During Reconstruction and the Fusion period, their accounts of the events and arguments leading up to secession rarely emphasized states' rights as a cause, probably for two reasons. First, most people had been alive when South Carolina seceded and knew better. Second, states' rights had no contemporary relevance. Since neo-Confederates didn't control Southern state governments during Reconstruction, they had no reason to argue that federal power was usurping the rightful power of state governments. By the 1890s, neither reason held. Meanwhile, slavery as a social institution had become completely indefensible. Historian William C. Davis puts it starkly: "builders of the Lost Cause myth sought to distance themselves from slavery." Therefore, now that they again securely controlled Southern state governments, Confederates and neo-Confederates began to claim the South seceded for, rather than against, states' rights, and certainly not for slavery. We include an excerpt from an 1895 history of the South by Jabez Curry showing this mystification within a few paragraphs, leading finally to "rights of the States" as somehow the crux of the matter. Examining these claims, Davis notes, "When asked to enumerate those rights that were thus threatened, champions of secession at the time and defenders of the states rights excuse today are silent. . . . No one at the time complained that the federal government was interfering in state taxation, road building, internal commerce, militia, elections, civil or military appointments, external trade, or anything else."[8] Not all Confederates participated in this grand rewrite of the past. John S. Mosby, the Gray Ghost of the Confederacy, grew disgusted at such obfuscation. "In February 1860 Jeff Davis offered a bill in the Senate which passed making all the territories slave territory," writes Mosby in 1907 in a piece we include. "He was opposed to letting the people decide whether or not they would have slavery." So much for the states' rights theory of what the war was about!

Confederate conduct during the Civil War became more stainless as time went by. Now forgotten were women's riots for bread, the prisons set up for disloyal white Southerners, and the war crimes committed against black Union soldiers. In 1925, Mississippi congressman John Rankin gave an address at Brice's Cross Roads, a minor but famous Confederate victory won by Nathan Bedford Forrest. During the war, Forrest presided over massacres of surrendered black troops here and at Fort Pillow, Tennessee, in line with Confederate policy, as detailed in Chapter 3. Rankin literally reverses this record, calls the United States Colored Troops "members of a semisavage race," and writes, "All their bestial passions and instincts had been aroused." In reality, black soldiers typically behaved with decorum and were frequently assigned to guard Southern homes after U.S. forces had taken new territory. At Brice's Cross Roads, the United States Colored Troops made possible an orderly retreat for most of the Union army. It was Confederates who behaved with "bestial passions" after they took black POWs.[9]

After the 1890s, African Americans had no political power, so neo-Confederates were free to construct an upside-down history of Reconstruction, when blacks did have some power. In this view, terror was visited upon white Democrats rather than upon African Americans and leaders of the Republican Party. In a 1904 speech we include to the United Confederate Veterans, Mississippi congressman John Sharp Williams says, "You will remember the ten long years of so-called reconstruction which made the four long years of war itself seem tolerable by comparison, the ten long years during every day and every night of which Southern womanhood was menaced and Southern manhood humiliated." Of course, Reconstruction was hardly "ten long years" of menace for whites.

Mystifying what happened during Reconstruction throughout the decades of the Nadir still takes a toll on historical literacy today. Like the teachers described in the introduction to this book who still think the South seceded for states' rights, many adults still believe what my black students at Tougaloo College in Mississippi replied in 1969, when I (Loewen) asked them, "What was Reconstruction? What happened then?" Sixteen of seventeen students in my first-year seminar told me, "Reconstruction was that time, right after the Civil War, when African Americans took over the governing of the Southern states, including Mississippi, but they were too soon out of slavery, so they messed up and reigned corruptly, and whites had to take back control of the state governments." In reality, African Americans never took over the Southern states. All Southern states had white governors; all but one had white legislative majorities throughout Reconstruction. Moreover, the Reconstruction governments did not "mess up." Mississippi, in particular, about which Hinton and Rankin say so much in this chapter, enjoyed more honest government under Republican governor Adelbert Ames (1868–70, 1874–76) during Reconstruction than under any administration later in the century.[10] Across the South, governments during Reconstruction passed the best state constitutions the Southern states have ever had, including their current ones. They started public school systems for both races. They tried out various other ideas, some of which proved quite popular. Therefore "whites" did not take back control of the state governments. Rather, *some* whites—Democrats, the party of overt white supremacy throughout the nineteenth century—ended this springtime of freedom before full democracy could blossom. Spearheaded by the Ku Klux Klan, they used terrorism and fraud to wrest control from the biracial Republican coalitions that had governed during Reconstruction. We include several pieces valorizing the Ku Klux Klan and its clones, such as the Red Shirts, as the answer to these coalitions. Each of them accurately portrays the Klan as a continuation of the Confederate cause, struggling for white supremacy.

This neo-Confederate mythology spread nationally. Having done nothing to stop the Nadir, Northerners were complicit in denying black Southerners citizenship. Partly to rationalize having done so, many embraced racism in the form of imperialism, Social Darwinism, and eugenics. Literary history provides a lens to see the change in white thinking. Two novels have dominated the literary scene in the United States far beyond any others—one in each recent century. Both were written by white women; both treat slavery. The novel dominating the nineteenth century—*Uncle Tom's Cabin*—depicts the pathos of slavery and helped end it, while the twentieth-century blockbuster, a product of the Nadir of race relations, laments slavery's passing as *Gone With the Wind.* Movies also played an important role. *The Birth of a Nation,* the first great epic, valorized the Ku Klux Klan. So did the film version of *Gone With the Wind,* the first great color feature and still the most successful movie of all time.[11] No longer were secessionists the villains; now abolitionists played that role. Now white Americans—North as well as South—rebuilt slavery plantations like Hampton in Maryland, Kenmore in Virginia, and Magnolia in South Carolina to honor their owners and ignore their workers. Now Southern historians like Frank Owsley and Northerners like Claude Bowers and William Dunning claimed that the Civil War had been about tariffs, railroad subsidies, the conflict between industry and agriculture—anything *but* slavery or race.[12] Now Americans celebrated the war (but not Reconstruction) as an American pageant of bravery and honor. In a 1976 national survey, the most popular choice of first-year college students to a question on Reconstruction was that it led to "unparalleled corruption among the entrenched carpetbagger governors and their allies in the black dominated legislatures of the defeated states"—precisely the neo-Confederate myth of Reconstruction.[13]

Present and past now entwined. The neo-Confederate mythology of slavery, secession, the Civil War, and Reconstruction put forth during the Nadir taught that white supremacy is the correct way to order society. Racial equality had been tried and had failed during Reconstruction and would now be a disaster. On that the North and South now agreed.

* * *

J. L. M. Curry (1825–1903), *The Southern States of the American Union*, 1895.[14]

Jabez Curry grew up in Georgia and Alabama, graduated from the University of Georgia, and attended Harvard Law School. He was a congressman from Alabama and then served in the Confederate Congress. After the war he held various positions: professor of education, officer of funds that helped Southern schools (including black schools), and ambassador to Spain. In this excerpt from his Southern history, he seems to argue that Lincoln's 1860 victory itself somehow involved "the perversion of the Government from its originally limited character." Of course, an election in itself could hardly do so, and Curry does not quite say this; he says the Southern states *regarded* Lincoln's election as such a "perversion." Even so, he is wrong: most arguments that Southern states put forth as they seceded do not emphasize or even mention issues about the "limited character" of the national government. As they seceded, Southerners indeed invoked the triumph of a party that showed "hostility towards her institution," as Curry then points out. However, Curry goes on to obfuscate this reference to slavery by claiming the South felt "hopelessness in any effort to conserve the Constitution." In 1860–61, Southerners raised no such constitutional issue. They did bemoan their loss of control of the federal government to a Northern sectional party, which is what Curry means by their loss of "equality of the States." By thus sliding repeatedly from concerns that Confederates actually voiced—slavery, Lincoln's victory—to nonfactual vague assertions like "the action of Congress" and "conserve the Constitution," Curry mystifies the reasons for secession.

When the election of Mr. Lincoln became an established fact, notwithstanding the formal legality of the election, it developed a sectionalism so pronounced and powerful as to be able and willing to organize the Federal Government apart from and irrespective of all Southern support. The Southern States, as previously and most solemnly announced, regarded the election as involving necessarily the perversion of the Government from its originally limited

character, and the overthrow of all those guarantees which furnished the slightest hope of equality and protection in the "irrepressible conflict" thus precipi-
tated upon the minority section.

It is often said as conclusive of rash impetuosity, or of a predetermination
to dissolve the Union, that the South did not wait for some overt act of wrong
before entering upon the fatal step of secession. It may seem to have been imprudent and precipitate, viewed in the subsequent experience of subjugation
and abolition, but that same experience is the confirmation of the apprehen-
sions entertained and the proof that the South was not blind as to what was the
purpose, nay, the inevitable logical result, of the triumph of sectional and hostile
anti-slavery organization. What was the South to suppose had been the meaning
and the motive of the nullification acts of all the Northern States, of the bitterness of hostility towards her institution, the canonization of John Brown, and
the growth and dominancy of the abolition sentiment? In 1840 the Abolitionists
were a despised sect, with nearly as little favor in Boston as in Charleston. In 1844
and 1848 the Liberty and Free Soil parties had candidates for the Presidency; in
1856 the Republican party had absorbed the Whig party at the North and carried eleven States, and in 1860 it was triumphant in the executive and legislative
departments of the General Government.

When it appeared evident to the Southern States that there was utter hopelessness in any effort to conserve the Constitution and the equality of the States,
or to have them recognized in the administration of Federal affairs, the sole alternative was submission to, or acquiescence in, the revolution which had been
wrought, or an effort to secure the benefits of the Government as originally constituted. Shall the Constitution and the rights of the States be maintained under
new relationships, and a Federal constitutional union of States be preserved, or
shall the existence of a nation be maintained, irrespective of the Constitution
and the autonomy and the parity of the States? Stripped of all extraneous matter,
that was the naked issue submitted to the Southern States. . . .

We omit quotations from a speech "by Lamar" on John C. Calhoun.[15]

The action of Congress, of Northern States and Legislatures, in direct and hostile contravention of the theory of Government which had been maintained
consistently from the beginning of the Federal Union, the utterances of newspapers, books, party conventions, judicial decisions, the increasingly virulent
public sentiment, adverse to constitutional guarantees and the equality of the
States, culminating in the hostile and treasonable incursion of an organized
band into Virginia, and in the election of a President by a purely sectional vote,
satisfied the Southern States that the Union could not permanently exist, composed of "free and slave States," that the Constitution would no longer furnish

any protection to a minority, and that the rights of the States were contingent upon and determinable by the popular will of a dominant and a passionate section. Originally, the States antedated the Union, and were, by separate action, a sufficient number spontaneously concurring, the creators of the Union and stood on a plane of absolute political equality. In course of time new States, carved out of common territory, had their territorial organizations, their enabling acts, their school funds, their admission into the Union, through the will of the Central Government at Washington, and they thereby seemed unable to realize that Iowa was as Massachusetts and California as New Jersey....

Again, we omit a passage by Lamar.

The new States were slow or unwilling to believe that they were on a plane of perfect equality with any of the original eleven who began the Government.[16] Then grew up the notion of an aggregate people, of an unrestricted democracy, of the absolute right of a popular majority, whenever existing, however ascertained, to rule without check or restraint, independent of constitutional limitation or State interposition. The will of the majority, for the time being, becomes *vox Dei*, and must be immediately executed, irrespective of law or constitution.

These two adverse theories clashing and making an "irrepressible conflict," war was inevitable....

* * *

Stephen D. Lee (1833–1908),
"The Negro Problem," 1899.[17]

Stephen D. Lee, no relation to Robert E., was an important general during the Civil War. Afterward, he was the first president of what is now Mississippi State University and the second commander in chief of the United Confederate Veterans.[18] He was a delegate to the 1890 Mississippi constitutional convention, called to disfranchise African Americans. There he argued for women's suffrage, partly because he knew that taxpaying white women would vastly outnumber taxpaying black women.[19] He died at the Vicksburg battlefield after giving a welcome to some Northern soldiers. The following selection consists of sections from Lee's essay, "The South since the War," in a popular multivolume Confederate military history published in Atlanta in 1899 that is still reprinted and sold today. Its inclusion in such a set shows how neo-Confederates saw Reconstruction as a continuation of the Civil War by other means. Ellipses are in the original. Here Lee states accurately that ex-Confederates and neo-Confederates focused upon "holding the political power in the hands of the white people" during the Fusion era. By the 1890s, the white South and white North "were again permanently cemented together in good feeling." Granting citizenship to African Americans "is now regarded as a great political mistake," Lee notes, also accurately. To justify taking black citizenship away, he then concocts a fantastic history of Reconstruction that blames African Americans for the inequalities they suffered, oblivious to the terror the white power structure had visited upon them. Beginning with his claim that African Americans "were greatly demoralized" by the end of slavery, his portrayal of Reconstruction is absurd and his account of corrupt state governments wildly exaggerated. Lee is remembered by the Sons of Confederate Veterans for his 1906 "charge" to them, which they still proclaim to be their mission. From the introduction of his essay:

They found at home 4,000,000 slaves suddenly emancipated as a result of the war. They realized that the greatest problem any people had ever had to solve on sudden notice faced them. The negroes, as was natural that it should be, were greatly demoralized, and had but a faint conception of the responsibility of the freedom that was theirs, and that they knew had been brought about by the defeat of the Southern armies. Large numbers of them thought that freedom meant a cessation of labor on their part, and that the great government which had freed them by force of arms would feed, clothe and provide for them. They generally left their work in the fields and went in crowds to the cities and towns, where they were fed and cared for at the expense of the United States government. All this added greatly to the chaos and confusion of the time.

Later in his essay:

National Patriotism at the South

These two circumstances first evoked a display of national patriotism by the South. The people were then intensely considering the happy restoration of local self-government in their respective States. The national government, by its severe and radical treatment, had partially destroyed local self-government everywhere. Under its policy enormous debts had been piled upon them while they were facing the bayonet in the hands of the military power. To them local self-government and a stoppage of corrupt government were the great present boon, and the growth of national feeling was slow but steady, as the two sections better understood each other. Their time was taken up in undoing the false legislation then in force, and when necessary, in constructing new constitutions, in steering between Scylla and Charybdis by keeping within the new amendments, and at the same time in holding the political power in the hands of the white people; also in preventing a return to power of the negro element, which was in a majority in many sections of the South.

To accomplish this required the greatest skill, courage and patience. The means resorted to at times varied as the occasion demanded, not always approved by the best citizenship, but deemed necessary generally to effect the purpose. This period was a very trying one, and brought out prominently the leading characteristics of the Southern people in their resolve never again to submit to negroism and its baneful results. The Southern people knew that they alone could solve the great social problem of the races. They, white and black, lived together; they had seen that the effort made by strangers from the North, who had attempted to administer their affairs when local self-government had been suppressed, had proved to be a woeful failure.

They felt that the people of the North would soon see that it was better to permit the people of the South to solve their own difficult problems themselves and without further interference. As the people felt more secure, a more liberal legislation and policy were adopted toward the negro race, and they themselves see how much better everything works since they ceased to give so much attention to politics and more to their material wants and education. This period from 1885 to 1895 was really a period of readjustment to normal conditions in the South, and the people were really too busy and too anxious in their hard work of restoration and in making permanent their new boon of self-government, to take any great interest in national affairs.

The year 1895 was really the year when the North and South were again permanently cemented together in good feeling and in a broad national spirit. It is true this feeling had grown steadily since the inauguration of President Cleveland, but it bore substantial fruit in 1895. Then were the three prominent events of the year to emphasize fraternal feeling, and to encourage and broaden the people of the South in their attachment to the government. They now fully recognize that theirs was the best government in the world; that the people had more freedom than under any other government; that all were getting back substantially to the government of their fathers; that the Constitution was once more erect in its majesty, true without the principles for which they had fought (State rights), but with a restoration of prosperity and a full acceptance of results, a good and beneficent government to them.

Lee describes the dedication of a monument to Confederates who died in prison in Chicago, the dedication of the Chickamauga battlefield in Georgia, with Confederates and Union soldiers given equal burials, and the Atlanta exposition, all in 1895. He then tells of new railroad lines and manufacturing plants in the South.

The Negro Problem

With the account of the great strides made by the South since 1880, one will ask, What became of the great negro problem, which for nearly three hundred years has been a running sore in this country? In nearly every stage of our history, this vexed problem has caused division, irritation, bitter political discussions, sectional animosities, and conflicting interests in material development. Even in the constitutional convention of 1789, our wisest statesmen knew and said that the States were divided between those having slaves and those not having them, or about getting rid of them. This division existed down to the war between the States; in fact, slavery was the irritating cause which divided the North and the South on sectional lines in the construction of the Constitution. The negro since the war was still the irritating cause which kept the sections wide apart, and was responsible for the harsh reconstruction epoch. He owed his freedom to a war necessity. He was the cause of the drastic political experiments inaugurated by Northern statesmen. From a slave he was made a full citizen, with full political rights.

These were thrust upon him suddenly, without any previous training or preparation. At the same time he was made to face the white man in the great problem of competition, while his aspirations and instincts were entirely different from the stronger ruling race; the one race thrifty, dominating, accumulative and full of enterprise and progress, the other not inclined to lay up wealth or better its condition. For awhile the negro was the ward of the nation, and money was lavishly spent to hold him in his new responsible position, but this had its end.

Thinking men knew that while he was not expected, owing to his unfortunate past, to be able to fight the battles of life with the superior race, still it was disappointing, as shown by the statistics, that the masses have been but little advanced in the acquisition of property and education. He is inclined to be wasteful and improvident; inclined to spend his money in baubles rather than in surrounding himself with comforts. It cannot be denied that he has improved in many ways, educationally, materially and morally, but as yet the signs are not of the most encouraging character that he will ever be successful in the great competition in life, which he will necessarily encounter side by side with the white man.

I hardly think it can be denied that prejudice exists against him as a race, both North and South. In his work he cannot compete with the white man in quality or amount. It is also evident that in all lines of employment except agriculture, he is steadily disappearing in numbers at the North, as compared with his hold in those employments years ago, when there was a sentiment in his favor. He is being more and more restricted in all the avenues of the various industries affording a living to workers. The places are being filled more and more by white employees. He is constantly failing in his ability to keep abreast of the white man in the struggle for employment. He is being pushed aside as the white man needs work and tries to get it, to such an extent that at the North he has but few lines of employment now left. Labor unions are discriminating against him in all mechanical trades, and in fact in all lines of work controlled by guilds, and this discrimination also exists where there are no labor unions. For a long time and until recently this feeling did not pervade the South, but it is growing, and where many negro mechanics got work for a long time, white mechanics are now strongly competing and demanding preference, and as they generally give better work, they are getting it more and more to the exclusion of the negro. The white immigrants, too, from the North to the South, have little use for the negro after a few years, and more and more the negro will have to fight and struggle for a living like every other race; and it remains to be seen how he can run side by side with his more progressive and assertive white neighbor, as the white race outnumbers him more and more, and becomes more aggressive.

Mr. Henry Garnett, in the summary of negro statistics in the Census Bureau for 1890, gives the following results: ... [I]n one hundred years the whites have multiplied eighteen times and the negroes nearly ten times. In 1790, the whites were 80.73 per cent of the population, the negroes 19.27 per cent. In 1890 the negroes constituted only 12_ per cent of the population.

In the criminal statistics, the proportion of negroes in jails was nearly four times as great as that of native white extraction, and the commitment of negroes for petty offenses is in much greater proportion than among the white race. The negroes also marry earlier and their lives are shorter than in the white race....

From a statistical standpoint, the outlook for the negro is not encouraging. I do not believe that any one can forecast the future of the negro. One thing is certain, when left to himself without the strong will and example of the white man in the black belts, he tends to retrograde; when outnumbered by the whites in the white belts, he assimilates more to the habits of white men, becomes a better laborer and a better citizen. The negro is certainly improving as a laborer all over the South since the last three or four years, and farming is getting more and more in its normal condition. Experimenting is passing away and both white and black races understand each other better, and all work is more strictly on business principles. Labor has got over its disorganization, and is realizing that unless good service is rendered, it is difficult to get on good lands or with good employers. Both white and black have paid old debts and are more careful in incurring new ones. Many mortgages have been lifted in the last three or four years, and good crops have been produced.

The white people are realizing fully now that the negro is a constant quantity at the South; that he has no idea of moving away and settling at the North and elsewhere; that he must be educated and fitted for citizenship as rapidly as possible; that it is better to help and encourage him than to repress him; and the whole drift now is to elevate him by education. It is worthy of remark that although he was freed as a war measure, still the great government which freed him has done nothing to remove his illiteracy, poverty and ignorance; but the great burden has fallen on the impoverished white people of the South mainly, which was the most disorganized section of the Union as a result of the war, and they are taxing themselves with as liberal and unselfish a spirit as has been shown by any people under similar circumstances anywhere on the globe. It is not just to say either that the negro, who was and is the principal farm laborer, is not entitled to a large credit for the great and valuable crops raised in the South since 1880. It is true he was directed by the white people who owned the land, but the crops were made mostly through his labor. The white people went to work also on the farms and made a large part of the crops themselves. They worked harder and more industriously than ever, and in the white belts raised a large per cent of the crops. I believe that the next census will show a much better record for the colored race. I remark, then, that the great progress of the South is explained in the energy and push of the Southern whites, under the great necessity to retrieve and save their country and transmit its Anglo-Saxon civilization unimpaired, and as far as possible untarnished by negroism or its consequences; that the rapid accumulation of wealth was brought about in spite of the incubus of an inferior race, which was forcibly carried along and made to do its part. The negro has seen the great difference and feels it is best for both races. Repression of the negro vote will gradually pass away, and he will become as regular a voter as his white brother, when he loses his identity as a political factor separate and distinct from others. White immigrants will move so rapidly now that the negro will be over-shadowed everywhere, as he is now in the localities where the whites outnumber him two or three to one; they will be assimilated to the whites in thrift and citizenship; never the equal but always the weaker vessel which must not be imposed upon but must be protected.

Morality of Southern People

The morality of the Southern white people will compare favorably with any country or section in the world. Unsympathizing pens have not considered their untoward surroundings in having contact with "an unassimilated and inferior race," that the "submersion of brains, political experience, land ownership, and habits of domination by ignorant members could have but one issue," which was plainly brought out in the reconstruction days and for many years following. The white people have given evidence of their morality in the growth of the religious denominations, and more especially in the prevalence of prohibition in the liquor business by local option laws, especially in Mississippi and Arkansas. About 90 per cent of the counties of Mississippi have prohibition by virtue of local option. It is even better in Arkansas, but in all these elections, the negro votes almost solid for whisky.

Social Matters

It is a wise provision also that the races are kept separate in the schools, in churches and in railroad cars. Equal accommodations are granted under the laws. In some of the States no separation appears in railroad cars, and soon it will be the rule in all the States in this particular, but it will be a long time, if ever, before the children of the two races will attend schools in common, so long as the negro is numerous in particular localities.

The race instinct is implanted by a stronger hand than that of man, and a different arrangement where the races are anyway equal or the blacks more numerous, would result in constant collision and disorder. The young generations of whites and blacks have far less disposition to adjustment in such matters than the older members of the respective races. The sensible negro never aspires to social equality; the broad men of the race distinctly state this; and any tendency in this direction is found only with the worse element and those disposed to create disorder and trouble. At the North it is hypocrisy to pretend that the negro is admitted in social circles equally with the whites. He is held more at arm's length than even at the South, this, too, in face of the fact that the negro is the exception there and seldom met, as compared with the South, where in several States he outnumbers the whites, and in many localities, the same condition exists in almost every State.

Of late years one hears more of negroes not being admitted to hotels and restaurants and public resorts at the North than at the South. Social equality is not recognized North or South, and the sentiment is the same among the whites and blacks in both sections.

Lynchings

Lynching to the extent it has existed in the South is indefensible. The crime invoking it began and has been continued solely by the irrepressible and worst element of the negro race, inaugurating a new crime, which was unknown and impossible in the days of slavery, and which, from that fact and the existence of slavery, invested it with peculiar horror and atrocity. That the race instinct is strongly implanted in human society is undeniable; and when this crime is committed under the peculiarly harrowing surroundings of isolation in sparsely-settled communities, upon helpless and unprotected white women, combined with the murder in many cases of the outraged female, it arouses a fierceness and revengeful spirit uncontrollable at times.

Lee then supplies a fantastical pseudo-history of Reconstruction and its overthrow to "explain" the alleged commonality of interracial rape by black men after 1890.

Those who engaged in lynching put themselves outside of the law, but at the same time those who committed rape put themselves also outside of the law. It would always be better to abide by the law, for human society and civilization are based on the principle that the individual gives up his right of protection of life and property to the State which must perform this duty. But in the isolated spots where the crime was generally committed, it was almost impossible in many cases to get this legal protection promptly, and when it was needed, the community was swayed by a terrible cyclone of excitement and horror.

The conditions evoked, too, are most peculiar. The whites felt themselves outraged, and by a state of tutelage of the negro for which they were not responsible. This is no excuse for the crime of lynching. It is only stated to bring out the unfortunate facts incident to a great political crime in thrusting responsibilities on a weak and unfortunate race by a too rapid hotbed process of development, a procrustean operation.

Lee then writes three more long paragraphs that excuse lynching by claiming blacks do it too, it happens in the North too, and whites are victims too. He closes:

... [T]he people of the South are as moral and law-abiding as any people anywhere in the world. It would be well if those who judge them harshly would consider what they would have done themselves, surrounded by the most grave social problem the world has ever seen; viz., the race problem in its ugliest presentation in the South, and by the provocation of the mistake of statesmen.

This is the version of Lee's charge used by the Sons of Confederate Veterans today. Lee may not have written its last sentence, the origin of which is unknown.[20]

To you, Sons of Confederate Veterans, we will commit the vindication of the cause for which we fought. To your strength will be given the defense of the Confederate soldier's good name, the guardianship of his history, the emulation of his virtues, the perpetuation of those principles which he loved, and which you also cherish, and those ideals which made him glorious, and which you also cherish. Remember, it is your duty to see that the true history of the South is presented to future generations.

* * *

White Mob Burns Black Businesses in Wilmington, North Carolina, November 10, 1898.[21]

Figure 11: Proud of what they have done, members of the white mob pose in front of a black business they burned. "Revolution at Wilmington, 1898." Courtesy of the North Carolina Office of Archives and History, Raleigh, North Carolina.

Wilmington was one of the largest cities in the South in the 1890s. In its 1897 municipal elections, an interracial Republican coalition elected the mayor and six of ten aldermen. Democrats fought back the next year, mounting a statewide white supremacy campaign that emphasized the alleged lust that African American males felt for white women. Vote Democratic, party leaders urged, to keep your wives and sisters safe from black rapists. Red Shirts, the terrorist arm of the party in South Carolina, now spread to North Carolina, menacing African Americans and their white allies across the eastern part of the state. On election day, many African Americans were afraid to vote, and the considerable Republican majority evaporated. After the election, 2,000 whites paraded through downtown Wilmington, demolished the office of the black-run newspaper, and forced the Republican mayor and aldermen to resign. This riot effectively ended black political participation in North Carolina until the civil rights movement.

* * *

S. A. Cunningham (1843–1913), "M'Kinley, Roosevelt, and the Negro," January 1903.[22]

During the Civil War, S. A. Cunningham served as a private in the Confederate army. After the war, he edited various Tennessee newspapers until founding *Confederate Veteran*, which became the official publication of all the Confederate veteran and memorial associations.[23] The first article defends the 1898 attacks by white supremacists upon the African American community in Wilmington, North Carolina. Cunningham's phrase, "blood ran in the streets," is all too accurate: the mob killed between 6 and 100 African Americans. He goes on to praise President McKinley for allowing this coup d'etat to stand. Cunningham's second article argues that whites should be kind to blacks but should repeal the Fifteenth Amendment that granted them the right to vote.[24]

The Southern people will remain "solid" on the race question. The most clannish of them are not fearful of disturbance upon that point. They concede that their Northern fellow citizens may not realize the necessity of white supremacy and that good men among them, in undertaking to disturb the natural relations, deserve prayer from knowing not what to do.

All the world remembers how the South grieved in the death of McKinley, and how her people respect his memory. They cherish his noble utterance in behalf of caring for the graves of the Confederate dead, and are comforted in the memory of his Christian resignation when shot down by an assassin. They prefer to remember these things to his early official acts. It may be well, however, in this connection to review his administration on the negro question. Elected by as partisan a class as any of his predecessors, and misguided as much by that question as any of them, he began appointing negroes to office in spite of the protestation of white people directly concerned. This emboldened the negroes to think that the bottom rail would indeed be on top, and they became more insolent than ever. The sin of it was so demonstrated in Wilmington, N.C. to note a single illustration, that the white people of that noted, conservative city determined, in spite of the power of the United States or all the world, that they would not submit to the outrages being there perpetrated. It was so bad that the white ladies could not walk the streets in safety. The wife of a merchant, for instance, was accosted by a burly negro, who walked up close by her on a public street and said, putting his face close to hers: "Won't you kiss me darling?" Public meetings were held, defiant speeches were made, and an organization was publicly perfected to annul the acts of the President of the United States. The men bound themselves by their sacred oaths to submit no longer, and blood ran in the streets.

These things induced the good McKinley to pause and consider his course on that subject. Impatient negroes held mass meetings and condemned the President. One of the speakers at such a gathering in the national capital demonstrated the animus of his race by saying that he "would concentrate those issues into one McKinley neck" and he "would hold the razor to cut the jugular vein."

The Spanish war coming on just then, men of the South rallied as promptly as those of the North to fight the battles of the United States, and the negro problem ceased to be considered. It is well remembered that McKinley did not further meddle with that question.

In the succeeding national campaign, McKinley's election was not regarded as the usual calamity in the election of a sectional and a partisan President, and many Southern people were not displeased that the remarkable leader of the "Rough Riders" in the Spanish-American war was ticketed with him. For his many admirable qualities that they had much hope that should he occupy the Presidency, Roosevelt would be a non-partisan, and that the deplored sectionalism would be obliterated before the patriotic soldiers of the Union and Confederate armies had all answered their last call. The last-named class is at least equally as anxious for it as the former. The most opportune conditions possible were anticipated. President Roosevelt had the best opportunity that has ever occurred to restore primitive relations to the country. His versatility, his integrity, and his independence might have made him the most popular President that ever occupied the White House in the memory of any now living; but the worst mistakes are being made, and the writer voices the sentiments of many millions, surely, in expressing sorrow and anguish in the Booker Washington incident and for other events that have followed on the race question. Aside from the principle issues, those who know President Roosevelt personally—those who have been fascinated and charmed by his qualities of good fellowship—are the more grieved.

Surely his best friends should importune him to pause and mediate upon human imperfections. He has not the power, and the armies can't be made large enough, to force into the kind of subjection he seems to desire the white people of the South who were compatriots of his noble ancestors and their children.

These expressions are not of sectional consideration, but from a principle as old and as deep as the creation of white and black—and the distinctive color odor. Let every possible influence be brought to bear with the President for the good of all people, black as well as white. Let his friends in the South be diligent to communicate with him upon the disastrous and grievous results that will come of playing with unquenchable fire.

It is our due to the President to state that his Southern blood induces our people to be much more exacting, and these remarks are as a plea to him rather than a criticism to injure.

* * *

S. A. Cunningham,
"Problem of the Negroes," January 1907.[25]

The VETERAN has been silent on this most important question; but every phase of it has been considered constantly and diligently, especially from the standpoint of friendship for that thriftless but most amiable race. Antagonisms exist as they never did before, and the neglect of white people in behalf of these issues has been greatly to their discredit. We all like the old negroes, and those of the fast-decaying remnant of ex-slaves are still faithful and loyal to the families of their former masters. The same instincts are much more prevalent among their offspring than is generally realized. While the Associated Press flashes a horrible account of a fiendish deed by one negro, ten thousand others are going quietly about their business as law-abiding and worthy of consideration as could be expected of them.

It seems that education has been a curse rather than a blessing to them. The editor of the VETERAN soon after attaining his majority, early after the close of the war, took an active part in behalf of their education. He antagonized some of his people as editor of a country newspaper in advocacy of public schools, which required that as good facilities be given to the blacks as the whites. He attended a venerable divine, President of the Davidson County School Board, who, when the movement was quite unpopular, canvassed his native county of Bedford in their behalf from purely benevolent motives, making the one argument that all men should learn to read the Bible. It seems, however, that when a negro has learned to read he ceases to work, and his idleness begets mischief, and often of the worst kind.

There is not sufficient cooperation of the two races. Besides, many whites are not justly considerate of negroes. White people should confer with the better classes of blacks for the common good, and they should cooperate cordially.

The separate car laws are proper, and became a necessity because of the insolent presumption of negroes. It was quite the rule for them to string out the length of cars, so as to compel whites to sit among them, and every act toward social equality has proven a tendency to insolence. The negroes made this isolation a necessity, and they may expect its perpetuity. With these laws in force the whites should be very considerate and see that no injustice is done the negroes. Again, there is a sore lack of consideration for negroes in conversations by white people. The negro is not to blame for his color and not wholly so for his odor; and, inasmuch as we declare his inferiority we should be diligent that justice be done him. Often are remarks made in the presence of negroes that instinctively create hatred not only toward those who are inconsiderate but against the white race. Every white person should be on guard to avoid giving offense in this manner.

At the first annual dinner of the Alabama Society (of one hundred and fifty members) in New York near Christmas day the Hon. Seth Low, of that great city, was a special guest. This race question was the theme of the evening, and Mr. Low, with exquisite deference, suggested that the white people of the South consider these unhappy disturbances as fairly as possible, looking at the situation from the standpoint of the negro. The condition confronts us, and the sooner we grapple it the better. White people intend to control, and the negro will be the greater sufferer in the end for all disturbances, so that both races should do all in their power for the friendliest relations possible. Southern whites know the negroes best, and they should do their best to restore helpful relations.

No more negroes should be admitted to the army, and the amendment to the Constitution giving negroes the ballot should be repealed. This ballot feature is the luring one in social as well as political strife. In compelling the negro to keep his place the highest instincts of life should be exercised to treat him kindly and justly in every way.

The servant problem should be solved. Many white women succeed in making earnest friendships with their servants, and all goes well. There is a certain way of being kind to servants which wins. Dignity must be maintained, and yet a kindly consideration shown to the servant that commends the spirit of justice.

Let us confront the problem honestly. The negro did not come among us of his own accord, and they can't all get away. If proper tact were exercised, it would be quite sufficient. Let the white people of the South revive the old rule of kindness, and never, anyhow in their presence, speak ill of the negro race.

* * *

JOHN SHARP WILLIAMS (1854–1932), "ISSUES OF THE WAR DISCUSSED," NOVEMBER 1904.[26]

John Sharp Williams was a congressman and then senator from Mississippi. This piece is taken from a speech to the United Confederate Veterans in Memphis. Williams begins by asking why do we celebrate the Confederacy? Mere bravery? No. A lost cause? No, lost causes are not celebrated. Secession? No; he admits that secession was a mistaken remedy. Slavery? No, he says, "slavery was only the occasion of the quarrel and the fight." Was states' rights the cause? Yes, he claims, "the right to local self-government." Of course, his own state, when seceding, stressed nothing but slavery, as Chapter 2 shows. But then Williams immediately refers to "even a greater cause . . . for which we fought . . . the supremacy of the white man's civilization."

But there was something else, and even a greater cause than local self-government, for which we fought. Local self-government temporarily destroyed may be recovered and ultimately retained. The other thing for which we fought is so complex in its composition, so delicate in its breath, so incomparable in its symmetry, that, being once destroyed, it is forever destroyed. This other thing for which we fought was the supremacy of the white man's civilization in the country which he proudly claimed his own; "in the land which the Lord his God had given him;" founded upon the white man's code of ethics, in sympathy with the white man's traditions and ideals. Our forefathers of the forties and fifties and sixties believed that if slavery were abolished, unless the black race were deported from the American States, there would result in the Southern States just such a condition of things as had resulted in San Domingo, in the other West Indies Islands, and in the so-called republics of Central and South America—namely, a hybridization of races, a lowering of the ethical standard, and a degradation, if not loss, of civilization. . . . Slavery is lost, and it is certainly well for us and the public—perhaps for the negro—that it has been lost. But the real cause for which our ancestors fought—back of slavery, and deemed by them to be bound up in the maintenance of slavery—to wit, the supremacy of the white man's civilization, the supremacy of the ethical culture, which had been gradually built up through countless generations—has not been lost.[27] We have not had the experience of the countries to the south of us; but I ask you, my friends, in all soberness and candor, to ask yourselves how and why we escaped the evils which befell others from identical causes, under similar, though not identical, conditions? What prevented the Africanization of the South? We escaped, but those of you, even no older than I am, will remember by what a slender thread we held to safety. You will remember the ten long years of so-called reconstruction which made the four long years of war itself seem tolerable by comparison, the ten long years during every day and every night of which Southern womanhood was menaced and Southern manhood humiliated. . . .

The brethren of our own race, in our own country—the country whose pen had been Jefferson, whose tongue had been Patrick Henry, and whose sword had been Washington—were against not only us but the race itself—its past, its future—were seemingly bent only on two things—our humiliation as a race in the present, our subordination as a race in the future. . . . There is no grander, no more superb spectacle than that of the white men of the South standing from '65 to '74 and '75 quietly, determinedly, solidly, shoulder to shoulder in phalanx, as if the entire race were one man, unintimidated by defeat in war, unawed by adverse power, unbribed by patronage, unbought by the prospect of present material prosperity, waiting and hoping and praying for the opportunity which, in the providence of God, must come to overthrow the supremacy of "veneered savages," superficially "Americanized Africans"—waiting to reassert politically and socially the supremacy of the civilization of the English-speaking white race. But what gave them the capacity to do this sublime thing, to conceive it and to persevere in it to the end? to wait like hounds in the leash—impatient, yet obedient to the call of the huntsman's horn—which came upon the heels of the autumn elections in the Northwestern States in 1874? What gave this capacity to the "easy-going, indolent, life-enjoying" Southerner? What if not four years of discipline, training, hardship? Four years which taught the consciousness of strength and mutual courage, the consciousness of capacity for working together, the power and the desire of organization, and which gave them, with it all, a capacity for stern action when required by stern events? But for the war—the lessons which it taught, the discipline which it enforced, the capacity for racial organization which was born with it—I, for one, do not believe that conditions in Louisiana, South Carolina, and Mississippi to-day would be very far different from what they are in Hayti, Cuba, or Martinique.

Neither of these causes is a lost cause. . . . The very men who told us in the sixties and the seventies that "one man was as good as another," no matter what the state of his civilization, no matter what his race traits and tendencies, are the very men who now, in establishing new governments in the new insular possessions, not only admit, but strenuously contend for the necessity of making such provisions of law as will prevent the white men in those possessions from being ruled by other races. The act of Congress for the government of the islands of Hawaii is almost identically the Mississippi Constitution reenacted, and the reason for its passage was the same—namely, to secure, as far as possible, without violation of the Fourteenth and Fifteenth Amendments, the white man's supremacy there, and this, too, although the native Kanakas in the Hawaiian Islands have a percentage of illiteracy less than that of any State in the Union except one, and although the white men in the islands do not constitute one-fifth of the population.

My friends, there is no other instance that I know of where men having apparently lost a cause by four years of fighting subsequently preserved it by ten years of unterrified solidarity, superb patience, and magnificent common sense.

Williams then closes with paeans of praise for the character of the Confederate soldier and the (white) Southern people.

* * *

John Singleton Mosby (1833–1916),
Letter to Sam Chapman, July 4, 1907.[28]

Owing to his daring cavalry raids in northern Virginia, Mosby was known as the "Gray Ghost" during the Civil War. The Confederacy defined his men, along with Quantrill's Raiders and other groups, "partisan rangers" who operated in the gray areas between authorized troops and independent guerrillas. After the war, Mosby became a Republican, but as this letter tells, he never repented of his service for the Confederacy. He did insist on recognizing honestly what the Confederacy was about. "The South went to war on account of Slavery," he points out: "South Carolina went to war—as she said in her Secession Proclamation—because slavery wd. not be secure under Lincoln. South Carolina ought to know what was the cause for her seceding." He goes on to show that Virginia had the same cause.

June 4th 1907   Department of Justice, Washington
Dear Sam:

I suppose you are now back in Staunton. I wrote you about my disgust at reading the Reunion speeches. It has since been increased by reading Christian's report. I am certainly glad I wasn't there. According to Christian the Virginia people were the abolitionists & the Northern people were pro-slavery. He said slavery was a "patriarchal" institution. So were polygamy & circumcision. Ask Hugh if he has ever been circumcised. Christian quotes what the old Virginians said against slavery. True, but why didn't he quote what the modern Virginians said in favor of it—Mason, Hunter, Wise, etc. Why didn't he state that a Virginia Senator (Mason) was the author of the Fugitive Slave Law & why didn't he quote the Virginia Code (1860) that made it a crime to speak against slavery or to teach a Negro to read the Lord's Prayer. Now, while I think as badly of slavery as Horace Greeley did, I am not ashamed that my family were slave holders. It was our inheritance. Neither am I ashamed that my ancestors were pirates & cattle thieves. People must be judged by the standards of their age. If it was right to own slaves as property it was right to fight for it. The South went to war on account of Slavery. South Carolina went to war—as she said in her Secession Proclamation—because slavery wd. not be secure under Lincoln. South Carolina ought to know what was the cause for her seceding. The truth is the modern Virginians debated from the teachings of the Fathers. John C. Calhoun's' last speech had a bitter attack on Mr. Jefferson for his amendment to the Ordinance of '87 prohibiting slavery in the Northwest Territory. Calhoun was in a dying condition—was too weak to read it. So James M. Mason, a Virginia Senator, read it in the Senate about two weeks before Calhoun's death—Mch. 1850. Mason & Hunter not only voted against the admission of California (1850) as a Free State but offered a protest against it wch. the Senate refused to record on its Journal. Now in the Convention wch. Gen. Taylor has called to form a Constitution for California, there were 51 Northern & 50 Southern men—but it was unanimous against slavery—but the Virginia Senator, with Ran Tucker & Co., were opposed to giving local self-government to California. Ask Sam Yost to give Christian a skinning. I am not ashamed of having fought on the side of slavery—a soldier fights for his country—right or wrong—he is not responsible for the political merits of the cause he fights in. The South was my country. In Fby. 1860 Jeff Davis offered a bill in the Senate wch. passed making all the territories slave territory. (See Davis' book) He was opposed to letting the people decide whether or not they would have slavery Wm. A. Smith, President of Randolph-Macon, quit his duties as a preacher & in 1857–8–9–60 traveled all over Virginia preaching slavery & proving it was right by the Bible.

Yours Truly

Jno. S. Mosby

* * *

E. H. Hinton (1852–1916),
"The Negro and the South: Review of Race Relationships and Conditions," August 1907.[29]

In this remarkable essay, Hinton, a railroad owner who died in Atlanta in 1916, begins with a wondrous depiction of slavery. His account of Reconstruction gets the facts equally wrong. He calls the rule of Mississippi governor Adelbert Ames a "malodorous memory," but historians now agree that Ames was honest and capable, until lack of federal support left his administration exposed to the terrorism of white Democrats. Hinton is correct, however, in claiming that African Americans in the Vicksburg area chafed under Jim Crow seating in auditoriums and other public spaces, and some disagreed with laws forbidding marriage across racial lines. Other than these facts, however, Hinton's depiction of "a negro politician named Davenport" leading a mob to "take the white women for our wives and concubines" is contrary to fact. Whites attacked African Americans in and around Vicksburg in 1874 and 1875 to expel Republican officeholders from the county and replace them with white Democrats. G. W. Davenport was chancery clerk, and along with the sheriff, Peter Crosby, he did try to mobilize Republicans, black and white, to keep white Democrats from throwing them out of office. Hinton's description of what came to be called "the Vicksburg riot" was vague but accurate: "How many negroes were killed in that riot will probably never be known, but it was sufficient."[30] Hinton then justifies any acts taken on behalf of white supremacy, even annihilation of blacks, by invoking, without ever quite saying so, the allegation that African Americans seek to rape white women.

Hinton's use of the phrase "'bloody shirt' speeches of Republican politicians of the North," also requires correction. Today, "waving the bloody shirt" has come to mean attempts to divert voters' attention from real issues by making demagogic references to opponents' misdeeds in the distant past. Specifically, it has come to refer to Republican attempts to delegitimize Democratic opponents by referring to their questionable loyalty during the Civil War.[31] Actually, the shirt in question was worn in

Aberdeen, Mississippi, in 1870, well after the Civil War, by A. P. Huggins, a white Republican and superintendent of Monroe County public schools (a majority-black school system), who was helping African Americans during Reconstruction. White Democrats warned him to leave the state, but he refused, so they rousted him from bed in his nightshirt and whipped him nearly to death. His bloody shirt was taken to Washington as proof of Democratic terrorism against Southern Republicans, where former general Ben Butler, congressman from Massachusetts, allegedly waved it on the floor of Congress. Thus "waving the bloody shirt" referred to the violent means Democrats used between 1870 and the 1890s to interfere with elections and governance across the South. Gradually it came to be distorted into the claim that Republicans were still bringing up the old charge that Democrats were the party of secession and rebellion.[32] After 1890, Republicans did not bother to contest the phrase, because they no longer pushed for black civil or voting rights in the South. So the distortion came to hold the day in history.[33]

In one of your recent issues, commenting on the Atlanta riot of September 22—an unfortunate incident which no good Southerner defends—you used this language: "How does it happen that the blacks who took care of the helpless women and children during the war cannot now be trusted to live in the same town?"

I have not seen this question answered directly by any Southern journal. And yet it goes to the very foundation of all our race troubles. It might be answered briefly by the statement that the negro has changed since 1865, and that in many important particulars he has changed decidedly for the worse. This fact is perfectly patent to intelligent observers in this territory, but it is due you that I particularize.

In order that you may understand that I am fitted by personal experience and observation to write on this subject, at least from our view point, it is proper for me to tell you that I am the son of a former large slaveholder of Mississippi who had from one hundred and fifty to two hundred slaves. Though a small boy when the war began, I was thoroughly familiar with plantation life. I lived on the plantation during the war and during the dark days of reconstruction. Prior to and during the war and after it I was thrown in daily contact with the negroes on our own plantation and others.

I cheerfully admit that during the war there was scarcely a plantation in the South where the mistress and her children were not left alone at the mercy of the slaves a great part of the time, and that the record shows unswerving loyalty on their part. This happy condition was the result of years of training until it had become an inherited tendency. No thought of social equality, and the vile thought inevitably incident thereto, ever entered the heads of the negroes. The discipline of the plantation was firm but kind, and the relation between the owner and owned took on a paternalistic character, the owner feeling as he might toward a lot of children and the slaves looking up to him as a superior whom they held in highest respect. There naturally grew up an affection, a bond of sympathy, and a mutual feeling of interest that was as beautiful as a poem, whatever may be said about the institution of slavery as a whole. (And I wish to say just here that none of the old slaveholders nor any of their descendants would restore the institution if they could.)

The end of the war came in the spring of 1865. Immediately a lot of adventurers, most of them unscrupulous, came into the South from the North, not for legitimate enterprises nor honest investments, but for plunder. They immediately began by precept and example to instill into the minds of the negroes the doctrine that they were in every way the equals of the whites, that they were entitled to every privilege, social or otherwise, which their former masters had enjoyed, and that the United States government had spent millions to guarantee this to them.

From the very first of this infamous propaganda there was created between the two races a strong propulsive force to drive them apart, placing on the defensive the white, with all his pride of race and every instinct of self-preservation, and on the part of the inferior black arousing an envy and hatred inevitably born of a feeling that in being debarred from social equality by the native whites he was being deprived of something to which he was entitled by right.

As strongly supporting the attitude of the "carpetbaggers," the people of the North recognized the negro as an equal by admitting him into all public places, such as theaters, Pullman cars, and hotels; and these facts, coupled with the intemperate utterances of the Republican politicians of the period in Congress and out of it, made it appear to the negro that the proud aloofness of the white people of the South was the stubborn unreasonableness of race prejudice, and therefore unjust to him; and all our race troubles date from the baleful dissemination of this idea.

It is but a step from the nursing of a supposed wrong to thoughts of righting it, and there gradually grew into the negro's mind a suggestion, if not a well-defined determination, to take by force this coveted privilege. I say gradually, for with the older negroes the instinct of deference and respect for the white race was too firmly planted by the growth of years to be easily supplanted by a contrary teaching; but in the young men and with the youth as they grew to manhood their new-found counselors from the North had receptive listeners until in the early seventies the question of social equality was frequently adverted to in public speeches by the negro politicians and preachers and by the white scoundrels and adventurers associated with them.

At that time the negroes were more than the political equal of the whites. Backed by Federal bayonets, they had voted themselves into practically every office in the State, and had elected as Governor an adventurer from Massachusetts, a miscreant whose offensive misrule is a malodorous memory in the State to this day. The Legislature was known as the "Black and Tan" Legislature on account of the great number of negroes and mulattoes that constituted it. It is safe to say that there was scarcely a self-respecting white man in the State holding office.

I reluctantly revive these unhappy recollections of experiences that linger in my memory as a hideous nightmare, but it is necessary to do so in order to emphasize a pivotal point in this discussion—to wit: That as far as political equality went, the negroes certainly ought to have been more than satisfied at that time. But they were not. There was a constantly growing unrest and turbulence among them, and why? Simply because the Southern whites sternly and proudly refused to recognize them as in any way their social equals. . . .

Here Hinton provides three paragraphs describing and justifying the Vicksburg riot of 1875. He concludes:

That fall the white men organized and took over the government of the State. Nearly all the harpies from the North fled between two suns; and after ten years of rank misrule, a saturnalia of official crime, of public plunder, and of spoliation of a proud but defeated people that dispassionate history will some day record as a foul blot on the escutcheon of the Republican party, the Anglo-Saxon of the South came into his own again. By the shotgun policy? Yes. I am in no sense a disciple of Machiavelli, and I am persuaded that my code of ethics is on as high a plane as that of any other Anglo-Saxon, regardless of latitude or of environment; but I shall always believe that in wresting their State from the thieves and plunderers who were desecrating its temples the end to be attained fully justified the means adopted by Mississippi's whites.

The history of Mississippi during the reconstruction period was a fair sample of the conditions in the other Southern States. Some of them escaped from the incubus sooner than others; but all of them suffered the same ills that afflicted Mississippi, and in all the misguided, if not malevolent, teachings of the Republican leaders of the time left their poisonous leaven in the heart of the negro.

Of course no further organized or open demonstrations looking to social equality were made by the negroes, but the venomous germ was none the less active that its operations were secret. It was kept alive, too, by the "bloody shirt" speeches of Republican politicians of the North, who made the political atmosphere lurid for so many years succeeding 1875, as well as by the actions, writings, speeches, and other public utterances of possibly sincere, but we think misguided, preachers, teachers, publicists, and would-be philanthropists of the North, who, according to Charles Francis Adams (see Century Magazine for May, 1906, page 109), have been talking and writing a lot of "rot" on this subject for the last forty years. Considering the gravity of the results to the Southern people, it is very mild, not to say flippant, criticism to call it "rot." We are reaping to-day the bitter fruit sown in this "rot" by our brothers of the North.

The negroes have all deep down in their hearts the false and dangerous notions gathered during reconstruction days, and every perpetration by them of the one most heinous and revolting of crimes may be traced to the dominant thought that they are only taking by force what is theirs by right, but which is denied them by what they have been taught to regard as the unreasonable prejudice of the Southern whites.

As a race the negroes do not regard this monstrous offense a serious crime, for they not only do not cooperate with the officers of the law in apprehending this class of criminals, but they actually protect and harbor them and aid their escape. It is inconceivable that any people would habitually shield criminals of whose crimes they sincerely disapproved, and next to the crime itself this phase of the race problem is one of the most conspicuous features of the diseased condition of the mind of the negroes from the industrious dissemination by your people of the kind of "rot" which Charles Francis Adams now denounces.

Forty years of freedom and this "rot" have transformed the negro from a docile, kindly, confiding, good-natured, dependent servant into a jealous, envious, distrustful, resentful, and independent citizen. The difference between a faithful dog and an undisciplined wild animal is not materially greater than the measure of this contrast. If you can appreciate the full significance of this transformation, you should be able to understand "why the blacks who took care of helpless women and children of the South during the war cannot now be trusted to live in the same town."

What remedy do I propose? It is this: Let your people undo the wrong they have done. Let them recognize the fact that in clothing overnight with full-fledged citizenship, including the dignity of suffrage, millions of barbarous or at least semibarbarous blacks only a few years removed from the utter savagery of African jungles they committed a crime against the Anglo-Saxon that is without a parallel in the history of that proud race. Let them in a measure make reparation for this crime by wiping out the Fifteenth Amendment of the Constitution of the United States. Then, instead of spending millions to send missionaries to the Orient, in an effort to supplant the teachings and philosophy of Buddha, of Confucius, and of Mohammed with the gospel of Christ, let your people divert these honest, God-fearing religious enthusiasts to the blacks of the South, to spread among them the plain gospel of honesty and of decent living, and to serve as an antidote for poison left by the horde of unsavory characters whom you sent down to us immediately after the war. Let them teach the negro the honor and dignity of labor and to be ashamed of his present idleness and shiftlessness. Let them teach him that to work three days out of the workday week and to loaf the other three, as at present, is a crime, and that if he would practice ordinary providence, thrift, and industry with the opportunities he has in the South he would soon be the richest laborer in the world.

If he could be kept busy, it would be a material help in curbing his criminal tendency. Above all, let them teach the negro that social equality is impossible, and that it will ever remain so, and that even political equality is an "iridescent dream" to be realized only by his faithfulness in good works. Let them make it clear to the negro that the Anglo-Saxon, unlike the Latin races, in a thousand years of achievement has always held himself proudly aloof from any amalgamation with an inferior race—an important factor in his progress; that as long as he has in him one spark of pride of race, one impulse of worthy ambition, or one trace of lofty purpose or high ideal this will be his attitude; and that if the negro would escape ultimate annihilation he must recognize and scrupulously respect this unwritten but inexorable law of the Southern whites.

Your people could further help the situation by trying to look at this question sometimes from the standpoint of the Southern white man and by refraining from any public deliverances on this subject until they have carefully studied both sides of it.

Our brothers north of the Ohio and Potomac Rivers can be of material help in solving this problem if they would; but not until the scales have fallen from their eyes, as they have from the eyes of the distinguished New Englander just quoted, and not until they escape from the "bog of self-sufficient ignorance" in which they are now enveloped in connection with this topic—until then (and we devoutly pray that that time is not far distant) your people do harm by interfering; until then urge them to be neutral, and let us "tread our wine press alone."

* * *

South Carolina Confederate Women's Monument, 1912.

Figure 12: Although women took the lead in memorializing the Confederacy, often men took the lead in memorializing women. The United Confederate Veterans endorsed this monument in 1896. The woman sits passively, a Bible in her lap, looking into the distance. According to historian Thomas Brown, men on the committee rejected two more active designs as "too Amazonian."35

Across the South, and even as far away as Helena, Montana, the United Daughters of the Confederacy put up monuments during the Nadir. Moreover, they placed most of them not in cemeteries, where they would memorialize the dead, but in courthouse squares and city parks, where they symbolized neo-Confederate resurgence. This monument stands on the grounds of the state capitol.

One of the UDC's stated objectives is "to record the part taken by Southern Women in patient endurance of hardship and patriotic devotion during the War and Reconstruction." Unlike statues to Confederate soldiers, those to "the women of South Carolina" (and Mississippi etc.) are to an ideal. Women were "unchanged in their devotion, unshaken in their patriotism, unwearied in ministrations, uncomplaining in sacrifices," in the words on this monument opposite the capitol in Columbia. Actually, women were not all pillars of the Confederacy; historian Drew Gilpin Faust ends her essay on Confederate women, "It may well have been because of its women that the South lost the Civil War." Nevertheless, during and after the Nadir, neo-Confederates could boast, as they do here, that it was around their women that "civilizations rallied and triumphed."[34]

* * *

C. E. Workman, "Reconstruction Days in South Carolina," July 1921.[36]

Workman's account of postwar life in the South exaggerates the destruction caused by the war and implicitly blames it all on U.S. troops. This is still common practice at historic sites controlled by neo-Confederates. Yet according to the best scholarship on the matter, retreating Confederates set most of the fires in Atlanta, Columbia, Richmond, and smaller towns as well, to deny provisions and cotton to oncoming Union forces.[37] Workman's errors continue into the Reconstruction period. Like other neo-Confederates during the Nadir, he raises the specter of rape of white women by black men to excuse Ku Klux Klan terror. He professes to believe that renters pay no taxes, while any landlord could tell him that their rents make tax payments possible. He does admit, "By all kinds of devices the Democrats polled a heavy vote" and tells some of the devices used in subsequent elections. "Devices" hardly does justice to the terror visited upon interracial Republican rallies in South Carolina, however.

There are hundreds—nay, thousands—of men and women who have grown up since the war closed in this beautiful Southland of ours who have but little idea of what their parents went through to bring about the prosperity they now enjoy. There are also thousands of true and noble men who wore the blue that have but little idea of the degradation heaped upon the Southern people by placing the ignorant negroes in power over their former masters.

I take it to be a duty I owe to the race of men who are rapidly passing away to record in my humble way from personal experiences some of the trials endured by them.

At the close of the war the Confederate soldiers with sorrowful hearts retraced their steps homeward. Great sacrifices they had made in behalf of their beloved country, but they had no regret for what they had given for the Southern cause, as, foot-sore and ragged, they plodded their weary way back to their native States and homes.

It is difficult to imagine a more deplorable state of affairs than existed at their homes. Thousands of them had not a single dollar, a bushel of corn, or a horse or mule; in most cases all that was left was the bare ground. Houses, furniture, fences, and everything that could be destroyed had been wantonly burned, all slaves freed, and they, exulting in their freedom, refused to work on any terms. All the Southern soldier had was the ground and the love of his wife and children.

With the same bold heart with which they had faced for four long years the columns in blue they now faced the wolf of poverty and fought to keep him from the door, and it was a hard, bitter fight. A still more bitter trial than defeat was before them, for as punishment for the South the powers in Washington resolved to place the negro in power, giving him the right to vote without any qualifications whatever. It did not matter that he knew less than the beasts of the fields; all that was necessary was that he had once been a slave. Armed troops were kept at every county seat to uphold negro rule and encourage him to vote the Republican ticket as often as he pleased, the Republicans by this means running up great majorities.

This state of affairs continued over all of the South from 1865 to 1876. Every office in South Carolina was filled by negroes, carpetbaggers, or renegade native whites known as scalawags.

"The bottom rail was now on top, the negro proudly pranced, The authorities at Washington piped for him to dance."

From the close of the war until 1876 South Carolina was under negro rule upheld by Federal bayonets. Adventurers from the North, mostly from the lowest walks in life, flocked South with all their possessions packed in carpetbags, from which they derived the name of carpetbaggers. These men encouraged the negro against his former master and instigated him to commit many heinous crimes.

The books written by Thomas Dickson [sic, Dixon], such as the "Leopard's Spots," etc., are not exaggerated conditions of this period. Crimes became so unbearable that the Confederate soldiers had to organize for the protection of their wives and daughters. They joined together in the Ku-Klux Klans, which inspired terror in the negroes and checked somewhat the crimes that were being committed.

At every election for State and national offices the white (Democratic) party put out a ticket, generally giving one-half of the offices to the best of the negroes, hoping in this way to get some of the whites into office; but they were continually defeated, as the negroes were taught that if the Democrats ever got into power they would be put back into slavery.

As a rule the negroes did not pay taxes of any kind. All the expenses of government were paid by the whites, and three-fourths of it was openly stolen by the plunderers in office for this purpose alone. An account of the disgraceful scenes at the statehouse in Columbia would not be fit for publication.

As all efforts of the whites to elect a mixed ticket had failed, in 1876 they determined to bring out a straight white man's ticket, and not to solicit a negro vote. That grand old cavalry officer, Wade Hampton, was nominated for Governor, and a full ticket for all other offices selected from men who had always been true to the South was placed in the field.

New life came into the hearts of the whites. A voice passed from the mountain to the sea, crying: "Arise, white men!" Like the dead arising from their graves, the Confederate soldier arose with his son, and all answered: "Yes, by the grace of God and with his help we shall redeem our land, fairly, if possible, but at any cost of blood or money."

In all counties cavalry companies were formed, arms secured, and a uniform, consisting of a red shirt and black hat, adopted. Weekly meetings were held at each county seat. It was resolved that the rule of the carpetbagger and negro should end; that he should not longer be allowed to incite the negroes to violence at their political meetings; that if he would agree to have joint debates all would be quiet, and each speaker should have a respectful hearing, but if not there should be no speeches made by the Republicans.

These terms the Republicans would not accept, so they were notified that their meetings should not be held, and in all cases where they attempted to speak the meetings were broken up by the "Red Shirts" making so much noise that the speakers could not be heard at all. One instance illustrating this will be cited.

Sumter, S.C., was a special stronghold of the Republicans, and they resolved to hold a mass meeting there, when Governor Chamberlain and other high officers of the State would address them. And they gave notice that if interfered with they would burn the town. The gage of battle being thus thrown down, the whites eagerly accepted it. The county chairman sent out messengers to all clubs and companies in Sumter, Kershaw, Lancaster, and adjoining counties, requesting full attendance and to come well armed and prepared for any emergency. Generals Hampton, Butler, and many other distinguished ex-Confederate generals were to be present to make speeches and take command of the forces in case they were needed. The eventful day arrived that the carpetbaggers had set to intimidate or test the courage of the "Red Shirt" Brigade. The club I belonged to arrived in Sumter about 9 a.m. after a ride of twenty miles. We found awaiting us members of clubs from other parts of the county and others arriving every hour until we had a force of about one thousand men, all mounted and armed. Opposing us were at least fifteen thousand negroes. We seemed a mere handful compared to the black cohorts assembled, but there was no fear in the hearts that beat beneath the red shirts. The flower of South Carolina was in the field, and the old war horse, Hampton, was at the head.

One or two hours were spent riding up and down the streets in close formation, the whites cheering for Hampton and the blacks for Chamberlain. About 11 a.m. the Republicans erected a platform in a grove of large trees near the depot, and Governor Chamberlain, surrounded by the thousands of negroes assembled, commenced his address. He was interrupted by a messenger from the Democratic assemblage requesting a joint debate, Chamberlain to be answered by Hampton, etc., but the request was refused. They declared that the Democrats should never speak at any of their meetings. On this refusal the "Red Shirts" surrounded the crowd and made such a noise by shouting that it was impossible for the speakers to be heard, so the meeting was broken up. General Hampton was then called to the platform to address the whites, Chamberlain and all his blacks going back into the town. Hampton had hardly begun to speak before the fire bells rang a general alarm, which meant either a fight or a fire. Every "Red Shirt" wheeled his horse and dashed wildly toward the courthouse. Generals Hampton, Hagood, and other officers soon gained the head of the column and by entreaty and commands succeeded in checking the men and causing them to fall into order. We advanced on the courthouse, which was surrounded by a dense mass of negroes, while above their heads could be seen bright bayonets and troops formed into line. While we did not know whether these soldiers were friends or foes, we surrounded the negroes on all sides, and two or three old cannons were loaded down with nails, scrap iron, etc., and placed at the corners of the streets, the courthouse being in a square.

We found that the surrounded troops were a company of citizens of the town. A fight had started between a negro and a white man. The citizens had placed their guns in the courthouse, and when the disturbance began they rushed to the courthouse and had been surrounded by the negroes. Our coming up and surrounding the negroes on all sides, with the old cannons at each corner, made things look very squally. Through the coolness of our leaders the hotheads were kept quiet. The negroes, being caught between two forces of whites, were intimidated, and after a good deal of entreaty by the leaders of both parties the crowds were quieted.

I am sorry to say that all meetings in the State did not end so peaceably. There were several bloody riots in which a few white men lost their lives. These skirmishes and losses plainly showed the African that he was not a match for the white man; that the Anglo-Saxon was thoroughly aroused and determined to regain his land at any cost of blood or money. Their leaders encouraged them on, but when trouble arose they took pretty good care to be elsewhere.

The elections came off in November, 1876. The negroes voted the straight Republican ticket, as usual; the white vote was solid for Hampton. By all kinds of devices the Democrats polled a heavy vote. Both parties claimed to have carried the State by heavy majorities. Two sets of State officers and Governors were sworn into office. The whites refused to pay any taxes to the Chamberlain government, and great confusion existed.

This state of affairs existed in other Southern States. It was finally agreed that the electoral vote of these States should be allowed to be cast for Hayes, and in return for this the national government would withdraw all Federal troops from these States, which was done and a fraudulent President was installed into office. But by this means war was averted, and the South was freed of negro rule.

Since 1876 the South has made rapid progress in wealth, which it would never have done under such a government as existed up to that time, and peace, happiness, and prosperity abound.

In 1878 the Republicans made their last attempt to regain control of the State and brought out the last Republican ticket for State and county offices that was ever put in the field in South Carolina. The whites again selected a straight Democratic ticket. At this time the Republican party was known only as the "negro party," and any white man voting that ticket was completely ostracized, both himself and his family. They were treated with the utmost contempt except those Northern men who had made their homes in the South and who voted only the national Republican ticket, voting always with the whites for all other offices. They were well treated and respected.

In 1878 we again brought out a white man's ticket. The result of this election was, of course, an overwhelming majority for the Democrats. In the presidential election of 1890 we selected a new plan of carrying the election. Seven boxes in which the votes had to be deposited were put out, and on each box in large Roman letters the name of the office was printed, and each ticket had to go in the right box or it would not be counted. If the vote for Governor was placed in the box for a county officer, that vote was not counted at all. If a voter did not have education enough to read his ticket and the name on the box, the chances of it being counted was perhaps one in a hundred. This disheartened the negro from any further attempt to control elections.

The law in effect at present is that each voter shall register sixty days before election and shall produce his poll tax receipt; that he also must be able to read and write and to explain any paragraph in the Constitution to the satisfaction of the judges of the election. To keep from depriving any white men of their votes, the grandfather's clause was inserted, which is that if the grandfather or father fought in either the Revolutionary War or War between the States a man was entitled to vote on account of the services rendered to the State by that ancestor.

The first time I ever voted in South Carolina the negroes marched boldly to the polls with guns on their shoulders, stacked them in a hundred yards of the polls, placing a heavy guard over them, and kept the white men pushed away from the polls.

None of us will ever regret the part we took in these measures or would hesitate to do the same again or even worse should the same conditions arise.

* * *

Mildred Rutherford (1852–1928), "The War Was Not a Civil War," January 1923.[38]

The United Daughters of the Confederacy was organized in 1894. Today it has almost 20,000 members, less than half as many as it did when Mildred L. Rutherford was its historian general. Rutherford taught at Lucy Cobb Institute, a private school for wealthy white girls in Athens, Georgia, for almost a half a century and was principal for more than a quarter century. Rutherford gave addresses to the national conventions of the UDC supplying neo-Confederate interpretations of the Civil War and Reconstruction and published her articles in pamphlets she called *Miss Rutherford's Scrap Books*, from which this selection comes. Critiquing a similar piece, historian James McPherson noted, "It mattered little to Rutherford's avid readers that . . . every one of her 'facts' and 'truths' . . . was false." She had immense influence on U.S. history as taught in Southern high schools. At the request of the United Confederate Veterans, she prepared *A Measuring Rod to Test Text Books, and Reference Books in Schools, College and Libraries* that prompted publishers to put out special Southern editions of otherwise national textbooks that called the Civil War "the War Between the States" and otherwise reflected neo-Confederate views. Rutherford also led the successful campaign to keep Georgia from ratifying women's suffrage.[39]

Ours was not a CIVIL WAR, so let us correct that wrong first. The United States was a Republic of Sovereign States. We were not a Nation until after the surrender, and even now the States have not surrendered their rights. A civil war must be in one State between two parties in that State. If we acknowledge that ours was a CIVIL WAR, we acknowledge we were a Nation, or one State in 1861 and not a Republic of Sovereign States, and therefore had no right to secede. This is what the North would like us to acknowledge.

It was not a WAR OF SECESSION as some would have us to call it. The Southern States seceded with no thought of war. They simply wished to have a government where their rights, reserved by the Constitution, should be respected. The war was caused by the North attempting to coerce us back into the

Union, contrary to the Constitution, and for no reason save that the States of the South demanded their rights. If we call it a War of Secession we admit the seceding States brought on the war.

The Northern States seceded from the Constitution.

It might be called a WAR OF COERCION, for the North did coerce the seceding States.

It was not a WAR OF REBELLION, for Sovereign States cannot rebel, therefore secession was not rebellion. This is acknowledged now by all thinking men.

DR. CHARLES STOWE, son of Harriet Beecher Stowe, said:

> "There is no doubt that there was a rebellion, but the rebellion was on the part of the North, not the South. The North rebelled against the Constitution—the South stood by Constitutional rights."

It was not a WAR OF SECTIONS. The North did not fight the South, for brothers were arrayed against brothers in many cases. There were men of the South who enlisted on the Union side. There were many men of the North who enlisted on the Southern side. Both North and South were contending for a principle and not because they hated each other.

It was the WAR BETWEEN THE STATES, for the non-seceding States of the United States made war upon the seceding States of the United States to force them back into the Union. Please call it so, and teach it so.

* * *

SUSAN LAWRENCE DAVIS (1862–1939),
"THE FIRST CONVENTION," 1924.[40]

Susan Davis was an Alabama native. Shortly before her death, she sued the publisher of *Gone With the Wind*, accusing Margaret Mitchell of plagiarizing her book, *The Authentic History of the Ku Klux Klan*, from which this excerpt comes. In dismissing the suit, the judge noted that *Gone With the Wind* was "partly historical and partly fictional." However, Davis and Mitchell shared a view of the Klan as the savior of white supremacy and good government across the South during Reconstruction. Davis's account of Robert E. Lee's role in the founding of the Klan was believed throughout the South throughout the Nadir, but the encounter has not been proven to have occurred. At their 1924 national convention, the United Daughters of the Confederacy endorsed Davis's book as one "that every southerner ought to read."[41]

Previous to the assembling of the Convention the Pulaski Ku Klux Klan had given permission to men in Fayetteville, Lincoln County, Tenn., and Huntsville, Madison County, Alabama, to form Ku Klux Klans. It was around these four adjoining counties, that the Ku Klux Klan pivoted throughout its entire existence.

The Pulaski Ku Klux Klan at this time had decided fully that, at this proposed Convention, a leader for all Ku Klux Klan activities which might develop throughout the South should be chosen, and toward that end, they sent emissaries to place before General Robert E. Lee, the fact that the Ku Klux Klan which had started merely in sport, was rapidly reaching tremendous proportions as a force for meeting distressing conditions in the South, and to ascertain if its continuance would meet his approval.

The men who were chosen to see General Lee were Major Felix G. Buchanan of Lincoln County, Captain John B. Kennedy of the Pulaski Ku Klux Klan, Captain William Richardson of the Athens Ku Klux Klan, Episcopal Bishop Richard H. Wilmer, and Captain John B. Floyd of the Alabama Ku Klux Klan.

General Lee was told in the most impressive manner possible of the good already done by the Ku Klux Klan, in the hope that he would express a wish to join them, but he did not make application.

He said to them, "I would like to assist you in any plan that offers relief. I cannot be with you in person but I will follow you but must be invisible; and my advice is to keep it as you have it, a protective organization."

When this message was delivered to the Convention it led to the christening of the United Ku Klux Klan, the "Invisible Empire," for they felt that General Lee was their "guiding spirit."

Captain William Richardson suggested General Nathan B. Forrest for the leader of the Ku Klux Klan, if it met with General Lee's approval, and he said: "General Nathan B. Forrest is the only man I know who could lead so large a body of men successfully. You may present to him my compliments and ask him if he will accept the leadership."

* * *

John E. Rankin (1882–1960),
"Forrest at Brice's Cross Roads," August 1925.[42]

John Rankin was born in Mississippi, attended Ole Miss, and became a lawyer and Democratic politician in what was then a one-party state. He then
won sixteen terms in Congress.[43] Like Williams, his fellow Mississippi congressman, Rankin denies that Confederate soldiers were fighting "merely to
maintain the institution of slavery." Therefore "the lost cause" is not really
lost: "You have won the great cause of white supremacy," he declares, and
indeed, white supremacy ruled unchallenged during the Nadir. However,
like most neo-Confederates during the Nadir, Rankin makes a brief bow in
the direction of states' rights as the cause of secession.

We are gathered to-day upon sacred ground. This hallowed spot was consecrated by the blood and sacrifices of the noblest army that ever followed a flag.
To this historic place the eyes of the world will one day be turned, and upon
it future history will forever pour its light. Here was won the most signal and
complete victory of the War between the States, by either side, and that, too,
against the most overwhelming odds. Here, sixty-one years ago to-day, was one
of the greatest demonstrations of military genius ever manifested, when Nathan
Bedford Forrest, that untrained soldier of the South, rose to the emergency of
the occasion and wrote his name among the immortals of the ages.

Critics of all countries agree that the greatest evidence of military genius is
for a general to divide his army into two or more parts and then successfully
concentrate them upon the field of battle. Napoleon did this at Austerlitz, and
the sun of fortune rose upon the most brilliant military career in the history
of all Europe. He tried it at Waterloo, and failed, which terminated that career in ignominious defeat. The genius of Robert E. Lee, combined with that of
Stonewall Jackson, astounded and thrilled the world by the execution of that
great feat at the second battle of Bull Run, which resulted in one of the most
glorious victories of all time.

But here, in the darkest days of the dying Confederacy, this daring, brilliant
soldier matched his genius against skill and numbers, and, in the face of a well-

fed, well-equipped army that outnumbered his more than three to one, divided his small band of half-naked, half-starved veterans into three separate parts, and so successfully concentrated them upon the field of battle as to sweep all before them in a wild riot of inglorious defeat. He killed and captured more men than his own army contained, an accomplishment that, I dare say, was never duplicated in any other pitched battle on American soil.

I stood some time ago upon the field of Manassas where Stonewall Jackson received his baptism of fire in that conflict as well as his immortal name, and my heart swelled with pride as I looked upon the scene of those two marvelous victories won by the soldiers of the South. I recently surveyed the heights of Gettysburg and caught the thrill that must come to every unbiased soul that scans that sacred field, as I glanced back across the lapse of sixty years and saw with imagination's eye that thin gray line of Confederate veterans march across that open field and up that deadly slope in the face of the most withering fire that was ever concentrated upon the legions of men.

But there is no place on earth that more thoroughly challenges our admiration than the ground on which we now stand, not only for the valor and courage of our brave men who conquered here, but for the matchless plan of their dauntless leader, as well as the precision and thoroughness of its terrible execution. They were our relatives, our neighbors, and our friends, defending our homes. What could be more gratifying or more inspiring to the children of the Southland than to look upon this historic field and contemplate the glorious achievements here, sixty-one years ago, of those brave men we are so glad to call our own? I would rather have their record to my credit than all the monuments wealth could buy. Their monuments, as well as their sacred memories, are in our hearts. Let us cherish them as the most priceless treasures of our time and transmit them with renewed devotion to the generations yet to come.

But, so far, this great field is unmarked. If it were in Massachusetts or Pennsylvania, and the victory had gone to the other side, it would to-day be bristling with towering monuments and covered with markers to show where each and every detail of the fight occurred. Volumes would have been written in commendation of the valor here displayed, and its every detail would have been perpetuated in history, song, and story.

Let us neglect it no longer. We should organize a Brice's Cross Roads Battle Field Association for the purpose of securing title to this ground, charting and mapping it off, and erecting hereon markers telling to the world the thrilling story of that great struggle. Let us place upon this eminence a monument to Forrest and his followers that will stand as a sentinel finger throughout the coming ages to guide the footsteps of future pilgrims to the ground upon which was achieved one of the most brilliant military accomplishments in the history of mankind, so that when the people of America come to realize the truth concerning the great cause for which those heroes fought and died, and when the world shall come to appreciate the great genius of the matchless leader who commanded here, they may come in humility and gratitude to scatter their flowers of admiration and affection and to draw an inspiration from the examples of valor and heroism enacted here by those men who wore the gray.

It seems to me that it would be quite improper to refer to you, or to address you, as veterans of the "lost cause." The cause for which you fought and sacrificed was not lost; it was the cause of civilization. It is as much alive to-day as it was in sixty-one, and it will live as long as our free American institutions shall endure. It will be lost only when the ideals of our race shall have vanished from the earth.

Slavery was not the cause that actuated the soldiers of the South in that dreadful conflict. We are all glad that human slavery has disappeared; but the dread of the horrible alternative which some of our opponents would have imposed—that of placing the negro upon terms of social and political equality with the white man—aroused the latent indignation of the Anglo-Saxon South and called forth from the deep wells of human nature the most powerful resentment that ever inspired a human soul to willing sacrifice or battered down the barriers of self-restraint.

Not only would they have placed the negroes on equality with the whites, but some would have placed them in control. To-day, the sons of those men who sixty years ago preached the doctrine of a black South, tell us that the South, with its pure American stock, its high ideals, and its inflexible fidelity to the great principles upon which our civilization rests, will some day be called upon to save this republic.

Our people had before them at that time the horrible examples of negro insurrections in Haiti and Santo Domingo, where the blacks had revolted and put to death, in the most cruel and unspeakable manner, the white men, women, and children of those unfortunate provinces. Such wanton cruelty was applauded by the opposition and was cited as conclusive evidence of the negro's fitness for self-government. Some of them even proclaimed that he had proved himself superior to the white man. Sixty years have passed away, and the negroes of Haiti and Santo Domingo have lapsed into a barbarism that would shame the jungles of darkest Africa. With three hundred years of training behind them; with a modern civilization thrust upon them; with a government already organized; with the sympathy and encouragement of the civilized nations of the earth; in a land extremely rich in climate, soil, and resources; with every possible advantage that could be laid at their feet—the negroes of Haiti have gradually drifted back into savagery, voodooism, and cannibalism, until to-day it requires the constant guard of American Marines to save them from themselves and to protect them from one another.

Yet those misguided individuals who advocated a black South would have had the world believe that the Confederate soldiers, who were fighting against those and similar possibilities, were doing so merely to maintain the institution of slavery.

A lost cause! You have won the great cause of white supremacy, by which alone our civilization can hope to endure!

But some will tell you that you lost the cause of secession. It was not a cause; it was a means by which you attempted to maintain the cause of State rights, or local self-government. We all rejoice that the country is reunited; but the great cause of self-government was not lost. Even those who scorned it in those days are now invoking its salutary protection against the dangerous tendencies of the times.

As I look upon this small band of battle-scarred heroes of the Confederacy, I am reminded of the expressions of Daniel Webster as he stood before the veterans of Bunker Hill on that historic field just fifty years to a day after that battle, in which he said:

> "Venerable men, you have come down to us from a former generation. Heaven has bounteously lengthened out your lives that you may behold this joyous day. You are now where you stood fifty years ago, this very hour, with your brothers and your neighbors, shoulder to shoulder, in the strife for your country. Behold, how altered! The same heavens are indeed over your heads; the same ocean rolls at your feet; but all else—how changed! You hear now no roar of hostile cannon, you see no mixed volumes of smoke and flame rising from burning Charlestown. The ground strewed with the dead and the dying; the impetuous charge; the steady and successful repulse; the loud call to repeated assault; the summoning of all that is manly to repeated resistance; a thousand bosoms freely and fearlessly bared in an instant to whatever of terror there may be in war and death—all these you have witnessed, but you witness them no more. All is peace; and God has granted you this sight of your country's happiness ere you slumber in the grave."

We hail and congratulate you, veterans of the Confederacy, the thinning remnant of the greatest army, man for man, that ever wore a country's uniform. Divine Providence has also granted you this wonderful sight of your country's happiness ere you pass to your eternal rest.

On that fatal day, sixty-one years ago, the clouds hung low and dark above the horizon of the Confederacy. In front of you, deployed upon yonder slope, was a black mass of recently liberated slaves, members of a semisavage race which our forefathers had elevated from the position of savage to that of servant and had shown the light of civilization for the first time through the unfortunate institution of slavery. All their bestial passions and instincts had been aroused. With badges bearing threats of violence as terrible as any ever perpetrated by the vicious members of their race upon the helpless women and children of Haiti and Santo Domingo, they were threatening the safety of every Southern home, as well as the life of every woman and child. It was a test that tried men's souls. You rose to the occasion and gave to the world an exhibition of that courage and determination which carried the South through that terrible war and through those darker years of reconstruction that were yet to come.

Suppose you could have looked beyond those lowering clouds to behold this glorious day. What a consolation it would have been! God grant that the venerated shades of those departed heroes who fell at your sides may be granted a vision of our Southland to-day, that they may realize the blessing which their sacrifices have brought, and know that they did not die in vain.

You have lived to see the principles of self-government and white supremacy survive the wreck of war and the chaos of reconstruction. Instead of following in the wake of Haiti and Santo Domingo down into the implacable mire of mongrelism, degeneracy, and decay, the South has risen like a Phoenix from the ashes of her destruction to assume the leadership in the onward march of the greatest civilization the world has yet known. Instead of the black South, which some of our critics predicted, Dixie has become the lasting abode of the purest Anglo-Saxon population to be found on American soil—the race that has built and maintained our modern civilization and upon which its future destiny depends.

You have not only lived to see the survival of those fundamental principles for which you fought, but you have seen the South gradually recover her lost prosperity, until to-day the eyes of the world are turned upon her. The cry used to be, "Young man, go West," but now the slogan is: "Young man, go South." It is the coming section of the world: As Henry Grady once said: "With a gentle climate above a fertile soil, she yields to the husbandman every product of the temperate zone." It is the most delightful and the most desirable portion of God's great commonwealth, and the world is to-day finding it out—as is evidenced by the continuous stream of people from other sections of the country hunting homes in that Southland which you have defended in time of war, protected in reconstruction, and preserved and improved in times of peace. It is filled with the happy homes of your children and your children's children, growing in wealth and prosperity, holding high the torch of civilization, and leading the way in the onward march of modern progress.

We congratulate you, and congratulate ourselves, that we are given this opportunity to lay at your feet the flowers of love and affection and to manifest in our humble way a small portion of that boundless gratitude which we owe and feel for the great sacrifices you and your comrades made, that our Anglo-Saxon civilization might not perish from the earth.

May you spend the remainder of the evening of your eventful careers in quiet and ideal peace. May you serenely rest in the loving care of those about you, mindful of your country's gratitude, conscious of a well-spent life, and confident of its good; and may you "greet the coming of another age of youth and usefulness in another radiant Easter beyond the gates of night."

* * *

CHAPTER 6

THE CIVIL RIGHTS ERA, 1940—

Around 1940, the Nadir of race relations began to ease. As with its onset, three underlying processes were at work. First, the Great Migration of African Americans from the South to the North produced black voters. Moreover, the prohibitions that barred African Americans from sundown towns and neighborhoods across the North concentrated them into a few places in a few larger cities. Soon these concentrations produced black aldermen, state legislators, even a congressman from Chicago. Now to use racial slurs was impolitic. Second, imperialism declined in intellectual and social power. American leaders saw that they would have to deal with nations governed by people of color. Overt racism would only off-put them. Third and most powerful, all nations demonize their opponents in war, but the Third Reich made it easy. As Americans learned about Hitler's racial policies, they grew appalled. That he was committing genocide against people—Jews—whom we considered white made it all the worse. As well, service in World War II gave African Americans a new rhetoric of legitimacy with which to demand an end to discrimination.

The title of the first reading in this chapter, "The Southern Tradition at Bay," foretells the declining influence of neo-Confederate ideas. Writing in 1943, Richard Weaver, a professor of English, hopes that by supplying a philosophical underpinning to Southern traditions, he can help them endure and prevail. Another English professor, Clifford Harrison, foresees the same decline and counters partly by making vague the Confederacy's reason for existence. (The previous chapter provides earlier examples of this tradition of mystification.) Next come reports from the Dixiecrat convention of 1948, when Southern Democrats revolted against their national party's increasing willingness to discuss and even enact policies favoring civil rights. The Dixiecrat revolt represents a high water mark for the explicit use of Confederate symbols, this time in the service of segregation and states' rights, not slavery and nationhood. We include a later speech by Strom Thurmond, Dixiecrat candidate for president.

Beginning with *Brown v. Board of Education* in 1954, a series of decisions by the U.S. Supreme Court placed neo-Confederates further on the defensive.[1] Georgia reacted by making the Confederate battle flag the prominent element of its new state flag in 1956; South Carolina reacted by raising the Confederate battle flag over its state capitol from 1962 to 2000. Running for office in Florida in 1958, Sumter Lowry raised fears that Communists were behind such attempts to force "race mixing." Across the South, the largest response was by a newly formed organization, the [White] Citizens' Councils. We include several articles and two cartoons from its magazine, along with its logo and slogan, "States' Rights / Racial Integrity." Like the Dixiecrats, these writings repeatedly make use of Confederate symbols and leaders.[2]

In January 1970, school districts in the Deep South finally desegregated, in response to the Supreme Court opinion in *Alexander v. Holmes*. Sixteen years of defiance was now at an end. Despite efforts by state governments and white citizens from Virginia to Arkansas, white and black children now attended school together; white and black teachers now taught together. Having failed to keep schools segregated, white Southerners no longer believed they could keep neighborhoods segregated; African Americans now moved onto previously all-white blocks from northern Virginia to Jackson, Mississippi, and beyond. As the civil rights movement reverberated through American culture, U.S. history textbooks began to present slavery as a burden to slaves, rather than a blessing. Some public officials, aware that African Americans again can vote, now support proposals to rename "Confederate Park" or "Nathan Bedford Forrest High School," causing consternation among the Sons of Confederate Veterans and United Daughters of the Confederacy.[3]

All is not lost for neo-Confederates, however. Their interpretations of secession, the Civil War, and Reconstruction, developed in the Nadir as the last chapter shows, still hold great influence in American popular culture.[4] In 1995, for example, the U.S. Postal Service issued stamps commemorating the end of the Civil War. The set's motto was "Once Divided. Now Perforated," and it was carefully balanced to equate the United States with the Confederate States. Thus it paired Lincoln and Davis, Grant and Lee, Clara Barton and Phoebe Pember (who helped run a military hospital in Richmond), Generals Sherman and Jackson, the ships *Monitor* and *Virginia* (*Merrimack*), Harriet Tubman and Mary Chestnut (planter/diarist), and the battles at Gettysburg (Union victory) and Chancellorsville (Confederate victory). Across the top ran two titles: "Civil War" and "War Between the States." As Chapter 4 showed, "War Between the States" is an anachronism, a later invention for rhetorical purposes. As well, the two sides were not moral equals. The sheet reflects the success of neo-Confederates—even after the Nadir of race relations—to redefine why states seceded, rename the war, and launder Confederate policies and objectives to make them more appealing.[5]

Beginning in 1964, the Republican Party openly courted white suprema-cists, who responded handsomely. Republican presidential candidate Barry Goldwater, notorious for opposing the Civil Rights Act of that year, carried South Carolina, Georgia, Alabama, Mississippi, and Louisiana, the only states he won outside his home state of Arizona.[6] In 1968 and 1972, Richard Nixon continued the courtship with his "Southern strategy." As Republican strategist Lee Atwater put it, "By 1968, you can't say 'nigger'—that hurts you. Backfires. So you say stuff like forced busing, states' rights, and all that stuff."[7] It worked. Gradually, the party of Lincoln became the party of Jefferson Davis. We include a map of votes for George W. Bush in 2004, showing the remarkable Republican solidarity of white Southerners and its similarity to support for Lincoln's three opponents in 1860. In 2008, Democrat Barack Obama won just 10% of the white vote in Alabama and 11% in Mississippi. In return for their support, Republican leaders, including Senator Trent Lott and Governor Haley Barbour of Mississippi; Pat Buchanan, candidate for president in 1992, 1996, and 2000; and polemic columnist Ann Coulter lent legitimacy to neo-Confederate orga-nizations and publications by speaking before them, being interviewed by or writing for their publications, and defending them when they came under fire. Occasionally neo-Confederate ideas and rhetoric influenced Republican think-ing overtly, such as at some nationwide tax protests on April 15, 2009. At such protests in Texas, Governor Rick Perry made cryptic statements about secession to crowds chanting "Secede!" At least four of the six candidates campaigning in 2009 for the 2010 Republican gubernatorial nomination in Georgia—including the three frontrunners—likewise supported secession if Congress were to pass laws that Georgia thought unconstitutional and wrong.[8]

From time to time, new neo-Confederate organizations arise, notably the League of the South. At its founding, Thomas Fleming, a founding director, declared: "The national government has been using armed force to suppress the South ever since the 1950s. They have beaten us black and blue with their civil rights legislation that has nothing to do with the rights of black Americans and everything to do with the imposing of the tyranny of Federal judges." On its website, the League's president, Michael Hill, explains its current stance: "Abe Lincoln and his minions have sired a long line of domestic terrorists, including most recently George W. Bush and Barack Hussein Obama (and all who aid them in their misrule). We might throw the larger part of Congress into the mix as well." Hill adds that the League's "ultimate goal is a free and independent Southern republic."[9]

A new magazine appeared in 1979, *Southern Partisan*; we include one short passage on Martin Luther King Day and a photo of a T-shirt it sold to provide a sense of its rhetoric. *Southern Partisan* promotes a hierarchal view of society run by white conservative Christian men, with women in their place at home.

Typical articles oppose immigrants, gay rights, feminism, modern trends in Protestant Christianity, multicultural education, interracial marriage, and international intervention by the United States. Older organizations survived, notably the United Daughters of the Confederacy and Sons of Confederate Veterans. In 2000, openly far-right neo-Confederates took over the SCV; it then launched a new magazine, *Southern Mercury*. Although much smaller than the Citizens' Councils, the Council of Conservative Citizens carries on their legacy and has ties to Republican Party leaders. Several foundations and think tanks, including the Rockford Institute in Illinois and the Ludwig von Mises Institute at Auburn, Alabama, support a neo-Confederate agenda. Neo-Confederates have also found a niche in the larger part of the diverse home-schooling movement; we excerpt a textbook on the Civil War aimed at that audience.

To cope with the new era, neo-Confederates continue to claim that the Southern states seceded for anything *other* than slavery. As part of this argument, some go further, maintaining that many African Americans fought for the Confederacy. Supposedly this proves that secession could not have been for slavery or white supremacy. We quote Georgia governor Sonny Perdue's declaration of Confederate History Month in 2008 and include a photograph of the Confederate monument in Arlington National Cemetery, which has evolved into "evidence" in support of this assertion. The chapter closes with an article from *Southern Mercury* that provides a good summation of what many neo-Confederates currently believe about their cause.

As of this writing (2010), it is too early to tell if having an African American in the White House will lead to a new era of race relations that will further marginalize neo-Confederates, or if it will prompt some of the almost 90% of whites in the Deep South who voted against Obama to coalesce, thus breathing new life into the neo-Confederate movement.

* * *

Richard Weaver (1910–63), Selections from *The Southern Tradition at Bay*, 1943.[10]

Richard Weaver was born in North Carolina and grew up in Kentucky. He became a disciple of the Southern Agrarians, the conservative writers group, while at Vanderbilt. This book was originally Weaver's 1943 dissertation, "The Confederate South, 1865–1910: A Study in the Survival of a Mind and a Culture," at Louisiana State University for his doctorate in English. Weaver taught English at the University of Chicago and was a major influence on Russell Kirk, William F. Buckley Jr., Young Americans for Freedom, and other conservative organizations and leaders. He died in 1963; in 1968 his dissertation was posthumously published with two editors, George Core and M. E. Bradford, the latter a campaigner for George Wallace. Donald Davidson, a founder of the Agrarians and still a segregationist in 1968, wrote the foreword.

Weaver held that white Southern culture needed to be distilled into a conscious ideological framework:

The South possesses an inheritance which it has imperfectly understood and little used. It is in the curious position of having been right without realizing the grounds of its rightness.

Weaver sees white Southern culture as being antimodern, antidemocratic, hierarchal, and oriented to place. He advocates restoring this culture as the solution for what he sees as the problems of modern society. In his book he paints slavery and large plantations as idyllic.

The feeling of being bound to a locality, which has been almost wholly lost by the deracinated population of the modern metropolis, was a part of the plantation dweller's daily consciousness and an important factor in his self-respect. In the midst of traffic in human beings there was, paradoxically, less evidence of the cash nexus than in the marts of free labor, and even the humble could have the deep human satisfaction that comes of being cherished for what one is. Between the expression "our people," euphemistic though it may have been, and the modern abstraction "manpower" lies a measure of our decline in humanity.

Weaver thinks giving women the vote is a bad idea:

Distinctions of many kinds will have to be restored. . . . I think that women would have more influence actually if they did not vote, but . . . made their firesides seats of Delphic wisdom.

Similarly, he sees emancipation as a bad idea for African Americans:

That the presence of the African had been the chief source of Southern misfortunes was a common admission; yet his very childlikeness, his extraordinary exhibitions of loyalty, and his pathetic attempts to find his place in the complicated white man's civilization rather had the effect of endearing him to his former owners. . . .

The Negro's first disillusionment came when he tried to grasp tangible form the benefits which the new dispensation was expected to confer. Stories are told of his coming to town with a sack to carry back the franchise which was to be given him, and of his confusion of the "Freedmen's Bureau" with the well-known article of furniture. "Whar's dat bureau? Was sure to be the first question," Virginia Clay wrote.[11]

* * *

M. Clifford Harrison (1893–1967)
"The Southern Confederacy—Dead or Alive?"
December 1947.[12]

Clifford Harrison did graduate work in English at the University of Virginia and then taught English at Virginia Tech for 45 years, retiring in 1960. Here he strikes a common theme in neo-Confederate writing: opposition to immigrants, other than from the United Kingdom and perhaps northern Europe. Also, he makes the cause for which Southern states seceded almost content-free: "a cause so grand" and "pure principles."

. . . The Southern Confederacy represented the purest Anglo-Saxon idealism. Beauty and virtue were their own reward. With the collapse of the Confederacy, America saw a premium put on the materialistic, the uncouth, the raw, the callous, and the crude. Encouragement was given to the false philosophy that mere bulk or size constitutes greatness and grandeur.

The North itself paid an awful price for its triumph. In order to provide replacements for the myriads of dead and wounded that had fallen before the glorious aim of Southern marksmen, the North opened wide its seaports to European immigration of all sorts and through tempting bounties recruited its ranks. In the later part of the War between the States many blue-coated privates of the Federal armies could not speak English at all. They were not Americans, they were not good soldiers; but they filled the gaps. And what has been the ultimate result? The gates of America, once unlocked, have, like the gates of Hell in Milton's *Paradise Lost*, remained open. The Hauptmanns, the Dillingers, and the Capones have been the answer. . . .

And let us look toward the future. Even some people in the North, whose own problems have grown darker with the passing of years, have come convinced that the salvation of America rests with the South. For in the South almost exclusively persists the idealism of the Anglo-Saxon, which, with the power of Christianity, safeguards the ultimate hope of the world. . . .

Is the Southern Confederacy dead or alive?

If we preserve a wholesome pride without haughtiness, and a sincere humility without subserviency; if our sons are honest because it is their inherent nature to be honest and not because they fear a punishing law; if our daughters personify refinement, virtue, and unselfishness, and can, should the need arise, starve with a smile on their lips, as did their great-grandmothers of the eighteen-sixties; if the youth of the South will, like their forefathers, defend pure principles even when it runs counter to expediency, and prefer defeat with honor to the bribe of mammon,

Then—

I do not hesitate to assert that the Southern Confederacy is still alive.

* * *

Dixiecrat Convention, Birmingham, Alabama, July 1948.[13]

Figure 13: Battle flags of the Army of Northern Virginia and a portrait of Robert E. Lee exemplify Dixiecrats' use of Confederate symbols. On the surface, doing so makes no sense, since Dixiecrats did favor states' rights while Confederates seceded "against" states' rights, as documents in Chapter 2 show. There is a deeper logic, however: underlying and unifying both movements was the maintenance of white supremacy. Courtesy of the Atlanta History Center.

Marion Johnson, photographer for the *Atlanta Constitution*, took this photo at the 1948 organizing convention of the "States Rights Democratic Party," better known as the Dixiecrat Party. Dixiecrats splintered from the Democratic Party owing to their opposition to President Harry S. Truman's support for civil rights for African Americans. They met in Birmingham to nominate South Carolina governor Strom Thurmond for president and Mississippi governor Fielding Wright for vice president.

* * *

BIRMINGHAM POST STAFF WRITERS, UNTITLED SIDEBARS ABOUT THE DIXIECRAT CONVENTION, JULY 17, 1948.[14]

Three sidebars to the *Birmingham Post*'s account of the Dixiecrat convention show further appropriation of Confederate symbols and heroes. Their 1948 ticket won only the electoral votes of South Carolina, Alabama, Mississippi, and Louisiana, but Dixiecrats never believed they would win. They hoped to defeat President Truman's reelection, but Truman upset Republican candidate Thomas E. Dewey nevertheless. The front page of the *Birmingham News* for the same day featured a photo of University of Mississippi students with Confederate flags. In the words of the *News*, "Something like hysterical excitement swept the auditorium as Bull Conner, Alabama delegate, called walkout delegates from Mississippi and Alabama to the stage. The audience whooped and gave out rebel yells as walkouters bore their state flags and Confederate flags to the front of the auditorium." The next day, the *News* again noted the theme: "The magic names were Robert E. Lee and Jefferson Davis. They never failed to bring swelling roars from the audience."[15] Clearly, organizers worked to conflate their cause with the Confederacy.

Hats Go Off for Stars and Bars

The entire audience stood silently with hats over hearts at 10:18 a.m. when a delegation of University of Mississippi students marched to their seats behind the Confederate battle flag.

It was the most impressive and best organized stunt of the convention until that hour and gave the anxious crowd a "break" in their wait for the delayed opening of the conclave.

They were followed into the hall seven minutes later by 10 Birmingham-Southern College students wearing string bow ties and carrying both Confederate battle and Alabama state flags.

Voice is Willing But Mike is Dead

Thomas Maxwell, Tuscaloosa political figure who once advocated "shipping the Negroes back to Africa" in a campaign address for the U.S. Senate took the limelight early, trying on several occasions to talk to the assembled delegates over a "dead" mike.

Lee's Picture Brings Cheers

Best "prop" brought onto the convention floor was a picture of Gen. Robert E. Lee, carried high by a group of from 30 to 40 Birmingham-Southern students, most of them members of Kappa Alpha fraternity.

The stunt pulled at 10:40 a.m. brought a spontaneous cheer from the near capacity crowd of some 4800 delegates and spectators.

* * *

STROM THURMOND (1902–2003), "ADDRESS TO THE STATE CONVENTION OF THE UNITED DAUGHTERS OF THE CONFEDERACY AT WINTHROP COLLEGE, SOUTH CAROLINA," OCTOBER 17, 1957.[16]

In 1948, Thurmond had run for president on the Dixiecrat ticket. Defeated, he then spent almost half a century as U.S. senator from South Carolina. Here he blames "agitation" for upsetting African Americans. Otherwise they would have been content to be segregated, he claims, just as neo-Confederates during the Nadir blamed abolitionists and "carpetbaggers" for upsetting African Americans who supposedly had been content to be slaves. In 1964, Thurmond left the Democratic Party permanently to become a Republican, one of many white Southerners to embrace the Republicans' "Southern strategy." We have noted that Thurmond correctly assesses the liberating potential coming from black voting in "pivotal" Northern states. This potential prompts Thurmond to conclude, not that African Americans should be allowed to vote in the South, but instead that black voting would be folly.

This is an age of wonders. It is the atomic age and we stand at the threshold of an even more wonderful age in which man is about to learn the secrets of outer space.

But, I must say also, the people of the United States are facing what could be a second "tragic era" if the Federal Government persists in following the policies it has adopted with reference to the rights of the States.[17]

I hope and pray that the Federal Government will cease its unwise, unnecessary and unconstitutional actions and avoid dragging our people into a second tragic era.

We of the South are a proud people. We come from a stock that has never flinched even in the face of defeat or rule by federal bayonets.

No one should be mistaken or misled. We are going to fight as long as we have breath, for the rights of the States and for the rights of our people under the Constitution of the United States.

Many of our leading national figures—including leaders of the Democratic National Party—have made a practice of insulting the South and striking at the heart of our institutions established under the Constitution. I want to remind these leaders of the contribution the South has made to the building of this nation.

The Southern States first issued the call for a Declaration of Independence. It was the great Southerner, Thomas Jefferson, who wrote that immortal document. What the sage of Monticello proclaimed by pen, another great Southerner, George Washington, won with his sword.

After we had won our independence, we were without the machinery of government to preserve and perpetuate it. From the South came the movement that resulted in the Constitutional Convention of 1787. Washington presided over that convention. The main principles which the delegates wrote into the Constitution were taken from plans drafted by James Madison of Virginia and Charles Pinckney of South Carolina.

We have only to read the proceedings of the Constitutional Convention to know the part played by the States we represent in creating our Government.

Of the first 25 Presidents, the South contributed 10. In those critical formative years of our Republic, Southern Presidents held the reins of government for 53 years.

Not only in the affairs of government, but in economics, in science, in social development, in education, in religion, and in every field of endeavor that contributes to human progress, the South has made its full contribution in the building of our country.

Our progress was set back many decades by the War Between the States and when the war was over, we were subjected to the bitter Reconstruction Period. We experienced first hand the ordeal of a conquered and occupied land. Our economy was destroyed, and we had to rebuild on the foundation of a shattered civilization.

Throughout the whole period which has elapsed since the Reconstruction, we of the South, and we alone, have cared and provided for the Negroes in our midst. The progress which has been made, by that race is a tribute, to the efforts of Southerners, and of Southerners alone.

The people of the South—whites and Negroes together—have succeeded in lifting themselves to a new and high standard of living in spite of the many handicaps which have been placed in our way.

Until the agitation of recent years, the people of the South—white and Negro alike—knew and respected each other. They understood each other.

Our racial relations have been excellent and violence is abhorred by the white Southerner as much or more than by the persons of any race anywhere.

We must not let the pressures which have been exerted upon us destroy the understanding which so long existed between the white and Negro races in the South. Violence can not be condoned. Violence must be prevented. The States must punish lawbreakers.

But neither South Carolina nor any other State needs the assistance or the interference of the Federal Government to protect its citizens. The power of the Federal Government should not be exerted to interfere in the affairs of any State.

If a Governor should need the help of the Federal Government to preserve the peace, the Constitution provides that he shall call upon the President to provide the assistance required.

The use of federal troops to force the integration of the races at Central High School in Little Rock, Arkansas, was ill-conceived, ill-handled, and certain to be ill-fated in its result.

Here Thurmond supplies sixteen short paragraphs quoting Eisenhower's attorney general and the president to the effect that troops were not likely to be used to enforce school desegregation.

Nevertheless, the administration, which had scoffed at the idea it would exercise such power, on September 24, 1957, ordered troops to enforce the order of the Federal Court at Little Rock to integrate the races at Central High School.[18]

Three sections of Chapter 15 under Title 10 of the United States Code were relied upon for authority to use the battle-trained-paratroopers for law enforcement. The Federal Government superimposed itself upon the sovereignty of Arkansas. Military rule was imposed upon Little Rock. Bayonets and rifle butts were used upon the citizens. Racial mixing was substituted for education.

The inevitable result was and has been the increasing of racial tension not only in Little Rock, and not only in Arkansas, but throughout the nation.

The order issued by the Federal Court at Little Rock for the integration of the Negro children into the white school was based upon the decision of the United States Supreme Court which was handed down on May 17, 1954.

That decision was based on the opinions of psychologists and sociologists rather than on the Constitution.

The Supreme Court sought to find justification for ruling against racial segregation in the public schools by asking certain questions about the 14th Amendment to the Constitution during the hearings in the school segregation cases. However, the answers provided the Court were not to its liking, so the evidence presented was disregarded.

The preponderance of evidence presented in the briefs showed that the Congress which approved the 14th Amendment, and the States which ratified it, did not understand the Amendment as prohibiting racial segregation in the schools.[19]

There were 37 States in the Union when the Amendment was submitted. A total of nine States did not have segregated schools and two abandoned them permanently after ratification of the Amendment.

On the other hand, 26 States were either operating segregated schools and continued to operate them or else established or re-established segregated schools after ratification of the Amendment.

The 39th Congress, which drafted the 14th Amendment, itself provided further evidence that it did not intend for the Amendment to be used to abolish segregation in the schools. That same Congress provided for segregated schools in the District of Columbia and for the establishment of Howard University, an institution exclusively for Negroes.

In addition to all the evidence that the 14th Amendment was never intended to apply to segregation in the public schools, many authorities believe the Amendment was never legally ratified. . . .[20]

Even if the 14th Amendment were legally ratified, the fifth section of the Amendment must be considered. It provides that:

"The Congress shall have the power to enforce by appropriate legislation the provision of this Article."

Congress has never exercised the power contained in that provision of the 14th Amendment to enact legislation for the purpose of destroying segregation in the public schools. Congress has never by legislation interpreted the "equal protection" provision of the first section of the Amendment or any other part of the Amendment to apply to segregation in the public schools in the States.

In spite of all this evidence, the Supreme Court rendered its unconstitutional decision on May 17, 1954.

Even while the school segregation cases were being heard by the Supreme Court, it was predicted that a generation of litigation would result if the Court attempted to end racial segregation in the public schools.

To my regret, I must say that today the prospects of a generation of litigation would be welcome in comparison with the second tragic era into which we have been plunged by the use of federal troops to enforce integration in our public schools at the point of bayonets.

The President should immediately withdraw the federal troops from Little Rock. He should return the Arkansas National Guard to its normal status of State Militia.

He should direct the Attorney General to withdraw from Little Rock all federal agents not normally assigned to that city. He should leave to the Governor

of the State and to other duly empowered officials of the State, the city, and the school district, the matter of administering school affairs in Little Rock.

I am sure that tranquility would soon return to the community if the Negro children who have been used as pawns in this game of power politics were transferred from the 30-year-old Central High School back to the new million-dollar Negro school with the 700 other Negro pupils in attendance there.[21]

The people of Arkansas decide whether their duly elected and appointed officials are properly performing their duties. Neither the President of the United States nor the Attorney General has the Constitutional authority to make such a determination. The sovereignty of a State rests in the hands of the people.

During my fight in the Senate to prevent the passage of H. R. 6127, the so-called Civil Rights Bill, I stated:

"The laws of the nation are dependent upon the customs and traditions of the people. Unless law is based upon the will of the people, it will not meet with acceptance."

I believe that the result of the seizure of Little Rock by federal troops proves that Executive actions should not be taken without regard for the customs and traditions of the people.

In view of what has happened since the Supreme Court decision of 1954, let us examine the reason for the game of power politics which has made pawns of innocent children. I think that Stewart Alsop, the newspaper columnist, stated the simple facts of the case most succinctly in an article published during August.

He said that "behind the shifting, complex, often fascinating drama of the struggle over civil rights, there is one simple political reality—the Negro vote in the key industrial States in the North. That is, of course, in hard political terms, what the fight has been all about."

The 1956 political platforms of both the Democrats and the Republicans contained planks supporting the Supreme Court decision in the school segregation cases. Both political parties fear the bloc voting of minorities in the pivotal States.

Both parties want to be in position to claim credit for the advancement of what has been called civil rights. Both parties want to capitalize on the Supreme Court decision and on the passage of the so-called Civil Rights Bill this year. They hope to benefit in the Congressional elections of 1958 and then to extend those gains into the Presidential election of 1960.

Mr. Stevenson, the defeated Presidential candidate of the National Democratic Party in 1952 and 1956, fully approved the action of the President in sending federal troops to Little Rock. On September 24 he declared in a statement that "the President had no choice . . . federal power must in this situation be used to put down force."

On September 29 at Chapel Hill, North Carolina, he again expressed approval of the President's action. He also criticized the President for [not] having taken a strong position for civil rights enforcement before the Little Rock seizure.

Democratic National Chairman Paul M. Butler, on September 17, 1957, declared that "the Democratic Party will not pull back" from its position approving the decision of the Supreme Court in the school segregation cases. His statement was made in Raleigh, North Carolina, after a two-day conference with 60 Democratic Party officials from nine Southern States.

Mr. Butler also stated that the possibility of a third political party being organized would not prevent the Democratic Party from taking a strong stand on civil rights. Mr. Butler criticized the President for not taking a more courageous stand on integration.

Thus the people of the South find themselves in the position of being persecuted by both political parties. They want to offer us as a sacrifice in return for the bloc votes of minorities who exert their influence through pressure and propaganda in the pivotal States of the North.

As long as we permit ourselves to be led meekly to the sacrificial altar of politics and offered up to appease the minority blocs, we deserve no respect or consideration.

The only consideration that will be given to our views will be that given to secure our votes if the national parties believe they need our support.

In South Carolina, there is no hope in the Republican Party. But there should be hope in the South Carolina Democratic Party.[22]

The officials of the South Carolina Democratic Party should demand that the National Party give consideration to the principles of the South Carolina Democratic Party. The National Democratic Party should be called upon to dismiss the present National Chairman. He has made it absolutely clear that he is not interested in the views of the South.

As Chairman, it is his duty to represent the interests of all Democrats in every State, not just the Democrats who want to integrate the schools. The National Democratic Party cannot truly represent the best interests of all the Democrats in every State unless its Chairman is willing to listen to the views of our people. The present Chairman has proved that he does not qualify.

On the same day that the National Chairman declared that the Democratic Party would not compromise on civil rights, the South Carolina State Chairman was quoted in news reports as demanding that the National Chairman resign or be fired. Two days later on September 19 the State Chairman was quoted by The Associated Press as denying that he asked for the removal of the National Chairman.

If the State Chairman demanded the resignation of the National Chairman, he should stick by that demand. If he has not made such a demand, he should now do so officially. This is no time for passive resistance. This is a time for massive resistance against the insults and disregard of the National Party.

State Democratic Parties are independent bodies and not subject to the dictation of the National Party. The State Party cannot be committed to any course of action not approved by the State Democratic Convention.

However, the officers of the State Party should secure from the Democratic National Committee a positive statement on whether the National Party is willing to give real consideration to the views held by South Carolina Democrats. The reply of the National Party should be given immediate publicity, so that every Democrat will have an opportunity to know what is to be expected from the National Party.

Then South Carolina Democrats can go to their precinct meetings and elect delegates to carry out their wishes at the County Conventions. The County Conventions can elect delegates to the State Convention who will stoutly support the principles of the South Carolina Democratic Party.

Delegates at the State Convention, composed of such real Democrats, would take appropriate action in choosing delegates to the National Convention and in other matters which might be considered.

Whatever course of action South Carolina Democrats decide upon in 1958 and in 1960 must be determined on the basis of the information available at the time of the State Conventions. Due consideration must be given to the actions of the National Democratic Party between now and then.

I would not, and should not, attempt at this time to predict what course the South Carolina Democratic Party will take in the next election. As time goes by, I expect to have further comments to make on this subject.

Failing to secure proper recognition from the National Party, South Carolina Democrats will have to choose a course to meet the situation in 1960. The South Carolina Democratic Party should not hesitate to pursue whatever course is deemed to be in the best interests of the people of our State.

* * *

SUMTER L. LOWRY (1893–1985), "THE FEDERAL GOVERNMENT AND OUR CONSTITUTIONAL RIGHTS," ADDRESS TO THE UNITED DAUGHTERS OF THE CONFEDERACY, OCTOBER 15, 1958.[23]

Born in Florida, Lowry attended Virginia Military Institute and served in both world wars, as a brigadier general in the second. An insurance executive, in 1956 he ran for governor of Florida as a Democrat; his campaign emphasized segregation and white supremacy and advocated interposition to stop the federal government from enforcing integration.[24] Since Americans saw Communism as a grave threat, it was easy for Lowry and other neo-Confederates to see Communism behind the decrees of the U.S. Supreme Court requiring school desegregation. "Mongrelization" is Lowry's other fear. Of course, racial purity does not exist. Such groups as "white," "Caucasian," "Negro," and "mongrel" are social constructs that refer imperfectly to physical characteristics, as do terms like "Jew" or "Italian" to some users. In addition, Lowry makes explicit that his concern about a "mongrel race" refers to the marriage of black males and white females. Logically, informal sexual relations between, say, white males and black females "bred" similar children. Since such children were defined "Negro," however, they posed less threat to white supremacy.

It is a pleasure and a privilege for me to address this group of patriotic Southern women. My forebears on both sides were staunch supporters of the Southern Cause during the War Between the States. My father, Dr. Sumter L. Lowry, throughout his life, kept up his intense interest in all Confederate organizations. He was a National Commander of the Sons of the Confederate Veterans and I believe the only honorary member of the UDC in Florida. This being a luncheon meeting it might be expected that I would speak on some light subject, but with the grave situation confronting our nation today, I feel that I must not let the opportunity go by to present to you my ideas on the greatest issue before the American people today—that is the effort being made by the Federal Government to destroy our Constitutional Rights.

I want to spend what time I have outlining the fundamental fact involved in this struggle, what is behind it and where it will lead our nation.

The driving force and the master plan in this crisis stems from the Communist International conspiracy to capture and destroy the United States of America—that organization well knows that if they can deprive the people of their constitutional rights by deceitful propaganda and divide them over internal issues, we will be an easy prey, and our country will fall.

In May 1954 the Supreme Court, by arbitrary and unlawful decree ordered the integration of the white and colored races in the public schools and public institutions. By so doing they struck a body blow at our constitutional rights. The 10th Amendment to our Constitution clearly gives the local communities the right to control the operation of their school system—yet, the Supreme Court, through a distorted and illegal interpretation of the 14th Amendment, at one blow destroyed the freedom given to us under the 10th Amendment, and opened the door to Federal control of our local schools.

The strategy behind this decree was to establish the precedent that the Federal Government can control the school system, forcing the people to accept this fact and then to move in on all other fields of local control reserved to the States and communities, thereby completely destroying the 10th Amendment. The issue of integration, with all of its emotional appeal, was selected as the hammer to crack open and destroy our constitutional rights. Keep always in mind that integration is only the first step in a master plan to take away all of our freedom and liberty.

Now there immediately occurred a violent and bitter reaction against the idea of forcing white and colored children to associate together in public schools and institutions—there have been millions of words written and every conceivable reason given why the people of the South so violently oppose the integration of the races. But when you get right down to the underlying cause, it leads to just one place, that is the definite and certain knowledge that if you mix male and female together in intimate, social relationship from childhood to maturity, it will bring on intermarriage—it will do this regardless of race or color.

Now the conspirators who wish to destroy our nation well know if you mix people of different color in marriage and if you infuse the blood of fourteen million negroes into the blood stream of the white American, you will breed a mongrel race, neither white nor black, and the history of the world shows that when a nation becomes mongrelized, it dies.

There has been a great effort on the part of the integration people to soft-pedal the fact of intermarriage as a result of integration—to make you believe it is not a threat or anything to worry about—but if you throw little white and colored children of both sexes together in an intimate social relationship from the time they are five or six years of age, and have this relationship continue through grammar school and high school, it can end only at one place—it can lead to only one door, and that is to the bedroom, with or without benefit of marriage. Anyone who has the slightest knowledge of biology, psychology, social relationship or history is aware that the absolute and certain end result of mixing the male and female together is sex relations. It has never stopped short of that and it never will—race or color is no barrier.

Now many sincere but misguided people try to overlook this fact, they just won't face up to it. But the fear and the certain knowledge that this is what will happen is the one thing that has made the southern white people band together to fight the illegal decree of the Supreme Court of the United States forcing the integration of the races. It is the rock around which the South must rally—it is the real heart of the issue!

Let me say here that I have only the most friendly feeling for the colored people—I want to see them given the finest schools, churches and facilities of all kinds. I want them to have every opportunity to succeed in life like every other American. But I do not believe in the mixing of the races. I am proud that I am a white man—I believe the negro should also be proud of his race, and I am sure that God intended it that way. I am also sure the negro's future will be brighter and happier if he will repudiate those voices who tell him he must force himself on a hostile and unwilling white society.

One of the most potent factors in influencing many people to meekly accept integration of the races, is the position taken by a great many preachers and churchmen in this country—there is no doubt, a large majority of the preachers believe in the integration of the races and are doing all in their power to get their congregation to accept integration—these men in high places in our churches do not understand or will not accept the realities and results of the continuous intermingling of the white and colored people of opposite sexes. They think somehow that little white and colored children can grow up together, go to public schools together, to Sunday School, to Church, engage in all the intimate social affairs put on by schools and churches, and then when they get to marriageable age, the white girl and colored boy will shake hands, say goodbye and that will be the end of their relationship—that theory simply is not true!

Do you mean to tell me there is even any justice in leading the negro to believe that you are accepting him as your social equal, and then turn him away at the marriage altar? I ask those preachers who believe in the theory of mixing of the races in their churches if they would be so cruel as to have a white girl and negro boy grow up together with binding social and religious ties, and then say to the colored boy, when he comes of marriageable age, "you can go so far, but no further, this is where the line is drawn." The truth is, that any white person who believes in integration, must in his heart, right now, accept the fact that some day he may be called on to take his daughter or granddaughter down a church aisle to join her in holy matrimony with a colored man.

Now I realize that the left-wing press have tried to put a stigma on any man who will openly discuss this phase of integration—they make the public feel it is rude and vulgar to mention, the possibility of intermarriage between the white and the black. But it must be done, because it is the heart of the matter, and the cornerstone around which Southern people rally to fight integration. Also, it is only fair to colored and white people that the facts be openly discussed and understood.

There is no doubt that the goal of the NAACP is the complete integration of the races in every phase of life—schools, churches, housing, public places, society and finally intermarriage—there can be no complete integration without intermarriage—the NAACP has tried to soft-pedal this fact, but it is true and nothing can change it.

The Communist conspirators who are behind this integration movement are past masters in the use of propaganda to win their battles.

For instance, after the Supreme Court's decision in 1954, which only said that there should be no discrimination between white and colored children in public schools, the communists immediately coined the propaganda phrase "the law of the land"—this phrase has been taken up on all sides, from our President on down—it is an effort designed to make law-abiding citizens believe that if they do not submit to integration they are not good Americans and that they are violating the law—this is not true! The Supreme Court cannot make any law, they only interpret the meaning of laws passed by Congress. The Congress of the United States is the only body that can make a Federal law. And they have never passed any law saying that white and colored children must go to school together—yet, those who wish to integrate the races have led our people to believe that the forced integration of white and colored school children is "the law of the land." This is a false and cruel propaganda hoax!

Another propaganda phrase so effectively used by those preachers in our churches who favor integration, is the phrase, "the brotherhood of man"— pointing out that Christ taught, that love of your brother was the first duty of all men. Well no Christian or truly religious person will have any quarrel about "the brotherhood of man." However, the real test on the part of the white man in his practice of "the brotherhood of man" and his regard for the negro, is whether the white man will feed the negro when he is hungry, nurse him when he is sick, give him money when he is broke and risk his life to save him from mob violence—that is the real test of the love of the white man for the colored man. Yet, some ministers with their great prestige and influence are using "the brotherhood of man" as a lever to force integration in their own churches. This action will lead only to disunity in their congregation, to heartbreak and disappointment for the negro, to intermarriage, a mongrel race and to the destruction of the United States of America.

The sad part about this whole situation is the almost total disregard for the rights and wishes that some bishops and clergy have for those people who believe in the separation of the races in the church—they run rough shod over these helpless men and women—giving them little opportunity to have their side of the issue heard in the high councils of the church or to have their views presented through church literature and publications—all this in the name of "the brotherhood of man" as preached by Jesus Christ. To continue this unfair treatment will destroy the church as surely as the sun rises tomorrow morning.

Please do not think that because I make this statement I do not love my church or respect its ordained leaders. It pains me greatly to openly differ with my church or criticize the fine men who are its leaders. I have been a life-long member of the Episcopal Church. I love it dearly and will continue to do so— but I must publicly say what I do because I know so well that the church is wrong in its doctrine that "integration is a Christian mandate." For me to remain silent would betray my children and my church.

The leadership to preserve our Constitutional Rights and prevent forced integration on the people must come from the elected representatives of the people, in the United States Congress, and from our State officials. But above all, the leadership should come from the highest elected officer in each State—the Governor. It is his duty to give fighting leadership—I repeat the word "fighting" to the people in their effort to preserve their rights and freedom. Most of the Governors of our Southern States understand the issue and have the moral courage to lead the people in this conflict—they are doing their duty in a courageous manner.

Unfortunately, in our own State of Florida, we have a Governor who has publicly surrendered to the forces of integration—he long ago quit the fight— this statement is not a matter of opinion, but a public record of his own voice. He has said over and over that he believes in gradual and moderate integration, which means gradual defeat, gradual surrender, intermarriage, mongrelization and the end of our nation. He adopts this course even though he is sworn to uphold the Constitution of the State of Florida which specifically prohibits the mixing of the races in our public schools.

The people of the South are in a great struggle, yet our leader, the Governor, says to his Florida people "now we will put up a token resistance, we will just fight for a limited time, we will sacrifice a given number of casualties, then we will surrender and the battle will be over."

Now this is a struggle in which there can be no compromise. Integration is wrong and should be resisted to the end, or it is right, and should be accepted now. There is no middle ground! It is a matter of principle, will our nation be mongrelized and destroyed, or will it continue a strong nation with white and colored people living side by side in peace and unity?

Yes, integration must be met head on—it is a cowardly thing to pass on to the next generation obligations which should be met now—never forget for one minute that total integration means intermarriage—also fully understand that the gradual integrationist is a man who flinches from the idea of his daughter marry a colored man, but is perfectly willing to have his granddaughter do so.

The policy of gradual surrender as adopted by Governor Collins is a far cry from the "never surrender" spirit of the great Southern leaders during the War Between the States. Can you imagine General Stonewall Jackson calling in his officers before the battle, and saying: "We will fight for three hours this morning, then we will run?" Or, can you imagine General Lee telling the people of Virginia that: "we will defend the soil of this State for six months, then quit?"— NO—these men never knew the word "quit" or "surrender"—all never passed their lips.

I want you fine ladies here this morning to always remember that the issue at stake right now is the same issue your southern forebears fought and died for.

During the war our southern men gave their lives and our southern women made every sacrifice to fight for a cause in which they believed—their battle cry was "honor" and "courage"—not "compromise" and "surrender"—and now the torch held so high by these men and women is passed on to you to carry forward—you must not fail them!

The time is here for the people of this State to rise up and say to the nation— "we DO NOT believe in the integration of the races"— "we WILL NOT see our nation destroyed by mongrelization"—"we WILL resist the illegal edict of the Supreme Court with every means at hand," and "we WILL repudiate and disown any office holders, no matter who he is, who attempts to influence the people to 'quit' and 'surrender' in our struggle for survival."

May the spirit of Lee and Jackson and the long line of departed southern heroes be with you, guide and strengthen you at this time so that this great organization of patriotic southern women can use its power to save our people and preserve our nation.

* * *

THE CITIZENS' COUNCIL LOGO, MARCH 1957.[25]

Figure 14: The Citizens' Council logo and slogan.

Incorporating the Confederate battle flag makes plain the Citizens' Councils' claim to Confederate ancestry. "Racial Integrity" also fits both the Citizens' Councils and the Confederate movement. "States' rights" does not, however. Earlier chapters have shown that—other than the right of secession itself—Confederate states did not emphasize states' rights except to deplore their exercise by Northern states against slavery.

* * *

"His Example Inspires Our Efforts of Today," The Citizens' Council, June 1956.[26]

Robert Patterson organized the Citizens' Councils of America, at first called the "White Citizens' Councils," in Indianola, Mississippi, in 1954. The organization spread rapidly and soon set up national headquarters in Jackson, the state capital. In many towns, all white business and civic leaders were expected to join, and did. Mississippi law required publishing the names of citizens who applied to register to vote. Citizens' Councils encouraged members to fire African Americans who dared to register, call in any bank loans, and refuse to sell them fuel or supplies. They claimed to eschew violence but often published names and home addresses of parents of the few black children who dared to try to integrate white public schools. They published a magazine, first called *"The Citizens' Council,"* later, *"The Citizen."* Today, the Council of Conservative Citizens is their descendant organization.

During the Civil War, Jefferson Davis often complained of being hamstrung by states' rights. He tried in various ways to force the will of the central government on the leaders of Georgia, North Carolina, and other sometime recalcitrant states, and usually succeeded.[27] In 1956, of course, the Citizens' Councils favored states' rights and worked to maintain the ability of the Southern states to keep African Americans from enjoying their rights under the Fourteenth and Fifteenth amendments. To enlist Davis in this cause, the magazine quotes words that are so vague as to be almost content-free.

Although official observance of his birthday is limited annually to June 3, Jefferson Davis affords a constant reminder that the modern South can derive strength and inspiration from his noble example during each of these critical hours facing us at present.

There has never been an abler or more ardent champion of the States' Rights cause which Jefferson Davis defended with all his strength and vigor. His memory will endure as long as free men cherish constitutional liberty and are willing to fight for it.

In the face of overwhelming odds, amid scorn and ridicule from the South's unrelenting enemies, Jefferson Davis fought the good fight. He never compromised a principle nor betrayed the trust reposed in him by the people and cause which he represented.

His inaugural message as first and only President of the ill-fated Southern Confederacy contains much inspiration for modern Southerners and other Americans who still adhere to eternal truths which Jefferson Davis prized above life itself. His words spoken in 1861 are just as true today. He said:

"In the midst of perilous times, our people must be united in heart. . . . Obstacles may retard but they can never prevent the progress of a movement sanctified by Justice and sustained by a virtuous citizenry

"Reverently let us invoke the God of our fathers to guide and protect us in our efforts to perpetuate the principle which by His blessing they were able to vindicate, establish and transmit to their posterity, and with a continuance of His favor, ever gratefully acknowledge, so that we may hopefully look forward to success, to peace and to prosperity."

* * *

W. E. Rose, "The Warning of Robert E. Lee," *The Citizens' Council*, February 1957.[28]

We can find no biographical information on W. E. Rose. Rose has a point, however. In Chapter 5, Susan Lawrence Davis tells of Lee's support for white supremacy and the Ku Klux Klan (pages 322–23), which this poem's imagery suggests.

The Warning of Robert E. Lee

A clatter of hoofs in the leaden rain
That pattered and tapped on my window pane,
The clinkity-clink of a bridle-chain
And the sound of steps on the iced terrain;
I sprang from bed with a muffled curse,
Wondering what in the world was worse
Than touching my feet to the frigid floor,
When a hoarse "haloo" came through the door—
Followed by blows and "Open, friend", . . .
And the neigh of a horse in the driving wind.
I groped my way across the room
With sleep-filled eyes in the semi-gloom,
Fingers flicking a deadened switch
Forgetting the power-pole in the ditch,
Which had left me in this plight
With only a candle to give me light;
A rattling key and a squeaking door
And the click of spurs across the floor,
As before the hearth my caller turned
Where the dying logs and embers burned.

A hasty match to the candle-wick
With trembling fingers, numb and thick,

And a tingling chill along my spine
As stern gray eyes looked into mine:
"What are you doing cowering here?
Has all the South succumbed to fear?
What has happened to Southern pride—
Was it all in vain that free men died?
Has a craven judge and a court's decree
Shackled the limbs of Liberty?
Open you,—mouth and speak to me—
Answer the ghost of Robert Lee!"

A sudden wave of blinding shame
Suffused my face as he gave his name,
With upraised hands and bended knee
I shrank from the wrath of Robert E. Lee;
A sabre clanked as he left the room
While I crouched there in the semi-gloom—
Breathing a prayer that fools like me
Should heed the warning of General Lee.

* * *

The Citizens' Councils,
"Old Censored Joe," November 1957.[29]

Figure 15: This cartoon shows support from the Citizens' Councils for the whites who harassed the Myers family. The Councils were always delighted when "The Race Problem Moves North," the title of a talk by its head, William J. Simmons.

When the William and Daisy Myers family moved into Levittown, Pennsylvania, in 1957, a sundown town that did not allow black residents, white supremacists occupied a nearby house that happened to be vacant and made it the center of organized opposition. They raised a Confederate flag and played "Dixie" over a loudspeaker at high volume and all hours. People from the house phoned the Myerses with threats.[30] The Myerses persevered. Decades later, in 1999, Levittown honored Daisy Myers (her husband had died) by naming a blue spruce in front of the municipal building for her and designating it the township Christmas tree.

* * *

THE CITIZENS' COUNCILS,
"MAU MAU PARTY," DECEMBER 1958.[31]

Figure 16: Mau Mau was a name applied to the anticolonialist movement in Kenya. It came to connote antiwhite violence in general.

This cartoon from the Citizens' Councils magazine lampoons the anticipated result if members let African Americans vote and run for office.

* * *

The Citizens' Council,
"Conditions in U.S. Today Offer Alarming Parallel to First Reconstruction Era of a Century Ago," August 1960.[32]

As this use of it by *The Citizens' Council* shows, by getting what happened during Reconstruction dead wrong, Margaret Mitchell's famous romance, *Gone With the Wind*, makes a potent case for white supremacy. Mitchell's novel is by the far the most popular book ever published and movie ever made in the United States. Unfortunately for the cause of democracy, *Gone With the Wind* is not an accurate historical source on Reconstruction.[33]

"Only the negroes had rights or redress these days," states Mitchell, quoted in *The Citizens' Council* with emphasis. As a description of Reconstruction, like other accounts concocted during the Nadir, this is wrong. Chapters 4 and 5 tell of the continuing violence visited upon African Americans and white Republicans during Reconstruction. It was they who could not get redress from juries dominated by white Democrats. The 1868 Georgia legislature, its first to be elected by blacks as well as whites, expelled all its black members. In 1870, Democrats won legislative control of the state, ending Reconstruction in that state after less than two years—years that Mitchell and the Citizens' Council portray as an eternity.[34] The Council quotes Mitchell's hair-raising account of "outrages on [white] women," but interestingly, white complaints of sexual outrage across racial lines were rare during Reconstruction. Whites raised this specter during the Nadir, when Mitchell wrote, partly to legitimize lynchings. Readers who have not previously questioned Mitchell's historical accuracy might begin their education with a novel by another Margaret—Margaret Walker's *Jubilee*, which supplies a more accurate portrayal of the actions of newly freed African Americans in Georgia during Reconstruction.[35]

Numerous references are being made to the current political madness as "Reconstruction II." To grasp the full significance of the comparison presupposes an understanding of "Reconstruction I."

Earlier generations of Southerners gained a vivid knowledge of the "tragic era" from their parents and grandparents who lived and suffered through the twelve-year period following the War Between the States. But later generations, preoccupied with different problems and taught from history books designed to suit the tastes of the victors, are largely unaware of the grim and successful struggle for survival waged by their forefathers after military defeat in terrible war.

Unfortunately, Northerners are almost completely unversed in the hard facts of this period. We recommend that they enlighten themselves. For "Reconstruction II" is aimed at them too, and by both political parties.

What was "Reconstruction I" like? Gone With the Wind, the famous novel by Margaret Mitchell (The MacMillan Company, New York), contains a graphic account, written in simple and striking language, that remains unsurpassed in modern literature.

One of the most widely read novels of all time, Gone With the Wind was not only a best-seller, but had an impact amounting to an historical event.

Most of us have read it at one time or another since its publication in 1936, and were entertained by Miss Mitchell's superior ability to tell an exciting story and her poetic grasp of things uniquely Southern.

But have you read "GWTW", as it became popularly known, in the light of political and racial developments of the past year or two? If not then we suggest that you are in for a new experience, no matter how many times you may have read Miss Mitchell's classic in the past.

For example, let's take a look at just a couple of passages. Change the Freedmen's Bureau to the Civil Rights Commission, the military to the Supreme Court, change the frame of reference only slightly, along with a few other transpositions, and a startling parallel between the events of 1866–78 and 1954–(?) will become apparent. Emphasis is ours, to point up the illustrations.

"Looking about her in that cold spring of 1866, Scarlett realized what was facing her and the whole South. She might plan and scheme, she might work harder than her slaves had ever worked, she might succeed in overcoming all of her hardships, she might through dint of determination solve problems for which her earlier life had provided no training at all.

"But for all her labor and sacrifice and resourcefulness, her small beginnings purchased at so great a cost might be snatched away from her at any minute. And should this happen, she had no legal rights, no legal redress, except those same drumhead courts of which Tony had spoken so bitterly, those military courts with their arbitrary powers. **Only the negroes had rights or redress these days.**

"The Yankees had the South prostrate and they intended to keep it so. The South had been tilted as by a giant malicious hand, and those who had once ruled were now more helpless than their former slaves had ever been.

"Georgia was heavily garrisoned with troops and Atlanta had more than its share. The commandants of the Yankee troops in the various cities had complete power, even the power of life and death, over the civilian population, and they used that power. They could and did imprison citizens for any cause, or no cause, seize their property, hang them.

"**They could and did harass and hamstring them with conflicting regulations about the operation of their business, the wages they must pay their servants, what they should say in public and private utterances, and what they should write in newspapers.**

"They regulated how, when and a where they must dump their garbage and they decided what songs the daughters and wives of ex-Confederates could sing, so that the singing of 'Dixie' or 'Bonnie Blue Flag' became an offense only a little less serious than treason. They ruled that no one could get a letter out of the post office without taking the Iron Clad oath and, in some instances, they even prohibited the issuance of marriage licenses unless the couples had taken the hated oath.

"The newspapers were so muzzled that no public protest could be raised against the injustices or depredations of the military, and individual protests were silenced with jail sentences. The jails were full of prominent citizens and there they stayed without hope of early trial.

"**Trial by jury and the law of habeas corpus were practically suspended. The civil courts still functioned after a fashion but they functioned at the pleasure of the military, who could and did interfere with their verdicts, so that citizens so unfortunate as to get arrested were virtually at the mercy of the military authorities.**

"And so many did get arrested. The very suspicion of seditious utterances against the government, suspected complicity in the **Ku Klux Klan, or complaint by a Negro that a white man had been uppity to him were enough to land a citizen in jail. Proof and evidence were not needed. The accusation was sufficient. And thanks to the incitement of the Freedmen's Bureau, Negroes could always be found who were willing to bring accusations.**

"The Negroes had not yet been given the right to vote but **the North was determined that they should vote and equally determined that their vote should be friendly to the North. With this in mind, nothing was too good for the Negroes.** The Yankee soldiers backed them up in anything they chose to do, and **the surest way for a white person to get himself into trouble was to bring a complaint of any kind against a Negro. . . .**"

(Editor's Note—History has turned full cycle. Today, the Northern white people get into trouble by bringing complaints against a Negro. Tomorrow it will again be the turn for Southern white people unless Caucasians, both North and South, turn on their political leaders who are busily re-creating the Frankenstein of 1866.)

Continuing in Gone With the Wind, Miss Mitchell writes:

"Aided by the unscrupulous adventurers who operated the Freedmen's Bureau and urged on by a fervor of Northern hatred almost religious in its fanaticism, the former field hands found themselves suddenly elevated to the seats of the mighty. There they conducted themselves as creatures of small intelligence might naturally be expected to do.

"Like monkeys or small children turned loose among treasured objects whose value is beyond their comprehension, they ran wild—either from perverse pleasure in destruction or simply because of their ignorance.

"To the credit of the Negroes, including the least intelligent of them, few were actuated by malice and those few had usually been 'mean naggers' even in slave days. But they were, as a class, childlike in mentality, easily led from long habit accustomed to take orders. **Now they had a new set of masters, the Bureau and the Carpetbaggers, and their orders were: 'You're just as good as any white man, so act that way. Just as soon as you can vote the Republican ticket, you are going to have the white man's property. It's as good as yours now. Take it, if you can get it!'**

(Editor's Note—And to think that certain "liberal" editors have been making fun of witch doctors in the Congo for making almost identical promises recently! For shame, gentlemen. Brush up on the history of "Reconstruction I" and you will avoid such embarrassing inconsistencies.)

"Dazzled by these tales, freedom became a never-ending picnic, a barbecue every day of the week, a carnival of idleness and theft and insolence. Country Negroes flocked into the cities, leaving the rural districts without labor to make the crops. Atlanta was crowded with them and still they came by the hundreds, lazy and dangerous as a result of the new doctrines being taught them. Packed into squalid cabins, smallpox, typhoid and tuberculosis broke out among them. Accustomed to the care of their mistresses when they were ill in slave days, they did not know how to nurse themselves or their sick. Relying upon their masters in the old days to care for their aged and their babies, they now had no sense of responsibility for their helpless. **And the Bureau was far too interested in political matters to provide the care the plantation owners had once given. . . .**

"For the first time in their lives the Negroes were able to get all the whisky they might want. In slave days, it was something they never tasted except at Christmas, when each one received a 'drap' along with his gift. Now they had not only the Bureau agitators and the Carpetbaggers urging them on, but the incitement of whisky as well, and outrages were inevitable. Neither life nor property was safe from them and **the white people, unprotected by law, were terrorized.** Men were insulted on the streets by drunken blacks, houses and barns were burned at night, horses and cattle and chickens stolen in broad daylight, **crimes of all varieties were committed and few of the perpetrators were brought to justice.**

"**But these ignominies and dangers were as nothing compared with the peril of white women, many bereft by the war of male protection, who lived alone in the outlying districts and on lonely roads. It was the large number of outrages on women and the ever-present fear for the safety of their wives and daughters that drove Southern men to cold and trembling fury and caused the Ku Klux Klan to spring up overnight.**

"And it was against this nocturnal organization that the newspapers of the North cried out most loudly, never realizing the tragic necessity that brought it into being. The North wanted every member of the Ku Klux Klan hunted down and hanged, because they dared take the punishment of crime into their own hands at a time when the ordinary processes of law and order had been overthrown by the invaders.

"**Here was the astonishing spectacle of half a nation attempting at the point of a bayonet, to force upon the other half the rule of Negroes, many of them scarcely one generation out of the African jungles.** The vote must be given to them but it must be denied to most of their former owners. The South must be kept down and disfranchisement of the whites was one way to keep the South down. Most of those who had fought for the Confederacy, held office under it or given aid and comfort to it were not allowed to vote, had no choice in the selection of their public officials and were wholly under the power of an alien rule. Many men, thinking soberly of General Lee's words and example, wished to take the oath, become citizens again and forget the past. But they were not permitted to take it. Others who were permitted to take the oath, hotly refused to do so, **scorning to swear allegiance to a government which was deliberately subjecting them to cruelty and humiliation.**"

So wrote Margaret Mitchell of "Reconstruction I" in Gone With the Wind. It does not take a very astute observer of the current scene to detect an uncomfortable similarity between the conditions prevalent in that era and those on our threshold in "Reconstruction II" today.

* * *

RICHARD QUINN (C. 1945–),
"MARTIN LUTHER KING DAY," FALL 1983.[36]

Thomas Fleming published the first issue of *Southern Partisan* in 1979. Since then it has appeared irregularly but has been the leading voice of the neo-Confederate movement, winning praise from the United Daughters of the Confederacy, for example.[37] *Partisan* supporters seek to be included in the councils of the Republican Party and the national conservative movement. An array of conservative leaders have given interviews or contributed articles to the magazine, including Dick Armey, John Ashcroft, Thad Cochran, Jerry Falwell, Phil Gramm, Jesse Helms, Trent Lott, Wesley Pruden, Pat Robertson, Phyllis Schlafly, and others. Richard Quinn, its editor from 1981 through 1999, grew up in Charleston, South Carolina, and has operated a political consulting firm in Columbia since 1979. He has called Nelson Mandela a "terrorist" and advocated for Ku Klux Klan leader David Duke. He was a major paid consultant to John McCain's campaigns for the presidency in 2000 and 2008 and has played a similar role for several other Republican candidates.[38]

This excerpt avoids the extreme racial rhetoric of the Citizens' Council and Council of Conservative Citizens. However, the "institutional arrangements" that Quinn lauds were precisely those "laws, ordinances, and traditions" that make up white supremacy. The civil disobedience Martin Luther King Jr. promoted was a desperate attempt to change a system so unjust that other routes—schools, courts, ballot box—were blocked.

. . . Never mind who he really was or what he did or said; and forget how much a new holiday in his name will cost us or how many other Americans lived lives more deserving of honor. Forget all that. The Congress and the Senate decided that Martin Luther King Day was good politics. An election year is upon us. And that's all that mattered.

. . . Instead, the sponsors of King Day chose a symbol that presses salt in the wounds of those old enough to remember and lies to those too young to understand.

King Day should have been rejected because its purpose is vitriolic and profane. Congress failed us (again) in its tutelary capacity to sanctify and protect national symbols.

King's memory represents, more than anything else, the idea that institutional arrangements—laws, ordinances and traditions—should be subordinated to the individual's conscience. The brand of civil disobedience he preached (and for which he is remembered) exhorts his followers to regard social reform as a process to be carried out in the streets.

. . . Ignoring the real heroes in our nation's life, the blacks have chosen a man who represents not their emancipation, not their sacrifices and bravery in service to their country; rather, they have chosen a man whose role in history was to lead his people into a perpetual dependence on the welfare state, a terrible bondage of body and soul. And a bunch of smiling white politicians went along for the ride.

* * *

James Ronald Kennedy (1947–) and Walter Donald Kennedy (1947–), "Equality of Opportunity," 1994.[39]

One of the founding books of the modern neo-Confederate movement, *The South Was Right!* first appeared in 1991 but was republished, much expanded, in 1994. It has sold more than 100,000 copies and remains in print. The Kennedys repeat the factual errors about Reconstruction that marked neo-Confederate rhetoric during the Nadir, but they also go on to attack more recent developments. In this passage, they deplore the Voting Rights Act of 1965, concluding that the U.S. government does not have the right to determine who votes. That right is reserved to the "sovereign communities of the South." Of course, the Fifteenth Amendment confers precisely this right upon the federal government.

Analysis of governmental policies, political rhetoric, and candidates' character during the years in the South when African Americans could not vote (about 1895 to 1966, depending on the state)—compared to when they exercised the franchise freely (about 1867 to 1875 and 1967 to the present)—does not support the Kennedys' claim that requiring voter qualifications results in better governance. One reason is intrinsic: who better to represent the interests of, say, an uneducated voter than that voter? As well, allowing someone else to decide if a voter has adequate "knowledge of history, geography, and mathematics" opens the door for abuse, as Mississippi showed after 1890 (see Chapter 5). Nevertheless, in recent years the new Southern Republicans (see pages 380–81) have imposed various new requirements from North Carolina to Texas that limit universal suffrage. Meanwhile, the Supreme Court has invalidated a key provision of the Voting Rights Act.

The liberal concept of one man–one vote, or universal franchise, is so deeply entrenched in the liberal dogma of the Yankee government that very few are willing to challenge its legitimacy. This is especially true in the South. Here we are faced with the danger of being labeled as a society attempting to deny the franchise permanently on the basis of race. Where will anyone find a popular politician who is willing to confront charges of racism and bigotry just to promote an improvement of the quality of the electorate? ...

They then refer to John Stuart Mill and argue:

We must move away from blind faith in the liberal theology of one man–one vote. Voting is the means by which citizens control their elected officials. Those who exercise this privilege must first earn it.

The Kennedys conclude that voters "must be able to read, to write, and to demonstrate certain elementary knowledge of history, geography, and mathematics." They must also pay taxes. The Kennedys do not count sales or income taxes, so we can infer that they would never agree that renters pay taxes within their rent; thus this amounts to a requirement that voters must own taxable property or perhaps pay a poll tax. Citizens on "relief"— "welfare, public housing, etc."—are also to be disqualified, as are people who have declared bankruptcy. They conclude:

Some will protest that we are "repealing" the Voting Rights Act; this is not true! You do not repeal a fraud; you correct it. You do not recall a tyrant, you remove him. The same is true with the so-called Voting Rights Act. The Voting Rights Act, as with all other Reconstruction legislation ..., must be annulled to restore the balance between the federal and state governments. These Reconstruction acts violate the consent of the governed within each of the sovereign communities of the South, and therefore they were invalid in their inception and are discriminatory in their enforcement. Thus, the South must use its political strength to terminate this illegitimate use of governmental force. The federal government does not have the right to deny the sovereign community the right to establish legitimate, non-arbitrary voting qualifications!

* * *

"Sic Semper Tyrannis" T-shirt, 1999.

Figure 17: This T-shirt celebrating Lincoln's assassination was a best seller for *Southern Partisan* in the mid-1990s.

Immediately after shooting Abraham Lincoln, John Wilkes Booth cried "Sic semper tyrannis!"—"Thus always to tyrants!"—on the stage of Ford's Theater. In the 1990s, Save The South, an organization in Blue Grass, Virginia, run by Y. P. "Bill" Lanier, sold this T-shirt through ads in *Southern Heritage*, a neo-Confederate magazine no longer extant. *Southern Partisan* sold it through their Christmas catalog, *General Store: A Confederate Christmas*. On the back is a quotation from Thomas Jefferson, "The tree of liberty must be refreshed from time to time with the blood of patriots and tyrants." In his mug shot, Timothy McVeigh, who bombed the Murrah Building in Oklahoma City in 1995, killing 168 people, sports this shirt.[40]

* * *

Alister C. Anderson (c. 1924–), "Address at Arlington National Cemetery," June 6, 1999.[41]

Alister C. Anderson attended The Citadel in 1941, graduated from the United States Naval Academy in 1945, and served in the navy until 1947. He attended Union Theological Seminary and was ordained an Episcopal priest. He volunteered for military service in 1956 as a chaplain in the U.S. Army.[42] After retirement he became "Chaplain-in-Chief" of the Sons of Confederate Veterans. He resigned his Episcopal ministry and was ordained a priest in the Antiochian Orthodox Christian Church. His speech at the Confederate monument in Arlington National Cemetery explains its symbolism accurately, with one exception, which the illustration below describes. In all, Anderson conflates the Confederate cause with opposition to fourteen different ideological afflictions: abolitionism, transcendentalism, utopianism, state centralism, universalism, rationalism, pantheism, hedonism, moral relativism, narcissism, socialism, nihilism, totalitarianism, paganism, and, he adds, "a host of other 'isms.'"

. . . We are gathered here this afternoon in front of, what I believe to be, the most profoundly wise execution of a work of art that I have seen in my lifetime. . . . It reveals and concentrates in beautiful, rugged bronze nearly every idea that a true Southern historian, theologian, statesman and patriotic citizen could present about the religion, history, culture, morals, economics and politics of a civilization from out of which the Confederate States of America evolved. . . .

Anderson then writes a passage mostly lauding the sculptor, Moses Ezekiel.

Garabaldi accused him [Ezekiel] of fighting for slavery. He replied defiantly, "None of us had ever fought for slavery, and, in fact, were opposed to it. The South's struggle was simply a Constitutional one, based on the Doctrine of States' Rights and especially on free trade and no tariffs."[43]

Anderson then tells about Ezekiel's nearby grave. "This monument is the largest and most imposing one in Arlington Cemetery," he notes, but complains that the United Daughters of the Confederacy, not the federal government, maintains it.

What I want to do this afternoon is to explain in words what Sir Moses Ezekiel has created in bronze. He wanted to reveal the South's religious faith, her culture and morals, and how they effected [*sic*] the lives and politics of her people. He achieved this goal. . . .

Anderson then supplies several paragraphs about the imagery at the top of the column. He paints Northern religious leaders as post-Christians tending toward atheist, compared to Christian Southerners. He then works his way down to the figures and bas-reliefs depicting Confederate life.

As you approach the front of the monument again you will see another negro next to the group of Confederate soldiers.[44] This negro is also a soldier and carries a rifle over his shoulder.[45] Most Americans do not know that there were thousands upon thousands of black soldiers who fought in the Confederate army and navy. These black soldiers were integrated into the ranks of the army with the white soldiers.

Anderson is wrong, of course. The panels illustrating Confederate life during the war include an African American behind a Confederate soldier, but the black man is no soldier. As selections in Chapter 3 of this book show, the Confederacy policy did not allow black soldiers in its army until two weeks before surrendering Richmond, a change of policy that historian Bruce Levine calls "a desperate, last-minute attempt to save what could still be saved from the wreckage of the Old South." Even then, these soldiers were controversial; when they marched down the street in Confederate uniforms, white adolescents pelted them with mud.[46] Before those final days, Confederate troops protested the presence even of interracial men who had "passed" to become soldiers and got them removed.[47] James A. Seddon, Confederate secretary of war, made this policy perfectly clear on November 24, 1863. Replying to a request to allow the enlistment of a "company of creoles of Mobile," he wrote, "Our position with the North and before the world will not allow the employment as armed soldiers of negroes." Only "[i]f these creoles can be naturally and properly discriminated from negroes" can they serve.[48] Nevertheless, Anderson claims the monument's image as evidence of "thousands upon thousands of black soldiers who fought in the Confederate army and navy." Of course,

Figure 18: This is the detail of Ezekiel's monument. Note that the Confederate soldier carries the rifle, or else the African American body servant has a little finger where his thumb should be.

a memorial is hardly evidence as to what happened during a war.[49] As well, when the monument was dedicated, this image was not interpreted as a soldier. The pamphlet distributed at its dedication—put out by the United Daughters of the Confederacy, the group that funded the monument—calls this figure "a faithful Negro body-servant following his young master."[50]

What do these poignantly conceived vignettes say about Southern culture? They portray what Sir Moses believed about Southern life and culture which he loved so deeply. Here is depicted the Southerner's great reverence for God and the Bible.

Anderson goes on to laud Southern religiousness and courage. Then he discusses the bottom third of the monument, including the Latin inscription at its base, which he correctly translates, "The winning cause pleased the gods, but the losing cause pleased Cato." He supplies two pages of exegesis showing that the monument means to denigrate Lincoln by conflating him with "Caesar's inordinate ambition and his lust for total power and control," while the Southern cause was merely "to be left alone and be governed by [the Constitution]." He concludes: "The aggression-minded, totalitarian Northern government would not permit that and so she pleased the gods of abolitionism, transcendentalism, utopianism, state centralism, universalism, rationalism and a host of other 'isms.'" Anderson then concludes that the entire nation needs Confederate culture because "[w]e are degenerating into pantheism, hedonism, moral relativism, narcissism and worst of all, into socialism leading into nihilism and totalitarianism." He hopes this monument will help "change the defeatist idea of a Lost Cause into the 'Just Cause' or 'Righteous Cause' of our Southern ancestors."

* * *

Sons of Confederate Veterans, "Postcard Objecting to Mention of Slavery at Civil War Sites," 2000.[51]

In 2000, Jesse Jackson Jr., representative from Illinois, got Congress to pass a bill directing the National Park Service (NPS) "to recognize . . . the unique role that the institution of slavery played in causing the Civil War and its role, if any, at the individual battle sites." This was new; all battlefields save one had maintained a studied silence on the matter.[52] Some still do. To neo-Confederates, silence was appropriate. In response to Jackson, the Sons of Confederate Veterans sent 2,200 postcards and letters to the NPS protesting breaking that silence. Interestingly, although many neo-Confederates claim that secession and the ensuing war had nothing to do with slavery,[53] the cards did not engage that issue. Instead, they argued that battlefield parks should focus solely on who fought there and how, leaving out why.[54]

The postcard campaign failed. Visitors' centers at battlefields from Corinth to Gettysburg now present the dispute over slavery and its extension as the key reason for secession, as does an NPS folder available at all Civil War sites, "Slavery and the Civil War."

It is my understanding that National Battlefield Park Rangers are being instructed to explain to visitors to sites of important battles of the War Between the States that the institution of slavery caused the War. I also understand that the role of slavery at individual battle sites is to be emphasized.

I believe that the primary purpose of preserving battlefields is to understand the military actions which took place there and to remember the men who fought there. To attempt to change the way that a battlefield is interpreted to include social issues of the day does a great disservice to the military strategists and to the soldiers who sacrificed their all at these important battlefields.

* * *

John J. Dwyer (1956–),
"Introduction" to *The War Between the* *States: America's Uncivil War*, 2005.[55]

This book looks like a history textbook, but Bluebonnet Press only publishes books by Dwyer, so it seems self-published. Dwyer is a part-time adjunct professor at Oklahoma City Community College who formerly taught at a private school that works with home-schooling parents. His four coauthors are three pastors and the principal of a Christian private school. According to Dwyer's website, his book avoids the "twisted, truncated, and wrong-headed version propagated en masse by the organized socialist conspiracy that is modern-day American academia and media." Dwyer speaks before far-right audiences, including the Sons of Confederate Veterans and the John Birch Society.[56] *The War Between the States* is aimed at the larger portion of the home-school market, the Christian Right.[57] Unfortunately, many home-schooling parents have neither the time nor the knowledge to debunk such inaccurate claims as these, made on the book's back cover:

Did you know: Neither the Federal nor Confederate governments went to war over the issue of slavery?
Did you know: Tens of thousands of black Americans fought on both the Federal and Confederate sides?

To be sure, the U.S. government went to war to hold the nation together, rather than about slavery. Not so the Confederates. As Chapter 2 of this book shows, Southern states told why they seceded, and slavery was indeed the cause. As for the "tens of thousands of black Americans" who fought on the Confederate side, Chapter 3 reproduces documents showing that the Confederacy never *allowed* that to happen.[58]

Dwyer practices history by assertion. He offers no footnotes or bibliography and riddles his book with errors. For instance, he lauds the slave South for its sense of "responsibility to the land." Actually, care of the land has long been an Achilles heel of plantation agriculture, which emphasizes quick return on investment. That's one reason why the Cotton South kept moving southwest, to find virgin soil to despoil. Dwyer writes, "a person could walk for a hundred miles in some parts of South Carolina and never meet anyone who was not of Scots-Irish descent." Surely he knows that South Carolina was the blackest state in the nation. He declares, "[N]o significant monument had been erected to [James G. Longstreet] even by the beginning of the 21st century," when one of the most publicized stories of recent Civil War public history is the erection of precisely such a monument at Gettysburg in 1998. Dwyer claims "the murder of surrendered Federal soldiers at such places as Fort Pillow . . . were [sic] unsanctioned—even condemned—by the South's high command"; readers can compare actual statements in Chapter 3 by Confederate leaders on this point.

Our excerpt is from the book's introduction, which presents in compact form its argument. By describing a "Fifty Years' War," Dwyer can mystify secession and make it partly about tariffs. In reality, Southerners had passed the tariffs of 1846 and 1857, so tariffs were not an issue prompting secession in 1860.[59] He also ignores how the exigencies of war drove both the Confederacy and the Union to invest their central governments with more power; instead, he claims this to be a cause of the conflict. Finally, Dwyer makes the neo-Confederate claim that the Civil War was a theological war.[60] In reality, some important Southern leaders, including Thomas Jefferson and John C. Calhoun, were Unitarians, while some important Northern antislavery leaders, including John Brown and Theodore Dwight Weld, were traditional Christians.

Withal, our story is not that of a "Civil War" of 1861–65, but of a Fifty Years' War in America. By the late 1820s, economic conflict tore at the unity of the country's regions. In particular, controversy over the tariff ... engendered animosity between the geographic sections, as witnessed by the Nullification Controversy. Fury filled Southerners, who believed the tax, whether or not intentional, to be a colossal transfer of wealth from themselves to those in the North. This contention was connected to the larger issue of what role the Federal government should play in America and its growth. The North, by and large, maintained the necessity for high tariffs, and the need for the strong and energetic national government they would fund—a government more powerful and expansive than most Southerners believed the Founders intended.

These competing visions regarding the role of the Federal government stemmed back to the Federalist versus Anti-Federalist debates of the Constitutional era. But now their import multiplied, fueled by hardening geographic divisions and the other issues. As the Southerners' discontent escalated to a consideration of leaving the Union, the Constitutionality of that act flared on the national stage. Moreover, the debate over the national government's role became a referendum on whether it or the state governments had birthed the Federal Union and whose authority held primacy.

That debate found particular relevance for the Abolitionist minority in the North who wanted slavery (now concentrated in the Southern states) abolished by the Federal government where Northerners held the majority. It did also for the Southern minority who were staunchly pro-slavery, but disproportionately wealthy and influential, and depended on their state governments to protect their right to the practice.

Added to long-held regional, cultural, and even ethnic differences, as well as the size and diversity incumbent in the ever-expanding Union, the debates over the scope and scale of the Federal government meant that increasing numbers of Americans had differences with one another. And all the more as the burgeoning influence of the Scientific Revolution, the European Enlightenment, and rationalism carried the religious persuasions of the North farther from the still largely orthodox Christian South.

* * *

"Lincoln's Worst Nightmare," 1996–99.[61]

Figure 19: From 1996 to 1999, *Southern Partisan* had a catalog section, "Southern Partisan General Store." There readers could purchase merchandise from the publishers, like this T-shirt. The back of the shirt reads, "A States Rights Republican Majority from Dixie."

Abraham Lincoln would surely be astounded to learn that Southern whites had captured the Republican Party. "Lincoln's Worst Nightmare" refers of course to the transformation of the party after 1964. To be sure, not all Southern Republicans joined because of the party's "Southern strategy," and those who did were not all neo-Confederates. Nevertheless, as this T-shirt implies, neo-Confederates did revel in their newfound influence in the party.

From 1996 to 1999, *Southern Partisan* had a catalog section, "Southern Partisan General Store." There readers could purchase merchandise from the publishers like this T-shirt. The back of the shirt reads, "A States Rights Republican Majority from Dixie."

* * *

STATES VOTING FOR LINCOLN (REPUBLICAN, 1860) AND KERRY (DEMOCRAT, 2004).

Figure 20 and Figure 21: Note the remarkable reversal of Republican states, including the solid support of white Southerners for George W. Bush in 2004. Four years later, Barack Obama carried every state that Lincoln won in 1860, but as a Democrat. Meanwhile, he received minuscule proportions of the white vote in states that formerly were heavily proslavery—10 percent in Alabama and 11 percent in Mississippi, for example. Again, we do not imply that most Southern Republicans are neo-Confederates. Southern Republicans often do support neo-Confederate positions, however, not only on "heritage issues" such as the continued display of Confederate flags, but also on issues like restrictive immigration policies and opposition to affirmative action.

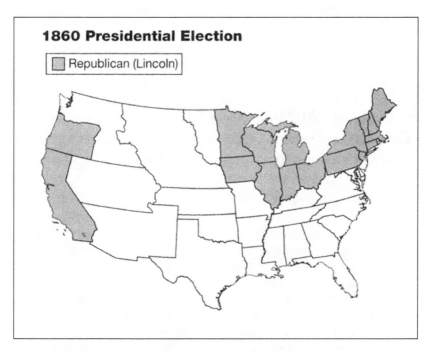

1860 Presidential Election

■ Republican (Lincoln)

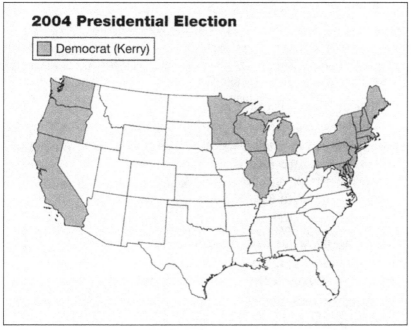

2004 Presidential Election

■ Democrat (Kerry)

Sonny Perdue (1946–),
"Confederate History Month Proclamation,"
March 5, 2008.[62]

Sonny Perdue is the first Republican to be elected governor of Georgia since 1868, during Reconstruction. Elected to the Georgia Senate as a Democrat, he became a Republican in 1998, following the lead of Strom Thurmond and many other white Southern Democrats.[63]

Every April, regardless of party, the Georgia governor proclaims "Confederate History Month." Like John Dwyer and Alister Anderson, in this proclamation Perdue emphasizes and falsifies the roles African Americans played on behalf of the Confederacy. It thus exemplifies neo-Confederate influence over some GOP officeholders. Of course, slaves literally served—as cooks, teamsters, ditchdiggers, and such—but not as soldiers, and often not voluntarily. Underlying this proclamation is the notion that if thousands of African Americans fought for the South, then the Confederacy could hardly have seceded and fought for four years for the maintenance of African slavery. Historian Robert Durden points out that the planter class indeed "went into the war to protect slavery and stubbornly maintained that goal."[64] Trying to derive cause from the alleged voluntary participation of the subordinate group is illogical from the start, which becomes obvious as soon as we change venues. Thousands of Jews *did* fight in Hitler's armies, including scores of officers, but that does not change the fact that Hitler pursued a policy of exterminating Jews.[65] Every system of oppression has its collaborators among the oppressed. The Confederacy would have had hundreds, perhaps thousands of African American soldiers in its ranks, had it allowed them before March 1865. Meanwhile, no annual governors' proclamations honor the nearly 200,000 African Americans who served their country in the army and navy of the United States during the Civil War.

Confederate History Month

Whereas: April is the month in which the Confederate States of America began a four-year conflict in the Civil War. Confederate Memorial Day on April 26 is a time when Georgians honor the more than 90,000 brave men and women who served the Confederate States of America; and

Whereas: Georgia joined the Confederacy in January 1861 when a convention ratified the ordinance of secession, and Georgia has long cherished her Confederate history and the great leaders who made sacrifices on her behalf; and

Whereas: Among those who served the Confederacy were many African-Americans both free and slave who saw action in the Confederate armed forces in many combat roles. They also participated in the manufacture of products for the war effort, built naval ships, and provided military assistance and relief efforts; and

Whereas: One such soldier who made a significant contribution to the state was Bill Yopp of Laurens County who served for four years in Co. H, 14th Regiment Georgia Infantry. Yopp helped to bring about reconciliation and healing after the war by raising money for Confederate Veterans, attending reunions and living in the Confederate Soldiers Home with his comrades. Upon his death on June 3, 1936, Bill Yopp was buried with full Confederate military honors in the Confederate cemetery in Marietta; and

Whereas: It is important that Georgians reflect upon our state's past and honor and respect the devotion of her Confederate leaders, soldiers and citizens; and

Therefore: I, Sonny Perdue, Governor of the State of Georgia, do hereby proclaim April 2008 as CONFEDERATE HISTORY MONTH in Georgia and encourage our citizens to learn about Georgia's heritage and history.

* * *

FRANK CONNER, "WHERE WE STAND NOW: AND HOW WE GOT HERE," SEPTEMBER 2003.[66]

Frank Conner, born in 1933, graduated from Newnan High School in Georgia and from the University of Georgia in marketing. In 2002, he published *The South Under Siege*, which was reviewed favorably in the same issue of *Southern Mercury* that featured this article as its cover story. He now lives in Newnan. Although not quite the most recent in publication, his essay is an appropriate final selection, because it summarizes the dominant neo-Confederate view of Southern history from the end of the Civil War to the present. *Southern Mercury* is an official publication of the Foundation for the Preservation of American Culture, the educational foundation of the Sons of Confederate Veterans.

Some of Conner's historical claims are nonsense. The South never teetered on "the knife-edge of mass starvation," and when cities or surrendered Confederates did face food shortages at the end of the war, the U.S. Army did what it could to help.[67] The secession statements in Chapter 2 prove that no one seceded because Republicans were "going to . . . tax the Southern states outrageously." The "bloody shirt" does not refer to Civil War casualties, as pages 306–7 show.

However, Conner also gets some things right. Across the South when he was growing up, and until at least the early 1970s, schools indeed taught history "from the [white] Southern viewpoint." It is of course true that "Confederates fought valiantly to defend their nation." Moreover, "the basic belief system and way of life predominant" in the 1940s, and until at least 1964, "were essentially the same as those of the Confederates"—at least so far as white supremacy was concerned. Conner is also correct when he notes that disfranchisement and segregation arose around the turn of the twentieth century, although hardly owing to "the blacks' transgressions." As he implies (but does not write), white Democrats disfranchised African Americans because they feared losing elections to interracial coalitions, such as Republicans in North Carolina, Readjusters in Virginia, and Populists in Alabama. He is also right that Northerners could hardly object to Southern segregation, because de facto segregation became widespread in the North as well. Lurking unmentioned beneath Conner's statements about schooling is the fact that as soon as Democrats eliminated blacks from voting, they slashed funds for black education. When Conner was a boy, Mississippi, for instance, spent $42 for each white pupil, $7.24 for each black pupil.[68]

The essay also embodies a distrust of the national government that is characteristic of neo-Confederates, although hardly limited to them, and shows their frustration at being on the defensive in recent decades. Conner attributes the reverses suffered since the end of the Nadir to "the liberals," who loom, omnipotent but vague, throughout his article. In *The South under Siege*, he is more specific: *Jews* are white Southerners' "dedicated and deadliest enemy."[69]

Any conservative Southerner who has read much about Reconstruction and post-Reconstruction is acutely aware that during those misery-encrusted 32 years, the Yankees did everything in their considerable power to break the spirit of the Southerners. They deliberately held the devastated South on the knife-edge of mass starvation, and continually waved the bloody shirt to fan the nation's hatred of the South. The North sought to crush the Southerners' Christian-based independence of spirit and belief in decentralized government and to coerce them into embracing the dominance of the national government and accepting meekly their new status as third-class citizens of the agricultural colonies of the industrialized North.

But no matter what cruel punishments the Northern leaders might heap upon the South, they could not break the spirit of the Southerners. In addition, the American public finally wearied of the constantly-repeated charge that the South had wantonly caused the deaths of 623,000 men in the War: the bloody shirt had faded to white.

Came the Spanish-American War of 1898, and Southerners enlisted in large numbers to defend the interests of the US while Southern leaders commented pointedly that it was time for the North to stop fighting the "Civil War." The North reluctantly agreed; and for awhile—it ceased attacking the South's history, belief system, and way of life, overtly. During the first half of the 20th century, the South was left free to revere publicly its own regional heroes as it saw fit and to teach its real history to the children.

What the South Was Like When I Was a Child

I was a youth in the 1940s. In school I was taught the history of Georgia and the history of the US, both from the Southern viewpoint. I was taught that slavery had been a longstanding lawful institution-in-being; that the Northern abolitionists had converted slavery into an emotionally-charged issue for condemning the South; that the Southern states began to secede in 1860–61 because the newly-elected Republican party was going to use the power of the federal government to tax the Southern states outrageously; and that when the North then invaded the South, the Confederates fought valiantly to defend their nation, their homes, and their families. The Confederates had been heroic fighters defending their homeland. They had been defeated, but not dishonored.

That was what most people in the towns across Georgia believed in the 1940s. Further, the basic belief system and way of life predominant in those towns in the 1940s were essentially the same as those of the Confederates—minus, of course, the acceptance of slavery.

On each Confederate Memorial Day, the schools in my town closed, and the students marched to the Confederate cemetery and joined the crowd of adults there. The main speech honoring the Confederates was always given by our US congressman or senator.

The school bands of that era regularly played Dixie—as did the radio stations. And to the Southerners, the Confederate Battle Flag symbolized the fighting spirit. That was the South I grew up in—the Old South of the 1940s, which was proud of its heritage. I did not then dream that within a decade the South would be under all-out attack again, resulting in the imposition of Reconstruction II upon us—which is still running strong.

The Liberals Infiltrate the South's Institutions

Although the 20th century began with a truce between the North and the South, the Northern liberals could not leave us alone. There was too great a disparity between the South's continuing belief in the importance of the individual and the need for limited, decentralized government, and the liberals' belief in the need for an all-powerful central government to impose social and economic equality upon every-one. And so the liberals began infiltrating the South's education establishment early in the 20th century.

It was begun by Robert Ogden, a dedicated liberal who administered John D. Rockefeller's philanthropic programs. He established the Southern Education Board, which established the General Education Board, to improve the quality and quantity of public education in the still-impoverished South, and then to gradually introduce liberalism into it. The liberals first accumulated in the humanities departments of the South's universities—beginning with Professor Howard W. Odum, who founded the sociology department at the University of North Carolina at Chapel Hill in 1920, under the tutelage of President Frank Graham, a liberal. They established committees of educators and other prominent people across the South, to push for the end of segregation.

Then liberals became the administrators of Southern universities. Meanwhile, liberal journalists were working their way upward in some of the South's newspapers (such as the Atlanta Constitution); and liberals were also infiltrating the South's other institutions. In the 1940s, these liberals began using the South's institutions, which they now controlled, to attack the traditional belief system of the South—beginning when Governor Eugene Talmadge of Georgia ordered the Board of Regents to fire Dean Walter D. Cocking of the School of Education at the University of Georgia, for promoting a policy of racial desegregation; whereupon the liberals fought back. And when the crunch came in the 1950s, these liberals were ready and aching to help destroy the existing order in the South. Under attack both from without and within, the South didn't stand a chance.

The Liberals Create a False Public Image of the Blacks
The 20th century liberals (North and South) decided to use black civil rights as their main moral weapon against the white South, just as their 19th century predecessors had done prior to the War of Northern Aggression.

After the turn of the 20th century, the white Southerners had disfranchised and segregated the blacks, in perhaps the mildest reaction possible at that time to the blacks' transgressions. The blacks—then a childlike people—had been selling their votes to the Democrats en masse for $.25 apiece in national elections. This so enraged the Northern Republicans (who believed that the blacks owed them) that in 1890 they almost succeeded at reinstating key elements of Reconstruction in the South (via the Force Bill). The white Southerners weren't about to undergo any part of that experience again, so they disfranchised the blacks lawfully via universal poll taxes, literacy tests, etc.

At the same time, due primarily to the ruinous practices of the Northern capitalists, many Southern blacks could no longer earn a living as sharecroppers; so they moved into the towns. But they did not understand town life, and the white Southerners lacked the money and other resources to teach them; consequently, the blacks' crime rates soared. Their homicide rate became seven times that of the whites. In sheer self-defense, the Southern whites segregated the blacks. The Northern liberals could not reasonably object to any of that. So instead, they began creating a false public image of the blacks.

Early in the 20th' century, the liberals took control of the humanities departments in the colleges and universities of America. Previously, anthropologists had routinely recorded the notable differences in IQ among the races; but at Columbia, a liberal cultural anthropologist named Franz Boas now changed all of that. He decreed that there were no differences in IQ among the races, and the only biological differences between the blacks and whites were of superficial nature. The liberals swiftly made it academically suicidal to challenge Boas' flat assertion. Meanwhile, the liberals in the media heaped special praise upon black athletes, musicians, singers, and writers—and treated them as typical of the black race. The liberals were creating a false image of the blacks in America as a highly competent people who were being held back by the prejudiced white Southerners.

The Liberals Destroy the Old South in the Name of Black Civil Rights

World War II came and went. Now the liberals began putting real pressure on the white Southerners to integrate the blacks into the Southern society (while leaving the North's de facto segregation untouched). Meanwhile, the segregated blacks (North and South) had spent 30 years studying the structure of the white society and learning how to duplicate much of it for a society of their own. In the post-WWII era, most Southern governors could measure the social progress of the blacks, and could also see the outside pressures building: it was time for a major change. But to integrate the blacks smoothly into the white society, the Southern states would first have to equalize the education of the blacks with that of the whites. So in the early 1950s, a number of Southern states pumped big money into the black school systems, to bring them up to par.

But gradualism did not suit the liberals' plans. As in the War of Northern Aggression, their objective was not to benefit the blacks despite their rhetoric, they've never cared anything about the blacks—but to destroy the belief system and way of life of the white Southerners. And so, beginning in 1947, Northern liberal writers launched a wide-spread hate campaign against the white South; and liberal Democrat Harry Truman pressured the Congress to enact a radical civil rights bill aimed squarely at the white South; and Truman did in fact desegregate the US government—including the armed forces—by presidential fiat that year, in 1954, the liberal Supreme Court rendered its patently-unconstitutional *Brown v. Board of Education of Topeka, Kansas* decision, to force the integration of white children and black children in the Southern schools. Had the Northern liberals attacked the white-Southern adults, that would have been bad enough; but they were going after the children. It didn't take a rocket scientist to forecast the disastrous results of that move, to be enforced by the hostile federal government; and the white Southerners did what they could to resist. But they never had a chance.

The Northern liberals funded and guided the black civil rights organizations; and the liberal news media gave them nonstop propaganda coverage which transformed them into national heroes. US presidents sent the US Army to enforce the integration of public schools and universities in the South. Black leaders such as Martin Luther King, Jr. carefully selected as their targets those Southern towns and cities with incompetent officials who were bound to react with violence. Literally thousands of white Northern liberals and radicals accompanied out-of-state blacks to register black voters in Southern towns, while the liberal Northern and scalawag TV news crews awaited the inevitable explosions.

The media, academia, and government at all levels vilified the white Southerners, their belief system, and their way of life in a propaganda campaign that blanketed America: the Southern blacks were saintly; the Southern whites were evil personified.

As the result, the US Congress enacted the patently-unconstitutional Civil Rights Act of 1964 and Voting Rights Act of 1965, both of which targeted only the South. Thus did the US government institute Reconstruction II, which is still in full effect. The Old South was destroyed, and its belief system and way of life were discredited outside the South.

Then came the social-welfare programs for the blacks and affirmative action and social promotions in the schools. The integration tactics employed by the liberals, along with these additional measures, largely destroyed the blacks' work ethic and academic learning and the black family resulting in insupportable levels of black illegitimacy, poverty, and crime. Had the liberals really cared about the blacks, they would have reversed course and repaired the awful harm they had done the blacks. The fact that they did not do so speaks much louder about the real motives of the liberals than their high-flown rhetoric. Black civil rights was simply the best moral weapon with which to destroy the white Southerners as a people—just as it had been in the 19th century.

The Liberals Begin the Final Stage of their Culture War Against the White South

A coalition of white liberals and black activists now expanded Reconstruction II via a series of campaigns in the private sector; some of them targeted the white South; others, the conservative whites nationwide. For example, in the 1970s, the motion picture and entertainment-television companies launched a comprehensive hate-the-white-South campaign which is still in force, and which has probably been more destructive of our beliefs and values than all else combined. The colleges and universities adopted multiculturalism—enforced by political correctness—as academia's official repudiation of the belief system and way of life of the white South. A coalition of black activists and the news media and the liberals in government now attacked the big corporations as racist, and made them adopt quotas and other preferential treatment of blacks. The same type of coalition attacked the criminal justice system in America and polarized it racially (epitomized by the O. J. Simpson criminal trial), thus ruining it. That coalition is presently promoting hate-crime legislation as the final weapon to intimidate the whites (particularly the white Southerners) into total impotence via thought-crime laws.

Thus reinforced, Reconstruction II is steadily shredding the traditional white society—first in the South and then in the rest of the nation. But the liberals are in a big hurry to replace Christianity with secular humanism and limited government with socialism. So now they are backing another major campaign against the white South.

In the late 1980s, the NAACP and other black civil rights organizations ran into a brick wall. The blacks had been given equality under the law and even preferential treatment; yet they were obviously not performing up to par with the whites. The problem was that the liberals' civil rights campaign had given the blacks a belief system which emphasized black inferiority. Politically, the black activists could not touch that problem; but they still had to explain the blacks' failure to perform in society. So they invented the concept of "institutional racism" on the part of the Southern whites: you couldn't see it, but it was there, and it was ruining the blacks' performance. This "institutional racism" was an integral part of the white Southerners' belief system—which they had inherited from their Confederate forebears. To destroy that belief system, it would be necessary to vilify and discredit the Confederates and their belief system.

And so in the early 1990s the process began whereby any obscure black could step up to a microphone and call the Confederate soldiers any vile name he could think up—such as "Nazi SS concentration-camp guards"; and the news media would not only run that as straight news, but would flood the South and the rest of the nation with it. The white South was swamped with such attacks, and had no way to respond to them. That discredited the Confederates' public image, and set us up for the liberals' next move.

In the late 1990s, the various liberal-dominated institutions joined that campaign. Liberal academia now swore that the South had fought the war solely over slavery, an unimaginably evil institution. Virtually the entire liberal media began calling the Confederates—and then today's white Southerners—names that were just as irresponsible and vicious as the ones the blacks were spouting. PBS began broadcasting miniseries that were blatant hate-mongering anti-white-South propaganda. Congress began legislating against the white South's heritage on the theory that we are all irredeemable racists. Local governments in the Southern states began restricting the public celebration of our Confederate heritage. Consequently, we conservative white Southerners are now aliens in our own homeland. And far worse treatment is awaiting us just around the corner—unless we fight back lawfully, and stop the attacks now.

Our Options

As we can see from this account, the liberals will not get bored and stop attacking us of their own accord; and we cannot appease them. The only way we can prevent them (and their black-activist catspaws) from finishing the job of destroying us as a people and destroying our belief system and our way of life is by counterattacking the liberals successfully and discrediting them in the eyes of the public.

The liberals continue to attack and destroy us only because we permit them to. For the first half of the 20th century, liberalism was the golden dream—and as such, it was bulletproof. But the tenets of liberalism have been official US government policy since 1965 (some will say 1933); and the public has now seen that it is unworkable because it ignores the realities of human nature. So liberalism is now vulnerable; it can be taken.

What I am about to say applies to all of the Southern-patriot organizations, but I address it specifically to the SCV, because that is the organization with which I am most heavily involved. Our traditional defensive-tactics—the indignant letter-to-the-editor, etc., employed by individual SCV members or camps will not work in today's culture war. The liberals are mounting huge institutional attacks against us and our heritage. To counterattack them successfully, the SCV must bring lawsuits, launch media campaigns, coordinate organization-wide protest demonstrations, etc. at the national level in order to prevail against the liberal institutions that are attacking us and our heritage. To do that, we must urgently reform the SCV, and convert it into a (lawful) effective fighting organization; and we must use it to fight back to restore our heritage. If we do not, we conservative white Southerners will soon have nothing left to anchor us to the South—not even a common language and mindset that we share with the rest of the Southerners.

* * *

CONCLUDING WORDS

Even today, visitors to the South will sometimes note upon their return, "they're still fighting the Civil War down there!" Although spoken with amused exaggeration, the statement carries considerable truth: the war still holds an unusual immediacy in the South, especially to neo-Confederates. Once we grasp that Confederates seceded to preserve slavery and maintain white supremacy—which this book proves—then we can understand why neo-Confederates still fight what might be called "the long Civil War." Neo-Confederates fight to maintain their ancestors' honor, which they do by obfuscating why their ancestors fought. They also fight to save "our belief system and our way of life," in Frank Conner's words—in short, to perpetuate the South's racial hierarchy. They accomplished this by law until the 1970s and still succeed by custom in some ways and places. The present-day function of this strife about the past explains the energy that still pours into it. No such ongoing struggle attaches to, say, World War I, which helps explain why no "Sons of WWI Veterans" exists.

This book appears as the nation marks the 150th anniversary of secession and soon of the bloody Civil War to which secession led. No one in 1860 would have predicted that a century and a half later, the exam given by the U.S. government to all foreign nationals who seek to become citizens would score either of two very different answers correct as causes of secession: "slavery or states' rights." In 1860, "all knew," as Abraham Lincoln said in his "Second Inaugural," that slavery "was somehow the cause of the war." No other question on the naturalization exam admits two "correct" answers, because no other question in our history has been subjected to a campaign of distortion and obfuscation lasting more than a century. That the U.S. Citizenship and Immigration Services Bureau cannot simply say the South seceded for slavery shows the influence that neo-Confederates still hold on our government.

Given this situation, every historian, every teacher of history or social studies, must make sure to use the documents in this book to counter the mythology and mystification that still enshrouds the Confederacy. For there is a reciprocal relationship between truth about the past and justice in the present. This relationship becomes apparent when one examines textbook coverage of our incarceration of Japanese Americans during World War II. Most textbooks published shortly after the war made no mention of the matter or brusquely justified it. Books written after 1988, when the United States paid $20,000 to every survivor, are much better. And why not? Now it had become another American success story. The nation misstepped, to be sure, but then it apologized and tried to make good. Thus justice in the present helps prompt a new willingness to write the truth about the past.

It can work the other way too. Solid research by Michael D'Orso helped persuade the state of Florida to apologize and pay reparations for whites' 1923 expulsion of black residents from the town of Rosewood, for example.[1] If Americans can face the unpleasant facts of Confederate and neo-Confederate history squarely—from the causes of secession to the treatment of black troops to the unsavory overthrow of state governments at the end of Reconstruction, and on to the use of Confederate symbols and ideology to oppose the civil rights movement and influence the Republican Party today—then doing so will help us understand the importance of white supremacy in our past. In turn, that understanding facilitates healing, justice, and better race relations in the present.

Such is the living significance of these documents, their "great truth" for us today.

NOTES

INTRODUCTION

1. Hammond, quoted in Jabez Curry, *The Southern States of the American Union* (Richmond, VA: B. F. Johnson, 1895), 189; on the Senate floor by L. Q. C. Lamar, 1/24/1878; and elsewhere.

    Notes use postal abbreviations for states; "NY" for New York City; "DC" for Washington, D.C.; "U" for "University"; and "P" for "Press." Dates after website URLs tell when they were retrieved.

2. E. E. Sparks, ed., *The Lincoln Douglas Debates* (Springfield: IL State Hist. Library, 1908), 485, at books.google.com, 8/2009.

3. Even given all these sources, a diehard handful of teachers—most recently one in Minnesota—still insist that secession was for the "states' right to secede." Sophisticated purveyors of this view note that a compact of independent states agreed to the Constitution; these states therefore had the right to break the compact. This was an open question when the Constitution was signed. Over time, it remained open, although Chapter 2 notes that Southern states opposed secession in 1815, when some New England Federalists made gestures in that direction. Those who proposed (then or later) that a state can unilaterally break the contract stipulated that it could only do so for good cause. Chapter 2 notes that no such cause existed; the Buchanan administration had done nothing to offend Southern states.

    Secession for the "states' right to secede" is a tautology. Even if secession had been a state's right, which the Civil War determined it was not, that right could never explain *why* states seceded, but only *how*.

4. Teachers getting it wrong included a majority black audience (Tennessee), very Northern audiences (Oregon, North Dakota, Minnesota), experienced teachers chosen to mentor others (Iowa, Ohio), and new and preservice teachers (several). Only in one group of teachers (Miamisburg, Ohio) did fewer than 50% vote for states' rights.

    As noted earlier, "the election of Lincoln" is correct as an immediate cause, and the South Carolina document says so. It makes no reference to any issue of tariffs or taxes.

5. Christopher Olsen, "Secession, Slavery, and Racism: Confederates vs. Neo-Confederates," review of Charles B. Dew, *Apostles of Disunion*, H-South, 1/2002, h-net.org/reviews/showpdf.php?id=5809.

6. Richard B. Harwell, ed., *The Confederate Reader: How the South Saw the War* (NY: Longmarts, Green, 1957); Rod Gragg, ed., *Illustrated Confederate Reader* (NY: Harper & Row, 1991).

7. It might be claimed that none of the documents in this reader could fit, since the Archives claims to have chosen documents that "have helped shape the national character, and . . . reflect our diversity, our unity, and our commitment as a nation to continue our work toward forming 'a more perfect union.'" This reasoning won't do, however, because many of the documents do *not* reflect "our unity" or "our work toward forming 'a more perfect union,'" such as the *Dred Scott* decision, the telegram announcing the surrender of Fort Sumter, and the Chinese Exclusion Act.

8. Loewen surveyed six textbooks published since 2000: Joyce Appleby, Alan Brinkley, and James McPherson, *The American Journey* (NY: Glencoe McGraw-Hill, 2000); Daniel J. Boorstin and Brooks Mather Kelley, *A History of the United States* (Needham, MA: Pearson Prentice Hall, 2005); Paul Boyer, *Holt American Nation* (NY: Holt, Rinehart, & Winston, 2003); Andrew Cayton et al., *America: Pathways to the Present* (Needham, MA: Pearson Prentice Hall, 2005); Gerald A. Danzer et al., *The Americans* (Boston: McDougal Littell [Houghton Mifflin], 2007); and David Kennedy, Lizabeth Cohen, and Thomas A. Bailey, *The American Pageant* (Boston: Houghton Mifflin, 2006). Amazingly, the last book does quote from the South Carolina document in a box on a page, but manages to select three long sentences that do not mention slavery. This is no easy task.

   We affirm that the ends for which this government was instituted have been defeated, and the government itself has been made destructive of them by the action of the non-slaveholding states. . . . For 25 years this agitation has been steadily increasing until it has now secured to its aid the power of the common government. Observing the forms of the constitution, a sectional party has found within that article establishing the executive department the means of subverting the constitution itself. [ellipsis in the textbook]

   The astute reader may infer that slavery lurks behind these vague words, but most readers won't. "This agitation has been steadily increasing"—agitation about *what*? Directly preceding that phrase, concealed by the textbook's ellipsis, South Carolina condemns "those States" that "have denounced as sinful the institution of slavery" and have "encouraged and assisted thousands of our slaves to leave their homes." We suspect that Houghton Mifflin simply did not want to include anything directly on point, lest some Southern state textbook adoption board might take offense.

9. *Holt* does go on without delay to mention slavery: "The issue went beyond states' rights, however. Also at stake was the determination of the southerners to protect slavery." Nevertheless, most readers would perceive states' rights as the primary reason, slavery second.

10. Southerners also had no use for secession when threatened by Northern states. Robert Hayne, for example, U.S. senator and governor of South Carolina, called New Englanders' conduct at the Hartford Convention during the War of 1812 "wholly indefensible," even though delegates never really threatened secession.

Three years later, he joined his state in threatening nullification and secession if the United States did not meet its demands for a lower tariff. See Theodore Dwight, *History of the Hartford Convention* (NY: N. & J. White, 1833), 435–46.

11. In "The Address of the People of South Carolina . . ." published by its convention on December 24, 1860, and included in Chapter 2, South Carolina does complain, "The people of the Southern States are not only taxed for the benefit of the Northern States, but after the taxes are collected, three-fourths of them are expended at the North." Georgia's "Report on Causes for Secession," also in Chapter 2, notes more accurately that the tariff controversy ended in the mid-1840s; "the principle was settled, and free-trade, low duties, and economy in public expenditures was the verdict of the American people."

12. Parts of this book, especially Chapters 2 and 5, rebut this obfuscation, especially the claim about states' rights. "Basic economic and social differences" is of course correct and can be summarized in a word: slavery. "Disagreements over tariffs" is flatly wrong; the South had written the two tariff bills prior to secession. Quarrels over "internal improvements at public expense" also does not stand up. Jefferson Davis himself put in motion one of the largest improvements, the Gadsden Purchase, buying land from Mexico for a rail route from New Orleans to California, because it would benefit the South and possibly extend slavery west.

13. William C. Davis, *The Cause Lost* (Lawrence: UP of KS, 1996), 177.

14. James McPherson, *Battle Cry of Freedom* (NY: Oxford UP, 1988), 241. I must add that our ellipses conceal McPherson's next words: "and freedom from the coercive powers of a centralized government." He is right that when white Southern Democrats lost control of the central government, they wanted freedom from it. Again, though, this is not "states' rights," but secession. Until the very moment of the November 1860 election, white Southern Democrats argued for *more* power in the federal government, so they could wield it to force the return of fugitive slaves and protect slavery in the territories, regardless of local sentiment or the actions of state or territorial governments.

15. James McPherson, *This Mighty Scourge* (NY: Oxford UP, 2007), 7, reprinted from "What Caused the Civil War?" *North & South* (11/2000).

16. Indeed, the Buchanan administration's newspaper, the *Washington Union*, by late 1857 favored extending the *Dred Scott* principle to states! "What is recognised as property by the constitution of the United States, by a provision which applies equally to all the states, has an inalienable right to be protected in all the states." If Buchanan or Taney had accomplished this goal, free states would cease to exist, at least legally, although the article does suggest that local "sentiment" could still suffice to make slaveowners feel unwelcome. The article goes on to denounce the ending of slavery in Northern states—which had mostly happened decades earlier—as "a gross outrage on the rights of property" ("Free-Soilism," 11/17/1857). Buchanan's was indeed a pro-Southern administration.

17. Chandra Manning, *What This Cruel War Was Over* (NY: Vintage, 2008), 107–8, 172, 204–10.

18. Quoted in Felix Okoye, *The American Image of Africa: Myth and Reality* (Buffalo, NY: Black Academy P, 1971), 37. See Leon Festinger, *A Theory of Cognitive Dissonance* (Evanston, IL: Row, Peterson, 1957).

19. William Harris and Judith Levey, eds., *The New Columbia Encyclopedia* (NY: Columbia UP, 1975), 1088.

20. James Hollandsworth, *The Louisiana Native Guards* (Baton Rouge: LSU P, 1995), 4, 10–11.

21. In May 1863, they participated in the Battle of Port Hudson, almost the first black troops to come under fire in the Civil War. U.S. general Nathaniel P. Banks praised their performance: "Their conduct was heroic.... Their charges upon the rebel works ... exhibited the greatest bravery and caused them to suffer great losses" (ibid., 62); see also "French Creole" website, frenchcreoles.com/military%20achievements/Louisiana%20Native%20Guards/louisiana%20native%20guards.htm, 3/2008.

22. Robert F. Durden, *The Gray and the Black: The Confederate Debate on Emancipation* (Baton Rouge: LSU P, 2000 [1972]); Bruce Levine, *Confederate Emancipation* (NY: Oxford UP, 2006).

23. Nat Brandt, "New York Is Worth Twenty Richmonds," *American Heritage* 22 #6 (10/1971), americanheritage.com/articles/magazine/ah/1971/6, 3/2008.

24. Mules result from mating between two different species, donkey and horse. All humans are one species, of course. Human races have always been defined socially, not biologically; their number and definitions have changed dramatically over time. "Interracial" offspring are therefore neither hybrid, mongrel, weak, degraded, nor wretched.

25. Neo-Confederates are adherents of the ideology portrayed by the selections in this volume, especially in Chapters 5 and 6. Thus James Longstreet and Jubal Early were both ex-Confederates in 1880, but only Early was a neo-Confederate.

26. Frank U. Quillen, *The Color Line in Ohio* (Ann Arbor, MI: Wahr, 1913), 120.

27. During slavery, whites always knew that blacks had been taken from Africa by force. They also recognized that slavery presented almost no opportunity for its victims to demonstrate their abilities or rise in social structure. In 1890, African Americans were still on the bottom, of course. Now, however, their lowly place could be construed as their own fault. After all, slavery had been over for a generation.

28. At the time, the conflict was called "the Civil War," "the War of the Rebellion," or "the Great Rebellion." See John Coski, "The War Between the Names," *North & South* 8 #7 (1/2006): 67.

29. James W. Loewen, *Lies Across America* (NY: New P, 1999), 252–58; Phillip H. Fall, "Welcome to United Daughters of the Confederacy Convention," Houston, TX, 10/19/1909, in *Minutes of the Sixteen Annual UDC Convention* (Opelika, AL: Post Publishing, 1909), 7.

30. Tennessee ratified it briefly but then rescinded its action.

31. Mildred Rutherford, "What Has the Negro Meant to the South? What Has the South Meant to the Negro?" in *Miss Rutherford's Scrap Book* (Athens, GA: 10/1925), 4–5.

32. During the Nadir, most labor unions were all-white. African Americans "protected" the South from strikes by forming, in Marxist terms, a "reserve army of the unemployed." White workers knew they might face black strikebreakers if blacks organized. One response would have been to organize an interracial union, but in the South that proved especially difficult.

33. For an extensive discussion of the use of the Confederate battle flag during the struggle for civil rights, see John Coski, *The Confederate Battle Flag* (Cambridge, MS: Harvard UP, 2006).

34. See Euan Hague, Heidi Beirich, and Edward Sebesta, *Neo-Confederacy* (Austin: U of TX P, 2008).

35. Kathy W. Nufer, "Racial Tensions Mount at North," *Appleton Post-Crescent*, 9/24/1999.

36. Ironically, the SCV then removed Lunsford from its heritage committee because he continued to attend meetings of the Council of Conservative Citizens in his official SCV capacity. Charles Lunsford, "Heritage Defense in the SCV: A Comment," *Southern Heritage* 2 #4 (7/1994): 14–17. The Council of Conservative Citizens is the explicit descendant of the [White] Citizens' Councils, a white supremacist organization whose publication we excerpt in Chapter 6.

37. P. Charles Lunsford, "The Forgotten Confederates," *Confederate Veteran* (11/1992), 12.

38. Service to the Confederacy by African American individuals could hardly prove such a proposition about a government in the first place. Self-preservation is a wonderful motivator.

39. See Thomas Edsall and Mary Edsall, *Chain Reaction* (NY: Norton, 1991).

40. This point is developed in James W. Loewen, *Lies My Teacher Told Me* (NY: Simon & Schuster, 2007 [1994]), 1–2, 363–64, note 4.

41. James W. Loewen, "Challenging Racism, Challenging History," foreword to Cooper Thompson, Emmett Schaefer, and Harry Brod, eds., *White Men Challenging Racism* (Durham, NC: Duke UP, 2003), provides a few examples.

CHAPTER 1

1. Arthur Zilversmit, *The First Emancipation* (Chicago: U Chicago P, 1967), 227–28; D. L. Robinson, *Slavery in the Structure of American Politics, 1765–1820* (NY: Norton, 1979), esp. 5–6; "Slavery in the North," slavenorth.com/index.html, 10/2008; Paul Finkelman, "Slavery and the Constitutional Convention," in R. Beeman et al., eds., *Beyond Confederation* (Chapel Hill: UNC P, 1987), 189–90; subsequent pages note passages that indirectly protect slavery.

2. Eric H. Walther, *The Fire Eaters* (Baton Rouge: LSU P, 1992), 57–58, 73–75.

3. In the nineteenth century, "Negro" was often not capitalized even by abolitionists such as Harriet Beecher Stow. We retain authors' capitalization. By about 1920, "Negro" was clearly preferred, especially by African American writers; use of "negro" after that date usually signals an antiblack point of view. Around 1970, "black" replaced "Negro" as the term of choice among African Americans; since then, "African American" has gained in popularity. A few neo-Confederate authors use "Negro" or even "negro" in recent years. Again, we retain their choices.

4. *Elliot's Debates*, vol. 5, 457–61. We have modified this text by adding speakers' first names and indicating their states in brackets.

5. Don Fehrenbacher, *The Slaveholding Republic* (NY: Oxford UP, 2001), 36–38, 218, 244; see also D. L. Robinson, *Slavery in the Structure of American Politics* (NY: Norton, 1979), 23–24 and ch. 5.

6. *Register of Debates in Congress*, 24th Cong., 2d sess., 13, pt. 2, 2184–88.

7. *Journal of the Democratic Convention Held in the City of Montgomery on the 14th and 15th February, 1848* (Montgomery, AL: M'Cormick & Walshe, 1848), 10–15.

8. Richard K. Crallé, ed., *The Works of John C. Calhoun*, vol. 6 (NY: Appleton, 1855), 290–313.

9. James Henley Thornwell, *The Rights and the Duties of the Masters: A Sermon Preached at the Dedication of a Church Erected in Charleston, S.C., For the Benefit and Instruction of the Coloured Population* (Charleston, SC: Walker & James, 1850).

10. Benjamin M. Palmer, ed., *The Life and Letters of James Henley Thornwell* (Edinburgh: Banner of Truth Trust, 1974 [1875]), 2–3, 82, 114–16, 147–55, 355.

11. Euan Hague and Edward Sebesta, "The U.S. Civil War as a Theological War: Confederate Christian Nationalism and The League of the South," *Canadian Review of American Studies* 32 #3 (2002): 253–84.

12. *Resolutions, Address and Journal of the Southern Convention, Held at Nashville, Tennessee, June 3d to 12th inclusive, in the Year 1850*, in H. V. Ames, ed., *State Documents on Federal Relations: The States and the United States: Slavery and the Union 1845–1861*, vol. 6 (Philadelphia: U PA Dept. of History, 1906), 23–29.

13. It also invalidates the Northwest Ordinance, enacted by some of the same Founding Fathers who wrote the Constitution. Of course, seven years later in *Dred Scott*, the Supreme Court would do just that.

14. From the section, *Journal of the State Convention of South Carolina Held in 1852, Together with the Resolution and Ordinance*, from the *Journals of the Conventions of the People of South Carolina Held in 1832, 1833, and 1852* (Columbia, SC: R. W. Gibbs, 1860), 137, 150–51.

15. Bills also depict buildings like the South Carolina state capitol; ships, trains, and landscapes; classical images including Greek goddesses; and Confederate leaders. Among activities, images of slavery predominate. Two major exhibitions have featured this theme: "Confederate Currency: The Color of Money, Depictions of Slavery in Confederate and Southern States," mounted in South Carolina and elsewhere in the early years of the twenty-first century (see its catalog by Gretchen Barbatsis, ed., and John W. Jones, artist [NY: New Directions, 2003]), and "Beyond Face Value: Slavery Iconography in Confederate Currency," a virtual exhibit (cwc. lsu.edu/cwc/BeyondFaceValue/beyondfacevalue.htm, 6/2009).

16. Loewen, *Lies Across America*, summarizes and cites recent scholarship on slavery (338–51) and tells of acts of freedmen around Fort Mill (273–79). See also William L. Barney, *Flawed Victory* (NY: Praeger, 1975), 139, 141; Stephen Ash, *When the Yankees Came* (Chapel Hill: UNC P, 1995), 190–92, 223.

17. Samuel A. Cartwright, "Diseases and Peculiarities of the Negro Race," *New Orleans Medical and Surgical Journal* 7 (5/1851): 691–715, included in Paul Finkelman, *Defending Slavery* (NY: Bedford/St. Martins, 2003), 157–73.

18. Genesis 9 and Numbers 12, in "The Bible, King James Version," etext.virginia.edu/ kjv.browse.html, 5/2009.

19. J. H. Van Evrie, *Negroes and Negro "Slavery;" The First an Inferior Race—The Latter, Its Normal Condition* (NY: Day Book, 1861), inside front cover (Davis), inside back cover (Clingman), and 1–12.

20. Stephen Jay Gould, *The Panda's Thumb* (NY: Norton, 1980), 173–75; George Frederickson, *The Black Image in the White Mind* (NY: Harper & Row, 1971), 92.

21. *Miscegenation*, 51, 57, 65, quoted in Sidney Kaplan, "The Miscegenation Issue in the Election of 1864," in Werner Sollors, ed., *Interracialism* (NY: Oxford UP, 2000), 245–47; see also Museum of Hoaxes, hoaxes.com/hoax/Hoaxipedia/ Miscegenation_Hoax/.

22. George Fitzhugh, *Cannibals All! Or Slaves Without Masters* (Richmond, VA: A. Morris, 1857), 25–32.

23. Cf. Thomas Jefferson, who knew better: "The whole commerce between master and slave is a perpetual exercise of the most boisterous passions, the most unremitting despotism on the one part, and degrading submissions on the other." Thomas Jefferson, *The Portable Thomas Jefferson* (NY: Viking, 1975), 214–15.

24. Henry Cleveland, *Alexander H. Stephens, in Public and Private, with Letters and Speeches, Before, During, and Since the War* (Philadelphia: National Publishing, 1866), 531–60. Also, *Appendix to the Congressional Globe*, 34th Cong., 1st sess., 723–29.

25. Jefferson Davis, "Speech of Jefferson Davis at State Fair at Augusta, Me.," in Dunbar Rowland, ed., *Jefferson Davis, Constitutionalist: His Letters, Papers, and Speeches*, vol. 3 (Jackson: MS Dept. of Archives and History, 1923), 312–14.

26. John B. Gordon, *An Address Delivered Before the Thalian & Phi Delta Societies of Oglethorpe University, Georgia at the Last Annual Commencement* (Macon, GA: Telegraph Steam Printing House, 1861).

27. Chapter 3 supplies a longer introduction.

CHAPTER 2

1. James L. Huston, *Calculating the Value of the Union* (Chapel Hill: UNC P, 2003), 28; Jefferson Davis, "Message to the Confederate Congress about Ratification of the Constitution," in this volume, pages 175–81.

2. Tennessee voters did not approve secession until June 8, 1861, but the legislature had withdrawn the state from the United States earlier.

3. Historian James O. Horton provides a persuasive account of the South's reasons for secession in "Confronting Slavery and Revealing the "Lost Cause," *CRM* 21 #4 (c. 1999), crm.cr.nps.gov/archive/21-4/21-4-5.pdf; John Marshall, *Austin State Gazette*, 4/20/1861.

4. *Reports and Resolutions of the General Assembly of South Carolina* (1859), 578, 579, from "South Carolina Proposes a Southern Convention: December 22, 1859," in H. V. Ames, ed., *State Documents on Federal Relations: The States and the United States: Slavery and the Union, 1848–1861*, vol. 6 (Philadelphia: U PA Dept. of History, 1906), 69–70.

5. Jefferson Davis, "Relations of States," *Congressional Globe*, 36th Cong., 1st Sess., 935.

6. *Official Proceedings of the Democratic Convention, Held in 1860, At Charleston and Baltimore* (Cleveland: Nevins' Print, Plain Dealer Job Office, 1860), 46–48, 55–65, 70–71.

7. Harry V. Jaffa, "Defending the Cause of Human Freedom," Claremont Institute, 4/15/1994, claremont.org/publications/pubid.667/pub_detail.asp#, 1/2009; italics in the original.

8. However, the new state would then face the issue of how to treat the property in persons that it was making illegal and how to compensate owners.

9. Eric Foner and Olivia Mahoney, *A House Divided: America in the Age of Lincoln* (NY: Norton, 1990), 68–69.

10. In "Constitutional Doctrines with Regard to Slavery," Robert S. Russel supplies a useful analysis of the issues surrounding Dred Scott and territorial slavery. *Journal of Southern History* 32 #3 (1966): 466–86.

11. Thomas Cary Johnson, *The Life and Letters of Benjamin Morgan Palmer* (Edinburgh: The Banner of Truth Trust, 1987 [1906]), 206–9.

12. Hague and Sebesta, "U.S. Civil War as a Theological War," 253, 257–58, 263.

13. Gaines M. Foster, *Ghosts of the Confederacy* (NY: Oxford UP, 1987), 50–51.

14. By St. Domingo he of course refers to Haiti, ruled by blacks after a nationwide slave revolt.

15. Paul Finkelman, "The Treason Trial of Castner Hanway," in Paul Finkelman, ed., *Articles on American Slavery*, vol. 6, *Fugitive Slaves* (NY: Garland, 1989), 145–47; Thomas P. Slaughter, *Bloody Dawn* (NY: Oxford UP, 1991), 66; Herbert Aptheker, *Essays in the History of the American Negro* (NY: Intl., 1964), 133.

16. Frank Moore, *The Rebellion Record: A Diary of American Events . . .*, vol. 1 (NY: G. P. Putnam, 1864), 3–4.

17. Davis, *Cause Lost*, 186; McPherson, *Battle Cry of Freedom*, 240.

18. South Carolina is outraged at states for "elevating to citizenship persons who, by the supreme law of the land, are incapable of becoming citizens." This passage refers to the *Dred Scott* decision, which sat in some tension vis-à-vis state constitutions and laws allowing people of all races to be citizens. However, *Dred Scott* does not make law on this point. As Justice Campbell's dissent noted, the Supreme Court knew that when the United States formed, at least five states, including North Carolina, allowed free blacks to be citizens. Like some other parts of its Declaration, this claim by South Carolina distorts the facts.

19. Convention, *Journal of the Convention of the People of South Carolina, Held in 1860, 1861, and 1862 . . .* (Columbia: R. W. Gibbs, 1862), 467–76.

20. Alexander H. Stephens, speech in Milledgeville, GA, 11/14/1860, quoted in William Freehling and Craig Simpson, eds., *Secession Debated* (NY: Oxford UP, 1992), 61–62.

21. "An Address: Setting Forth the Declaration of the Immediate Causes Which Induce and Justify the Secession of Mississippi from the Federal Union and the Ordinance of Secession," in *Commemoration of the Centennial of the Civil War* (Jackson: MS Commission on the War Between the States, 1962 [1861]), Appendixes 3–5.

22. Convention, *Journal of the Proceedings of the Convention of the People of Florida, Begun and Held at the Capitol in the City of Tallahassee on Thursday, January 3, A.D. 1861* (Jacksonville: H. & W. B. Drew, 1928), 20.

23. William R. Smith, *The History and Debates of the Convention of the People of Alabama, Begun and Held in the City of Montgomery, on the seventh Day of January, 1861* (Spartanburg, AL: Reprint Co., 1975), 24–25, 76.

24. Allen D. Chandler, ed., *The Confederate Records of the State of Georgia*, vol. 1 (Atlanta: Chas. P. Byrd, 1909), 349–61.

25. William Winkler, *Journal of the Secession Convention* (Austin, TX: State Library, 1912), 61–65.

26. As well, Texans complain that the federal government has not protected them adequately from American Indians and blame Northerners for that failure.

27. George Williamson, "Letter to President and Gentlemen of the Convention of the People of Texas," in Winkler, *Journal of the Secession Convention of Texas*, 121–23.

28. Williamson was born in South Carolina, graduated from South Carolina College in 1850, and became a lawyer in Louisiana. A signer of Louisiana's ordinance of secession, he then became a Confederate colonel. *National Cyclopædia of American Biography*, vol. 12 (NY: James T. White, 1904), 52; LA Historical Assn., online biographical dictionary, lahistory.org/site40.php, 8/2009. See also Charles B. Dew, *Apostles of Disunion* (Charlottesville: U VA P, 2001), 19.

29. Fulton Anderson, Henry L. Benning, and John S. Preston, *Addresses Delivered Before the Virginia State Convention* (Richmond, VA: Wyatt M. Elliot, 1861), 21–26.

30. He was surely wrong about the permanent Republican majority. While Lincoln did score a big victory in the electoral college, he won less than 40% of the popular vote. Certainly the Southern majority in the Supreme Court would not just go away. Nor would Chief Justice Roger Taney, as Lincoln found to his consternation. Among the congressmen elected in 1860 were just 108 Republicans. That provided a big majority, to be sure, but only because 66 representatives from seceded states withdrew. Adding them to the 44 Democrats remaining would have resulted in a tossup, to be determined by the 30 Unionist Party members (prowar Democrats) and 5 others. Moreover, in the next election Republicans dropped by 22 seats while Democrats picked up 28.

31. *Proceedings of the Virginia State Convention of 1861* (Richmond: VA State Library, 1965), vol. 2, 562–68; vol. 3, 127–203, 252–70.

32. Convention, *Journal of Both Sessions of the Convention of the State of Arkansas* (Little Rock, AR: Johnson & Yerkes, 1861), 51–54, 93–94, 98, 121–22.

33. Like Virginia, Arkansas indicates it would have been satisfied with a division of the territories along the Missouri Compromise line.

34. Isham Harris, "Message," in *Senate Journal of the Extra Session of the Thirty-Third General Assembly of the State of Tennessee* (Nashville, TN: J. O. Griffith, 1861), 6–18.

35. James Fertig, *The Secession and Reconstruction of Tennessee* (Chicago: U Chicago P, 1898), 22.

36. Tennessee was the last state to secede based on the date of the referendum but effectively left the Union when the legislature acted, if not before.

37. Robert H. White, ed., *Messages of the Governors of Tennessee*, vol. 5 (Nashville: TN Historical Commission, 1952), 294–300.

38. Donald Reynolds, *Texas Terror* (Baton Rouge: LSU P, 2007).

39. Some of these items are preposterous. Republicans did not exist when the Constitution was written, of course, so they hardly wrote the provision guaranteeing to South Carolina and Georgia the right to import slaves from abroad. The party took pains to distance itself from John Brown. Abraham Lincoln did not assert black equality. Probably no Republicans lived in North Texas, let alone Republicans who committed the crimes Isham denounces.

40. Frank Moore, *Rebellion Record*, vol. 1 (NY: G. P. Putnam, 1861), 155.

41. Tennessee also claims to be last, based on its referendum, but it had effectively withdrawn weeks before the vote.

CHAPTER 3

1. Ludwig von Mises Institute website, mises.org/store/Lincoln-Unmasked-P324.aspx, 12/2008; McPherson, *Battle Cry of Freedom*, 290; John Majewski, *Modernizing a Slave Economy* (Chapel Hill: UNC P, 2009), 7; Richard F. Bensel, *Yankee Leviathan* (Cambridge: Cambridge UP, 1990), 14.

2. Richard B. McCaslin, *Tainted Breeze* (Baton Rouge: LSU P, 1994), 1, 10–15, 27–49, 57–73, 100–114, 127–44, 169–70; Guttery, quoted in David Williams, *Bitterly Divided: The South's Inner Civil War* (NY: New P, 2008), 113.

3. For a detailed treatment of Confederate policy toward black POWs, see Gregory Urwin, *Black Flag Over Dixie* (Carbondale: Southern IL UP, 2004), especially 34–51.

4. In recent years, Lee's position on slavery has become important to neo-Confederates, who typically misrepresent it. For a summary of Lee's record as a slaveowner,

see Michael Fellman, *The Making of Robert E. Lee* (Baltimore: Johns Hopkins UP, 2003), 64–66, 96–97.

5. The address is at many websites, including the Jefferson Davis papers at Rice University, jeffersondavis.rice.edu/resources.cfm?doc_id=1507.

6. Senate website, senate.gov/artandhistory/history/minute/Jefferson_Davis_Farewell .htm, 9/2009.

7. This portrayal of Calhoun attempts the impossible: to paint nullification as stemming from "attachment to the Union." Davis cannot support nullification, however; Mississippi has just seceded because, in considerable part, it objected to efforts by Northern states to avoid complying with the federal fugitive slave law.

8. Davis's reasoning here is circular. Andrew Jackson did not agree that a state had the right to secede from the United States. Hence he had the right—indeed, the obligation under his oath of office—to "execute the laws" of the nation throughout the nation. Only if secession is legal is Jackson wrong. Davis makes a stronger legal case for secession in his Senate speech of January 10, 1861, which we quote in a note on pages 170–74.

9. Davis's characterization of the Declaration of Independence is surely accurate. For several years, Abraham Lincoln had been using the stirring words of its second paragraph—"that all men are created equal"—to argue against slavery; just three years later at Gettysburg, he would succeed, at least temporarily, in getting that phrase to apply to African Americans. But Davis is more precise in his reading of both founding documents on this point. Of course, Davis's argument here implies that secession was about the twin issues of slavery and race, which is also accurate.

10. Dunbar Rowland, *Jefferson Davis: Constitutionalist: His Letters, Papers and Speeches*, vol. 5 (Jackson: MS Dept. of Archives and History, 1923), 67–85.

11. Like South Carolina's "Declaration of the Immediate Causes," Davis's history lesson emphasizes the looseness of the "Articles of Confederation and Perpetual Union" while leaving out the last three words of its full title. Davis also goes on to discuss the Constitution without noting that its purpose, inter alia, was "to form a *more perfect* Union" (italics added).

12. Samuel P. McCutchen, *The Political Career of Albert Gallatin Brown* (Chicago: U. of Chicago Ph.D., 1930), 137–38. Historian Richard B Morris, *The Forging of the Union: 1781–1789* (NY: Harper & Row, 1987, 55–60), calls the compact theory "a continuing if fruitless debate from the nineteenth century to the present."

13. Morris (ibid.) points out that although colonies of course predated the national congress, the congress preceded and called for the formation of state governments, which in almost every colony overthrew and replaced the colonial governments. Moreover, the Congress predated the Articles of Confederation and Perpetual Union by almost seven years. He concludes, "a national government was in operation before the formation of the states" (59).

14. As Davis implies, the Constitution indeed set up a stronger central government and did not facilitate secession. His words here are an effort to explain away those facts. He made perhaps a stronger argument earlier, on January 10, 1861, in a "State of the Country" address to the U.S. Senate (reprinted in Jefferson Davis, *The Rise and Fall of the Confederate Government*, vol. 1, Appendix H [NY: Appleton, 1881], 613–23). There he admitted, "I know it has been argued here that the Confederation said the Articles of Confederation were to be a perpetual bond of union, and that the Constitution was made to form a more perfect union." But he pointed out that the Constitution "was not adopted by the mass of the people, as we all know

historically; it was adopted by each State; each State, voluntarily ratifying it, entered the Union: and that Union was formed whenever nine States should enter it." (No national mechanism existed, then or now, for referenda. Within each state, for that matter, representatives voted for the Constitution, not "the mass of the people," and Davis, no populist, would not have changed that. Hence his argument is not as telling as it might seem.) Davis goes on to argue that the Tenth Amendment to the Constitution "declared that all which had not been delegated was reserved to the States or to the people." If the Constitution does not explicitly grant to the federal government the power to prohibit a state from seceding, he asks, "must not this power be in that great depository, the reserved rights of the States?" (Davis devotes most of this speech to attacking the Buchanan administration for trying to hold on to the U.S. property in the South and the District of Columbia, so we do not include it here.)

Between Davis's January 10 speech and his April 29 message, Abraham Lincoln spoke to these points. In his "First Inaugural," Lincoln, like Davis, is trying to persuade Southerners who have not yet made up their minds about secession. He argues that the Constitution purposefully omits secession because no government provides for its own dissolution. Besides, even if the government had been formed as a compact, that still would not let a state withdraw unilaterally. As Lincoln put it, "If the United States be not a government proper, but an association of States in the nature of contract merely, can it, as a contract, be peaceably unmade by less than all the parties who made it? One party to a contract may violate it—break it, so to speak—but does it not require all to lawfully rescind it?" Lincoln, "First Inaugural Address," March 4, 1861, at Bartleby.com, bartleby.com/124/pres31.html, 9/2009.

Americans had broached secession before. The Kentucky and Virginia resolutions of 1798, written by Jefferson and Madison, do not suggest secession, but New Englanders had made noises about seceding in 1814, unhappy with federal policies during the War of 1812. At that time, Southern states argued that secession was no right, as the last chapter noted. See, for example, Gaillard Hunt, *John C. Calhoun* (Philadelphia: Jacobs, 1907), 31–33; Davis, *Cause Lost*, 180. President Andrew Jackson opposed South Carolina's threatened secession in 1832 with these words: "The Constitution . . . forms a government not a league. . . . To say that any State may at pleasure secede from the Union is to say that the United States is not a nation." Quoted in Harold C. Syrett, *Andrew Jackson: His Contribution to the American Tradition* (Indianapolis: Bobbs-Merrill, 1953), 36.

15. Davis conveniently ignores that the Preamble to the Constitution hardly limits itself to foreign aggression but also includes the phrases "to form a more perfect Union, establish justice, insure domestic tranquility," and "promote the general welfare." The Confederate Constitution omits that last phrase, but it is bad history for Davis to do so when discussing the U.S. Constitution.

16. Referring to Southern slaveowners as the "minority," Lincoln actually said the opposite: "If by the mere force of numbers a majority should deprive a minority of any clearly written constitutional right, it might in a moral point of view justify revolution; certainly would if such right were a vital one. But such is not our case. All the vital rights of minorities and of individuals are so plainly assured to them by affirmations and negations, guaranties and prohibitions, in the Constitution that controversies never arise concerning them."

17. Here Davis doubtless refers to Lincoln's "Speech from the Balcony of the Bates House at Indianapolis," delivered February 12, 1861, as Lincoln traveled across the country to take office. Lincoln had prefaced his remark about counties with a specific disclaimer: "I speak not of that position which is given to a State in and by the Constitution of the United States, for that all of us agree to—we abide by." He did question whether being a state confers any *moral* right greater than, say, a county with a similar number of citizens. Speech reported in *Indianapolis Daily Sentinel*, 2/12/1861, at quotesandpoem.com/literature/literaryworks/Lincoln/ Speeches_by_Abraham_Lincoln_1861-62/2.

18. On April 15, 1861, President Lincoln issued a call for 75,000 troops to, among other aims, "re-possess the forts, places, and property which have been seized from the Union." Readers can decide for themselves whether it was a "declaration of war." For the full text, see "Proclamation Calling Militia and Convening Congress" at The History Place, historyplace.com/lincoln/proc-1.htm, 9/2009. Moreover, a state of war had existed between the United States and the seceded states at least since Confederates opened fire on Fort Sumter on April 12. Indeed, in his January 10 speech to the U.S. Senate, Davis had predicted war if secession were not allowed: "If you will not have it thus—if in the pride of power, if in contempt of reason and reliance upon force, you say we shall not go, but shall remain as subjects to you— then, gentlemen of the North, a war is to be inaugurated the like of which men have not seen." Davis, *Rise and Fall*, 623.

19. Climate and soil were not the true hindrances to continued slavery in the North. Consider tobacco. The growth of this labor-intensive crop in early Virginia is often cited as a key reason why Virginia "had to" adopt slavery. Yet for centuries tobacco has been a major cash crop in Connecticut, Massachusetts, even Nova Scotia. Of course, growing tobacco is more economical with slave labor. Doing *anything* with unpaid labor is likely to prove profitable. It is also true that until recently, people transplanted tobacco seedlings, cut off the leaves from the bottom as they ripened, tied them in bunches, and hung them to dry—all by hand. On a small farm, one person can do all these things, however, and just as efficiently as 100 can do them on a plantation. Rather than soil and climate calling forth slavery, plantations called forth slavery. Plantations foment hierarchical values. Where the value system did not favor hierarchy, working-class and lower-middle-class whites held more power, and there slavery did not thrive. Conversely, where slavery thrived, working-class whites did not immigrate in great numbers, having no incentive to compete against unpaid labor.

20. James D. Richardson, *Messages and Papers of the Confederacy*, vol. 1 (Nashville, TN: U.S. Publishing, 1906), 37–53.

21. A young Canadian has mounted a full comparison: filibustercartoons.com/CSA .htm, 12/2008.

22. In reality, Democrats too had used federal monies for internal improvements. When he was secretary of war in the Pierce administration, Jefferson Davis himself "did much to help the South in its efforts to get a transcontinental railway," in the words of Mississippi historian John K. Bettersworth. Davis got "a South Carolina railroad man, James Gadsden," appointed minister to Mexico and supported Gadsden's purchase of southern Arizona to provide a good railroad route from New Orleans to Los Angeles. Bettersworth concludes, "Jefferson Davis was very much interested in the West . . . particularly because he hoped the area might be

divided into slave states." See John K. Bettersworth, *Mississippi: Yesterday and Today* (Austin, TX: Steck-Vaughn, 1964), 172.

23. The Confederate preamble also drops "promote the general welfare," in accord with its ban on federal revenue for internal improvements.

24. Perhaps the new government's most important bow to states' rights was extraconstitutional: it never set up the supreme court provided for in its constitution. In *The Confederate Constitution of 1861* (Columbia: U MO P, 1991), neo-Confederate political scientist Marshall DeRosa holds that this impasse resulted from states' rights issues (77).

25. Thanks to South Carolina historian Vernon Burton for this point (conversation, 12/2009).

26. According to Joshua R. Giddings, *The History of The Rebellion* (Chicago: Follett, Foster, 1864), Virginia got "greater income from the rearing and selling of slaves than from any other object of industry" (455).

27. Edward Alfred Pollard, *Echoes from the South* (NY: E. B. Treat, 1866), 77–102.

28. William C. Davis, *"A Government of Our Own": The Making of the Confederacy* (NY: Free P, 1994), 293–94.

29. Governor H. M. Rector to Colonel Sam Leslie, Commandant, 45th Regiment, Arkansas Militia, 11/28/1861, in Ted R. Worley, "Documents Relating to the Arkansas Peace Society of 1861," *Arkansas Historical Quarterly* 17 #1 (Spring 1958): 84–85.

30. Ted R. Worley, "The Arkansas Peace Society of 1861: A Study in Mountain Unionism," *Journal of Southern History* 24 (11/1958): 445–56. According to Ralph Young, ed., *Dissent in America* (NY: Pearson/Longman, 2005), "Many of those impressed into Confederate service wound up deserting to Union lines at the first opportunity" (242).

31. See George Henry Preble, *Our Flag: Origin and Progress of the Flag of the United States of America* (Albany, NY: Joel Munsell, 1872), 415–18; see also Coski, *Confederate Battle Flag.*

32. Guy Lancaster, review of Thomas J. Anastasio, et al., *Individual and Collective Memory Consolidation*, H-Memory (1/2013).

33. William T. Thompson, *Savannah Morning News* editorials, quoted in Preble, *Our Flag*, 390–97, 400–418; William Peterfield Trent, *Southern Writers* (NY: MacMillan, 1905), 252–53.

34. In fact, the second National Confederate flag *was* mistaken for a flag of truce. As a consequence, the Confederate Congress added a red vertical stripe at the end.

35. Preble, *Our Flag*, 417.

36. Dunbar Rowland, "Jefferson Davis to the Confederate Congress," in *Jefferson Davis Constitutionalist: His Letters, Papers, and Speeches*, vol. 5 (Jackson: MS Dept. of Archives and History, 1923), 396–415. Also in the *Journal of the Confederate Congress*, vol. 3, 58th Cong., 2d sess., 1904, S. Doc. 234, Serial 4612, 13–14.

37. In *What This Cruel War Was Over*, 175–76, historian Chandra Manning shows that Confederate troops welcomed Davis's policy against treating African Americans as prisoners of war.

38. This means the death sentence.

39. *Journal of the Confederate Congress*, vol. 3, 58th Cong., 2d sess., 1904, S. Doc. 234, Serial 4612, 386–87, 423, 425.

40. McPherson, *Battle Cry of Freedom*, 566.

41. *The War of the Rebellion: A Compilation of the Official Records of the Union and Confederate Armies* (hereafter cited as *OR*), Series 1, 24, Part 2, 457–61.

42. This Richmond is a hamlet in Louisiana.

43. *OR*, Series 2, vol. 6, 21–22, 115.

44. *Frank Leslie's Illustrated Newspaper*, 5/7/1864.

45. Pragmatic reasons support this rule: opponents who expect to be executed if captured may fight all the more fiercely, which is hardly in one's own interest. On the other hand, if one's own soldiers imagine that, if captured, they will be executed, they may refuse to attack. Rules of warfare thus usually win assent from both sides.

46. Davis, *Cause Lost*, 101–3; Williams, *Bitterly Divided*, 204; Urwin, *Black Flag Over Dixie*; John Cimprich and Robert C. Mainfort Jr., "The Fort Pillow Massacre: A Statistical Note," *Journal of American History* 76 #2 (12/1989): 832–37; David Ndilei, *Extinguish the Flames of Racial Prejudice* (Gainesville, FL: I. E. F., 1996); James Hollandsworth, "The Execution of White Officers from Black Units by Confederate Forces during the Civil War," *LA History* 35 (1994): 475–89; Loewen, *Lies Across America*, 250–57; Brian S. Wills, *A Battle from the Start* (NY: Harper, 1993), 77–78, 178, 186–93, 215; Nathan Bedford Forrest, 4/15/1864 dispatch, *OR* 32, Part 1, 609–10; Jack Hurst, *Nathan Bedford Forrest* (NY: Knopf, 1993), 161, 169–80.

47. John R. Eakin, "The Slave Soldiers," *Washington (AR) Telegraph*, 6/8/1864.

48. Francis Irby Gwaltney, "A Survey of Historic Washington, Arkansas," *AR Historical Quarterly* 17 (1958): 356–59; Mark Christ, "Engagement at Poison Spring," in *Encyclopedia of Arkansas Online*, encyclopediaofarkansas.net/encyclopedia/entry-detail.aspx?entryID=37, 1/2009; see also Mark Christ, *All Cut to Pieces and Gone to Hell* (Little Rock, AR: August House, 2003).

49. "*Brutum fulmen*" in Latin means "inert thunder" or empty threat.

50. Henry Hotze, "The Negro's Place in Nature," *Index* (London) 3 (12/10/1863): 522–23.

51. Robert E. Bonner, "Slavery, Confederate Diplomacy, and the Racialist Mission of Henry Hotze," *Civil War* 51 #3 (9/2005): 290.

52. *OR*, Series 2, vol. 3, 71, 710–11, 914.

53. Robert E. Lee, "Memoranda on the Civil War," *Century Illustrated Monthly* 36 #4 (8/1888), 600–601.

54. Daniel Mallock, "Cleburne's Proposal," *North & South* 11 #2 (12/2008): 66–70.

55. Editorial, *Macon (GA) Telegraph*, 1/6/1865.

56. *OR*, Series 4, vol. 3, 1009–10.

57. J. H. Stringfellow to Jefferson Davis, 2/8/1865, at "Lest We Forget," lwfaaf.net/cw data/ltrc_jhs.htm, 5/2009, referenced to *OR*, Series 4, vol. 3.

58. During the war, 500,000 to 700,000 former slaves fled to Union lines, according to Levine, *Confederate Emancipation*, 69.

59. G. Raymond Gaeddert, "First Newspapers," *Kansas Historical Quarterly* 10 #1 (2/1941): 9–10; Frank W. Blackmar, ed., *Kansas*, vol. 2 (Chicago: Standard Publishing, 1912), 770–71.

60. Actually, thousands of free blacks fought in the Union ranks. Chapter 12 of James McPherson, *The Negro's Civil War* (NY: Vintage, 1965), describes their initial reluctance, partly because Confederates threatened to kill or enslave them if captured, and their eventual splendid service.

61. Richmond, VA, 3/23/1865, reprinted in *OR*, Series 4, vol. 3, 1161–62.

62. Levine, *Confederate Emancipation*, 46; McPherson, *Battle Cry of Freedom*, 837. However, a Confederate eyewitness, Private R. M. Doswell, reported in the

Richmond Times-Dispatch of black Confederate soldiers guarding a wagon train on the retreat from Richmond. They successfully repelled an attack by some Union cavalry, then surrendered to the cavalry's second charge. "Union Attack on Confederate Negroes," *Confederate Veteran* 23 #9 (9/1915): 404 (hereafter cited as *CV*).

CHAPTER 4

1. Reconstruction ended in different years in different states, from 1870 to 1877. The period known as "Fusion" then lasted until as late as 1902 in some states.
2. Many selections in this chapter and the next make this clear. So does Ludwell Johnson in *North Against South: The American Iliad, 1848–1877*, a book republished by the nonprofit arm of the neo-Confederate magazine *Southern Partisan* (Columbia, SC: Foundation for American Education, 2002; originally *Division and Reunion: America, 1848–1877* [1978]). John J. Dwyer tells of a "fifty year war" in a book we excerpt in Chapter 6 (pages 367–78).
3. Some colonial possessions, including Cuba and Puerto Rico, also maintained slavery.
4. See James W. Loewen, *The Mississippi Chinese* (Prospect Heights, IL: Waveland, 1988), 22–26.
5. Davis, *Rise and Fall of the Confederate Government*, vol. 1, 66 (italics in the original).
6. Stephen Budiansky, *The Bloody Shirt* (NY: Viking, 2008), 23–26.
7. Daily Chronicles of the Civil War, cw-chronicles.com/blog/?p=1763, printed 8/10/09; Robert Barnwell Rhett Papers in Wilson Library, UNC, lib.unc.edu/mss/inv/r/Rhett,Robert_Barnwell.html, printed 8/10/09.
8. "History of the White Line Organization in Mississippi," *Republic* 7 #4 (11/1876), 225–28, at books.google.com. The laws are lightly edited, to remove "be it enacted," for example.
9. *Jackson Daily News*, c. 8/1865, quoted in James W. Loewen and Charles Sallis, eds., *Mississippi: Conflict and Change* (NY: Pantheon, 1980), 147.
10. "Black Code of Mississippi," *Chicago Tribune*, 12/1/1865.
11. Today about $75 and $1.50/mile.
12. Today perhaps $150 to $1,500.
13. *Report of the Joint Committee on Reconstruction at the First Session Thirty-Ninth Congress* (DC: GPO, 1866), 135–36.
14. Rushmore G. Horton, *A Youth's History of the Great Civil War in the United States from 1861 to 1865* (NY: Van Evrie, Horton, 1867), 75–81.
15. Sidney Kaplan, "The Miscegenation Issue in the Election of 1864," *Journal of Negro History* 34 #3 (7/1949): 316–17; J. W. Duffy, "A Twice-Born Book," *CV* 34 #1 (1/1926): 118; "History of the White Line Organization in Mississippi," 229–30. See also *CV* 34 #6 (6/1926): 238; *CV* 35 #1 (1/1927): 38.
16. Loewen, *Lies Across America*, 250–61; Mary Royden Winchell, *Where No Flag Flies: Donald Davidson and the Southern Resistance* (Columbia: U MO P, 2000), 290–95; Scott Barker, "Nathan Forrest: Still Confounding, Controversial," *Knoxville News Sentinel*, 2/19/2006; David Ribar, "Monumental Failure: A Statue That Doesn't Honor Anybody," *Nashville Scene*, 7/16/1998, nashvillescene.com/1998-07-16/news/monumental-failure/1; SCV Camp #28 Nathan Bedford Forrest Memorial

Park website, tennessee-scv.org/camp28/project7.htm; *Citizens Informer* 29 (Spring 1998): 6.

17. Edward A. Pollard, *The Lost Cause Regained* (Freeport, NY: Books for Libraries P, 1970 [1868]), 13–14.

18. Alexander H. Stephens, *A Constitutional View of the Late War Between the States,* vol. 1 (Philadelphia: National Publishing, 1868), 539–43.

19. In notes on a conversation late in the war with Maryland politician Francis P. Blair, Jefferson Davis said that Blair would like to see "the war between the states terminated." That is the only use of the term we or historian John Coski has found during the war, although we have not performed an exhaustive search. See *OR* 46, Part 2, 1037; Coski, "War Between the Names," 67.

20. *OR,* Series 1, vol. 46, Part 2 (DC: GPO, 1895), 1037–38.

21. "Political Affairs: The South," *NY Times,* 9/5/1868.

22. John B. Gordon, "To the Colored People," *Columbus (GA) Weekly Sun,* 9/29/1868.

23. Ralph Lowell Eckert, *John Brown Gordon: Soldier, Southerner, American* (Baton Rouge: LSU UP, 1989), 323, 339; Biographical Directory of the U.S. Congress, biogu ide.congress.gov/scripts/biodisplay.pl?index=G000313, 8/2009.

24. Robert Lewis Dabney, "Women's Rights Women," *Southern Magazine* 8 #3 (3/1871), 322–34; reprinted in Robert Lewis Dabney, *Discussions,* ed. C. R. Vaughn, vol. 4 (Richmond, VA: Presbyterian Committee of Publications, 1897), 489–505.

25. Tennessee also ratified but two years later rescinded its ratification.

26. Jubal A. Early, *Proceedings of the Southern Historical Convention Which Assembled at the Montgomery White Sulphur Springs, Va., on the 14th of August, 1873* (Baltimore: Turnbull Bros., 1873), 26.

27. For Early's violent Negrophobia, see Jack P. Maddex Jr., *The Virginia Conservatives* (Chapel Hill: UNC P, 1970), 103, 193; Jane Dailey, *Before Jim Crow: The Politics of Race in Postemancipation Virginia* (Chapel Hill: UNC P, 2000), 119–25; Charles C. Osborne, *Jubal: The Life and Times of General Jubal A. Early, CSA* (Chapel Hill, NC: Algonquin, 1992), 417–18. Osborne writes, "In Virginia, the presence of freed blacks induced dread and loathing in Early."

28. This is surely a reference to James Longstreet, Lee's former right-hand man, who now supported equal rights for African Americans and commanded the state mili tia in New Orleans.

29. Davis, *Rise and Fall of the Confederate Government,* vol. 1, 65–72.

CHAPTER 5

1. In "The Nadir: Incubator of Sundown Towns," in *Sundown Towns* (NY: New P, 2005), 24–44, Loewen explains why the Nadir developed.

2. Historian Rayford Logan began to establish the term in his 1954 book, *The Negro in American Life and Thought: The Nadir,* reprinted as *The Betrayal of the Negro* (NY: Macmillan Collier, 1965 [1954]). He used "1877–1901" in the subtitle of his book but actually treated 1877–1921. We use somewhat different dates—1890 to the 1930s— but Logan's work infuses our thinking. See also C. Vann Woodward, *The Strange Career of Jim Crow* (NY: Oxford UP, 2001 [1955]).

3. The original name was the United Sons of Confederate Veterans, but because the initials USCV were also the initials of the United States Colored Volunteers,

African American troops in the Civil War, they dropped the "United" from their name; see Foster, *Ghosts of the Confederacy*, 108.

4. Jones County, MS, exemplifies the former; Cleveland, MS, the latter.

5. Moreover, before 1890 most Confederate monuments went up in cemeteries and mourned the dead. After 1890, most went up in courthouse squares and public parks and proclaimed the rightness of the "Lost Cause." See Paul Shackel, *Memory in Black and White* (Walnut Creek, CA: Alta Mira, 2003), 78–81.

6. The Vietnam Veterans Memorial offers a case in point: we *lost* that war, and that monument goes *down*, not up; it is a gash in the earth, a memorial to the dead, not a symbol of triumph.

7. Shackel, *Memory in Black and White*, 86–87, notes that some UDC members, remembering that most slaves did not remain loyal to their owners after the war, opposed building a proposed "faithful slave" monument or "mammy" memorial. As a result, none got built.

8. Davis, *Cause Lost*, 180.

9. Noah Andre Trudeau, *Like Men of War* (Boston: Little, Brown, 1998), 180.

10. See Loewen and Sallis, *Mississippi*, 164; Blanche Ames, *Adelbert Ames* (NY: Argosy-Antiquarian, 1964).

11. See Loewen, *Lies My Teacher Told Me*, 136–37, 144, and 389, note 8.

12. No matter that the North had many farmers, or that many Southerners were trying to bring industry and railroads to their region.

13. Allen Bragdon, *Can You Pass These Tests?* (NY: Harper & Row, 1987), 129–40. This is far from the picture supplied by studies of the period published during Reconstruction or since about 1980. For a modern corrective, see Eric Foner, *Reconstruction* (NY: Harper & Row, 1988).

14. J. L. M. Curry, *The Southern States of the American Union* (NY: Putnam's, 1895), 183–88.

15. Probably this is the dedicatory address at the Calhoun monument in Charleston, SC, by L. Q. C. Lamar, 4/26/1887.

16. In reality, new Southern states—Mississippi, Alabama, etc.—seceded exactly like older Southern states—South Carolina and Georgia. New Northern states—Iowa, Illinois, etc.—opposed secession, just like Pennsylvania and Massachusetts. Again, Curry is mystifying the situation.

17. Stephen Dill Lee, "The South since the War," in *Confederate Military History*, vol. 12 (Atlanta: Confederate Publ., 1899), 271, 340–42, 346–60.

18. Foster, *Ghosts of the Confederacy*, 167.

19. Also, increased voting by white women might mask the drop-off in voting by black men. Then the United States might not slash Mississippi's representation in the House of Representatives, per the Fourteenth Amendment. Lee was also a genuine advocate for women's rights. See Herman Hattaway, *General Stephen D. Lee* (Jackson: UP MS, 1976), 175–76.

20. Charles L. Rand III, "The Charge Revisited," *CV* 66 (2/2008): 18–21, 49.

21. "The Revolution at Wilmington, NC," *Collier's Weekly* 11/25/1898; Image from NC Department of Cultural Resources, Iconographic Collection N.66.7.120.

22. S. A. Cunningham, "M'Kinley, Roosevelt, and the Negro," *CV* 11 #1 (1/1903): 4.

23. "Mr. Cunningham's Life and Work," *CV* 22 #1 (1/1914): 9–10.

24. James W. Loewen, "Telling History on the Landscape," *Poverty & Race* 8 #2 (3/1999): 1–2, 5–6, reprinted in Chester Hartman, ed., *Challenges to Equality:*

Poverty and Race in America (Armonk, NY: M. E. Sharpe, 2001); David Cecelski and Timothy Tyson, eds., *Democracy Betrayed: The Wilmington Race Riot of 1898 and Its Legacy* (Chapel Hill: UNC P, 1998); Michael Hill, "Wilmington Race Riot Draft Report Offers Revelations," 12/8/2005; 1898 Wilmington Race Riot Commission, history.ncdcr.gov/1898-wrrc/1898rptdrftr.pdf, 2/2009.

25. S. A. Cunningham, "Problem of the Negroes," *CV* 15 #1 (1/1907): 8.

26. John Sharp Williams, "Issues of the War Discussed," *CV* 12 #11 (11/1904): 517–21.

27. For clarity, we added the dash after "fought."

28. John Singleton Mosby, *Take Sides with the Truth: The Postwar Letters of John Singleton Mosby*, ed. Peter A. Brown (Lexington: U KY P, 2007), 73–75. Original reference GLC 3921.21 John Mosby (Gilder Lehrman Collection, NY).

29. E. H. Hinton, "The Negro and the South: Review of Race Relationships and Conditions," *CV* 15 #8 (8/1907): 367–69.

30. See Christopher Waldrep, "Black Political Leadership: Warren County, Mississippi," in Christopher Waldrep and Donald Nieman, eds., *Local Matters* (Athens: U GA P, 2001), 227–29; Christopher Waldrep, *Roots of Disorder* (Urbana: U of IL P, 1998); Foner, *Reconstruction*, 558–60; and various *NY Times* stories, including "The Vicksburg Disturbances," 12/10/1874, and "The Vicksburg Massacre," 1/3/1875.

31. According to *Wikipedia* in March 2009, for example, "The phrase implied that members of the Democratic Party (which garnered much of their support from the 'Solid South') were responsible for the bloodshed of the war and the assassination of Abraham Lincoln." Prepublication readers lambasted our use of *Wikipedia* but failed to note that we cite it precisely to show how the misuse of the phrase has become commonplace.

32. Prohibition Party leaders did so in 1888, for example; see "Conscience in Politics; The Prohibition Party's State Convention," *NY Times*, 8/26/1887.

33. See Richard S. West Jr., *Lincoln's Scapegoat General* (Boston: Houghton Mifflin, 1965), 342–43; Stephen Budiansky, *The Bloody Shirt: Terror After Appomattox* (NY: Viking, 2008).

34. June Murray Wells, Talk at SC State House, 1/8/2000, electricscotland.com/history/America/udctalk.htm, 8/2009; Drew Gilpin Faust, "Alters of Sacrifice," in Catherine Clinton and Nina Silber, eds., *Divided Houses: Gender and the Civil War* (NY: Oxford UP, 1992), 199.

35. Thomas Brown, "The Confederate Retreat to Mars and Venus," in Catherine Clinton and Nina Silber, eds., *Battle Scars: Gender and Sexuality in the American Civil War* (NY: Oxford UP, 2006), 199–204.

36. C. E. Workman, "Reconstruction Days in South Carolina," *CV* 29 #7 (7/1921): 256–58.

37. See, for example, Marion B. Lucas, *Sherman and the Burning of Columbia* (College Station: TX A&M UP, 1976).

38. Mildred Rutherford, "The War Was Not a Civil War," *Miss Rutherford's Scrap Book* 1 (1/1923): 14–15

39. James M. McPherson, *This Mighty Scourge* (NY: Oxford UP, 2007), 103; Elizabeth McRae, "Caretakers of Southern Civilization," *GA Historical Quarterly* 82 #4 (Winter 1998): 801–3, 807–8, 822.

40. Susan Lawrence Davis, *Authentic History Ku-Klux Klan, 1865–1877* (NY: American Library Service, 1924), 80–81.

41. "Suit Over 'Gone With the Wind,'" *NY Times*, 4/29/1937; Stanley F. Horn, *"Invisible Empire": The Story of the Ku Klux Klan, 1866–1871* (NY: Smith Patterson, 1968

[1939]), 312–13; "Memorial Fund to Honor Wilson Boosted by U.D.C.," *Atlanta Constitution*, 11/22/1924.

42. John E. Rankin, "Forrest at Brice's Cross Roads," *CV* 33 #8 (8/1925): 290–92. Originally delivered at Brice's Cross Roads, 6/10/1925.

43. Biographical Directory of the U.S. Congress, bioguide.congress.gov/scripts/biodisplay.pl?index=R000056.

CHAPTER 6

1. To be sure, the 1954 decision had antecedents in a chain of opinions requiring Southern states to admit black students to graduate programs in higher education. Nevertheless, its impact on Southern public opinion was a bombshell.

2. As usual, the "Confederate flag" they used was the battle flag of the Army of Northern Virginia.

3. One neo-Confederate response is the new statue of Forrest shown in Chapter 4.

4. Teachers' erroneous answers to "Why did the South secede?" show this influence, as told in the Introduction.

5. Edward Ayers, "Worrying About the Civil War," in Karen Halttunen and Lewis Perry, eds., *Moral Problems in American Life* (Ithaca, NY: Cornell UP, 1999), influenced this paragraph.

6. Goldwater won the white vote of the Deep South, of course; few African Americans were allowed to vote there in 1964, a fact that helped lead a Democratic Congress to pass the Voting Rights Act the next year.

7. Atwater, quoted by Bob Herbert, "The Howls of a Fading Species," *NY Times*, 6/1/2009.

8. Joseph Crespino, *In Search of Another Country* (Princeton, NJ: Princeton UP, 2007), 274–75; Ann Coulter, "From How to Talk to a Liberal: The Battle Flag," *CV* 62 #6 (11–12/2004): 18–21, 57; AP, "Governor Says Texans May Want to Secede from Union But Probably Won't," at Fox News, foxnews.com/politics/2009/04/15/governor-says-texans-want-secede-union-probably-wont/, 5/2009; Cynthia Tucker, "Some GOP Hopefuls Talk 'Treason,'" *Atlanta Journal-Constitution*, 5/27/2009; Jay Bookman, "Poythress Calls the Secessionists' Bluff," *Atlanta Journal-Constitution*, 5/21/2009, blogs.ajc.com/jay-bookman-blog/2009/05/21/poythress-calls-the-secessionists-bluff/.

9. Michael Hill, League of the South website, dixienet.org/New%20Site/index.shtml, 5/2009.

10. Richard Weaver, *The Southern Tradition at Bay* (New Rochelle, NY: Arlington House, 1943), 52, 169, 265, 388, 394.

11. Virginia Clay was the wife of Confederate senator Clement Claiborne Clay. Suspected of involvement in the assassination of Abraham Lincoln, she was imprisoned for a year, then released. Later she became active in the United Daughters of the Confederacy. "Stories" like these are staples of white neo-Confederate thought; in reality, African Americans were closely attentive to the debate about their right to vote during Reconstruction and the Freedmen's Bureau.

12. M. Clifford Harrison, "The Southern Confederacy—Dead or Alive?" *United Daughters of the Confederacy Magazine* 10 #6 (12/1947), 6.

13. Marion Johnson, photographer, with thanks to the Atlanta History Center.

14. "Around the Hall—Wallace Pickets Greet Delegates," *Birmingham Post*, 7/17/1948. ("Wallace" refers to Henry Wallace, vice president of the United States under FDR before Truman. In 1948, he was also running for president, under the banner of the Progressive Party.)

15. "Thurmond Seems to Have No. 2 Spot for Sure," *Birmingham News*, 7/17/1948; "Orators Have Own Way as Revival-Like Fever Grips Great Throng," *Birmingham News*, 7/18/1948. "Walkouters" were delegates to the Democratic national convention who had walked out in protest when the party adopted a civil rights plank in its platform.

16. Strom Thurmond, "South Faces Second 'Tragic Era,'" *United Daughters of the Confederacy Magazine* 21 #1 (1/1958), 15, 18–19, 22–23, 25.

17. This use of "tragic era" refers to Claude Bowers's 1929 book of this title. Bowers, a journalist and Democratic politician, wrote an interpretation of Reconstruction along neo-Confederate lines, a common occurrence during the Nadir of race relations.

18. Of course, the president's oath of office includes the words "faithfully execute the office," and the Constitution defines the "Duties of the President" to include "take care that the laws be faithfully executed." The Supreme Court having ruled, there could be no doubt as to what the law was. Eisenhower would have been derelict of duty had he not acted to desegregate the Little Rock schools.

19. Thurmond is right in this claim.

20. Thurmond here echoes a common neo-Confederate claim. In fact, the Fourteenth Amendment was deemed ratified in 1868, so this claim in 1958 has no legal standing.

21. As in other Southern states, many black high schools in Arkansas had been built more recently than white ones. Until after World War II, many districts had no black high schools at all or rudimentary ones. To head off the legal campaign for desegregation, states belatedly rushed to make black schools separate but equal, which had supposedly been their policy all along. In its 1954 decision, the Supreme Court held that segregation on the basis of race, "even though the physical facilities and other 'tangible' factors may be equal," indeed deprives black children "of equal educational opportunities." In a famous phrase, the court summarized: "Separate educational facilities are inherently unequal."

22. Just seven years later, Thurmond would become a Republican. Thurmond's switch does not show inconsistency on his part but recognizes the reversal Republicans committed in 1964, appealing to opponents of that year's Civil Rights Act.

23. Sumter L. Lowry, "The Federal Government and Our Constitutional Rights," *United Daughters of the Confederacy Magazine* 22 #2 (2/1959), 32, and #3 (3/1959), 15, 22, 24.

24. Helen L. Jacobstein, *The Segregation Factor in the Florida Gubernatorial Primary of 1956* (Gainesville: U FL P, 1972).

25. *The Citizens' Council* 2 #6 (3/1957) and later issues.

26. "His Example Inspires Our Efforts of Today," *The Citizens' Council* 1 #9 (6/1956).

27. See Paul Escott, *After Secession* (Baton Rouge: LSU P, 1978); and Richard E. Beringer, *The Elements of Confederate Defeat* (Athens: U GA P, 1988).

28. W. E. Rose, "The Warning of Robert E. Lee," *The Citizens' Council* 2 #5 (2/1957).

29. *The Citizens' Council* 3 #1 (11/1957), 4.

30. David Kushner, *Levittown* (NY: Walker, 2009), 202, 205; exhibit on Levittown, PA State Museum, Harrisburg, 9/2002.

31. *The Citizens' Council* 4 #3 (12/1958), 4.
32. "Conditions in U.S. Today Offer Alarming Parallel to First Reconstruction Era of a Century Ago," *The Citizens' Council* 5 #11 (8/1960).
33. In a 1988 informal poll by the American Library Association, *Gone With the Wind* won more votes for "Best Book in the Library" than all other books ever published, combined; "A Favorite Still," *Burlington Free Press* (1/24/1988). See also Adrian Turner, *A Celebration of Gone With the Wind* (NY: W. H. Smith, 1992), 166, quoting *Variety* statistics; and "A Favorite Still, Iacocca's Book Sets a Record," *Free Press* (4/1986).
34. Foner, *Reconstruction*, 347, 423–24.
35. Margaret Walker, *Jubilee* (NY: Bantam, 1966).
36. Richard Quinn, "Martin Luther King Day," *Southern Partisan* 3 #4 (Fall 1983): 4.
37. Clara Erath, "Confederate Notes," *United Daughters of the Confederacy Magazine* 58 #7 (8/1995), 11; 60 #2 (2/1997), 13; 61 #3 (3/1998), 10; 62 #11 (12/1999), 9.
38. "Hesiod," "McCain Campaign Paid $50,000 to a White Supremacist," *Daily Kos*, dailykos.com/story/2008/2/15/85831/2516/354/457290, posted 2/15/2008, 5/2009, citing David Firestone, "The 2000 Campaign: The Strategist; McCain Aide's Conservatism Runs Deep," *NY Times*, 2/8/2000, and other sources.
39. James Ronald Kennedy and Walter Donald Kennedy, *The South Was Right!* (Gretna, LA: Pelican, 1994), 251–56.
40. Ad in *Southern Heritage* 2 #1 (11/1993): 35; see also *Southern Heritage* 2 #3 (3/1994): 38–39; *General Store: A Confederate Christmas* (Columbia, SC: Southern Partisan, 1995); *Southern Partisan*, personal communication, 12/5/1995; thesmokinggun.com/mugshots/mcveighmug1.html.
41. Alister C. Anderson, "Address at Arlington National Cemetery," Arlington National Cemetery Website (not connected with the National Park Service website), arlingtoncemetery.net/anderson-address.htm, posted 12/24/2000, 3/2009.
42. "First Friday," biographical note on speaker Alister C. Anderson, instituteontheconstitution.com/IOTC-NewSite/events/events_01FstFriday.html, 5/14/2009.
43. Readers can turn to Chapter 2 to confirm that states' rights, free trade, and tariffs played no role in prompting secession.
44. Although his address was posted in 2000, Anderson does not capitalize "Negro." Capitalizing the word became standard practice before World War II in most of the United States. For that matter, most African Americans stopped using "Negro" around 1970, in favor of "black." "African American" as well as "black" have been the terms used since about 1985. Anderson thus makes a deliberate choice to be incorrect.
45. The African American does not carry the rifle, as the next caption notes.
46. Levine, *Confederate Emancipation*, 157; Truman R. Clark, "History Gives Lie to Myth of Black Confederate Soldiers," *Houston Chronicle*, 8/29/1999, at chron.com, 11/2008. See also N. W. Stephenson, "The Question of Arming the Slaves," *American Historical Review* 18 (1/1913): 295–308.
47. In 1862, for example, the commissioned officers of South Carolina's Seventh Battalion petitioned to remove eight men "from our midst on account of their not being white men and not liable to do duty as soldier." All got transferred; most probably became teamsters, according to historian John Coski, "Library Collections Document Black Confederates," *Newsletter of the Museum of the Confederacy* (Spring 2001), 8–9.

48. James A. Seddon, reply to Gen. Dabney H. Maury, 11/24/1863, *OR*, Series 4, vol. 2, 941.

49. It's not even intended to be accurate; the sculptor lists fourteen Confederate states, for example, although only eleven really seceded.

50. Hilary A. Herbert, *History of the Arlington Confederate Monument at Arlington, Virginia* ([Richmond]: United Daughters of the Confederacy, 1914), 77.

51. In Dwight Pitcaithley, "'A Cosmic Threat': The National Park Service Addresses the Causes of the American Civil War," in James O. Horton and Lois E. Horton, eds., *Slavery and Public History* (NY: New P, 2006), 176.

52. According to Pitcaithley (e-mail, 8/2009), "in 1998, the only park to include slavery as a cause in interpretive exhibits was Fort Sumter which had a small exhibit out on the island."

53. Examples in this collection include pieces by Davis (in 1881, not earlier), Curry, Anderson, Dwyer, and Conner.

54. See Pitcaithley, "'Cosmic Threat,'" especially 176–78, for a good overview of the controversy. See also Jesse Jackson Jr.'s 2001 speech to the NPS, nps.gov/history/history/online_books/rthg/chap1.htm, 8/2009; and Shackel, *Memory in Black and White*, 169.

55. John J. Dwyer et al., *The War Between the States: America's Uncivil War* (Denton, TX: Bluebonnet, 2005), 20–21.

56. bluebonnetpress.com/wbts_interview.html, 2/2009; johnjdwyer.com/media.html#wbts, 2/2009.

57. Deanna Swartout-Corbeil, "Home Schooling," in *Gale Encyclopedia of Children's Health: Infancy through Adolescence*, at HighBeam website, highbeam.com/doc/1G2-3447200285.html, 2/2009.

58. In the book, Dwyer makes the astounding claim that "between 50,000 and 100,000" African Americans, "free and slave, served in the Southern military some time during the war." He does admit that the Confederacy did not allow them to be soldiers but claims "around 40,000" served "in combat roles" and provides five pages of details (407–12). Of course, slaves did serve as cooks, teamsters, ditchdiggers, etc., but not as soldiers and often not voluntarily. An SCV website claims "30,000 to 100,000"; evidence was "distorted or destroyed" by a Northern conspiracy (scvcamp469-nbf.com/theblackconfederatesoldier.htm). A book would be required to show the errors of these claims, and Bruce Levine recently provided it in *Confederate Emancipation*.

59. J. M. Ludlow, *A Sketch of the History of the United States* (Cambridge: Macmillan, 1862), 306–7.

60. 15 Southern Ministers, "The Moral Case for the Confederate Flag," *Southern Partisan* 16 (4th Quarter 1996): 16–21, is another neo-Confederate example of this argument.

61. *Southern Partisan* 16 #3 (3/1996) to 19 #1 (1/1998). *Southern Partisan* often published late, so dates are approximate.

62. Sonny Perdue, "Confederate History Month Proclamation," Governor's website, gov.georgia.gov/vgn/images/portal/cit_1210/2/32/107379793Confederate%20History%20Month%202008.pdf, 11/2008.

63. John C. Inscoe, "Sonny Perdue," *Georgia Encyclopedia Online*, georgiaencyclopedia.org/nge/Article.jsp?id=h-2801, 8/2009.

64. Durden, *The Gray and the Black*, ix–x.
65. Bryan Mark Rigg, *Hitler's Jewish Soldiers* (Lawrence: UP of KS, 2002).
66. Frank Conner, "Where We Stand Now: And How We Got Here," *Southern Mercury* 1 #2 (9/2003): 10–14.
67. As U.S. troops left Columbia, SC, for example, in February 1865, they left 500 cattle on the green of the University of South Carolina for the townspeople, provided transport for citizens made homeless by the Columbia fire to an abandoned college, and gave them blankets and rations. See Lucas, *Sherman and the Burning of Columbia*. Grant's army famously supplied rations to Lee's at Appomattox. See, inter alia, Horace Greeley, *The American Conflict II* (Hartford, CT: O. D. Case, 1866), 745. Residents of Richmond assuaged their hunger by looting shops and Confederate storehouses. See, inter alia, Warren F. Spencer, "A French View of the Fall of Richmond," *VA Magazine of History and Biography* 73 #2 (4/1965): 178–88.
68. Loewen and Sallis, *Mississippi*, 213.
69. In this article, he claims that "the liberals took control of the humanities departments in the colleges and universities of America." In the book, he writes, "Jews flocked to teaching posts in the various humanities departments in our colleges and universities." A subtitle in the article reads, "The Liberals Create a False Public Image of the Blacks," but in the book, "Jews in academia" accomplish this task. See Frank Conner, *The South under Siege* (Newnan, GA: Collards, 2002), 392–406.

CONCLUDING WORDS

1. Michael D'Orso, *Like Judgment Day* (NY: Berkley, 1996).

INDEX

abolitionism, 67, 73, 169, 282, 378, 386;
    attacked, 44, 47, 50–51, 76, 104–7,
    195; denied as reason for secession,
    271–76; petitions, 23, 30–35, 58–59;
    proposed by Confederates, 218,
    224–27; as reason for secession,
    5–7, 90–91, 127–28, 134, 139, 142,
    147–52, 160–63, 175, 243–45, 283
Adams, Charles Francis, 310
Adams, John Quincy, 30
Africa, 11, 17, 28, 33, 64–66, 85, 106, 178,
    190, 214–15, 257, 310, 326, 365
African Americans: as inferior, 14–15,
    213–15; loyalty to Confederacy, 63
African American soldiers
    in Confederate army, 19–20, 169,
    223–27; enlistment act, 228–29;
    Native Guards, 12–13; neo-Con-
    federate claims of, 372–74, 382,
    406n62, 415n58; opposed, 221–22;
    proposed, 216–18, 223–27
    in Union army, 14, 217; Confederate
    hostility toward, 13, 168–69,
    198–212; massacres of, 203–13, 377;
    in Reconstruction, 280
Agassiz, Louis, 73
Alabama, 8, 23, 36–39, 40, 92, 100–1, 168,
    213, 233, 283, 322, 332–33, 338–40,
    380, 384, 410n16; secession state-
    ment, 131–32
Alabama Society, 300
Alaska, 20
Alexander v. Holmes, 331

American Indians. *See* Native Americans
American Revolution, 22, 25, 176, 271; ref-
    erenced in secession declarations,
    113, 119, 120–21
Ames, Adelbert, 281, 306
Anderson, Alister, 371–72
Anglo-Saxons, 106, 258, 291, 309–11, 317,
    326–29, 336
Antiochian Orthodox Christian church,
    371
Arizona, 36, 332, 405n22
Arkansas, 92, 102, 104, 167–68, 181,
    191–92, 207, 209, 291, 343–45,
    402n33, 413n21; secession state-
    ments, 156–59
Arlington National Cemetery, 333, 371–74
Articles of Confederation, 111, 113, 176–77,
    181, 403n11, 403n13, 403n14
Ashcroft, John, 18, 366
Atchison, David, 40
atheism, 52, 107
Atlanta Constitution, 338, 387
Atwater, Lee, 332

Baldwin, Abraham, 27
Baltic nations, 20
Barbour, Haley, 332
Barton, Clara, 331
Baseball, 17
Beauregard, P. G. T., 195
Belgium, 20
Benning, Henry L., 6–7, 93, 149–52
Bensel, Richard, 168

Bible, 65–66, 82–85, 107, 299, 305, 312, 374
Birmingham Post, 339–40
Birth of a Nation, 282
Black Codes, 216, 231–32, 237–39
"bloody shirt," 306–9, 384–85
Blow, Henry T., 240–41
Boas, Franz, 387–88
Bonner, Robert, 213
Booth, John Wilkes, 370
Border Ruffians, 40, 82
Boston, Massachusetts, 172
Bowers, Claude, 282, 413n17
Bradford, M. E., 334
Brattleboro, Vermont, 19
Brown, John, 94, 127, 150, 163, 269, 274,
    284, 377, 402n39
Brown v. Board of Education, 17–18, 331,
    388
Bryan, William Jennings, 9
Buchanan, James, 8, 10, 31, 96, 112, 161,
    394n3, 396n16, 403n14
Buchanan, Pat, 332
Buckley, William F., Jr., 334
Bush, George W., 332, 380
Bushnell, Horace, 265
Butler, Paul M., 346
Butler, Pierce, 29

Calhoun, John C., 23, 30–35, 40–49, 62,
    171, 305, 377, 403n7
California, 7, 36, 44–46, 160–62, 285, 305,
    396n12
Carter, Mary D., 242
Cartwright, Samuel A., 24, 64–70
Central America, 15, 88, 91, 243–44
Chamberlain, Daniel Henry, 316–18
Charleston, South Carolina, 4, 50, 98, 251,
    257–58, 366
Charleston Mercury, 234
Chestnut, Mary, 331
Chicago, Illinois, 288, 330
Christiana, Pennsylvania, 109–10
Citizens' Councils [White], 18, 247, 331,
    333, 354–56, 359–60, 398n36
Civil liberties: in Confederacy, 167–68,
    191–92; in Union, 167–68, 370

Civil Rights Act (1964), 18, 332, 413n12
Clay, Virginia, 335, 412n11
Cleburne, Patrick, 13, 216
Clingman, T. L., 73–74
Cobb, Howell, 13, 221–22
Cocking, Walter D., 387
Colorado, 277
Confederate Reader, The, 8
Confederate Veteran, 16, 19, 242, 278–79,
    296–303, 306–11, 314–19, 324–29
Connecticut, 5–6, 27, 29, 113, 115, 141, 272,
    405n19
Conner, Bull, 339
Conner, Frank, 384–91
Constitution
    Confederate, 12, 74, 167, 175–76,
        181–88, 210, 221, 228
    Kansas, 82, 161
    Mississippi, 15, 277, 286, 303, 318
    United States, 15, 46–48, 59–61, 116,
        118–23, 131–33, 164, 255, 273, 284;
        convention, 22–29, 41, 96–97, 171,
        288, 342; and slavery, 25–29, 41–42.
        See also Constitution: Confederate;
        Fifteenth Amendment; Fourteenth
        Amendment; fugitive slave issue;
        slavery: and the territories; states'
        rights
Core, George, 334
Coulter, Ann, 332
Crosby, Peter, 306
Cuba, 91, 98–100, 302
Cunningham, S. A., 278, 296–301
Curry, Jabez, 280, 283–85, 410n16

Dabney, Robert Lewis, 232, 260–66
Dakota territory, 277
Dakotas (Native Americans), 278
Daniel, John W., 16
Davenport, G. W., 306
Davidson, Donald, 248
Davis, Jefferson, 3, 13, 19, 24, 40, 73–74,
    92, 167–81, 207, 223, 232, 249,
    280, 305, 332, 339, 355–56, 396n12,
    403n7, 403n8, 403n9, 403n11,
    403n14, 403n15, 403n17, 403n18,
    405n22, 409n19; on Emancipation

Proclamation, 198–200; for racial purity, 87–88; on slavery, 96–97, 178–80; on slavery as cause of war, 271–76; on states' rights, 180–81

Davis, Susan Lawrence, 322–23

Davis, William C., 9, 111, 280

Deep South, 6, 8, 23, 92, 111, 156, 183, 331, 333, 412n6

Democratic Party, 8, 112, 175, 180–82, 271, 380, 315, 332, 341, 380, 382, 396n14, 402n30, 405n22; against civil rights, 15, 230, 254–56, 278, 342–47, 384–85, 387, 413n15; for civil rights, 346, 388, 412n6; in Civil Rights era, 332, 348–53; in Civil War, 73–74; in Fusion, 230, 294; in Nadir, 277–78, 324; in Reconstruction, 14, 191, 230–31, 242, 254–57, 267, 306–7, 314–18, 361, 413n17; and slavery, 23, 36–39, 92, 96–104

Dewey, Thomas E., 339

Dickinson, John, 28

disfranchisement. *See* Fifteenth Amendment

District of Columbia, 17, 46–49, 157, 163, 344, 403n14

Dixiecrats, 17, 248, 330, 338–41

Dixon, Thomas, 315

D'Orso, Michael, 392

Douglas, Stephen A., 5, 96, 98, 187

Douglass, Frederick, 109

Dred Scott, 10, 98, 102, 150, 160–61, 275, 395n7, 396n16, 399n13, 400n10, 401n18

Dunning, William, 282

Durden, Robert, 382

Dwyer, John J., 376–78

Eakin, John R., 209–12

Early, Jubal, 232, 267–70, 409n27

Ellis, John W., 166

Ellsworth, Oliver, 25, 27

Emancipation Proclamation, 169; Confederate response, 198–202, 209–12

Enlightenment, European, 378

Episcopal Church, 322, 352, 371

Everett, Lloyd T., 242

Federal Elections Act, 233, 277

Fifteenth Amendment, 5, 14, 18, 112, 232, 368; opposition to, 15–18, 277, 287, 296, 300, 303, 310, 355

Filipinos, 278

Fillmore, Millard, 110

Finkelman, Paul, 22

"Fire Eaters," 5, 36, 40, 96, 118, 170

Fitzhugh, George, 24, 80–82

flags: Alabama state, 339; Confederate, 13, 17–19, 91, 168, 193–97, 331, 338–39, 354, 359, 380, 386, 397n33, 412n2, 423n60; Mexican, 19; U.S., 87, 90, 109, 193, 245–46, 354

Fleming, Thomas, 332, 336

Florida, 7–8, 92, 102, 207, 331, 348, 352, 392; secession statement, 130

Foner, Eric, 98

Forrest, Nathan Bedford, 206–8, 247–48, 280, 323–24, 329, 412n3

Fort Pillow, Tennessee, 206–8, 280

Fort Sumter, South Carolina, 153–56, 160, 167, 181, 405n18, 415n52

Fourteenth Amendment, 5, 14, 18, 232; and school desegregation, 343–44, 349, 355, 413n20; subversion of, 277, 287, 302–3

France, 27–28, 128, 136, 162, 169, 199, 222

Free-Soil Party, 82, 223, 284, 396n16

fugitive slave issue, 5–6, 10, 15, 30, 40–44, 47, 55, 59, 97–99, 109–15, 127–28, 138, 142, 150–51, 154, 156–58, 160–63, 172, 178–79, 274, 304, 396n14, 403n7

Fusion period, 230, 233, 277, 286–88, 387

Garabaldi, Giuseppe, 371

George III, King, 173

Georgia, 7–8, 12–13, 20, 24, 26–29, 63, 82–83, 89, 92–93, 113, 123, 187, 219, 221, 232, 243, 251, 257, 267, 272, 283, 288, 320, 331–33, 355, 361, 363, 382–87, 396n11, 402n39, 410n16; se-

cession commissioners, 6, 149–52; secession statement, 133–39
Gerry, Elbridge, 28
Giraldi, Giovanni Battista, 12
Gist, William, 94
Goldwater, Barry, 332, 412n6
Gone With the Wind, 18, 282, 322; Reconstruction and, 361–65, 414n33
Gordon, John B., 24, 89–92, 232, 257–58
Gorsuch, Edward, 109–10
Grady, Henry, 328
Gragg, Rod, 8
Graham, Frank, 386
Great Britain, 22, 89, 92, 112–13, 119–20, 123, 136, 169, 176, 199, 213, 263, 274
Guttery, Robert, 168

Hague, Euan, 50
Haiti (San Domingo), 69, 108, 152, 301–2, 326–29, 401n14
Hamlin, Hannibal, 131–32
Hammond, James Henry, 5
Hampton, Wade, 316–17
Harris, Isham, 160–65
Harrison, Clifford, 330, 336–37
Harwell, Richard, 8
Hawai'i, 278, 303
Helena, Montana, 312
Helms, Jesse, 366
Helper, H. R., 257
Hill, Michael, 332
Hinton, E. H., 279, 281, 306–11
historiography, 3, 15–16, 279–82, 330–33, 392–93
Hollandsworth, James, 12
home schooling, 333, 376
Horton, Rushmore G., 14–15, 73, 231–32, 242–46, 251
Hotze, Henry, 169, 213–15
Howard University, 344
Hunt, James, 213–15
Hunter, Andrew, 216–18, 304–5

Illinois, 5, 7, 115, 247, 272, 333, 375, 401n16
Illustrated Confederate Reader, 8
Index (newspaper), 213–15
Indiana, 5, 83, 115

Indianapolis, Indiana, 405n17
Indians. *See* Native Americans
Interposition, 285, 348
Interracial relations, 15–16, 18, 76, 237, 242–44, 311, 328, 333, 348–49, 351–53, 397n25. *See also* "miscegenation"
Iowa, 5–7, 115, 141–42, 285, 394n4, 410n16

Jackson, Andrew, 30, 175, 403n8, 403n14
Jackson, Jesse, Jr., 375
Jackson, Thomas (Stonewall), 232, 324–25, 353
Jaffa, Harry, 98
Japanese Americans, 392
Jefferson, Thomas, 342, 370, 377, 400n23
Jews, 330, 382, 385; biblical references to, 84–86, 267
John Birch Society, 376
Johnson, Andrew, 230, 234, 236
Johnson, Lyndon, 18
Johnson, Marion, 338

Kansas, 24, 40, 141, 151, 161, 162–63, 223; Alexander H. Stephens on the admission of, 82–86
Kansas-Nebraska Act, 40, 82, 275
Kappa Alpha fraternity, 340
Kennedy, James Ronald and Walter Donald, 368–69
Kentucky, 22, 149, 155, 167, 180, 183, 334, 403n14
Kenya, 360
Kershaw, Jack, 247–48
Kerry, John, 380–81
King, Martin Luther, Jr., 332, 366–67
King, Rufus, 28
Kirk, Russell, 334
Knights of the White Camellia, 15, 232
Ku Klux Klan, 15, 17, 89, 232, 248, 257, 259, 281–82, 314–15, 322–23, 366

Langon, John, 28
Latinos (Hispanics), 20, 24, 311–15
Lee, Robert E., 4, 14, 112, 169, 216–18, 243, 257–58, 259, 324, 338–40, 353, 402n4; and Reconstruction, 231, 240–41, 254–56

Lee, Stephen D., 278, 286–93
Levine, Bruce, 373, 415n58
Levittown, Pennsylvania, 359
Lincoln, Abraham, 9–10, 74, 156, 160,
    166, 175–83, 191–92, 217, 232, 243,
    245, 331–32, 374, 380, 392, 402n30,
    402n39, 403n9, 403n14, 404n16,
    405n17, 405n18, 411n31, 412n11;
    election of, as trigger for secession,
    4–10, 24, 30, 92, 94, 104, 108, 111,
    131–34, 139, 145, 147–51, 156, 160,
    170, 175, 199–200, 232, 243–45, 283–
    84, 304–5, 384, 386, 394n4, 402n30,
    402n39; T-shirts, 167, 370, 379. *See
    also* Emancipation Proclamation
Little Rock, Arkansas, 191, 343–46, 413n18
Lodge, Henry Cabot, 278
Longstreet, James, 4, 14, 21, 232, 377,
    397n25, 409n28
"Lost Cause," 14, 249–50, 267, 271, 280,
    301–2, 321, 324–27, 374
Lott, Trent, 18, 332, 366
Louisiana, 7–8, 12–13, 64, 88, 92, 101–3,
    108, 140, 203–5, 207, 232, 269, 302,
    332, 334, 339, 401n28, 407n41; se-
    cession commissioner, 145–58
Louisiana Medical Association, 64
Louisiana Purchase, 44, 272
Louisiana State University, 334
Low, Seth, 300
Lowry, Sumter, 331, 348–53
Loyal League, 257
Ludwig von Mises Institute, 167, 333
Lunsford, Charles, 19, 398n36
lynching, 16; excuses for, 292–93, 361

Mahone, William, 14, 232
Mahoney, Olivia, 98
Maine, 5–6, 24, 87, 115, 141
Majewski, John, 168
Martin, Luther, 25
Martin Luther King Day, 332, 366–67
Maryland, 7, 22, 26–27, 29, 43, 67, 109–10,
    113, 151, 155, 167–68, 282, 409n19
Mason, James M., 40, 304–5
Massachusetts, 5–6, 27, 29, 32, 100, 113, 115,
    141–42, 172, 251, 272, 278, 285, 307,
    309, 325, 405n19, 410n16

Mau Mau, 360
McCain, John, 18, 366
McKinley, William, Jr., 278, 296–98
McPherson, James, 9–10, 168, 228, 320,
    396n14
McVeigh, Timothy, 370
Mean, John H., 60
Methodist Church, 29
Mexico, 15, 23, 36–39, 44–45, 58, 87, 91,
    128, 135–36, 396n12, 405n22
Mexican War, 36–39, 151, 272
Michigan, 5–7, 115, 141–42
Mill, John Stuart, 369
Minnesota, 7, 394n3, 394n4
"miscegenation," 73–74, 242
Mississippi, 8, 15, 17, 18, 44, 65, 92, 100–1,
    161, 167, 170–72, 203, 207, 231, 234,
    237–38, 242, 247, 277, 280–81, 301–
    3, 306–9, 324, 332, 338–39, 355, 368,
    380, 385, 403n7, 410n16, 410n19;
    secession statement, 6, 127–29
Mississippi River, 145, 203, 206
Mississippi State University, 286
Missouri, 40, 42, 82, 136, 149, 155, 167, 223,
    240, 272
Missouri Compromise, 36, 44, 46, 55, 135,
    153, 275, 402n33
Mitchell, Margaret. See *Gone With the
    Wind*
Montana, 36, 312
Morris, Gouverneur, 29
Mosby, John Singleton, 304–5
Myers, William and Daisy, 359

Nadir of race relations, 11, 15–17, 21, 109,
    232, 247, 277–82, 312–14, 322, 324,
    330–31, 341, 361, 368, 385, 397n32,
    413n17
Nashville, Tennessee, 23, 247; convention,
    23, 55–59, 92
National Association for the
    Advancement of Colored People
    (NAACP), 351, 390
National Park Service, 375
Native Americans, 13, 20, 22, 141, 258,
    277–78, 401n26
Neshoba County, Mississippi, 18

Nevada, 36
New England, 22, 87, 123, 271–73, 311, 394n3, 395n10, 403n14
New Hampshire, 5–6, 29, 113, 115, 141, 272
New Jersey, 22
New Mexico, 36, 44–46
New Orleans, Louisiana, 12–13, 16, 22, 24, 64, 104, 146, 396n12, 405n22, 409n28
New York, 5–6, 37, 73, 110–15, 141, 272, 300
New York City, 22, 24, 73, 112, 242
Nixon, Richard, 18, 332
North Carolina, 4–7, 22, 26, 28–29, 63, 73, 83, 92, 99, 136, 167, 233, 259, 278, 294–96, 334, 346, 355, 384, 386, 401n18; secession statement, 166
North Dakota, 7, 16, 36, 394n4
nullification, 171, 284, 377, 395n10, 403n7

Obama, Barack, 20, 332–33, 380
Odum, Howard W., 386
Ogden, Robert, 386
Oglethorpe University, 89–91
Ohio, 6–7, 83, 115, 141, 163, 394n4
Ohio River, 136, 311
Oklahoma, 277, 370, 376
Oklahoma City, 370
Oregon, 7, 44, 46, 151, 238, 394n4
Othello, 12
Owsley, Frank, 282

Palmer, Benjamin, 92, 104–8
Panama, 89, 91
paternalism, 50, 62, 80, 104–5, 308
Pember, Phoebe, 331
Pennsylvania, 5–6, 29, 31, 67, 109–10, 113, 115, 141, 223, 272, 325, 359, 410n16
Perdue, Sonny, 333, 382–83
Perry, Rick, 332
Pinckney, Charles, 26–27, 342
Pinckney, Charles C., 27, 29
Pollard, Edward A., 14, 231–32, 249–50
polygenesis, 213
Postell, William Ross, 194
POWs. See African American soldiers: in Union army
Preble, George Henry, 194, 196

Presbyterian Church, U.S. See Southern Presbyterian Church
Presbyterian Church of America, 50
Puerto Rico, 408n3

Quakers, 29
Quebec, 20
Quillen, Frank, 16
Quinn, Richard, 18, 366–67

racism. See white supremacy
Raleigh, North Carolina, 166, 346
Randolph, Edmund, 29
Rankin, John, 280–81, 324–29
rape, 18, 292–94, 306, 310, 314, 361, 365
Read, George, 29
Reagan, Ronald, 18
Reconstruction, 4, 14–18, 74, 89, 230–41, 247–50, 254–59, 267–70, 279–82, 286–88, 302, 306–10, 314–19, 322–23, 342, 361–65, 385
Rector, H. M., 168, 191–92
Red Shirts, 15, 17, 232, 281, 294, 314–19
Republican Party, 11, 73–74, 131, 147, 150, 236, 242–45, 380–81; against civil rights, 345–46, 413n22; for civil rights, 4, 170, 230–33, 238, 254; in Civil Rights era, 18, 20, 332–33, 341, 366, 379, 393; in Fusion, 230, 294, 387; in Nadir, 277–78, 280; in Reconstruction, 4, 15, 194, 230–42, 249, 254, 257, 280–81, 294–95, 306–9, 314–18, 361, 364, 384
Rhett, Barnwell, 40, 118–26
Rhett, Edmund, Jr., 234–36
Rhode Island, 5–6, 22, 113, 115, 141
Rice University, 403n5
Richmond Examiner, 249
Robinson, Jackie, 17
Rockford Institute, 333
Roosevelt, Theodore, 296–98
Rose, W. E., 357–58
Rosecrans, William S., 254
Russia, 20, 211
Rutherford, Mildred, 16–17, 21, 320–21, 397n31, 411n38
Rutledge, John, 22, 25, 29

St. Cloud State University, 6
Savannah, Georgia, 12, 187, 219
Savannah Morning News, 13, 168, 194
school desegregation, 331; opposed, 248,
    341–53, 387–88, 413n21. *See also*
    segregation
Scotland, 20
Sebesta, Edward, 50
secession, reasons for. *See* Lincoln,
    Abraham: election of; slavery;
    states' rights; tariffs
Seddon, James A., 221–22, 373
segregation, 16–17, 330, 334, 384–88
Simpson, O. J., 389
slave trade: domestic, 47, 80–81, 163, 182;
    international, 12, 22, 25–27, 46, 108,
    179, 183. *See also* fugitive slave issue
slavery, 3, 12, 22–24, 83–86, 281–82, 331,
    375; as cause of secession, 4–11,
    15, 58, 61, 93–94, 104–8, 111–64,
    175, 178–79, 219, 249–52, 284, 288,
    304–5, 376, 382; distancing from,
    20, 50, 280; end of, 14, 216–18,
    223–27, 230–31, 235, 239, 254–55;
    portrayed, 62–63, 71, 279; as
    positive good, 30, 64–65, 70, 73–75,
    80–81, 89–91, 187–88, 252, 279,
    286, 306–7, 328, 334–35; religious
    justifications for, 51–54, 64–66,
    83–86, 305; said not to be cause
    of secession, 232, 271–72, 280,
    283, 301, 324, 326–27, 333, 371, 392;
    and the territories, 36–38, 44–47,
    55–58, 89, 92, 97–103, 137. *See also*
    abolitionism; Constitution: U.S.;
    fugitive slave issue
Slovakia, 20
Smith, Edmund Kirby, 168–69, 203–5
Sons of Confederate Veterans, 16, 19, 50,
    247, 278, 286, 293, 331, 333, 348, 371,
    373, 376, 384, 409n3; charge to, 278,
    286, 293, 410n20
South Carolina, 4–8, 10, 16–17, 22–30,
    40, 50, 60–63, 83, 92–95, 98, 101,
    104, 109, 127, 131, 140, 156, 171, 175,
    201, 232–35, 257, 269, 282, 294,
    302–5, 312–19, 331–32, 338–47, 366,
    377, 394n4, 395n8, 395n10, 396n11,

399n15, 401n18, 401n28, 402n39,
    403n14, 410n16, 414n47, 416n67;
    secession declarations, 111–26
South Dakota, 36, 277
Southern Historical Society, 104, 267–70
Southern Mercury, 333, 384–91
Southern Partisan, 332–33, 366, 370, 379,
    408n2
Southern Presbyterian Church, 50
Spanish-American War, 278, 297, 385
states' rights, 16, 32, 40, 182–83; as issue
    after 1954, 18, 20, 330–32, 338, 355;
    and secession, 4–11, 20, 111–12, 125,
    153, 177, 183, 271–72, 279–81, 301,
    324, 354, 371, 392
Stephens, Alexander H., 12–16, 24, 82–86,
    167, 187–90, 231–32, 251–53
Steven, Thaddeus, 110
Stowe, Charles, 321
Stowe, Harriet Beecher, 74, 321
Stringfellow, J. H., 223–27
Sumter, South Carolina, 316

Taft, William Howard, 278
Talmadge, Eugene, 387
Taney, Roger, 98, 161, 275, 396n16, 402n30
tariffs: as cause of earlier conflict, 272,
    377; as cause of secession, 4–8, 118,
    133, 175, 274, 279, 282, 371
Taylor, Richard, 203–5, 208
Taylor, Zachary, 36, 305
Tennessee, 7, 55–59, 92, 167, 206, 209, 232,
    237–48, 280, 296, 394n3, 400n1,
    402n36, 402n41, 409n24; secession
    statement, 160–64
territories. *See* slavery: and the territories
Texas, 8, 17, 20, 44, 57–58, 92–93, 102, 128,
    145–49, 161–63, 168, 260, 272, 332,
    403n39; secession statement, 6,
    140–44
textbooks: for home schoolers, 333,
    376–78; treatment of issues in,
    8–12, 17, 320, 331, 392, 395n8
Thompson, William T., 193–97
Thornwell, James H., 23, 50–54
Thurmond, Strom, 17, 21, 248, 330, 338,
    341–47, 382, 413n19, 413n20, 413n22

Tougaloo College, 281
Truman, Harry S., 17, 338–39, 388
Tubman, Harriet, 331

Uncle Tom's Cabin, 218
Underground Railroad, 40, 43–44, 175, 179
Unitarians, 377
United Confederate Veterans, 16–17, 257, 278–80, 286, 301, 312, 320
United Daughters of the Confederacy, 17, 19, 242, 247, 259, 278–79, 312, 320, 322, 331, 333, 341, 348, 366, 372, 374, 412n11
United Daughters of the Confederacy Magazine, 336–37, 348–53
United States Postal Service, 331
University of Chicago, 334
University of Georgia, 283, 384, 387
University of Mississippi, 339
University of North Carolina, 386
University of South Carolina, 50, 416n67
University of Virginia, 336
Utah, 36
Utes, 278

Van Evrie, J. H., 24, 73–79
Vanderbilt University, 334
Vermont, 5–6, 19, 115, 141
Vicksburg, Mississippi, 63, 203, 286
Virginia, 6–7, 14, 16, 22, 26–27, 29, 40, 64, 67, 71, 92–93, 95, 113, 115, 136, 149–52, 167, 169, 180–81, 187, 207, 216–17, 223, 231, 233, 240–41, 247, 251, 267–68, 272, 282, 284, 304–5, 370, 384, 403n14, 405n19, 406n26; secession statement, 153–55
Virginia (Merrimack), 331
Virginia Military Institute, 348
Virginia Tech, 336
Voting Rights Act, 19, 368–69, 389, 412n6

Walker, Margaret, 361
Walker, Robert, 161
"War Between the States," as term for Civil War, 16, 251, 320–21, 331
Washington, Arkansas, 209
Washington, Booker, 297
Washington, George, 247
Washington Telegraph, 209–12
Washington territory, 151
Weaver, Richard, 330, 334–35
Webster, Daniel, 32, 327
Weld, Theodore Dwight, 377
West Indies, 35, 48, 214–15, 301
Whig party, 36, 38, 40, 150, 182, 187, 262, 284
white supremacy, 11–20, 30, 35, 73–78, 83–84, 93, 169, 187–90, 195–202, 230–32, 249–52, 267–69, 271, 275, 278, 281, 296, 301–3, 306–9, 324–29, 338, 348–52, 359–66; abandoned by some neo-Confederates, 19, 333; adopted by Republicans, 332; contradicted in Bible, 65
Williams, John Sharp, 280–81, 301–3
Williamson, George, 145–48
Williamson, H., 28
Wilmington, North Carolina, race riot, 278, 294–98
Wilson, James, 28
Wisconsin, 5–6, 19, 115, 138, 141
women, 280–81, 286, 300, 312–13, 320, 348; seen as subordinate, 17, 77–78, 232–33, 260–66, 286, 320, 332, 335, 410n19
Workman, C. E., 314–19
Wright, Fielding, 17, 338

Yancey, William, 36–37
Yopp, Bill, 383